THE RADICAL NOVEL RECONSIDERED

A series of paperback reissues of mid-twentieth-century
U.S. left-wing fiction, with new biographical and critical
introductions by contemporary scholars.

Series Editor
Alan Wald, University of Michigan

Kelly,
I wish this book
was longer.

Johnny

THE GREAT MIDLAND

ALEXANDER SAXTON

THE
GREAT
MIDLAND

With an Introduction by the Author
and an Essay by Constance Coiner

University of Illinois Press   Urbana and Chicago

© 1948, 1997 by Alexander Saxton
Editor's note, bibliography, and "The Old Left and
Cross-Gendered Writing" © 1997 by the Board of Trustees
of the University of Illinois
Manufactured in the United States of America

P 5 4 3 2 1

This book is printed on acid-free paper.

Library of Congress Cataloging-in-Publication Data

Saxton, Alexander.
The great midland / Alexander Saxton ; with an introduction
by the author and an essay by Constance Coiner.
    p.   cm. — (The Radical novel reconsidered)
Originally published: New York : Appleton-Century-Crofts,
1948.
Includes bibliographical references.
ISBN 0-252-06564-6 (paper : alk. paper)
1. Working class women—Illinois—Chicago—Fiction.
2. Communists—Illinois—Chicago—Fiction. 3. Chicago
(Ill.)—Fiction. I. Coiner, Constance. II. Title. III. Series.
PS3537.A976G76   1997
813'.54—dc21
97-7008
CIP

Contents

Editor's Note

ALAN WALD

A distinguishing feature of The Radical Novel Reconsidered series is the original introduction, by an outstanding scholar in the field of U.S. radical culture, that accompanies each reprinted novel. These essays aim to acquaint the general reader with pivotal issues in the biography of the novelist and with the social, historical, and cultural context in which the novel was conceived. Moreover, such introductions open the door to further intellectual inquiry by raising concerns by contemporary students and scholars in the areas of gender, multiculturalism, "race," ethnicity, literary value, the mass culture industry, genre theory, and other flash points of current research and debate.

In the instance of Alexander Saxton's *The Great Midland,* the director of the University of Illinois Press, Richard Wentworth, and I thought we had located the ideal person to write such an introduction. Constance Coiner was a devoted scholar of left-wing fiction with a national reputation as the author of *Better Red: The Writing and Resistance of Tillie Olsen and Meridel Le Sueur* (1995) and a unique relationship to Saxton and his novel. As revealed in the brief essay that follows, Constance (it is hard to call such an ebullient personality and inveterate anti-elitist "Dr. Coiner") had read *The Great Midland* early in her graduate school career and was inspired by its female protagonist, Stephanie Koviak, to devote herself to studying issues of gender, class, and the Left. Moreover, as Alexander Saxton discloses in his own thoughtful and moving introduction to this reissue of his work, Constance's prodding occasioned him to rethink his novel in light of gender issues and to aggressively pursue its republication.

It was a great loss to Constance's family, friends, students, colleagues, and The Radical Novel Reconsidered project (for whom Constance served as part of my "brain trust" when the plans were first hatched) when she and her daughter, Ana, were killed on TWA

Flight 800, which exploded in July 1996, shortly after departing New York City for Paris. Even though we knew that Constance had not yet completed her essay, we held onto the hope that at least some publishable portion of a draft might exist. Six weeks later we were informed by Steve Duarte, Constance's bereaved companion, that, indeed, a manuscript had been located. In the meantime, Saxton had revised the autobiographical afterword he had prepared into an full-fledged introduction.

When we compared the usable portions of Constance's unfinished draft with Saxton's work, we were heartened to find a perfect fit. In her manuscript, which I have titled "The Old Left and Cross-Gendered Writing," Constance traces the evolution of her thought in relation to gender issues raised in *The Great Midland* and explains their importance in the context of extant scholarship about women and the Old Left. Saxton, in turn, includes in his introduction his own recent thoughts on the part played by Stephanie Koviak in his novel, which he gratefully attributes to the influence of Constance's enthusiasm for and her observations about gender in *The Great Midland*.

Following Saxton's introduction appears the series's standard bibliography of works by and about the author, which I have prepared from a combination of my own and Constance's resources. Thus Constance Coiner has indeed remained a full-fledged contributor to and collaborator on this edition. Saxton's eloquent dedication, following his introduction, speaks for all of us who had the privilege of working with Constance in the endlessly complex and difficult task of reconstructing the radical cultural tradition in the twentieth century. Salud, Constance.

"The Old Left and Cross-Gendered Writing"

CONSTANCE COINER

I entered graduate school in English literature in the late 1970s with a special interest in U.S. working-class—and particularly U.S. working-class women's—writing. I eagerly enrolled in the pioneering "women in literature" courses being offered in my graduate program, excited that women's writing had recently emerged as a legitimate category of literary analysis and delighted to have female professors for the first time in my educational experience.

In many ways, the professors—who were knowledgeable, conscientious, and personable—met my high expectations. But their syllabi were emblematic: the canon of privileged male writers of northern European heritage was being augmented, at this time, largely with women writers of similar class, racial, and ethnic origin—Kate Chopin, Jane Austen, the Brontës, George Eliot, Edith Wharton, Virginia Woolf, Doris Lessing, Louisa May Alcott, Charlotte Perkins Gilman, Sylvia Plath, and the like. Chopin's *The Awakening* and Gilman's *The Yellow Wallpaper,* for example, were rapidly becoming chestnuts of a "new canon," prefiguring the current status of greatest hits by women writers of color—e.g., Toni Morrison's *Beloved,* Zora Neale Hurston's *Their Eyes Were Watching God,* Maxine Hong Kingston's *The Woman Warrior.* But in 1978–79, even at a major research university in California, issues of race and ethnicity were not perceived as inseparable from issues of gender and sexuality—not in the English department, in any case. And class? *Class?* Class was—and remains, among most English professors—the last taboo, the Great Unmentionable.

I didn't do what I now urge my own students to do—discuss with the professors in question why the syllabus included only middle- and upper-class WASPs. Instead, I confessed my disappointment to only two friends and informal mentors outside my department, who, fortunately, happened to know about Alexander Saxton's working-class novels, by then long out of print. I immediately checked out all three from the university library—*Grand Crossing* (1943), *The Great Mid-*

land (1948), and *Bright Web in the Darkness* (1959)—and read them in quick succession. Thereafter, the trajectory of my academic work would be, to borrow grandly from one of the high canon's head boys, "changed, changed utterly."

I puzzled over how a fiction writer—especially a *male* writer—could have produced a female character such as Stephanie Koviak (*The Great Midland*) before feminism's second wave. I was also struck by the connections in the novels aross racial and ethnic boundaries—Michael Reed, Ben Baum, and William Christmas (*Grand Crossing*); Dave Spaas, Stephanie Koviak, Pledger and Ruby McAdams (*The Great Midland*); Joyce Allen and Sally Kallela (*Bright Web in the Darkness*). What I knew about the 1940s I had learned as a high schooler and undergraduate in traditional surveys of U.S. history. I knew almost nothing about U.S. labor history and about the history of American radicalism. I thought the women's movement had disintegrated after suffragists won the vote in 1920, not to reappear until the 1960s, and that the civil rights movement originated in *Brown vs. Board of Education* and the Montgomery bus boycott.

There were no dust jackets—and so no biographical blurbs—on the library copies of Saxton's novels. I wondered what had contributed to the consciousness of a male writer to enable him to fashion a female character—in what would now be termed "cross-gendered" writing—as conflicted, depression-prone, ambitious, and independent as Stephanie Koviak? What experiences had enabled a WASP to hear, and then replicate in his fiction, the speech patterns of immigrants such as Polish-American Roman Koviak? What associations had led him to depict African Americans such as Pledger and Ruby McAdams? When I asked my friends about Saxton's background, I learned that his father had been, for many years, chief editor at Harper and Brothers; that Saxton had been educated at Exeter and at Harvard but had rejected the elitism of the northeastern establishment; that he loved the desert and mountains and could keep up with backpackers and mountain climbers a third his age; and that he had been a Communist party member.

It was evident which lead I needed to follow. To historicize these novels, then, I began to probe the Party's positions on gender and race issues—as well as the Party's literary debates—during the thirties and forties. Such excavation, leading to a dissertation/book, corrected my notion that the civil rights and women's movements had emerged spontaneously during the fifties and sixties (that is, without ties to earlier radicalism). More common starting points for

xii

(the relatively few) materialist-feminist Americanists interested in radical and working-class writers are Tillie Olsen, Meridel Le Sueur, Agnes Smedley, Josephine Herbst, Tess Slesinger, Myra Page. But, as I indicated in the acknowledgments of *Better Red,* it was Stephanie Koviak (*The Great Midland*) who "got me started on the whole thing."

Daniel Horowitz's lead article exposing the radical origins of Betty Friedan's *The Feminine Mystique* in the March 1996 issue of *American Quarterly* (and highlighted as "controversial" in the 12 April 1996 issue of the *Chronicle of Higher Education*), then, came as no surprise to me. If Rosa Parks refused to take a seat at the back of a segregated bus not simply because her feet hurt, then Friedan did not write *The Feminine Mystique* simply because she was an unhappy housewife.

But, as Horowitz acknowledges, some scholars have for many years insisted that important connections exist between the Old Left and feminism's second wave. Rosalyn Baxandall, for example, observes that "a number of the women's liberation movement activists of the late 1960s were Red-diaper babies, grew up with such terms as 'male chauvinism' and the 'woman question,' and heard frequent gossip about which Party families were backward about women." Baxandall reminds us that "the 'woman question' was a radical nineteenth-century term, and only the Communist party continued its use."[1] Betty Friedan's identifying in *The Feminine Mystique* a "problem that has no name" may for many signal the beginning of feminism's "second wave." But few are aware of Friedan's ties to the labor movement and the Old Left. And few are aware of other radical voices during the "conformist" fifties. Betty Millard, a member of the *New Masses* editorial board, for example, published a two-part article, "Woman against Myth" (30 December 1947, 6 January 1948), echoing Rebecca Pitts's prescient "Women and Communism" (*New Masses,* 1935) and anticipating many "second wave" concerns. Millard reports that despite misgivings about "Woman against Myth" among some *New Masses* editors (with the exception of Millard, all of them were male), it received substantial support from some Party members, and *New Masses* printed letters responding favorably to it. That the Party issued Millard's two-part article as a pamphlet (International Publishers, 1948) indicates its willingness to draw attention to her views.

What Sara Evans observes about the New Left also applies to the Old: "The new left did more than simply perpetuate the oppression of women. Even more importantly, it created new arenas—social space—within which women could develop a new sense of self-worth and independence . . . and having heightened women's self-respect,

xiii

it also allowed them to claim the movement's ideology for themselves."[2] As I said near the conclusion of chapter 2 in *Better Red*, the Party's work among women in the thirties should be carefully evaluated as part of the struggle for women's liberation in the United States. Many women developed an awareness of their own potential, a sense of collectivity, and an understanding of America's social system through Party-related activities. As I have said, that the Party leadership was overwhelmingly male and that its bureaucracy functioned undemocratically "from the top down" is a matter of record. But the creative maneuvering within that patriarchal hierarchy—by Party women, its "loyal opposition," and its rank-and-file members—has yet to be thoroughly explored.

NOTES

1. Rosalyn Baxandall, "The Question Seldom Asked: Women and the CPUSA," in *New Studies in the Politics and Culture of U.S. Communism*, ed. Michael E. Brown et al. (New York: Monthly Review, 1993), 159.

2. Sara Evans, *Personal Politics* (New York: Knopf, 1979), 244.

Introduction

ALEXANDER SAXTON

Not many novelists enjoy the privilege of commenting on one of their own novels half a century after publication. *Enjoy*, however, is not the right word: confrontations with the past may be humiliating, overpowering, inspiring; scarcely enjoyable. It is hard to imagine being young again. It is difficult to believe that America of the Great Depression ever existed. The burden of hoping to convey so much leaves one spaced out between speechlessness and reincarnations longer than the book itself.

When for reasons not altogether of my own choosing I quit writing novels, I taught U.S. history for many years and often used novels (never my own) for assigned reading. Fiction, drama, poetry, I believed—treated as primary source material—could offer valuable historical evidence. Usually I arranged such evidence at two levels, which I called reportorial and ideological. It is under these headings that I want to comment on my novel *The Great Midland*.

I have always thought that imaginative writing rests on, or takes off from, a conscious reproduction of human experience. However fanciful, utopian, or ultimate the project, it must be put together from segments of everyday living in much the same way that it is composed of words and sentences. And like words and sentences, these ingredients are socially constructed. I regarded Melville as a great working-class writer because of his reconstruction of the labor process on a whaling ship. Work, subjectively, even aesthetically experienced, has seldom entered the mainstream of American fiction. Having worked in the railroad yards, I hoped to fictionalize the work processes of the yards as a precondition of fictionalizing lives lived in and around those processes.

So what does reportorial, or mimetic, fiction amount to as historical evidence? Could it not be duplicated out of newspapers and old photographs, manuals, trade journals? It easily could; but not the taste and smell, the simmerings of intention and despair. Rereading my own text offers no basis for judgment in this respect because the same images and phrases punch the same buttons fifty years later. I may be shaken up again but I don't know that anyone else will be. Coming from New York, a commercial city, I was stunned by the beauty and horror of industrial Chicago. More a romantic then than now, I believed the essence of human acts and relationships somehow infused sensual perception. I struggled at each juncture to fix the certain slant of light. Too much, I think now.

The reportorial level focuses on people in place, but especially people. The most important people in *The Great Midland* are Communists. How do they stack up as historical evidence? I joined the Communist party in 1941 or 1942. The Communist party in those days attracted young people across class lines. A college student whose middle-class adolescence had coincided with the trough of the Great Depression, I believed America's brightest hope lay in industrial unionism, in getting beyond the political hodgepodge of the New Deal to a mass politics based on industrial labor, driving toward socialist democracy. The Communist party seemed to me an intensely serious advocate of such politics. No, I was not brainwashed, scarcely even recruited. I went looking for the Communist party.

So I called on an acquaintance, Conrad Komarowsky, to ask for application forms, which he happened to have in his desk drawer. Comrade Conrad, as we called him, had been a doctoral student in philosophy at Temple University but never finished. When we knew him in Chicago, my wife and I were living in one of the rental apartments at Hull-House and Komarowsky was doing research for our next-door neighbor, a left-wing author named Harvey O'Connor, who specialized in exposés of capitalist industrial concentration with titles such as *Mellon's Millions* and *Steel—Dictator.* After the war, Komarowsky edited a Polish working-class newspaper in Detroit. He came closer, I think, than anyone I have known to embodying Antonio Gramsci's concept of the organic intellectual. But we had not yet heard of Gramsci.

I remained in the party while I wrote *The Great Midland* and for a good many years afterward. To portray party members positively was my deliberate intention, but that did not seem to me in conflict with accuracy. Shaw observed that revolutionary movements attract the best and worst. Although well acquainted with some of the worst, I understood then, as I know now, that many of the most admirable people I ever met were members of the Communist party. Party membership cost me dearly in some ways; it also was a privilege I would not wish to have missed.

I had forgotten (until I reread *The Great Midland* for this introduction) the Chicago neighborhood circle to which I assigned the novel's heroine, Stephanie Koviak. With the exception of Jessica Mitford's *A Fine Old Conflict*, I think it offers one of the most accurate portrayals of rank-and-file party membership that exist in American print. From this distance perhaps the best way I can recall these people is to mention that they were readers. Each neighborhood circle (they were officially called "branches") had its literature agent, whose task was to keep the members up to their quota. Of course the agent plugged current party literature but also distributed books such as W. E. B. Du Bois's *Black Reconstruction*, Howard Fast's *Freedom Road*, Mike Gold's *Jews without Money*, Richard Wright's *Native Son*—not to mention Marx and Lenin, Jack London's *Iron Heel*, and Tom Paine, Walt Whitman, Mark Twain. I remember vividly those cluttered little living rooms of South Chicago flats with all the pamphlets and books in their bright jackets spread across the footworn carpet while the hostess of the evening handed out coffee and doughnuts and the literature agent worked up a discussion of the dramatized version of *Native Son*, then playing at a downtown theater.

By contrast to the neighborhood branches, the railroad sequences in *The Great Midland* are more complex and more fictionalized. They remain reportorial to the extent that the handful of Communist railroad workers during the late thirties and early forties were trying to do exactly what they are shown trying to do in this novel and in the sense that I knew "real people" whose life experiences paralleled those of Pledger McAdams, Roman Koviak, Red Brogan, Dave Spaas. But Communists on the railroads were so totally unsuccessful that their story in isolation seems like an invocation of despair. That we did not despair at the time was because we could see unfolding across the street in the can factory, the stockyards, the steel mills, precisely what we hoped to bring about on the railroads. The prototype of Pledger McAdams, in reality, never reclaimed his skilled trade. I had never heard of a white shop steward on any railroad who defended black workers. Yet working-class alliances of white and black workers were being pushed successfully by Communists in other industries. I knew, or read, of many such in automobile manufacturing and rubber and coal mining, in the shipyards and maritime trades—even in the rural South. So I borrowed from across the street, allowing my characters a bit more elbow room than they enjoyed in real life. Perhaps that takes us to the level of ideology, which is next on my agenda. First, however, I need a final point at the reportorial level.

If my claim to historical accuracy has any validity it tends to negate the theory of American Communism as a conspiracy by party bureaucrats at the New York headquarters to gain power and prestige by serving as running dogs of a foreign power. The neighborhood and industrial branches I knew in Chicago linked into sequences that ran separately from national leadership. As organizational forms, they preceded the party. Some of the older members had been Wobblies or Socialists. Many came through the language federations of the old Socialist party. I learned later (after I became a historian) that had I been young in 1905 and joined a Socialist club I would have met older people who once were Populists and Bellamy Nationalists; or if I had signed into a Populist local in 1892, I would have found members who had been Grangers or Knights of Labor (or both); and so on back, generation by generation, to the National Labor Union, the Fanny Wright neighborhood circles, and the Workingmen's parties. Typical educational presentations at Fanny Wright gatherings in 1829 would have focused on the oppression of blacks and tyranny by men over women. So did they in Stephanie Koviak's neighborhood branch in 1939.

I am not dreaming of a secret illuminati who somehow penetrated these organizations. What I mean is that in American towns and cities the neighborhood branch and the industrial caucus—often associated with trade unions or city centrals—were logical, almost inevitable forms of political activism. Their continuity and reproduction have provided the lifeline of American radicalism. Conspiracy theorists of American Communism—some of whom, like Victor Hugo's single-minded detective in *Les Miserables,* dedicated professional lifetimes to their pursuit—have remained studiously oblivious to this aspect of radical history.

Every expression of creative imagination, every attempted work of art brings forward an ideological statement. At first glance, the ideological statement of *The Great Midland* seems beguilingly naive: join the Communist party and help bring America (and the world) to the highest mode of political economy, which is socialism. A political leaflet could say as much. Hostile critics—clearly in the majority when the novel first appeared in 1948—generally read it that way. Yet there is not much about socialism in *The Great Midland.* While both Stephanie and Dave seem to take socialism for granted, it is as a goal in the remote future. What more immediately concerns them is a commonplace question yet one with deep-delving implications: whether or not consciously willed human actions can reshape human history. If so, then every individual is responsible for the history of the human species. The implications cut deep because to admit such a possibility entails the obligation to act on it. Dave (whom Stephanie once described as "a stolid, persistent person") answers affirmatively. Stephanie, appalled at the implications, hesitates.

Thus the ideological statement is not simply declarative, but conditional, and hangs on the relationship between Dave and Stephanie. In 1948 there actually were a few favorable reviews of the novel, mostly in left-wing journals, and these concurred that the novel's outstanding achievement was to have brought forward (for the first time in American literature, some said) a "believable" Communist hero. They referred of course to David Spaas; apparently none perceived Stephanie as a hero of any kind, let alone a Communist hero.

If they ventured any judgment on Stephanie, it was as a victim of bourgeois hang-ups, an impediment to Dave's heroic trajectory. At the time, I was grateful for favorable comments on Dave, since a believable Communist was what I had striven for. Afterward I began to puzzle over the neglect of Stephanie. By then however, the pattern had been reversed: readers since the 1970s have favored Stephanie over Dave, and it is largely due to Stephanie that *The Great Midland* is being republished.

I had not thought of Stephanie and Dave as making antithetical statements. Dave has so fully internalized his class experience that he adheres without ambivalence to values drawn from that experience. He might debate or compromise over ways of pursuing values but would never revalue the values. Stephanie by contrast is always revaluing. It falls to Stephanie not only to establish the intellectual and scientific premises of their commitment but also to assess the emotional costs that Dave dismisses as irrelevant. Thus it is Stephanie who will see the black snow on the railroad embankments and hear the engines whistling in the new year; Stephanie—knowing that a materialist world grants short shrift to spiritual renderings of the human condition—who will dread the obliteration of her own perceptions of beauty. To Dave she quotes Whitman's poem: "Out of the rolling ocean, the crowd, came a drop gently to me whispering. . . ." What will we remember of making love, she asks, at our final rendezvous as random particles in the ocean of matter? How can there

xix

be anything against that nothing? Yet also it is Stephanie, acclaiming the strength and courage of the human mind, who will define mind empirically as the functioning of the brain.

When I was writing *The Great Midland* Dave was always difficult, Stephanie came easily. I seemed to know without much strain how she would respond to any situation. Looking back, I see how consistently I identified with Stephanie. The city, the railroad, the university are realized through her awareness. Even Dave, stolidly objective though he may be, has his existence largely through Stephanie's perception of him. This recognition puts me under some pressure to reexamine the opinion expressed by left-wing reviewers in 1948 that Stephanie embodied bourgeois hang-ups. I don't know what I would have come up with had I undertaken such a reexamination then. Today I would begin by saying that class cannot encompass the entirety of human experience. In a curious way this is like saying that mimesis, or reportage, by itself cannot encompass a whole work of art. Without the ultimates of birth and love and utopian desire and death that potentially compress all humanity into a single identification, the mimesis of social and political intercourse remains superficial and banal. Such ultimates by themselves, on the other hand, separated from a social existence in our time primarily governed by class can be only abstract and repetitious. I see Stephanie as stretched between the mimetic and the ultimate, between the immediate imperatives of class and the ultimate consciousness of our human species adrift in the rolling ocean. In the end, I think, she may be a better dialectician than Dave, because she confronts the absurdity and terror of the human condition at the same time that she struggles to fill out its intellectual and aesthetic openings.

Some of my own story line is relevant to this introduction. I shipped out as a merchant seaman during World War II and my wife and I moved to California after the war. My first novel, *Grand Crossing* (Harpers, 1943), had received favorable reviews in major newspapers and did well financially. *The Great Midland* (Appleton-Century-Crofts, 1948) was my second novel. I signed a contract in the spring; the book came out in December. Immediately after the November election (in which I served as a county campaign director for Henry Wallace), the so-called cold war shifted into high gear; Appleton-Century-Crofts, embarrassed by *The Great Midland,* tried to pretend it had never published it. Stonewalled by reviewers and booksellers alike, the novel's sales in the United States stood at virtual zero. In

Europe, in translations, it circulated quite widely. The European royalties were helpful but scarcely supported a family of four. My wife was working; and I learned the trade of construction carpenter at which I worked for the next fourteen years—trying to write novels and short stories over the weekends or on rainy days when construction work closed down. I always liked the carpenter's trade and fortunately was good at it. Growing older, however, I noted that forty hours left diminishing energy to put into writing and reading on those long-deferred Saturday and Sunday mornings.

In 1951 the House Un-American Activities Committee summoned me to Washington to discuss my political activities and tell the committee members about people I might have known or been associated with. What I told them was my date of birth and home address, which they already knew; and I laid claim to all protections contained in the Bill of Rights as well as any others I might not yet know about. Doubtless the committee members could have cited me for contempt—a sentiment I conveyed as cogently as I could, although not perhaps in the legal sense; but after all I was not a very important bird, especially since I declined to sing for them; and it was just before Christmas recess; and the courts were now beginning to uphold the Fifth Amendment.

So I enjoyed a free ride back to California. There was of course a price tag attached. During the war Paramount had invited me to join its stable of script writers. Soon after the war, the English department at San Francisco State University invited me to teach creative writing. Such positions traditionally provide safety nets for novelists who may not always turn out best-sellers. Now, however, as a witness who refused to cooperate with the committee, both were closed to me. I sold three short stories, one each to three slick, well-paying magazines; after that, none. I published one more novel, *Bright Web in the Darkness* (St Martin's Press, 1959), based on the struggles of black shipyard workers to overcome racial discrimination by their employers and by the craft unions. But it took ten years to write that book; and in the effort to hit on some mode of expression that might be saleable yet not shameful to me, I found myself increasingly distanced from what I really wanted to write.

I had admired John Dos Passos's trilogy, *U.S.A.;* and while I was at sea read (for the first time) *War and Peace.* Soon afterward I was into Sean O'Casey's memoirs of his Dublin boyhood and Martin Andersen Nexo's marvelous working-class sequences, *Ditte, Daughter of Man* and *Pelle the Conqueror.* As the titles suggest, I wanted to be thinking in epic terms and hoped to construct perhaps a trilogy of the maritime industry in which I could intertwine the lives of men and women of different race and class backgrounds and divergent political outlooks. *Bright Web* was to have been a step in that direction. Several people from whom I heard accounts on which the novel is based were Communist party members deeply involved in the shipyard fight against racial discrimination. But—after *The Great Midland*—neither I nor my literary agent thought there was any chance of finding a publisher if I portrayed leading characters as Communists. So I compromised reportorial accuracy: in the interest of telling the story of black shipyard workers (which never had been told), I sacrificed the story of black and white Communists in the shipyard. To that extent I falsified history and to that extent contributed to the monstrosities of the cold war. I remain bitterly ashamed of the compromise, although when I think it through again, as I have often done, I don't know how I could have called it much differently. In any case, the novel ten years in process brought home less than a few months at carpenter's wages.

The FBI went to the trouble of hounding my wife as if she occupied a post in high-tech defense; actually she was a social work consultant to diagnostic clinics for crippled or birth-damaged children. That of course is a profession. So far as I know the FBI never hassled the small building contractors I worked for. But, did they perhaps drop in at editorial offices? Was my inability to earn a living as a writer due to the drying up of my own aesthetic imagination or to blacklisting? Under such circumstances one vacillates between internalizing the fault and blindly projecting it. Both are bad medicine because the first erodes self-esteem while the other flames out in self-serving anger.

At the beginning of this introduction I mentioned that I quit writing novels for reasons not altogether of my own choosing; and these I have now sketched in. I had an A.B. degree in history from before the war and I began to consider going to graduate school and trying to get a job teaching—perhaps in one of the new community colleges that were proliferating around San Francisco. Such a route had become possible (theoretically at least) because the courts had set aside the California loyalty oath. My friend Clint Jencks, who had an A.B. in economics, was thinking along similar lines.

Jencks had been an organizer in the Mine, Mill, and Smelter Workers' Union (CIO), damaged but not quite destroyed under the Taft-Hartley Act by attacks from more conservative unions. In the marvelous film *Salt of the Earth*—collectively produced by an embattled local of the Mine, Mill, and Smelter Workers in New Mexico (under the direction of the blacklisted Hollywood director Herbert Biberman and scripted by the Academy Award–winning and also blacklisted screenwriter Mike Wilson)—Jencks had played his own role, that of union organizer. *Salt of the Earth* defied not only the Hollywood blacklist but also the House Un-American Activities Committee as chief instigator of the blacklist. Completed under incredible difficulties, the film was virtually banned from American screenings, at the same time that it was winning film festival awards and audience acclaim in Europe. For Clint Jencks—under other circumstances—*Salt of the Earth* might have opened a new career in labor-oriented filmmaking. Under the circumstances of the 1950s it left him jobless and broke.

It was Jencks who explored the possibilities of graduate study at Berkeley.[1] When he seemed to be surviving in that rarefied atmosphere, I made my own journey across the bay to apply for admission to the doctoral program in history. I have always been grateful to the history department at Berkeley for taking me in out of the rain, so to speak, and encouraging me to do what I could. What I did turned out to be sufficient (I believe) to justify the confidence. Starting graduate study in 1962, I completed a master's degree the following year and a doctorate in 1967. My first teaching job was at Wayne State University in Detroit. Later I returned to California to teach U.S. history at UCLA. My dissertation, published in 1971 by the University of California Press under the title *The Indispensable Enemy: Labor and the Anti-Chinese Movement in California,* remains in print twenty-five years later. It was reissued by the University of California Press in 1996.

There is one more thread of personal history I ought to tie off before moving to final assessments. I dropped out of the Communist party about 1959, not with a bang or even much of a whimper. Although I had been stunned by the unveiling of Stalinism in 1956, it was not for that reason I dropped out. I never held the American party, or myself as a member of it, responsible for Stalinism. I dropped out because I thought the party had ceased to be politically effective. With friends who stayed in, I remained on friendly terms. We began groping for a broader synthesis of the Left. Joining with Trotskyists and ex-Trotskyists and a scattering of Socialists, we set up a Socialist forum in San Franciso. The forum itself was short-lived but out of it came something of greater historical importance: the

Bay Area Committee for Fair Play for Cuba. I served as chair; the secretary was a longshoreman, a Trotskyist, Asher Harer. Striving to project an image of a non- (or at least post-) sectarian Left, we found ourselves not only fellow workers but close friends. Together we helped organize the largest radical mass meeting San Francisco had seen since the 1940s—an angry protest against the Kennedy administration's counterrevolutionary policy toward the revolution in Cuba led by Fidel Castro.[2]

What made the San Francisco Cuba committee effective was that a newly politicized generation of students at the University of California and San Francisco State turned out in support of the Cuba demonstrations. Many of those young people already had taken part in the civil rights movement, some had journeyed South to put their bodies on the line against white supremacy. The Cuba committee in San Francisco provided a channel of communication between segments of militant labor and the Old Left, on the one hand, and the upcoming New Left of the 1960s, on the other. Later, when I was teaching nineteenth-century American history on various college campuses, I marveled at the courage and achievements of young Americans of the New Left; and I grieved over the disintegration of their movement.

I would consider myself delinquent if I did not indicate how the ideological statement of *The Great Midland* now looks to me fifty years later. Almost everything I have written as a novelist and subsequently as a historian has focused on racial exploitation and white racism in the United States. Yet when I was a college student during the thirties majoring in American history at Harvard and the University of Chicago, I learned absolutely nothing about either of these problems. Although I was born in the same small New England town as W. E. B Du Bois (Great Barrington, Massachusetts), I never heard of him as a child; and although Du Bois was, one would suppose, memorable as the first African American to complete a doctorate at Harvard, I never heard of him at Harvard either. What I learned about Du Bois, and most of what I learned about racial discrimination in U.S. history, I learned in the Communist party. On race, as on the condition of women, the American Communist party stood fifty years ahead of most of the rest of this country, including its government, its educational apparatus, its organized labor movement, and its mainstream churches. Had American communism done nothing else but to push forward these two issues, that would have been enough to have earned an honorable place in political and intellectual history.

I feel scant sympathy for one-time Marxists whose revulsion for Stalinism led them to become cold war champions, even less for some of my former colleagues who pled they had been lured or deceived into communism. We were not deceived. As I look back on world crises that have dominated our lifetimes, I think the positions taken by the American Communist party stack up well enough to need no apology by contrast to those, say, of the American State Department, the CIA, or the Democratic and Republican parties of the United States. Power, military power especially, corrupts manipulators of power. Both antagonists of the cold war were by power possessed—and corrupted.

To evaluate the cold war, however, in terms of relative degrees of guilt or innocence is to collaborate in obscuring its historical context. That context was the rise of industrial capitalism in the nineteenth century and the Marxist criticism of industrial capitalism as at once compulsively productive and compulsively exploitive. Capitalism, in the Marxian analysis, contains no structural limits to either of these imperatives; consequently it accentuates social inequality and universalizes human exploitation. To propagate exploitive inequality is to destroy the only possible basis of social morality: that was (and remains) the bottom line of the Marxist indictment of industrial capitalism.

As a positive alternative to its critique of capitalism, Marxism projected the image of an industrial order without human exploitation—socialism. Millions of people around the world have seen in that image a road to the future. Capitalism responded to the Marxian criticism, and to the utopian image, by marshaling the immense powers of national governments for a century-long series of bloody repressions (in which the cold war forms only one phase) that stretch from the Paris Commune to the CIA intervention in Chile.

The cold war, for many who lived through it, was an exceptionally dirty war in the sense that its complexity permitted no clear choices. To support Washington and the Pentagon in their confrontations with the Soviet Union was also to support a global war of extermination against socialist beginnings—even against the possible sparks of such beginnings. To support the Soviet Union in its confrontations with the United States was to support the Stalinist dictatorship that murdered socialism in the name of socialism. Living in America, I chose to stand against the cold war policies of the United States in every way I could. Thus I signed and circulated the Stockholm petition against atomic armament, tried to protect the Cuban revolution from American invasion, opposed war in Korea and Vietnam. I never believed these were perfect choices; they were the best I could find.

Marxist criticism through the past hundred years, together with mass imaging of a nonexploitive social order, has furnished the ideological framework of working-class (and middle-class) resistance to industrial capitalism. Within the boundaries of national politics, such resistance took the form of labor organization, labor politics, agrarian populist movements, the Social Democratic parties in Europe. Beyond these national boundaries, resistance sometimes exploded in rebellions against capitalism itself. What resulted, for so-called "democratic" industrial nations in the West, has been a grungy stalemate generally known as welfare statism. Welfare states promise to their own national working classes—in return for capitalist control of the economic system—certain protections against being reduced to the absolute level of the world labor market. While in one respect this compromise rests upon fears of accelerating class conflict at home, its cutting edge during the twentieth century has been at the periphery, in actual or potential revolutions aimed at breaking out of the capitalist industrial world. Thus welfare statism, which during the Great Depression and again at the end of World War II proved the salvation of capitalism, owed its survival in large measure to the existence of the Soviet Union and Communist China—as well as to anticapitalist insurgencies in the Third World.

Any such symbiotic connection was of course denied in the West, especially so by leaders of partially co-opted labor movements and cautiously reformist Social Democratic or Eurocommunist parties. Yet the reality of the symbiosis seems confirmed precisely by its demise. No sooner had the Soviets self-destructed and Communist China signaled a switch to the capitalist road—no sooner, in short, had the cold war bottomed out in celebrations of free market capitalism—than welfare states began to wither. The cold war had functioned at several different levels. Its earliest phase created a setting appropriate for isolating, demonizing, and disarming the domestic defenders of welfare state institutions. Its final phase eliminated any immediate likelihood of anticapitalist revolts at the periphery. Now the welfare states of the West, one by one, are surrendering their strongholds to the vivisectionist politics of free market capitalism. Tomorrow the new world order of exponentially accelerating affluence and misery: a bleak prospect for survival of the human species. Thus the Marxian indictment of capitalism stands out more cogently at the end of the cold war than when it was first written one hundred fifty years ago. And yes, our aspirations for a society without human exploitation remain unrealized—yet why should that be so for minds that can learn to explore cosmic space?

In the final pages of *The Great Midland* Stephanie is climbing the steps of an elevated train station west of the university. It is evening, winter. Dave is away again, at war. She looks out over the snow-patched rooftops of working-class Chicago. One day, she thinks, one day out of the yards and alleys and little houses that stretch endlessly beyond the embankment the fire would crackle up. The fire of Stephanie's hope is the fire of collective commitment and revolutionary change. My most recently published book, *The Rise and Fall of the White Republic* (1990), a work not (intentionally at least) of fiction, but of history, contains the following in its next-to-final paragraph:

> in the long run the ancient wisdom seems likely to prevail: a camel will pass through the eye of a needle sooner than a rich man enter the kingdom of heaven. Wealth, privilege, power, tend to narrow the vision of ruling classes and their mercenary retainers. If this is true, far-reaching prospects of the human condition are more likely to be constructed in the ghettoes of great cities and Third World barrios (or in the work of intellectuals whose socialization has somehow contained "organic" links to such experience) than among skilled industrial technicians or within military-industrial complexes.

Noting the similarity of these two passages, an unfriendly critic might suggest that their author had learned nothing new in half a century. My own conclusion is that what I learned in the 1940s remains substantially true in 1997. Would I revoke if I could the decision I made in 1942 to join the Communist party? I would not.

NOTES

1. Jencks wrote his dissertation on labor in British coal mining and taught for many years in the economics department of California State University at San Diego. *Salt of the Earth*—an affirmation of the rights of working people to equality and respect and the need for union organization to protect those rights—contained within its labor narrative a beautifully evoked story of women's struggle for equality and respect inside their own class, from their lovers and husbands and sons. It is this inner story—rediscovered by the feminist movement in the 1970s—that gives *Salt of the Earth* its status as a classic in American film.

2. Asher Harer wrote me (December 1995): "Ruth and I are still Trotskyists—although we do not belong to any political organizations except the Gray Panthers and the Labor Party Advocates. In February we are to going to Cuba (our first trip!) on a Global Exchange tour. We'll talk about it when you come to SF."

BIBLIOGAPHY

Books by Alexander Saxton

Grand Crossing. New York: Harper and Brothers, 1943.
The Great Midland. New York: Appleton-Century-Crofts, 1948.
Bright Web in the Darkness. New York: St. Martin's Press, 1958.
The Indispensable Enemy: Labor and the Anti-Chinese Movement in California. Berkeley: University of California Press, 1971.
The Rise and Fall of the White Republic: Class Politics and Mass Culture in Nineteenth-Century America. London: Verso, 1990.

Reviews of *The Great Midland*

Canwright, Norman. "Alexander Saxton and *The Great Midland*." *People's World,* 13 Jan. 1949, 5.
Conroy, Jack. "*The Great Midland*." *Chicago Sun-Times,* 16 Nov. 1948, 11.
Fast, Howard. "The Railroad Men." *Masses and Mainstream* 1.9 (Nov. 1948): 81–84.
"*The Great Midland*." *Booklist* 45.6 (15 Nov. 1948): 103.
"*The Great Midland*." *Kirkus* 16 (1 Sept. 1948): 450.
"*The Great Midland*." *New Yorker,* 6 Nov. 1948, 131.
Match, Richard. "*The Great Midland*." *New York Herald Tribune Weekly Book Review,* Nov. 7, 1948, 20.
McG., J. B. "*The Great Midland*." *Providence Journal,* 12 Nov. 1948, 16.
R., M. "*The Great Midland*." *San Francisco Chronicle,* 28 Nov. 1948, 11.
Smith, Bradford. "Labor's Pains, 1919–41." *Saturday Review* 31.49 (4 Dec. 1948): 34.

Other Sources

Buhle, Paul. "Race and Democracy—II." *The Nation,* 17 June 1991, 822–25.
Humboldt, Charles. "Communists in Novels, II." *Masses and Mainstream* 2.7 (July 1949): 44–65.
Stern, Frederick C. "Sexton's Late-Proletarian Triptych: To Chicago and West." *MidAmerica* 7 (1980): 125–55.
Rideout, Walter. *The Radical Novel in the United States, 1900-1954.* Cambridge, Mass.: Harvard University Press, 1956. 268–69.
Wald, Alan M. *Writing from the Left.* London: Verso, 1994. 187–91.

To Constance Coiner

ALEXANDER SAXTON

The introduction that precedes this commemoration was originally intended as an afterword. The real introduction to the second edition of *The Great Midland* was to have been written by Constance Coiner, a young scholar teaching American literature and women's studies at the State University of New York in Binghamton. Constance Coiner had done her doctoral work at UCLA, where I had the good fortune to be a member of her dissertation committee. As a scholar, Constance Coiner was intense and thorough. As a literary critic she was relentlessly probing and unerringly constructive. I think she was the most gifted teacher I have ever known.

My relation to Constance was mediated through a third person who actually existed only in our respective imaginations—the fictional character Stephanie Koviak in my novel *The Great Midland*. I had already been working several years with Constance on her dissertation research before I learned she had even read *The Great Midland,* then long since out of print. Happening on the novel in the library, Constance explained to me, she identified parts of her own life with Stephanie Koviak, whose story somehow opened for her doors of possibility. I might have been inflated with pride at this information but instead felt humiliated because, although I had in a sense created Stephanie Koviak, I had not known she possessed such powers until Constance pointed them out to me.

Thus it was from Constance I learned that Stephanie was really the central character of my novel. I could never have written what I wrote about Stephanie Koviak in my introduction had it not been for Constance's critical perception of Stephanie.

Along with her other multiple enterprises, Constance took up advocacy of *The Great Midland.* That the novel is being republished fifty years after its first run is due in large part to her relentless (but good-humored) badgering of potential publishers. That she did not herself write the introduction is because, with her twelve-year-old daughter Ana, she died in the crash of TWA Flight 800 off Long Island in June 1996.

My wife and I—like many others—loved Constance and wept at her death. During almost eighty years of living we had accumulated some familiarity with death. One of our two daughters died of cancer; and in that case, after a year of struggling and suffering, death wore the gentle disguise of rational and benign resolution. O sane and sacred death, as Walt Whitman wished to believe it. I have never so starkly encountered the insane contingency and arrogance of death as in the deaths of Constance and Ana.

Among Constance's favored quotations were lines from Antonio Gramsci in which he defines the *summum bonum* of human existence as pessimism of the intellect held in tandem with optimism of the will. I am trying to will that optimism. This new printing of *The Great Midland* is dedicated to Constance Coiner, who, while she lived, helped to make the earth a saner and more sacred place.

THE GREAT MIDLAND

THE FIRST WAR

1912

EDDIE SPAAS sat in the door of the boxcar and dangled his feet. He held his guitar on his knees, strumming and singing over the noise of the wheels,

> "You will eat by and by
> In that glorious land above the sky;
> Work and pray, live on hay,
> You'll get pie in the sky when you die."

Out from the tracks, the emerald-green cornfields swept away, rolling and folding to the horizon. The fields shimmered under the July sunlight. Eddie leaned through the door of the car and looked up ahead at the engine, sawing along like an old horse under its column of smoke. A few buildings appeared over the edge of the prairie, while beyond the buildings lay a bank of smoky-looking haze out of which the sun had just risen.

"Wake up, Uncle Jennison, you lazy yellow dog," Eddie called over his shoulder. "We're coming into Chicago." Uncle Jennison, who was stretched out on the floor of the car with his head on his satchel, groaned and pulled his straw hat farther down over his eyes. "Wake up," Eddie shouted, "you rotten good-for-nothing Wobbly bastard. Wake up, I tell you." Turning around, he twanged his guitar close beside Uncle Jennison's ear, and improvised words to the tune of Yankee Doodle:

> "Uncle Jennison came to town
> A-riding in a boxcar,
> He stuck his finger up his nose
> And said it smells like coal tar."

Uncle Jennison opened his eyes abruptly and sat up. "You and your damn caterwauling. It's a wonder I put up with it." They both moved into the doorway now and sat smoking their pipes, looking out at the cornfields while Eddie strummed notes at random. Buildings and streets sprang out of the prairie in front of them. The train slowed and Eddie and Uncle Jennison, to keep clear of the company police, dropped off as they reached the edge of the yard. They slid down the embankment, crossed an open field to the corner of Kedzie and Lake, and took the streetcar downtown.

An hour and a half of clattering past long blocks and crowded intersections brought them at last to the south side of the city. Eddie was looking for an address which his younger brother Joe had sent him. This turned out to be a three-story brick building on Halsted Street, a boardinghouse with a lunchroom on the ground floor. The landlady who met them on the steps told them, yes, Joe Spaas lived there but right now he was sleeping and they ought not to wake him because he had worked all night. But they pushed past her, threw open the doors along the second-floor landing until they found the room Eddie's brother Joe was sleeping in. Joe Spaas sat up in bed and rubbed his eyes, and Eddie piled on top of him, shaking his hand, slapping him on the back. "How are you kid? I'm glad to see you, young fellow. Want you to meet my buddy, Uncle Jennison—but hell, you know him already, don't you?" Eddie, talking in a rush, pulled Uncle Jennison down beside him and put an arm around each of them. "So how's the old turnpike treating you since we left? Made a chewing, spitting brakeman out of you, hey? Didn't know when you was well off, but you had to go railroading. Haven't seen you in a coon's age, my lad—"

Wrestling free of Eddie, the boy went over to the bureau where he pulled on his pants. He kept looking back uneasily at the two men on the bed. "Are you going home?" he asked.

"No sir," Eddie said. "Don't reckon I'll ever get back to Albany as long as I live."

"What did you come for?" the boy asked. "You going to work at the yard again?"

"No, we come to attend a convention. But—anyhow, my boy, we got delayed on the way so the convention's all over. We'll just hang around long enough to see how you're getting along. Can you put us up, hey? Can you take care of a couple of hard-working stiffs?"

"I guess the landlady has another room if you want it."

4

"We'll tell the landlady to go fry her ass. You won't be using your bed tonight if you're working night shift. We'll just turn in here. Say, Unc, will you look at the kid; he shaves already!" Eddie jumped up and stroked his brother's cheek with the back of his hand. "Smooth as goose fuzz. And you're a brakeman—!" He hooked his arm in Joe's and pulled him towards the door. "Come on, we'll go set up some suds for ourselves. Saw a place on the corner when I come in."

Joe shook his head violently and broke away again. "Listen, Eddie, I'm glad to see you and all like that. But I don't want any beer, and I want to catch some sleep because I got to work tonight."

Eddie's mouth dropped open in amazement, but Uncle Jennison said, "Let the kid alone. He's all right. You shouldn't have woke him up to start with, you lame-brain." He pushed Eddie into the corridor, and Joe called after them, "I'll get you a room from the landlady. I got money enough; I can pay for it. But I don't want you sleeping in my bed."

"Can you tie that?" Eddie asked.

He and Jennison went down to the street again and rode the trolley car to the IWW hall on the Near North Side. Here they found four or five men and a couple of girls putting together the minutes of the convention—which, as one of the men told them, had ended two days before. The secretary stepped out of the inner office and took them downstairs for coffee and doughnuts. Uncle Jennison explained how they had stopped to make a speech in a little town near Fargo, North Dakota, and it was two weeks later before they got out of the jug. That was how they had missed the convention.

"Where you from?" the secretary asked.

"Montana. Near Butte."

"Miners?"

"No," Eddie said. "We're railroad workers. I'm a brakeman, and this bald-headed stink-finger is a carknocker."

"Well, brothers," the secretary told them, "that's what the working stiff has got to put up with. Delegates to the American Federation of Labor conventions ride in Pullman cars, but the IWW's travel by freight and get thrown in the hoosegow into the bargain." When they had finished the coffee and doughnuts, the secretary gave them the minutes and resolutions of the convention so they could at least make a report to their membership

5

in Montana. Then they all shook hands and Eddie and Jennison went back to the boardinghouse on South Halsted Street.

Eddie's brother Joe had not come down yet, so they borrowed a bucket from the landlady and Eddie fetched a gallon of beer from the saloon on the corner. They sat down on the back porch which looked out over a little vegetable garden, and the landlady joined them to help with the beer. The landlady's daughter came out too, bringing a pan of spuds, and she lay on the grass in front of the porch peeling the potatoes, and looking up grinning at Eddie sometimes while he joked back and forth with the landlady.

"You fellows ever work for a living?" the landlady asked.

"Haven't had much need to work," Eddie told her, "ever since we located that gold in Nevada—"

"You located some gold?"

"Show her that bag of gold dust you got in your pocket, Unc." Jennison took off his hat, wiped his bald head, but said nothing. He whistled at the birds in the garden and refilled his glass steadily from the bucket. "Unc don't like to show that gold dust around too much," Eddie explained, and the landlady laughed and said that was one story she hadn't ever heard before. But Eddie after a short time grew tired of the conversation and moved down on the grass beside the girl. He chewed up a raw potato and talked to her about the places he had been—San Francisco and Portland, the valley of the Columbia, and Tallefer, high up in the Rockies. The girl asked him what the mountains looked like and what kind of trees grew there, and if you could see flowers popping right up beside the snowdrifts like the books said. As she listened to him, she stopped her work and kept putting the same half-peeled potato into the pan and then taking it out again.

Finally the landlady yelled, "Quit pounding your gums down there. We need them spuds for supper."

It was about five o'clock when Joe came down, puffy-eyed and cross from sleep. They ate together at the counter in the lunchroom; Joe told Eddie how he had gone back home at Christmas time and how everybody at home was getting along, and then he began talking about his job. He was hind man already after only a year, and the yardmaster told him he'd get to be a conductor in a few months more. Talking steadily in a low voice, he explained how he knew all the tracks in the yard by heart and now he could switch out cars where they belonged without even asking the yardmaster most of the time. Uncle Jennison winked at Eddie. The landlady's daughter was waiting on the counter and every time she came past with an armful of dishes, Joe stopped talking and ducked his head over his plate. The girl set pie and coffee down for them. She said to Joe, "Here y'are, Mr. Conductor," and Eddie and Uncle Jennison almost keeled over laughing.

After supper they walked out into Halsted Street. Uncle Jennison and Eddie lighted their pipes and they strolled down to the corner and back. Joe struck up a black cigar which he held clenched between his teeth with his lips drawn back from it.

"Look out, my lad," Eddie said. "That seegar is liable to explode and blow your head right off." He felt cross because he wanted to tell Joe about Montana and what it was like braking in the mountains; but Joe didn't ask any questions, and soon began telling them all over again how well he knew the tracks in the Great Midland yard. By the time it got dark, Joe took his lantern, picked up his lunch from the landlady, and went off to work. Eddie and Uncle Jennison wandered down to the saloon for a glass of beer.

The landlady gave them a room under the eaves, with a gable window and a big double bed. Eddie woke at daybreak and saw that Uncle Jennison was up already, climbing into his clothes. He watched suspiciously.

"Thought I'd drop over to the Great Midland yard for a little bit," Jennison explained. "Shake your keester out of that flea-tick, Eddie. We haven't seen the boys over there in a couple of years."

"Don't care if we never see those boys for a couple hundred years," Eddie said. But he crawled out from under the blanket, dressed, and followed Jennison downstairs, complaining all the way about missing his sleep. As they waited on the corner for the southbound Halsted streetcar, Jennison said, "Let's just see how your kid brother works. And we'll say hello to all the boys."

In the yard, they found Eddie's brother Joe running up and down with a sheaf of papers in his hand, lining up switches for the boxcars that came rumbling along in batches of two and three, as the switch engine kicked them down the lead. The brakemen whom Eddie and Uncle Jennison knew came over joking and whistling to welcome them back. A lot of cars were in the yard and three engines mauling them around; plenty of work for all summer, the brakemen told them.

Uncle Jennison stooped down and said into Eddie's ear, "What would you think of getting our old jobs back?"

"Are you off your noggin?" Eddie shouted.

Jennison shook his head. "Maybe I'll step in and see the foreman. We could pick up a little work here for a month or so, hey Eddie?"

Eddie grabbed him by the arm. "You must be getting dizzy spells. Come along with me, Unc. We'll have a drink and catch the hotshot west."

But Jennison pulled his arm free. "Let go my arm, Eddie. I'll just drop over and say hello to the foreman." He crossed the tracks to the yard office, and Eddie remained staring after him. He glanced around at the crowd of brakemen who were still busy talking about all the work in the yard and urging him to hire out again. Then he saw Jarvis, the union chairman for the car repairmen, push into the circle. "Hello, Eddie," Jarvis said. "Was that my old buddy Jennison I see going into the office?"

Eddie nodded without answering.

"What's the matter," Jarvis asked. "They run your ass out of Montana?"

"Gets too cold there in the summers," Eddie explained. He turned and looked the other up and down. Jarvis was a short little man beginning to grow plump, with a round face and round beady eyes. He wore a necktie, a clean blue shirt, and spotless overalls, as if he had not come within several yards of any grease or mud in a number of years. "Who you representing now?" Eddie asked. "The union or the company?"

The brakemen began to snicker and Jarvis flushed. "I'm union chairman just like I always was," he said. "If you and Jennison figure to come back here, you better lay off that Wobbly talk."

Eddie suddenly shouted in his face, "You AFL company fink! I thought they'd promoted you to foreman by this time." He and Jarvis immediately began yelling at each other while the brakemen slapped their legs in delight.

"Eddie ain't changed a bit," they howled. "Give it to him, Eddie!" Men came running from all over the yard to find what the commotion was about. Eddie waited till he saw Jennison and the foreman come flying through the door of the yard office;

then he stepped back, kicked Jarvis in the stomach and punched him in the eye as he doubled up. He was swinging his foot back to kick Jarvis again, when his brother Joe jumped him and two or three others piled on top. After that there was a free-for-all with everybody kicking and punching, and Eddie on the bottom getting the worst of it. The next thing he knew, he saw Uncle Jennison up above him swinging a brake club; it took only a few thuds and yells before the pile had cleared off. Uncle Jennison pulled Eddie to his feet, and together they took off across the yard with five or six carmen and a couple of railroad cops after them. They scrambled down the embankment and caught a street-car on the run.

When he had got his breath back, Uncle Jennison asked, "What did you do that for, Eddie?"

Eddie did not answer, and Jennison patted him on the knee. "You done it on purpose, Eddie. I know you. But I guess I didn't really want to go back to the yard at that."

That evening they sat on the back porch, watching the twilight filter down through the leaves of the trees that grew in a row across the end of the back yard. A gang of kids with a bicycle raced up and down the alley. The leaves overhead stirred faintly, and from somewhere in the distance drifted the reedy voice of a calliope at a street carnival. Joe came out and stood behind them.

"Listen Eddie," he said. "I'm glad to see you and all like that. But why do you have to come over here and make trouble for me? I'm getting along good at the yard. I know all the tracks and I'll be a conductor in a couple months more. And now you got to come over and start trouble."

"Relax, my boy," Uncle Jennison said. "We won't be going back to the yard."

Eddie fetched out his guitar and was getting started on his stock of Wobbly songs when the landlady's daughter in a long blue dress with blue ribbons under her chin came down from the kitchen. She was a lithe, dark-haired girl and she swung herself over the porch railing without disarranging her skirt; then glanced back at them for a moment and set off between the rows of vegetables.

"Where you going all dressed up?" Eddie called.

"What do you care?"

"I only asked to be polite."

9

"I'm going to the carnival. You can hear the music, can't you?"

Eddie crouched forward on one knee with his hand cupped behind his ear as if he were listening for an Indian whoop. "That sure is a sour machine," he said. "Would you like some company?"

The girl shrugged her shoulders. "It's a public place. I can't stop you going to a carnival."

Strapping the guitar across his back, Eddie vaulted the porch railing into the garden. "Come along, Joe," he shouted. But Joe got up without answering and went back into the house, while Uncle Jennison propped his feet on the railing and puffed dreamily on his pipe.

There was only a two-by-six ferris wheel at the carnival, but it swung them up over the chimneys and treetops so they could see the city stretching out below them in the gray evening. "You're not like your brother," the girl said. "Are you?"

"Maybe not. But he's a good lad, ain't he?"

"I guess he's all right."

"Well then, what's wrong with him?" Eddie demanded.

The girl wrinkled her nose and laughed. "I call him Mr. Conductor. He's always talking about that railroad where he works, and it makes him mad that I call him Mr. Conductor." Eddie paid for three rides on the ferris wheel; after that, they tried the merry-go-round, looked in all the booths and peep-shows, and then settled down at the beer counter behind the carnival. Eddie unlimbered his guitar and began teaching the girl how to sing "Pie in the Sky":

> "Long-haired preachers come out every night,
> Try to tell you what's wrong and what's right;
> But when asked how 'bout something to eat
> They will answer with voices so sweet:
> You will eat by and by
> In that glorious land above the sky;
> Work and pray, live on hay,
> You'll get pie in the sky when you die."

A knot of people gathered around; everybody drank a lot of beer and they made Eddie go through all the songs he knew. He sang the verses in his shrill voice, and the others joined in if they remembered the words.

It was after midnight when he and the girl headed back to the boardinghouse weaving a crooked path down the middle of the street. "We're wobbling all over," the girl said. "Look at us." Then she wrinkled her nose at him and told him how just because she had wrinkled her nose that way, the Catholic sisters had expelled her from their school; but she was glad because she hadn't liked it there anyway. She told him about the boardinghouse and how tired she got fixing food and waiting on table; and how one evening at supper, she had thrown a dinner plate right through the glass door into the street.

"What made me do a thing like that, Eddie?" she asked. "I got mad and stamped my foot and let it fly. The boarders all thought I was going crazy." She opened the gate from the alley into the vegetable garden. "You been a lot of places, haven't you?"

"I been around."

"I'm not going to stay here long," she told him. "I want to see places too. A girl wants to have a good time and go places like anybody else." Between the rows of beans and summer squash, Eddie put his arms around her, and she dropped her head back, opening her lips under his.

"Will your ma hear us if we go up to your room?"

"Yes, she'd hear us."

"We'll have to stay down here then."

The girl shook her head. "It's too wet. You go up to your room and wait by the window. I can get there."

"But Unc's in the room," Eddie said. "That's my buddy, I mean, Uncle Jennison. Well, I'll throw him out, that's all. The old bald-headed bastard can sleep in Joe's bed."

"Is he really your uncle?"

"Him? No, everybody calls him Unc. I don't know why."

She giggled suddenly. "He's funny. He hasn't any hair and he always wears that hat." Pushing Eddie away, she ran across the garden to the kitchen door.

Eddie walked around to the front entrance. Upstairs, when he lighted the lamp, he found the room empty, and a note on the dresser from Uncle Jennison. *"There's no use arguing with guys that got skirt fever,"* the note said. *"I'll see you some other time. The bedsprings squeak bad, you better set the mattress on the floor."*

Eddie posed for himself for a moment in front of the mirror. He needed a haircut, and the skin was peeling off his bony and sunburned nose. But he shrugged his shoulders and slipped the note from Jennison in his pocket. Then he dragged the mattress down from the four poster bed, blew out the kerosene lamp, and stood by the window. Below him, the shingles slanted steeply down to the eaves. A faint mist, rising out of the garden, trailed through the branches of the trees, and the musky smell of wet earth hung in the night air. He heard a noise above him. Leaning around the corner of the gable window, he watched the girl climb over the ridge pole and feel her way down the slope of the roof. She jumped in the window and stood in front of him, laughing.

"I guess you better tell me your name," he said.

"Oh, you don't know my name yet? My name's Ann." She pressed against him, supple in his arms, laughing at him, biting at his lips and cheeks.

Every evening after supper, they went out together. Sometimes they would go to the carnival, or sometimes to the White City over on Sixty-Third Street. Sometimes they took the trolley car east and walked along by the lakeshore. Then late at night when the house was quiet, she came over the roof to him and stayed until daybreak. They waked and slept and lay whispering together. She told him the things she wanted to do and the wild ideas that went through her head; she wanted to know the names of all the girls he had gone with, and the places he had seen; and he told her about the Wobblies, and how many hoosegows he had been inside of. During the day, he did not know what to do next and he felt dizzy and drunken with looking forward to the evening.

One Sunday night as he stood by the window waiting for her, he heard the sound of feet clumping up the stairs, and Uncle Jennison kicked the door open.

"Hello, Unc," Eddie said. "Where you been?"

"You got skirt fever, Eddie. I can see it by looking at you. I don't suppose there's any use my talking to you."

"What do you want to talk about?" Eddie asked. "Go ahead and talk."

"I got my old job back in the yard after all, Eddie. I told 'em you was drunk and didn't know what you was doing."

"So you're going to get planted? Well, I figured that was what you wanted."

"Why don't you drop over to the yard, Eddie? Buy Jarvis a couple of drinks and let on you're sorry it all happened. They need brakemen. They'll hire you back."

Eddie shook his head.

"Listen," Jennison said. "I'll tell you the truth: my gut's bothering me, Eddie. I got no heart for hitting the road again; I've rid so many boxcars I don't want to set foot in one of them things ever again. And what about this girl, Eddie? What do you aim to do with her?"

Eddie stared in silence at the wallpaper peeling down the slant of the roof. Finally he said, "Maybe I'll take her with me."

"You're out of your mind. What do you figure to do, buy yourself a Pullman car all the way out? Are you going to take a girl like that in boxcars? And what the hell would you do with her in Tallefer? You'll have fifty-one guys climbing in your window every time you hit the night run."

"They better not."

"And how about when you want to move? You won't stay put in Tallefer; you're a worse boomer than I ever was. You'll just about get ready to pull up stakes, and she'll say: Can't move right now, daddy, I'se a little bit pregnant. You got skirt fever, you damn lighthead. Get hold of yourself."

Eddie without answering looked at the wall. At last Uncle Jennison said, "All right, Eddie. I'll be going now."

"So long, Unc."

"If you change your mind about the yard, you know where to find me."

Uncle Jennison slammed the door behind him, and Eddie stood at the open window peering into the darkness. It was raining and the smell of the vegetables and wet leaves drifted up from the garden. After a long time, he heard her whistle to him, and she slid down the shingles; he caught her and lifted her in through the window.

"Ooh," she whispered, "it's raining. I'm soaked through." Tossing her head back, she shook the water from her hair like a wet dog; then unfastened her dress, dropped her clothes in a heap on the floor, and jumped into bed. She went to sleep in his arms at last, but Eddie did not sleep. He thought how it would be to come home to her like this every night—to find her waiting for him, his all day and all night always. His throat was hot and dry with his hunger for her. Then he wiped his eyes and spat on the floor because he knew Uncle Jennison was right. He couldn't take her with him, and he couldn't stay.

In the morning, Eddie dropped a letter for her in the mailbox and caught the Northwestern hotshot to Minneapolis. He hung around the Minneapolis Wobbly hall for almost a month, and it was there he got an answer from her, three or four lines long, saying she was going to marry his brother Joe. Eddie put the letter in the bottom of his grip and tied out for the West.

For the first time in his life he felt as if he were in a hurry to get where he was going. Instead of the freights, he hopped the coal car of a mail train from Minneapolis; and as they pulled into Brainerd, Minnesota, he could see the yard dicks waiting for him in a bunch across from the depot. He climbed down the back of the coal car and dropped off. The train was going fast; Eddie turned a somersault in the cinders, and stumbled up again, bleeding from scratches all over his hands and face. The yard dicks came over to get him, but taking off across the right of way, he dived under a fence into a cornfield. He waved and whistled to them from the other side of the field, and set out along the dirt road to circle the town.

1919

IT smells like America," the man shouted. He flung his arms into the air and stamped on the familiar American pavement. "It don't smell like no foreign country. It smells like America. We're home, man!" Pledger McAdams laughed, but he could not speak. He heard the white lieutenant call them to attention. The band began to play, and they swung up Fifth Avenue with their bayonets flashing in the winter sunlight. Marching to the stamp and swing of the boots, Pledger held his head stiff beween his shoulders, but sometimes he twisted his eyes sidewise to catch a glimpse at the white people lined up along the sidewalks. The white people were shouting and waving little flags which said, "Welcome home to our heroes." In front of the public library stood the Mayor of New York City with his hat in his hands, and a lot of big officers were with him, saluting the flags which went past, while company by company, the men snapped their heads to the left.

14

The band struck up again, the men sang as they tramped up the windy sweep beside Central Park. Then at last they came into Harlem, their wives and girls broke through the lines and marched with them, arm in arm up the length of Lenox Avenue.

"Ain't your wife here to see you, Pledger?" the man next him asked.

Pledger shook his head. "I got to wait a little while yet. She's with her folks in Chicago."

Between the flashing bayonets, he could see the first flag of the regiment with the ribbons of the French Croix de Guerre streaming back across it. Happiness welled up in Pledger's chest till it almost choked him. He threw back his head while tears rolled down his face. All about him, the men and their girls were laughing and weeping at the same time. Thank God, thank God, we come back, he kept saying half aloud.

Pledger gave part of his mustering out pay for a ticket to Chicago. Through the long night, the wheels of the train hammered beneath him. Gusts of wind whirled down the coach, stirring the dust under the yellow glare of the electric lamps. Half asleep, he lay with his head against the arm of his seat, dreaming how it would be when he stepped down from the train and Sarah came towards him along the platform, when he reached out to her and pulled her against him. The wheels banged over the rails; the cold of the winter night seeped through the windows. Pledger huddled down into his khaki overcoat.

Towards midmorning, the train stopped in an Indiana town. He shook himself awake and jumped down to the platform, where he stumbled back and forth, clapping his hands and stamping his feet. Then, seeing the brakemen uncouple the engine, he walked across the street from the depot for a cup of coffee. A few people were in the restaurant eating breakfast, and Pledger sniffed the American smell of coffee and toast and bacon. Grinning with pleasure, he sat down at the counter and picked up the menu.

The counterman was standing over him. "What do you want in here, fellow?"

"Coffee and fried eggs straight up," Pledger said.

"We don't serve no colored in here."

Pledger stared at the other for a moment before he understood. "We don't serve no niggers in here," the counterman said again. Getting up from the stool, Pledger lifted his square-knuckled

15

brown hands. Then he let them drop, turned and walked to the door. He saw the other people in the restaurant watching him with expressionless faces. The door banged shut behind him. He was no longer hungry and now he did not even feel angry. He crossed the street and walked down to the end of the train. Here he could see beyond the tracks, the winter gray plains stretching away under the gray sky. Patches of snow lay in the hollows, and overhead the clouds rolled endlessly past.

He felt empty and strange. He felt ashamed to think of his wife Sarah because of what had been done to him. For a moment, he remembered that a Marshal of France had pinned to the flag of his regiment the Croix de Guerre; he remembered the French girls who had kissed them and wept over them, and the Mayor of New York standing with his hat in his hands. But now it was as if he were waking from a dream, and the friends who had been his friends vanished with the warm shadows of sleep. He found himself alone in the winter daylight, staring across the snow-patched fields.

The whistle blew and he climbed aboard the train. Stiff in his seat, he sat through the long hours as the train hammered across the prairies. But at evening, he looked out over the roofs of Chicago, at the lights glowing through the smoke of the winter twilight.

■　■

In the spring of that year, Pledger McAdams returned to his old job as car repairman in the coach yard of the Great Midland Railroad. Through the long afternoons, he and his partner worked down in the wheel pit, fixing the axles and wheels of the damaged cars. Their young white apprentice handed them tools and craned his neck down trying to follow the work. To Pledger, after three years of walking and waiting, it felt good to be back at his trade again. He sang to pass the time, and as he worked, he looked forward to supper hour and the cake and sandwiches his wife Sarah had fixed for him. When the eight o'clock whistle blew, Pledger crawled up from the pit, stretching and yawning. He and the white apprentice squirted water on their hands, trying to wash the grease off. Pledger's partner, Andrew Masters, walked off into the coach yard, and returned after a few minutes with a bottle of coffee.

"Better not let Upstairs Jarvis catch you swiping coffee off them diners," the young white apprentice said.

"Didn't swipe no coffee," Andrew Masters told him. "The chef gave it to me." His black face wrinkled up when he laughed and his gold teeth flashed. "And don't you worry none about Upstairs Jarvis. He'll have to step out right lively to catch anything on me."

They sat down in a row on the bench outside the wheel-pit house to eat their sandwiches. In front of them, the yard gang was making up the midnight express. The coach cleaners scrubbed the sides of the cars with their long-handled brushes, while the Pullman commissary men pushed along trucks loaded with bedding, towels, and food. From the rear end of the train, Pledger saw the little Polish carknocker working his way forward, tapping the wheels with his hammer and flashing his lantern at the coupling connections. By the time the carknocker reached the head end of the coaches, the passenger engine came backing in from the round house, the carknocker eased it toward the train with motions of his lantern until the coupling knuckles clanged together. Then, setting his lantern on the ground, he crawled between the engine and the cars to hook up the air hose and safety chains. The engine puffed softly, and steam drifting across its flanks glowed red through the light from the firebox. In the cab window, Pledger saw the engineer leaning on his elbow smoking a pipe, while the night yard foreman, Upstairs Jarvis, stamped around beside the engine, waving his arms and yelling. The carknocker wriggled out from between the cars, blew out his lantern, and walked over to the bench by the wheel-pit house, where Pledger and Andrew Masters made room for him.

"What's eating Jarvis?" Pledger asked.

The carknocker held his wrist up to his ear as if he were listening for the tick of a watch. "Late. She supposed to be down to the depot now." He spread his lunch on a newspaper across his knees and began slicing raw onion with his jackknife. "How your wife feel today?" he asked Pledger.

"She felt bad last night. But she's all right today."

"That's the way a woman is when she gets a kid. Feel good one day, bad the next. She real big yet?"

"She sure is." Pledger held his hands out in front of his stomach. "Big and round as a watermelon."

The Polish carknocker's face lighted with pleasure. "It's good

17

to see a woman get big. It makes you feel good to see that. Me, I got two kids—one little girl and one boy. You want some onion?" As he passed around slices on the blade of his jackknife, he told them about his little girl. "She's only five years old, and she talks better than me already. Not that I talk so good; but my little girl don't talk this Polack-American like me—she talks real American." He bit into his onion and bologna sandwich, and when he came up for air, told Pledger, "You'll like having a kid around. It'll make you feel good—"

"Koviak!"

The carknocker stopped abruptly. In the distance they heard Jarvis, the yard foreman, yelling, "Where the hell has that dumb Polack got to now?"

Pledger, grasping the carknocker's wrist, said, "You finish your lunch, man. You ain't had fifteen minutes to eat in."

The carknocker grinned, drew one finger across his throat, and gulping down the rest of his sandwich, hurried off to work again. Jarvis, the yard foreman, spotted him coming. "I'll be a son of a bitch," his voice shouted over the clatter of hammers; "the Midnight's late already and you got to be taking banker's hours—"

The three on the bench remained a few minutes longer before the whistle blew for the end of lunch period. They watched the Midnight Express puff slowly out of the yard, come to a halt silhouetted darkly along the crest of the embankment, then roll backwards toward the depot. The yard seemed deserted now that the train had gone; the rails of the empty tracks gleamed red and green under the switch lamps. Rows of lights wavered through the mist that was rising out of the ground, and the few baggage cars and coaches still scattered across the yard loomed up like islands. They went back to their work in the wheel-pit house.

Pledger took up the sledge hammer to drive free a steel pin that had frozen in its place. Andrew Masters held the chisel with a pair of long-handled tongs. The apprentice spotted the lantern beam and Pledger, his head twisted sideways under the axle, gripped the hammer close by its throat and swung up underhanded from the level of his waist. He felt sweat running down his neck, and while he worked, he thought of his wife Sarah, how big she was getting, and how pretty she looked with her hands clasped under her belly. He began to sing and hum with the blows of the hammer. Then the pin shot free, clanged down against the concrete floor of the pit, and Pledger lowered the hammer, laughing.

At midnight, he and Andrew Masters rode home together on the Wentworth Avenue streetcar. They said good night in front of Andrew Masters' little frame house which stood by itself in an almost empty block. "Would you care to come in for a bite to eat?" Andrew Masters asked. The ground floor of the house, with the words, TRINITY SPIRIT CHAPEL painted across its window in a lopsided arc, was unlighted; but on the second floor the windows glowed, and Pledger heard the sound of pans rattling on a stove. "My sister always has a bite of something ready."

Pledger shook his head. "I got to get along home. My gal's waiting for me."

"Good night then, my boy. I want you to understand that it's a comfort for me to work with a young man like you. I'm growing too old for swinging a hammer that way. Just like what it says in the Bible: 'Two are better than one, but woe to him that be alone when he fall.' Did you read where it says that?"

"Yes, I read that."

Reaching out, Andrew Masters tapped Pledger's arm. "I think you are one who try to walk in the ways of God, son. Tonight I hear you singing while you swing the hammer. You're fine and strong, son, tall as Daniel. But you know the Bible says, 'Pride of the body is a vain thing, for the body is cut down like weeds in the field.' You read the Bible?"

"Yes, I read it," Pledger said.

"Only sure strength, son, is to walk in the way of God, for that is hope and strength of spirit. If you'd wish to come, you could pray with us on our prayer nights. We meet Sunday evenings."

"I'd like to come, thanks."

They said good night again, and Pledger hurried up the street to the flat-faced brick building in the next block where he and Sarah lived. The widow woman who ran the Chile Parlor next door was still sitting outside her shop, playing cribbage with a man by the light from the store window. "Would you like something cool to drink, Mr. McAdams?" she called; but Pledger shook his head and went into the building.

Inside, he stopped for a moment, his hand on the banister of the stairway, listening in the darkness to the sounds around him. From behind the many closed doors, he heard people moving, laughing, talking, whispering; the clatter of dishes, the creak of bedsprings, the sudden shrill cry of a child. Then he ran up the stairs. Sarah was in bed half asleep, but she got up and set his supper on the table for him while he washed in the bucket of warm water on the stove.

■ ■

Out beyond the last houses, the evening darkened over the prairie. The sun floated down towards the rim of the horizon. The long line of telegraph poles which had stood sharply against the sunset, wavered now and faded in the gathering dusk.

Mist floated up from the hollows; a chorus of crickets sang out shrilly. The stars blossomed one by one through the midsummer evening. Diagonally out of the west, following the line of telegraph poles from the still faintly glowing horizon on one side to the orange shimmer of the city on the other, the freight train rumbled northeastwards along the embankment. Its headlamp cut like the prow of a ship through the milky blue breakers of mist; the roll of its wheels grew stronger until it filled the whole night, echoing and reverberating, muffled for a moment beyond hearing, then thundering out louder than before.

Across the prairie, across the silver cornfields, past the first lonely street lamps at the intersections of streets where there were yet no buildings, past the vacant lots and back yards, past the dark factories and the slanting moonlit roofs of the city, the boxcars, coal cars, oil cars, hammered over the rails; the whistle wailed, the red lamps of the caboose dwindled into the distance. The swirling cinders pattered down like hail, the smoke drifted away over the rooftops, the endless moonlit rooftops of Chicago. . . .

"We sinned, oh Lord, but heal us with mercy. We transgressed, oh Lord, but it was weakness of flesh, not weakness of spirit. Make our flesh strong," Andrew Masters cried, flinging out his arms, "Lord, though men revile us, make our flesh strong to walk in the ways of the Lamb of Christ."

Teeth and the shining eyes flashed white in the lamplight. The people cried Amen and clapped their hands. The clapping flowed into a rhythm; the voices singing filled the chapel.

"Surely goodness and mercy shall follow me all the days of my life!"

"Goodness and mercy, Lord,
Sweetness and Life."

Pledger McAdams heard his own voice among the others. His heart swelled against his chest. He felt the hand of God come close to them, guiding them, stretching out to them over the breathless streets of the summer night. And after the prayer meeting, as he and his wife Sarah returned home, he put his arm around her, and she walked proudly leaning backwards, so that the widow woman sitting in front of the Chile Parlor giggled as they passed and called out, "It's a boy sure, Mis' McAdams."

Upstairs in their room on the top floor, they took off their clothes and crawled into bed. Pledger pressed his hands against Sarah's belly, laughing in wonder at the kicks and stirrings from inside.

He and Sarah went each Sunday evening to Andrew Masters' chapel. Most of the other Negroes from the railroad yard came with their families; the word passed around, and each week the congregation grew larger until all the seats were taken and people stood up along the wall at the back.

Sunday was the only day the men had free, and very often they did not get that. For every week there seemed to be more work in the Great Midland coach yard. The company built an extra wheel pit and put on more crews of car repairmen. After a few weeks the white apprentice whom Pledger and Andrew Masters had been training moved up to helper-apprentice on the day shift. Another white apprentice came to break in with Pledger and Andrew Masters in the wheel pit.

Now they began repairing cars that had not been painted or shopped since 1915, before the war. They worked overtime, three and four hours a night. The cars rolled endlessly on to the pit tracks; the days and nights moved past in the succession of eating, sleeping, waking, hurrying to the yard. Sometimes the yard got so jammed with broken cars that Upstairs Jarvis, the foreman, couldn't make up his trains; he raced back and forth yelling at the men and shouting, "Koviak, you dumb Polack carknocker, where the hell you got to now?" Then the big shots came down from the depot to find what the tie-up was, and when they had gone, Jarvis and the company policeman gumshoed all over the yard trying to catch somebody sitting down or smoking on the job.

The company kept hiring men as fast as they came in off the street; they started as coach cleaners at twenty-five cents an hour—

mostly Mexicans from Texas and Negroes just out of the South who still held their hats in their hands and said, "Yas suh," and "No suh" when a white man spoke to them. To Pledger and Andrew Masters they listened with respectful nods of their heads, because Pledger and Andrew Masters were regular carmen.

"How much a carman make a day, man?"

And when Andrew Masters told them, they winked and nodded and clicked their teeth. "Straight man, how long it take us to get to be carmen?"

"You got to learn the trade first," Andrew Masters told them. "Then before long you get on a carmen's job just like us."

Pledger, coming into the wheel pit one day at the start of the afternoon shift, found the white boy they had first trained as apprentice waiting for him. He was a long-legged kid with a freckled face and red hair. "Listen," the boy said, pulling Pledger into the corner by the forge. "They asked me today did I think I could handle a job as regular carman."

"Sure enough, Red? We must have trained you right good." Then Pledger stared down sharply into the boy's face.

"You know whose job they figure to give me?"

"Whose?"

"Yours. They say you ain't going to be working here much longer."

"Who? Who say that?"

"Upstairs Jarvis said it. I told him I don't want your job, Pledger, but it don't make any difference. One of the others will take it."

Without answering, Pledger nodded his head and turned away. Then he swung back suddenly, caught the boy by the wrists and forced him against the wall. "We trained you," he shouted. "We learned you your work and now you're ready to spit in our faces because we're colored. I tell you you better shag out of here before I break you in half." He shoved the boy across the wheel-pit house; but a moment later, running after him, put his arm around the boy's shoulders. "I got to apologize now, Red. I know it ain't your fault, boy. You acted square to tell me."

Pledger went the next morning to find the chairman of the Car Builders' Union. The chairman took off his hat and wiped himself with a bandanna which left blue streaks across his bald head.

"Nope, they can't get away with that, Brother McAdams."

22

"Who's to stop 'em?"

"*We'll* stop 'em, that's who. The union'll fight your case just like you was one of our own members. I sure wish you could join the union."

"I'll pay the dues if you ask me to."

The chairman shook his head. "The constitution don't allow you to join, that's all." Then stretching his long neck forward, he said in a low voice, "I'm a new chairman here, see. Just got elected a couple months back. My name's Jennison."

"Glad to know you," Pledger said.

"Between you and me, this constitution's got a lot of reactionary, yellow-dog, Jim Crow clauses in it. We're going to fight 'em and pretty soon we'll get 'em out. Keep that under your hat, Brother McAdams."

Pledger said that he would.

Just as there were more workers in the coach yard and more people crowding Andrew Masters' chapel, so it seemed to Pledger there must be more people everywhere. The family next door to the room where he and Sarah lived took in some relatives from Louisiana; they slept by shifts in the one bed, while the kids played all day on the stairs. And on his way to work, Pledger noticed the growing crowds along the avenues—Negroes in overalls and wide-brimmed straw hats, who wandered up and down staring in amazement at the city around them. To the gossip of the neighbors and the talk of the Negro workers in the coach yard, Pledger paid little heed; yet he felt a growing sense of uneasiness with the hot August days. The wind, stirring over the rooftops, blanketed the city with the pig smell of the stockyards. The streetcars were jammed. On the sidewalks, people waited in line while the loaded cars went past without stopping. Sometimes there were fights on the corners at the fringes of the colored section. Late at night gangs of kids ran shouting beside the streetcars, and once Pledger saw a stone crash through the window, cutting a woman's face with slivers of glass.

Pledger and Andrew Masters at dusk worked sweating in the wheel pit, slapping at mosquitoes that came whining into the beam of the acetylene lamp. Andrew Masters lighted a piece of oily waste in an old tin can to lay a smudge against the mosquitoes. For once, the Midnight Express had gotten off early to the depot;

the yard was quiet; the only sound was the puffing of a switch engine somewhere down the main line, setting out cars on the sidings. Pledger had sent the apprentice to fetch some journal-box packing from the storeroom; and the apprentice was taking his time about coming back.

"Damn those mosquitoes, Andrew," Pledger said. "They must like the smell of that smudge of yours. But I sure don't." Andrew Masters laughed, kicked over the tin can and ground out the waste under his boot. At the same moment, Pledger heard a voice behind him; he turned and saw one of the Negro coach cleaners kneeling at the edge of the pit, motioning them to come close.

"Your hear what happen?" he whispered.

Pledger and Andrew Masters shook their heads.

"Well, it done happen. It started now. We got to look out for ourselves!" The man's voice was shaking but there was a look almost of relief on his face.

Pledger clamped a hand on his wrist. "What do you mean? What started?"

"Over on the lake beach, they kill a colored boy with stones. That's what started. They out on the streets now with sticks and guns trying to kill us. It started, I tell you. Look out! Look out for yourselves."

The coach cleaner vanished and Pledger and Andrew Masters, only half believing what he had said, went on with their work. At supper hour when they came out of the wheel-pit house, they heard sounds of shouting, and on the far side of the yard they saw men lined up along the railing at the top of the embankment, looking down into the street. The backs of the men stood out in silhouette against the reddish glow from the sign over Sam's Restaurant. Pledger ran across the coach yard with Andrew Masters hopping behind him. When he shoved through to the railing, he saw below him a streetcar stalled at the corner and a crowd gathering around it; he thought at first the car had run over someone. Then he saw people fighting by the front entrance. A Negro with the shirt torn off his back broke out of the crowd and fell across the sidewalk. Five white men followed him, pulled him to his feet, propped him against the concrete embankment and pumped their fists into his face. Around them the crowd closed in, watching in silence.

Pledger began to shout, but no one seemed to hear him. He found the railroad policeman Morgan leaning over the rail, his head thrusting and jerking at the end of its long neck as he followed the movements of the men in the street. Pledger shook him by the arm.

"Morgan," he shouted. "Morgan!" The yard policeman turned slowly as if he had waked from a dream. "You got a gun. You could stop that."

After a long silence, Morgan said, "That's not my jurisdiction down there, mister. I'm a railroad policeman. They stay down there, I stay up here." He shook his head and leaned again over the rail.

Pledger ran toward the stairway that led down into the street. Andrew Masters, who tried to hold him, he knocked aside with a swing of his arm.

Now from the top of the stairs he saw the crowd close in around the streetcar again, while a bunch of young men smashed open the front entrance of the car. From the rear entrance two Negro boys jumped down, darted back and forth trying to find a way through the crowd. The young men swarmed after them yelling in shrill voices, "Get the bastards! Get those niggers!" But most of the people in the crowd only stared in silence, making no motion either to stop the Negro boys or to help them.

The red letters of the sign glowed over the entrance to the restaurant. Below Pledger, the faces of the crowd spread like a swirling reddish sea. He saw one of the boys fall and the crowd surge over him. The other boy reached the foot of the stairs before someone pulled him down and the men piled on top of him. Pledger stumbled down the steps. Faces swept forward to meet him. For a moment the faces seemed to fall away, he seized the Negro boy by the collar and dragged him towards the stairway. But on the first steps hands catching hold of him pulled him backwards and he fell on his knees under the press of bodies. Behind him the stair rail splintered and he and the boy toppled sideways into the crowd with the others on top of them.

The mass of bodies crushed and smothered him. A blade of pain stabbed into his chest and for an instant darkness rolled across his eyes. When he came to, he found himself wiggling his way free from the tangle of arms and legs. He still held the Negro boy by the collar, and together they dragged themselves on the stairs again and crawled to the top. The men on the embankment pulled them up the last two steps, and Pledger rose to his feet, holding his chest and gasping for breath.

Before him, the railroad yard sprang suddenly into a blaze of white light. A switch engine rolled towards them from the main line, and its headlamp picked out the gleaming web of rails, the blades of grass between the ties; lighted up the knuckles and cheekbones of the Negro and white workmen who stood around him. The boy shielded his eyes from the light and began to cry.

"Take it easy," one of the men said. "You all right now boy." Andrew Masters patted him on the shoulder; but the boy spun around like a cat in a box, lit out suddenly across the yard, tripping and stumbling over the rails.

"Stop him," Pledger cried. "Don't let him run like that." He started after the boy, but the pain stabbed through his chest and he bent double, hugging himself with his arms, biting his lips against the pain, and whispering, "Look out boy, look out—"

The boy was halfway across the yard. He disappeared behind a baggage car and came out again on the far side; a line of Pullmans blocked his path and he zigzagged one way, then another as if he did not know what direction he was going. From the shadow of the line of Pullmans, the policeman Morgan stepped out behind him.

"Where you going?" he called. "Halt there."

The boy kept on running, his head down and his hands reaching out in front of him. Morgan drew his pistol from its holster and sighted along the barrel. Against the side of the Pullman car, his thin figure cast a thin black shadow. After he fired, the boy ran a few steps farther through the glare of the engine headlamp before he collapsed into the cinders. As the men gathered around him, the boy seemed to come to life, clawed wildly in front of him, then stiffened suddenly as if his limbs had congealed.

"Wouldn't stop," Morgan told them. "I yelled for him to stop, but he wouldn't pay me no mind." In silence the men stared back. Morgan's eyes dropped and he wet his lips with his tongue. "You saw he wouldn't stop when I called to him," Morgan said—

Pledger, his broken ribs strapped in a cast, lay for eight days without moving. Sometimes he and Sarah heard shouts and fighting along Wentworth Avenue. At night they heard gunshots and the sirens of fire engines, and through their window, they saw the fires glowing against the sky. Pledger told Sarah to turn out their light, and then he listened to her sobbing beside him until she fell asleep. With the light out, the room seemed to grow smaller; the walls bent in, the ceiling pressed down, the black shapes of the stove, the chest of drawers, the pile of boxes in the corner, rose up, filling the darkness. A watery glow from the window washed across the ceiling, but no air stirred. The room was heavy with the sour smell of old plaster, the odor of wet boards around the drain pipe, the smell of food long since cooked. He listened to the whispering of the silence. Sometimes he heard the sound of feet echoing on the pavement four floors below, and sometimes the silence was shattered by the puffing of engines on the near-by embankment. The alarm clock over the stove ticked loud enough to deafen him, and a moment later he would be holding his breath to find if he could still hear it.

In the morning when Andrew Masters came to see how he felt, Pledger was half out of his head. He kept scratching at the plaster cast and talking over and over about something he had seen in the war. Sarah had squeezed herself into the farthest corner, where she sat staring at him as if she did not know him. Andrew Masters caught hold of Pledger's hands, whispering,

"No, no, son. Ask God to forgive you, boy. Ask the Lord's pardon."

But Pledger, lifting his head up, shouted exultantly, "That's just what I did, like you say. I stuck a bayonet into the man's guts and he grabbed ahold of the bayonet and rolled his eyes at me. A white man—it was awful to look at, it surely was. When I see what I done, I crawl in the mud and ask God to forgive me; I rub my head in the dirt and say, Oh Lord, strike me for what I done." He rocked the bed with his laughter until the pain of the broken rib sliced all the way down to the pit of his stomach, and he lay back, shaking silently.

On the fourth day, Sarah, looking out the window, saw soldiers with rifles and machine guns making camp in the vacant lots of Wentworth Avenue; after that, everything was quiet.

Part One

THE NEW YEAR 1939

I

DOWN at the end of Fifty-Fifth Street, the purple-colored sun glowed through the mist that lay over the lake. Buildings loomed up like islands in the murky twilight of autumn morning. As Martin and Stephanie crossed the street on their way to breakfast, the grocery stores were already opening, and Stephanie saw the windows full of apples, oak leaves, pumpkins, and jugs of cider.

"Hurry up, Martin," she said, tugging at his elbow. "I'm cold."

They walked and half ran the two long blocks to Fifty-Seventh Street. In the corner drugstore they sat down at their table by the window, ordered rolls and coffee, and Martin opened his book.

"What a delightful breakfast companion you are," Stephanie said.

"What's that?" He glanced up, marking the place with his finger. "Oh, the book? Well, I'm ready to talk. You got anything interesting to say?"

"I'm surprised you don't take that damn book to bed with you."

"Everything in its proper place. In the morning I hunger for learning. At night for other things."

"Ah?"

"Come, don't be cross. What shall we talk about?" He tapped her on the wrist. "Tell me, why do you always manage not to be present at our staff meetings?"

"I don't do that."

"But you are doing it."

"Only this time, Martin. My brother's getting married, I'll have to go."

"What for? Can't you go to the next one?"

"No, I think this will be my brother's first and last."

"But you've got two brothers."

Stephanie laughed and shook her head. "You don't understand. My family sets a lot of store by their boy getting married. You have

31

no relations with your own family, you forget what these things are like."

"Of course I have relations with my family. Financial relations. My mother sends me twenty-five dollars every Christmas."

"Then you've been holding out on me, you skunk. How long has that been going on?"

"Two years. Or three. I've forgotten."

"They're beginning to think you aren't a total loss after all, Martin. They'll be wanting you home again soon. So what shall we do with the money?"

"*We?*"

"Well, you know, we share things, don't we?"

"Of course we do. We'll pay part of my tuition with it."

"Oh no, that wouldn't be sharing."

The waitress set their breakfast on the table; Stephanie, breaking one of the rolls, dipped the pieces in her coffee. "This is more like a windfall; we should throw a party."

"The hell with the parties. What do we use for my tuition?"

A fattish bald-headed man came into the drugstore, and Martin announced in a loud voice, "There's that leach Hawkins again."

The bald man nodded acknowledgment, took off his coat, and sat down beside them. "Stephanie's welching out on our staff meeting," Martin told him.

Hawkins called to the waitress for boiled eggs and toast; then he asked, "What's the matter with her this time?"

"She's going to a wooden wedding. Hawkins, did you ever go to a wooden wedding?"

"If this is dirty," Hawkins said, "I don't want to hear it."

"Two Poles are getting married."

Stephanie and Hawkins regarded Martin coldly.

"Well, Stephanie," Hawkins said at last. "You don't like our staff meetings. I'm hurt."

"Why should I like them, Hawkins? I'm no philosopher."

"Nevertheless, your presence adds something to the meetings."

"Sure it does. I bring in the coffee and crackers. But you're big boys now. You can make your own coffee."

"It's not the coffee," Hawkins explained, "though don't misunderstand me, I think your coffee is excellent. But as I was saying, it's something even more tintillating than coffee—"

"That's not a word, Hawkins."

"You've no need to interrupt me. It's the pragmatic breath of scientific method you bring into our scholastic quibblings that I find so refreshing. Perhaps we debate the cosmological proof for the postmortal existence of the soul, and you tell us a worm's intestines pickled in picric acid will keep on wiggling forty-eight hours beyond the decease of the worm. That's a point of view we need on the *Philosophical Quarterly*."

Hawkins sniffed his eggs cautiously. Then his face brightened; he added salt and pepper and began to eat. "So you're going to a wedding?" he said after a moment. "Who's taking the vows, may I ask?"

"My brother."

"Your brother! Not brother Victor?"

Stephanie smiled and shook her head.

"That's what I'd want to see," Hawkins told her. "When your brother Victor gets married. But some women have the most unexplainable taste. They say there's a natural mate for everyone if you look far enough—"

"What a break for you," Stephanie said. "Come, Martin, it's five to nine, we'll be late." She winked at Hawkins as they got up, and while they walked towards the door of the drugstore, buttoning their overcoats, Hawkins, who had remained at the table, called after them, "The girl's sharp today, Martin. You'd best not cross her."

Late that afternoon, in the church with its half-veiled figures, Stephanie watched the priest marry her brother John and his young bride Rosa. Then she walked out to the steps where she waited for the others. The afternoon was fading now to evening; green streaks of winter sunset lay across the base of the sky. Beyond Milwaukee Avenue, the ragged line of roofs and chimneys stood up in silhouette, while around the tops of the two great gas tanks, red aircraft signals began blinking on and off. The wind blew sharply out of the west. She turned up her coat collar and breathed in the cold air, for the wind swept away the musty odor of incense from the church, which still seemed to cling to her. High over the gas tanks, she watched the evening star prick through the green twilight.

The guests began coming through the porticoes of the church. Her oldest brother Victor dragged himself down step by step, tottering on each step as he lowered the points of his crutches. One of the guests offered to help him, and Stephanie saw her brother's face contort with anger as he cried, "Get away. I don't need any help." Then the bridesmaids appeared, pulling on coats over their fluffy green dresses; and beside Stephanie a voice said, "You all right, Stevie? You're not cold?"

Her father Roman Koviak had come out behind her. "It went good, didn't it, Stevie?"

She nodded and turned towards him, smiling. "How long since you been inside a church, Roman?"

He shrugged his shoulders. "Couple months maybe."

"Don't lie to me. And right on the church steps too. I'll bet it's been five years."

"Couple months, I tell you." Roman was giggling and shaking his shoulders. "Five years! What kind of a man you think I am?"

"I know what kind of man you are. You can't kid me about going to church."

He laughed and patted her on the arm. "I guess so, Stevie. You and me always been bad about going to church." Then he said in a low voice, "It's good to get married in a church, Stevie. It makes everything start off good." He glanced at her quickly. "You don't think so?"

"It's good for Johnny and Rosa. It wouldn't be good for me."

"Oh you. Nobody ever ask *you* to get married in a church. But you know what I mean, for Johnny and Rosa, it's better this way. Rosa's a good girl, you think so, don't you, Stevie?"

"I think she is."

"She'll be good for Johnny." He was working his chin up and down, poking his finger at his shirt collar.

"Your collar's too tight," Stephanie told him.

"No, just I'm not used to a dress-up shirt. I can't move my neck."

"Now look." She unbuttoned the collar, adjusted the necktie so it covered the gap, and then watched him waggle his head in relief.

"That feels fine now. But a girl like Rosa will be good for him. She'll make Johnny feel happy and he'll settle down with her, don't you think, Stevie?"

Stephanie knew what was in both their minds. She nodded her head without answering.

On the steps in front of the portico, the fluttery crowd of bridesmaids began to wave and call. Through the doorway, Johnny and his bride Rosa emerged into a bombardment of rice and confetti. The bride covered her head with her hands, her feet tripped in her long white skirt, and Johnny half dragged her down the church

34

steps to the automobile, while the others closed in behind, still firing flowers and confetti. Roman and Stephanie followed them down to the cars.

Victor, in the slow progress of his crutches, had reached Roman's Chevrolet just ahead of them, and Stephanie waited while he yanked open the back door, pitched the crutches inside, and dragged himself in after them. As she sat beside him, he glanced up at her, then stared down at his knees. "Did you like the wedding?" he asked.

"I liked it all right."

"I thought it was divine," Victor said. "The bride looked so charming in white." He pressed his hairy, knob-knuckled hands together. "I thought I wanted to cry. Didn't you, Stephanie?"

She shrugged her shoulders without answering. In the front seat, Roman and Mrs. Koviak had settled themselves, and Roman was stamping on the starter. The cars moved in procession up Milwaukee Avenue with their horns blaring. "You have no feeling," Victor said. "But tell me, Stephanie, how could you tear yourself away from your love nest long enough to come to this rather primitive ceremony?"

"Oh shut up, Victor." Turning, she looked out the car window at the lighted shop fronts along the street, the bars and furniture stores, the funeral parlors with their blue neon signs.

"What about Martin?" Victor asked. "You don't think he would have enjoyed coming?"

"No."

"But think of Mother and Roman. Ought you not to give them a chance to make his acquaintance, now that he's—now that he's number one?"

Stephanie could hear Victor laughing and humming under his breath, and she bit at her fingers, trying to hold down her anger. Pressing her face against the window, she peered back at the line of cars behind them with their paper ribbons streaming into the wind. The procession stopped at the photographer's, and Johnny and Rosa posed for their wedding picture against a backdrop of snow-capped mountains.

Then the parade of cars moved up Milwaukee Avenue again to Smolinski's Restaurant and Assembly Rooms. The waiters ushered the guests to a special table at the back of the hall; Johnny and Rosa sat down in the places of honor, and the two families lined up on each side. Rosa's uncle ordered whiskey all around;

then Roman ordered whiskey, and jumping up from his place, tried to make Rosa a toast. But his English failed him, he muttered something in Polish, stretched out his hand toward his daughter-in-law, cried "To Rosa" and emptied his glass. Everybody clapped and shouted and somebody ordered more whiskey around the table. Roman's friends, the silent old railwaymen from the Great Midland car yard suddenly began shouting jokes back and forth with the relatives of Rosa's father, who came from the steel mills. After a time, the young people started talking too, and Stephanie listened to the rising and falling voices arguing about people she did not know, or whose names she had almost forgotten since leaving high school.

". . . saw the two of them at Walter's place last week."

"But I thought she was steady with George. . . ."

Johnny's voice shouted over the others, "The Pennsy's not a bad outfit. You get a job braking down to Elkhart, there's plenty of work through the summer. . . ."

"Sure the Pennsy's all right, Johnny. But you got to know somebody. You got to have a drag to get on the Pennsy."

Stephanie, who had not eaten since breakfast, began to feel pleasantly drunk. Leaning back, she looked around the restaurant at the bright-colored patterns on the walls, the bar with its bottles winking in the lamplight, the counter by the entrance where you could buy Polish cakes and pastry. She was hungry, and she sniffed the good smells of sauerkraut, beer, and roasting meat. Through the haze of smoke, the portraits of Pilsudski and Paderewski winked at her from the wall over the bar. After a moment, she noticed the bartender winking at her also; she raised her hand and waved back.

"Who are you waving to?" Victor asked.

"Pilsudski," she told him. "The brothers Pilsudski and Paderewski. They're up there over the bar."

Now the dinner had begun; a waiter set plates of soup in front of them, and Victor, as he crunched a handful of crackers into his plate, said, "You've been drinking too much of that whiskey."

Following the soup, the waiters brought on meat in sour-cream sauce, potatoes, rye bread, dishes of vegetables, stewed fruit, and pickled watermelon. All the waiters of Smolinski's Restaurant hovered over the wedding party, while at other tables, bald men with napkins tucked in their collars tapped their glasses and gestured angrily. But the waiters paid them no attention. When the

36

wedding party finished the main course, the waiters brought trays of pastry, coffee, and more whiskey. It was ten o'clock before everyone finished eating.

Now fiddlers and a piano player arrived and couples moved out on the dance floor. Stephanie saw Johnny and Rosa in the crowd of dancers; but a few moments later, Johnny was leaning over her shoulder. "Stephanie," he shouted through the sound of music and the clatter of dishes, "Want you to meet a friend of mine. He was the best man tonight. Swell dancer. Walter, want you to meet my sister—"

Stephanie found a little red-headed man in a tuxedo standing beside her chair. He began to kick his feet and snap his fingers. "You care to dance?" he asked. She got up, and as they moved out on the dance floor she felt his cheek against hers, and his bristly mustache bobbing up and down against her ear while he talked. "I bet you don't remember me from school," he asked. "Do you?"

"No, I guess I don't."

"That's what I said to Johnny. I said, it's been four—five years since she graduated high school and I bet she thought we was just kids then. I says, use your head Johnny, she won't remember me from a hole in the ground. Lot of water's flowed under the bridge since then. But you look younger than ever."

"I was hoping I'd grown up a little."

"You know what I mean. You look like a million dollars, I mean." Squeezing her arm, he said into her ear, "You're some looker now, kid."

"Thanks."

"Why, tonight when Johnny told me, That there is my sister Stephanie Koviak, I almost dropped a clinker. I told Johnny, you mean to tell me that romantic-looking armful is your sister! Why that ain't the way I remember her in high school. And he says that's her, that's Stephanie; and I says—"

As Walter, the best man, paused for breath, Stephanie asked, "What do you do, anyway?"

"I don't get you, kid?"

"What do you do for a living? Are you an insurance salesman or vaudeville comedian or what?"

"You mean what kind of work I do? I work with my old man. We got a place of our own just off Halsted near the railroad yard. Me and my old man are partners, see? I take care of the mixed drinks—that's my specialty. Whenever a customer wants a mixed drink, that's when they start looking for Walter. Didn't Johnny tell you about our place?"

"No, he didn't."

"I made a regular study of mixed drinks, see? I can mix eighty-eight different kinds. Would you believe that?"

"Gosh."

"Why, before I made this study, if some guy says to me there was eighty-eight different kinds of mixed drinks, I'd of told him he's a liar. Never use a book either; I do it from memory. Why, I could walk over to that bar and mix any one of those drinks right this minute. Some of them are whipsnorters too."

"I bet they are."

"Say, I'd like you to drop over to my place some evening, kid. I want to tell you, it's a strictly nice place; we got all chromium and genuine leather upholstery, and I tell you we don't put up with no rough stuff." Stephanie tried to move away from the little prickling mustache, but the mustache followed her ear whichever way she moved till she and the best man were both leaning sideways as they danced. "Why don't you come over some night after work?" he asked. "I'll get the old man to let me off and we'll take in a late show. How about it?"

"Thanks a lot," Stephanie said. "But I'm married. Johnny should have told you that."

Walter shrugged his shoulders. "Well, I wasn't quite sure."

"You weren't sure?"

"Don't get sore now, kid. Is your husband here tonight?"

"No."

"I wouldn't asked you, see, except they told me your husband wasn't—well they said he wasn't in Chicago."

"Did Johnny tell you that?"

"No, not Johnny."

"Oh I see. It was Victor told you."

"Don't get sore now."

She laughed and asked him, "Will you do me a favor? Move your mustache back about an inch. It feels like a caterpillar."

Walter hunched his shoulders and grinned at her, showing a gold tooth under the wisp of red hair. Then, leaning forward again, he said into her ear, "Let's not have any hard feelings at each other. I didn't intend to make you sore, see?"

"You didn't make me sore."

The music stopped and Walter pulled her over to the bar.

While he told her again about the drinks he could mix, she nodded her head now and then to indicate she was listening. Turning sideways, she looked out across the crowded restaurant. At the long table Roman, his friends from the railway yard, and Rosa's uncles, all had their heads together, talking in Polish and shouting with laughter. Stephanie's mother and Rosa's mother, side by side, were whispering into each others' ears. Beyond the two women and sitting alone at the end of the table, she saw her brother Victor. She tried to look past him, but his eyes caught hers across the moving heads and through the clouds of tobacco smoke. Under his stare she grew angry and uneasy, and at last twisted sideways, breaking her eyes away. As she turned back to the bar, she noticed the look of satisfaction on Victor's face that it was she who had dropped her eyes first. Why should I waste my time with that baby's game? she thought; but it made her angry to have given in. She swore under her breath and Walter, the best man, glanced up apprehensively.

Now the fiddlers had begun again, swinging into a polka. Her brother Johnny came tugging at her elbow. "Let's show them how to do it, Stevie."

"Won't Rosa dance it with you?"

"Says she can't in her long dress."

Stephanie stood for a moment watching the dancers. Pair by pair, they were dropping out, until only one couple was left—a boy and a stocky Polish girl, who whirled and stamped across the empty floor. She remembered how stupid Dave had been learning the polka the spring when she had tried to teach him.

"Come on, Stevie. Let's you and me show them how."

Johnny took her hand and they squeezed between the tables to the floor. The other couple made way for them and they ran out into the center, spinning, clapping, turning, stamping their feet. Stephanie saw the faces on all sides watching them, the other couple spun past, and she could see the fiddlers sawing at their fiddles and how the chief fiddler was up on his feet waving to them with his fiddle bow. The room rocked around her. Faces and lights poured into a whirl of color spinning across her eyes. But now her feet danced of themselves, fitting their steps precisely to Johnny's, who with one hand behind her back, swept her round and round the floor. The music halted abruptly. She and Johnny, laughing and blushing, and the other couple, bowed and curtsied to each other and to the audience.

"Now I really am thirsty," Stephanie said.

They returned to the bar where they ordered beer, and Stephanie, raising her glass to the light, watched the bubbles that streamed up through the clear amber. She drank, pressing her nose down into the foam.

"You got suds on your nose," Johnny told her.

She looked at him, laughing over the rim of the glass, then asked, "Is that fellow Walter a good friend of yours?"

"The best man? He's a laugh, isn't he, Stevie? He's always good for a joke."

"I guess he must be."

"Didn't you like him?"

She shook her head.

"He and his old man run a bar, see Stevie? It's right close to the yard. I stop over there for a beer sometimes when I get done work."

She nodded, and after a moment Johnny touched her arm. "Stephanie, Rosa's a swell girl, isn't she?"

"I think so, Johnny."

"It's screwy for me," he said in a low voice. "I'm scared."

"*You* scared, Johnny? But you've been around. You can show Rosa what to do."

"I don't mean that."

In embarrassment he bent his head over his beer glass, and Stephanie felt sorry for what she had said. "Johnny," she asked, "what's worrying you?"

"I don't know, Stevie. I never went steady with a girl until now. I hung around with a whole lot of different girls, and some of 'em bitches too. I told Rosa that and she said it was okay." He stopped, then asked in a low voice Stephanie could scarcely hear, "Do you think I'll be able to keep steady with her now?"

"Why not?"

"I been a hell-raiser ever since way back in junior high school. I went on the bum and drunk a lot and everything—"

"Most young fellows do that, don't they?"

"Some do."

"I guess you wouldn't be getting married if you didn't want to, Johnny. Maybe you're too old to be acting like a kid any more. You got a nice wife and you got a job; that's more than most people have." She watched him tugging at the frayed lapel of his rented tuxedo, and she thought, I wish I were as sure of that as I sound.

40

But Johnny looked up, reassured now and smiling. "Stevie, will you do something for me?"

"Of course I will." Across the restaurant, she saw the best man, Walter, guiding one of the bridesmaids toward the street door of the restaurant.

"What you laughing at?" Johnny asked.

"At your friend Walter. What do you want me to do for you?"

"Look, Stevie, Rosa and me are going to try to sneak out without the whole gang taking off after us. I guess Rosa's had enough rice and old shoes for one day. Would you bring the car for me? The old man's, I mean; he's letting us use it."

Stephanie took the car keys he gave her, put on her coat, and went out to the street.

It was cold outside. She heard the wind humming over the roofs of the buildings, and when she looked up she saw shreds of cloud racing across the black, star-sprinkled sky. November again, she thought, the snow comes soon, the black ice over the pavements; through the winter nights, the engines stumping back and forth along the embankments; Roman and Johnny going out in their boots and wool caps to work in the train yard. She shivered, hating the cold. Gusts of wind snapped at the skirts of her coat, and the wind whirled scraps of paper across the empty sidewalks of Milwaukee Avenue.

She found Roman's Chevrolet standing under a streetlamp, mud-spattered and dusty, but festooned with streamers. On the spare tire someone had hung a sign which read: JUST MARRIED. MIDNIGHT SHOW TONIGHT.

Stephanie smiled, but pulled the sign off because she knew it would embarrass Rosa. Then she climbed into the car; Rosa's chariot, she thought, to some little hotel by the lakeshore. For the big show—she shook her head slowly as she tried to start the cold motor—the flat west of Halsted, the little parlor, the little kitchen, Rosa keeping house all day while Johnny went out to work in the freight yard.

The car coughed and backfired. The motor began to run steadily at last. She drove to the restaurant, got out, and a moment later Johnny and Rosa raced through the door, jumped into the car, and took off down Milwaukee Avenue. The others ran out after them, shouting and waving, but no one tried to follow. They stood together on the sidewalk, watching the red taillight of Roman's Chevrolet disappear into the distance.

It was long after midnight when Rosa's father drove the Koviaks home from Smolinski's Restaurant. The Koviaks' house stood with its back against the embankment of the Great Midland Railroad, and Stephanie, at the window of her old room in the attic, looked out over the expanse of tracks. The rails gleamed blue in the moonlight. A line of boxcars was rolling slowly along the farthest track, and from the distance, she could hear the engine puffing and the wail of the whistle over the rumbling wheels.

So many nights she had stood at this same window listening to the sound of the trains; it now seemed to her as if nothing had ever changed. Five years, ten years, the twilight of spring evenings, summer and winter, the rain and snow, poured over the embankment of the Great Midland. The engines puffed past, sprinkling with soot her mother's wash hung out to dry in the back yard. The brakemen leaned out the windows of the cabooses, smoking their pipes. The sunflowers climbed up the embankment in July and withered and died under the autumn wind. It was four months since she had been in the room, but the window received her again as though she had not been away. It was as if there were some figure of herself standing always at this window, and no matter where she might be, waiting for her to come back. She shuddered and turned away.

Pulling off her clothes, she slipped into bed and pulled the counterpane up around her ears.

In the morning Stephanie woke hearing her name called. Misty light from the window lay in pale squares across the cracked plaster of the ceiling. She moved luxuriously under the covers. A churchbell was ringing somewhere for early-morning mass.

"Stevie, you awake?" Roman, in overalls and leather jacket, leaned over the bed.

"Yes, I'm awake. What time is it?"

"Seven."

"Oh, Roman." She raised up on one elbow and blinked, trying to get her eyes open. "You don't have to go to work today? Isn't this Sunday?"

Roman, laughing, sat down on the edge of the bed. "Don't you know even what day it is, Stevie? Yes, I guess I got to go to work today."

"Tell 'em to go to hell. You never get a day off."

He shook his head, grinning. "You be here tonight?"

"No, Roman, I got some work still to do this afternoon."

"You never get a day off either, I guess." He sat silent for a moment, patting her hand on top of the counterpane. Then he asked suddenly, "Stevie, you hear from Dave?"

"No."

"He don't write you at all, Stevie?"

"Why should he?"

"Maybe you should write him?"

"Oh hell, Roman, let's not go through this again. I'm all right; now let me alone. Even if I did write him, the letter wouldn't get through."

After a long time Roman said, "I guess if anything happen to Dave they let us know, won't they?" He pushed himself up from the bed, but hesitated, staring down into her face to see if she were still angry. "You come and see us next Sunday, eh Stevie? You do that?"

"All right, Roman."

After he left, she could not go back to sleep. She got up, dressed, and went downstairs. Her mother had gone out to church and Victor was not around yet. Stephanie found herself a cup of coffee left over from Roman's breakfast, wrote a note to her mother, which she hung on the oven door, and then hurried outside with a feeling of relief at leaving. She walked through the early morning sunshine and caught the streetcar to the University.

2

THERE were New Year's parties in all the apartments. The kitchens were lighted one on top of another, and back and forth across the windows moved the shadows of men and women with glasses in their hands. In the light from the windows the back porches, stacked on top of each other, stood up on gaunt and rickety legs. Beyond the porches, light from the windows shone on the branches of the trees that grew in the back yards. The branches moved constantly, bare and shiny and wet in the winter rain. Down below, the rain dripped into the blanket of snow.

Stephanie Koviak and Henry Martin, who shared the top-floor apartment, came out together on their back porch. They climbed down the three flights of stairs and crossed the back yard on tiptoe so the snow would not come up over their rubbers. Reaching the alley, they followed it to the street and walked up the block to the corner drugstore. They had each an armful of empty soda-water bottles which they exchanged for full ones. Then they returned to the apartment, avoiding the alley this time because of the deep snow there.

Along the quiet street the rain fell, pitting the snow; the rain fell through the darkness and pattered through the bare branches of trees that moved across the streetlamps. During the evening the snow had turned to rain, but across the yards, the fallen snow still appeared fresh and new. It covered the street and sidewalk, unbroken except for a single line of footmarks, so that the city street seemed in the snow like a road through a country village. The sounds of the city hung muffled and quiet; the distant puffing of a freight engine, the clatter of a streetcar along Cottage Grove Avenue, faded almost beyond hearing. There was only the quiet and the snow; the glowing windows, the winking green and red lights of Christmas trees on the doorsteps.

Over the roofs of the houses, the bells of the University churches rang out; the clocks one after another striking the hour: eleven o'clock. When the bells stopped ringing, the sound of the rain returned, pattering down through the branches.

"Isn't it quiet for New Year's Eve?" Stephanie asked.

Martin nodded, and Stephanie, who had been to parties where the men bawled and wrangled and sang from dark until daylight, was grateful for the quiet. She and Martin climbed the stairs to the top floor. Inside the apartment, someone was playing "Stormy Weather" on the phonograph, and she heard the shuffling feet of people dancing. Martin, putting down the soda-water bottles, reached for his key, when Stephanie touched his arm, reminding him. He laughed, pulled her against him, and kissed her. They stood for a moment close together; then he opened the door and they went inside.

Stephanie presided over the pouring of drinks until all the people dancing and all those talking in little knots around the room had their glasses refilled with Scotch and soda. Then she dropped down on the sofa in front of the fire; after working all day in the laboratory, she felt tired now, content to sit where she was, sipping from her glass and watching the flames flow upward over the bricks of the chimney. Martin settled on the arm of the sofa, leaning sideways with his hand on her shoulder. Hawkins and Smith and the others from the staff of the magazine gathered around Martin.

As always they were arguing about something and Smith, in his schoolmaster's voice, started off as if he were lecturing a classroom. Stephanie did not listen. She felt Martin's fingers on her shoulder and she lay back, rested her head against his side and stretched out her legs toward the fire. A cat on the hearth—if only we had a cat, she thought—a cat would lie on the hearth purring and flexing its velvet paws. Then the cat and I would feel alike, and if I were a cat instead of a scholar, I would lie here purring and stretching too, all the rest of my life—never push myself around, never force myself off to work, never wait on winter street corners for streetcars that do not come. Poor little kitty, lying quiet, disturbed by nothing, sleeping with my cheek against Martin's thighbone. Then we would sleep like the lotus-eaters; Martin, if only your thighbone were not so sharp—

She opened her eyes. Hawkins was punching her in the ribs. "See, I told you," Hawkins said. "You put her to sleep, Smith."

She saw Smith regarding her with a hurt look on his face. "I was thinking of something else," she explained. "I wasn't asleep."

"You've become a regular specialist," Smith told her. "You take no interest in anything, Stephanie, except your own particular field. I told you several years ago that going into physiology would simply be putting your mind in a straight jacket."

"Oh, Smith," she said, "I'll not argue with you tonight. You don't know anything about physiology. Why should I argue with you?"

"It isn't a question of knowing specific facts about physiology, Stephanie. I'm not a scientist, after all. My field is philosophy and ethics—"

"Which has nothing to do with science, I suppose?"

"In a general way, certainly. Science is the study of physical categories, while ethics deals with the human mind and soul."

Stephanie sat up angrily, and Martin on the arm of the sofa began to laugh.

"Look out!" Hawkins said to Smith. "Now Stephanie's going to deflate you by a couple of atmospheres."

"Oh, I'm not going to deflate anybody. Smith and I don't talk the same language, that's all. Physical categories and mental

45

categories! As far as I'm concerned my mind is a piece of me and thinking one of its functions. The more you see how your mind works, the better you can use it: that seems simple. I'll not argue about ethics; I haven't anything to argue about."

There was a knock on the hall door, and Stephanie's crippled brother Victor came in followed by Marguerite Strauss, who carried an armful of umbrellas and raincoats. Victor settled down in one of the armchairs by the fire, arranging his shriveled, steel-braced legs so that everyone who passed tripped over them. Marguerite propped his crutches in the corner, brought him a drink, and then wandered around uncertainly looking for a place to sit down, while Victor paid her no more attention.

"Sit here," Stephanie called. She made room on the sofa and Marguerite, who was broad across the beam, squeezed into the place, as Stephanie pressed up closer to Martin.

"It's a dreadful night out," Marguerite said.

"Yes, it's raining, isn't it?"

"I'm afraid I'm coming down with the flu, Stephanie."

"Do you think so? You look well."

"Oh, I suppose I *look* all right. But I've always had a tendency to sinus, Stephanie, and this damp weather keeps me run down all the time."

God, Stephanie thought, and I asked for it too.

"Do you know, Stephanie, I think sometimes, if only I could get to a dry climate where I could really make use of my energy—"

Stephanie nodded, but did not answer. After a brief silence, Marguerite turned away and tried to blast her road into the conversation that was going on among Victor and Smith and Martin. She kept throwing in observations several minutes too late, which the others did not bother to notice.

Stephanie let the talk go past without her. Sometimes their arguments made her angry and sometimes she felt contemptuous of these scholars with their Phi Beta Kappa keys on chains across their bellies. But at the same time, she knew she was proud of her position among them. She was proud of Martin, proud that he sat beside her; proud that the group always formed around Martin and dissolved again when she and Martin left. And she, Stephanie, being Martin's girl, held the place of honor among them; that was not bad for the kid from beyond the railroad embankment.

That was not bad. Even her brother Victor's shrill disposition could not deny her that. The scholars argued about their philosophy and ethics, but they could not ignore her as they ignored Marguerite Strauss; for when she fell asleep, they punched her in the ribs to make her wake up and listen to them. She felt at once annoyed and amused by her own vanity. Resting her head against Martin's side, she sipped from her glass and held the liquid far down in her throat, trying to find some way to imitate the purring of a cat. Martin, up above her on the arm of the sofa, was banging his hands together as he made his points. He had picked on Smith and now forced him back position by position, until Smith, angry and speechless, dropped into silence. For a moment Martin watched him, grinning. Then he heard the strange noise Stephanie was making with her whiskey.

"What are you doing, Stephanie, gargling?"

"I was trying to purr like a cat," she said. As she spoke, she swallowed the whiskey the wrong way, choked and almost strangled. Martin pounded her on the back while the others, laughing and yelling, milled around, giving her artificial respiration.

Just before midnight, Stephanie went to the kitchen for the sandwiches, and Marguerite followed along to help. The kitchen was crowded; people playing charades ducked back and forth from one room to another. As Stephanie arranged the sandwiches on the platters, Marguerite stood close by her elbow.

"Listen, Stephanie, I don't know if I have any right even to ask you this question—"

She hesitated and Stephanie said, "Well, go ahead and ask. I may not answer it."

"No, it's not about you, Stephanie."

"Who's it about?"

Marguerite whispered into her ear, "About Victor. Listen to me, Stephanie; one night he told me some things. He was in a terrible state of mind; I'm not sure he even knew what he was saying. It was about his legs, Stephanie, about what happened to them. I don't know if I dare ask you. But I'm certain that that experience, in his mind—something terrible psychologically— If I only knew, maybe I could help."

"There's no mystery," Stephanie told her. "He was stealing coal when he was a kid. He fell off the coal car and injured his back."

"I'm sure he didn't know what he was saying when he talked to me."

"I'm quite sure he did know." Stephanie moved the full platter aside and began to load the next one. "My brother Victor never does anything by accident. He probably wanted you to ask me about this."

"I don't believe that."

Stephanie shrugged her shoulders. "Where did you grow up, Marguerite?"

"In Pennsylvania."

"Well, I grew up here in Chicago. When I was little, the kids used to go out on the railroad tracks to pick up lumps of coal that fell from the trains."

"Yes, I've seen that."

"That's right, they still do it. I started that game when I was six years old, Marguerite. The day Victor got in trouble, we'd all gone out—Victor and I and half a dozen other little kids from down the block. It was midwinter and snow all over; the tracks had been picked clean, we couldn't find a lump anywhere. So I went home along with the other smaller kids, and Victor and—and a friend of his—went off by themselves. You want a sandwich?"

Marguerite shook her head and Stephanie said, "The bigger kids used to wait for the freights, climb up on the coal cars, and throw the coal down. That night the railroad police were laying for them, that's all. I don't know whether Victor slipped or jumped or got pushed. But he fell off the car and down a concrete wall—"

"Oh my God, Stephanie!"

"And of course it had to be me that went down to answer the bell when they brought him home. I remember that part very well. Here, let's send these sandwiches into the living room; it's almost midnight."

Marguerite took the platters, and when she had gone, Stephanie walked across to the back door of the kitchen. Through the glass panel of the door she peered out at the rain in the branches of the trees. For a moment, the things she had told Marguerite remained so vivid in her mind it seemed as if the pictures were moving across the darkness in front of her eyes—the children with scarves wrapped around their ears, hopping and running along the embankment, the snow-covered roofs on both sides, the red and green signals of the Forty-Seventh Street tower sparkling through the gathering dusk. She had heard Victor's friend—Victor's friend Dave—ask, "You want to try it tonight?" and Victor's tough-sounding voice reply, "What's there to be scared of?" Then both the older boys had turned angrily on the kids, shouting, "Beat it!

G'wan home"; and the kids had scampered off homewards, one after another sliding down the icy slope of the embankment into their various back yards. . . .

Stephanie glanced over her shoulder. The kitchen was empty now; the clock on the stove said five minutes before midnight. She slipped out through the back door and eased it shut behind her.

She did not want anyone to notice where she had gone. Lighting a cigarette, she leaned against the porch rail and looked at the trees and the rain. In a few moments the whistles all over the city would sound the New Year and she preferred to be alone. A tick of the clock, midnight, an artificial and meaningless division; yet she knew it would bring a tightening of her throat, a strange stirring of the flesh down her spine. Out of the darkness and rain, she imagined the moment of midnight moving towards her. She felt it breaking like a wave from east to west over all the parts of the earth, and she wondered how many other people were standing listening, as if for some signal. The earth spun by itself through the immensity of night, while on a thousand steps and doorways, people waited for the coming of the New Year. Only for a few moments, she did not want to hear anyone make a clever remark about Aristotle, or laugh at a joke, or debate the problems of the University English Department. She moved down the porch, out of sight from the kitchen door.

Through the criss-crossing branches, Stephanie looked at the lighted windows of the other houses. If I were making a New Year's wish, she thought, I would wish that all Chicago were bright warm windows like those, that trees grew in all the back yards of Chicago. The time had almost come now; she felt the pressure in her throat, the throbbing of her own blood against the veins of her throat. I would wish, she whispered, for a city with wide streets and trees, and houses for people to live in; where no one would ever again wait at daybreak in the lines before the relief stations. God, that wouldn't be wishing for much, would it? For a city that people could live in, for houses with windows, for trees in the back yards?

The simpleness of the wish she had thought of, the sudden vision of what the city might be, held her for a moment, transfixed, her hand with the cigarette half raised to her lips. But in the instant of lifting her hand the rest of the way, of drawing in and then breathing out the smoke, the wish and the vision faded. She had seen

49

too often the streets in the bleak lamplight; the drab gray fronts of houses etched in the lamplight, and the other houses, drab and bleak and ramshackled, stepping away one after another into the shadows. The railroad embankments, the glow of neon signs at distant corners; too often, Stephanie whispered, too often. And the sound of last year's sunflower stalks which thrust up stiffly through the rubble of vacant lots, she had heard the sound of them, rattling in the wind.

Beyond this small oasis of pleasant houses and trees, the apartments around the University, began those other streets, the streets of wooden houses backed against the railroad embankments, the streets she had seen so many thousand nights that even now, closing her eyes, she saw them as if she had never left.

Midnight caught her in a kind of horror, looking out at the lighted windows through the branches. Martin, who knew where she would be, came out to find her. She put her hand in his, and they stood silent, listening. After the twelve strokes of midnight from the churches of the University, came the other sounds: voices, horns, people singing in the distance. Then, drowning all these, there rose in chorus from all directions of the city the uneasy voices of the engines, whistling in the New Year.

"God, listen to the engines, Martin."

She could see the engines now as she had seen them so often, stumping along the embankments with their loads of boxcars, coal cars, tankers, rumbling along the embankments higher than the roofs of the houses. 1939 had come to Chicago; the engines had greeted it.

As Stephanie thought of the railway yards and the city that stretched west from the University, at once she thought of Dave. She could not think of one without the other. Like pepper and salt or humpty and dumpty, she said angrily to herself. They went together, they were one; you thought of one, you thought of the other. A perverse part of her mind formed the word deliberately: Dave. At the same time, she tried to check the anger that the name roused. She had freed herself from regret, but whenever the name rose in her mind, she felt angry that it should still be there. She knew she would not be completely free till she could say the name without anger, with no emotion whatever.

With a little catch of breath, Stephanie turned to Martin and dropped her head on his shoulder. Now she did not want to look at him, she felt that name of Dave hovering behind them, as if the name itself were a shadow that followed them through the shadows. Martin, who had never seen Dave, to whom the name was only a name, was aware of the shadow. Always she knew this from the troubled and sympathetic look of his face, or from his voice, which became suddenly as if he were talking to a child. Even at night, when she lay in Martin's arms with her head on his shoulder and her body pressed against his, sometimes the name would jump into her mind. She would go stiff and cold, and Martin, understanding at once, would whisper to her as if to quiet a child.

Dave, the perverse voice inside her mind repeated, and the other voice answered, I wish he were dead; I wish to God he were dead.

She straightened up. Gripping the porch rail, she stared into the darkness at the moving branches of the trees. She had wished he were dead; and now, shuddering, she felt there must be some fatality attached even to the thought of those words inside her mind. For it was so likely he was dead. Perhaps in the very instant of wishing, her wish had been answered. He was running forward, his breath warm in his throat from the running, his voice calling out over the crunch of booted feet in the snow; perhaps in that instant of wishing it had found him, and he had dropped down, burying his face in the snow of those cold hillsides.

The engines had fallen silent now. The New Year had come. But Stephanie could hear, somewhere in the distance, the solitary puffing of one lone engine, stumping along an embankment with its load of boxcars.

3

SOMETIMES the haze seemed to thicken in the engine room. The shafts and elbows of the engine flashed in front of his eyes more and more rapidly, as if they intended to leap from their casings. Then he would stumble forward to check the gauges. But it was not the gauges that were out of line; it was his eyes. His watch-partner, the little Englishman Ardwick, caught him by the arm and led him back to his place against the bulkhead. "Take it easy, Da-vey," he shouted over the drumming of the pistons. "I'll polish off the work for tonight. You'll do the same for me sometime."

"Thanks, Ardwick,"

The Englishman thrust his nobby bald head close and said into the other's ear, "You're bloody sick, mate. Stay away from the engine."

"You'd have a hell of a mess to clean up, wouldn't you . . . ?"

"Aw, forget it, Da-vey."

Ardwick went on with the work, hopping up and down the ladders and stagings, cleaning and oiling the moving arms of the engine. And Dave Spaas watched him for a time, then let his head drop sideways, fighting to hold his eyes open.

The bell rang at last. The relief watch came, and Ardwick and Dave Spaas climbed up to the crew's quarters. Ardwick said he was hungry and went to the mess hall; but Dave Spaas pulled off his clothes and rolled into his bunk. As soon as he drew the covers around his neck, a dry heat baked through him like heat from the hot bricks of an oven. The mattress knotted and bunched under him; no position he could find was comfortable. He rolled from side to side, but every muscle ached whether he turned to his right or to his left. At last he forced himself to lie quietly on his back, fighting the desire to move. All the pain of his body seemed to concentrate in those two red channels through his shoulder. He felt the jagged flesh again, and the hour when the doctor had probed into the wounds. Against the core of the wounds, he felt his heart beating. The dry heat consumed him. At the same time, he could not keep his feet warm, and drafts seeping under the blanket crept shuddering down the hollows of his back.

The ship was beginning to roll a little. He recognized the familiar motion of the ground swell and whispered to himself, we're almost in. These were comforting words, he repeated them over and over and at last fell asleep still whispering, "Almost in; we're almost in—"

Ardwick waked him an hour before the next watch. He had sweat during the night. His underwear and the mattress and blankets were sopping wet. But the fever seemed to have left him and he felt better. While he changed to dry underwear and pulled on his clothes, Ardwick, who was excited, kept fussing at him.

"Hurry up, Da-vey. For Christ's sake, you're the slowest bloody oiler this side of Austraylia." Ardwick hurried him through the alleyway to the deck and they stood together at the rail. Neither of them spoke for a long time. Already the ship had entered the Narrows and was moving at half speed down the inner bay. The water sparkled in the summer sunshine. Abreast of them, but in the opposite direction, a tugboat was towing two barges and pouring out a column of black smoke into the sunlight. A Staten Island ferry, inbound, swept past them, a white curl of foam under its bow and the decks crowded with men in light suits and women in bright-colored dresses. Dave Spaas nodded his head slowly. In the distance, beyond the blunt nose of their own ship, he saw the towers of Manhattan forming vaguely through the haze that lay over the city. Now a window here and there in the distant buildings caught the sunlight through the haze and flashed back like silver.

"Well, mate," Ardwick said, "you're 'ome."

"Yes. I didn't expect it would feel so good to come home." He remembered he had not looked forward to returning. He had told himself that home was wherever he happened to be; but now a strange feeling stirred through him. He felt like reaching out his arms to the city in the distance—the towers shining in the American sunlight.

"It's no shame for a man to be glad to come 'ome," Ardwick said philosophically. "It's just as natural as for a man to be glad to get back to his wife. Anybody shoved themselves as hard as you to get through a trip, ought to be 'appy to see the end of it."

"You're the one that shoved yourself," Dave told him. "You did all the work."

"Me? Little extra work don't make any difference. Helps pass the watch, that's all. But I used to look over at you, Da-vey, and think to myself, there's one young oiler we'll be dropping over the side in a canvas sack before ever we come to New York."

"Well, I made it."

"Sure you did. And now you're 'ome, you'll be all right. You'll be ready to ship out with me again in another couple of months."

Dave grinned and shook his head.

"No? Well, it's a matter of personal choice. I'd rather be going to sea than stay ashore. How do you feel now, Da-vey?"

"Not so bad."

Ardwick stepped back from the rail, tugging at Dave's elbow.

"Well, come on, let's get some chow. A man needs some grub in his stomach before he goes on watch."

■ ■

It was late afternoon when they finally cleared their papers with the customs and immigration inspectors, collected their pay from the captain, and climbed down the ladder to the wharf.

Dave Spaas drew a deep breath. "Thought we never would get out of there."

"Inspectors are the same bloody bastards the world over," Ardwick said.

They picked their way between crates and bales of cargo, crossed a railroad siding, and at last reached the gate of the pier. A small man in a gray hat and gray suit stepped forward to meet them. Dave Spaas stared at him, trying in the shadows under the gateway to recognize the man. Then he caught him by the hand and dropped an arm over his shoulders. "Nelson, I didn't expect you'd be here." He introduced Nelson to Ardwick, and the three of them walked across the cobblestoned avenue, almost empty now, to Nelson's car. They drove to the ferry slip and took the ferry across the Hudson River.

Already they could see the shadows covering the lower buildings of Manhattan and creeping up into the angles and planes between the skyscrapers. The banks of smoke faded to lavender; for a moment longer the sunlight sparkled over the highest peaks before the shadows washed up over them too. Three gulls wheeled above the river. It was evening; and in the city, lights began to wink on.

The ferry nosed into its berth on the New York side. Timbers creaked and bucked under the impact; the gangways locked down against the deck and the line of trucks and cars rumbled out into the crowded downtown streets. As they drove across the city, Dave Spaas stared out the window at the people on the sidewalks. It seemed unbelievable to him that every face, every expression and gesture, looked just as he had remembered it. Nothing had changed. The shrill voices, the blaring automobile horns, the roar of the elevated trains, the colored neon signs, the smells of beer and gasoline and cooking food—all were the same they had been. The day he had passed through New York two years ago might have been yesterday. The months in between might never have happened, a feverish night, a dream better forgotten—

54

He shook himself uneasily. He did not like daydreaming. He was afraid he would fall asleep, for the tiredness was gathering like fog behind his eyes. If he went to sleep, Nelson and Ardwick would think he was sick again. With an effort, he sat up stiffly.

"The city looks about the same as when I saw it last."

"It is about the same," Nelson said. "I'm afraid it isn't going to welcome you with any brass bands, or people throwing confetti out the windows."

"We didn't expect that."

"Whether you expected it or not, that's what you should have had. But you don't need any brass bands to know how we feel about it."

Dave Spaas nodded, and Nelson asked him, "What are you going to do now, Dave?"

"I'll go back to Chicago as soon as I can."

"Back to railroading?"

"If I can find a job."

"Why don't you stay here and rest up for a while?"

"If I have to rest up, I'll do it in Chicago."

"You got some people to put you to bed and fatten you up a bit? That's what you need."

"Maybe so," Dave Spaas said; but noticing the other's puzzled expression, he added, "Sure I have, Nelson. Don't worry about that."

After he spoke, he turned to look out the window again, and jerked his head up and down abruptly, trying to drive the mist away from behind his eyes. The car stopped. Nelson led them into a house, up some stairs to an apartment that was full of people. The lights seemed to be dim as if the room were thick with tobacco smoke. Dave Spaas had trouble breathing now and he started to ask someone to open the windows, but saw the windows were open already. Nelson was introducing him to a lot of people whose names he did not know. All around him, he saw faces watching him anxiously.

Nelson's voice was saying, "This is Dave Spaas, just back from the war in Spain—"

Dave Spaas reached out for a chair. The lights and the faces blurred before his eyes. He felt suddenly too tired to move or speak. The long return journey was over. Border patrols, police, consuls, immigration inspectors, customs and passport officials— all these were behind him. He was home, or almost home; the faces around him were the faces of friends. Within a few days he would be riding into Chicago . . . into Chicago again, Chicago. . . . Inside him, the tension of many months relaxed. He heard Ardwick's voice close to his ear, calling his name; but the voice faded farther and farther into the distance. Dave Spaas dropped asleep in the chair where he had sat down.

Part Two

THE PROSPEROUS YEARS

1920

IN the year 1920, a few months after Pledger McAdams had returned to Chicago from the great victory in Europe, Eddie Spaas, the wandering brakeman, was also returning from war—or rather from service in the army, since Eddie Spaas had never been within three thousand miles of the front lines.

But that three thousand miles was close enough for Eddie. Up in Tallefer before he had been drafted, he had told his friends that if Uncle Sam wanted him to go gunning for the Kaiser, Uncle Sam would have to come and get him. He had implied that there were lots of mountains around Tallefer, and Uncle Sam might have some considerable looking. But when the federal men raised this question with him, Eddie listened quietly to their conversation, and then accompanied them to the draft board. He contributed twenty-four months to the great victory—twenty of them switching boxcars at an East-coast port of embarkation; the last four in the guardhouse for going AWOL—or rather, as Eddie understood it, for being caught.

So in the summer of 1920, Eddie made his way back to the Middle West. He carried an honorable discharge in his pocket, more through an oversight on the part of the army than for any other reason. He was gray-haired and thin and stringy, packed what clothes he owned in his khaki overcoat, and his guitar case as always slung across his back. He moved from one town to another across Kansas. With Prohibition now, there weren't any saloons to play in and people seemed to have forgotten the old songs. He found a building with an IWW sign over the door; but it had been closed a year and a half.

Eddie took to the freights again. He panhandled when he had to and played his guitar in the hot-dog wagons and on the steps of the farmhouses for food and a cup of coffee. Up through Kansas and Nebraska, the wind and the sunlight and the dust driving across the prairie brought the color back to his face. His legs grew springy once again, and the wheels hammered over the rails with the old tune. At night he slept in the rolling boxcars, resting his head on his guitar case. One morning, waking, he saw through the open door of the car a bright blue river winding across a bed of yellow sand. Eddie let out a whoop and sat in the doorway dangling his feet. Across the valley, a jagged line of cliffs and mesas thrust up purple and brown in the morning sunlight. He lighted his pipe and unlimbered his guitar.

> "Casey Jones," *he hummed,* "oh Casey Jones
> There wasn't much left but a bag of bones.
> He went and rapped on the Pearly Gate—
> Saint Peter said, You're a little bit late.
> They've some fires in hell that'll suit you fine,
> You scabbing skunk from the S.P. line."

Whistling and singing, he strummed the guitar, while the freight chugged slowly along the Whitewater valley.

Eddie worked the harvest through August and September. Then he got a farmer to take him on as hired man for the winter in exchange for board and lodging. In the spring of 1921, he found himself a job on the Whitewater and Northern, braking the division west from Andersen, North Dakota. Six days a week, he used to take the way freight up the Whitewater valley into Montana. Before dawn, they would tie the engine on to half a dozen boxcars, pick up the caboose, and chug out along the bank of the Missouri River. Across the river, the bluffs and butt ends of hills piled up tier on tier to the eastern rim of the plateau. Then as the sun rolled up over the rim, the morning light poured into the valley, flooding down across the range lands and the yellow stubble fields, burning away the mist that hung between the cottonwoods on the river bank.

Every ten or twelve miles they stopped at a siding to set out a car or pick one up. By midmorning, they reached Fort Mason, where there was a station house, and a little brick hotel looking as if it had been built to fit a wedge-shaped city lot, but standing here by itself on a slope of sagebrush. They stopped for a cup of coffee, then switched the train onto the spur line and puffed across the Missouri River bridge. Eddie, sitting on the steps of the caboose, looked out at the delta half a mile upstream, where the Whitewater flooded across a spit of sand into the Missouri.

As they moved up the Whitewater valley, the land turned bone dry. Neither grass nor cottonwoods grew along the river, while strange-shaped cliffs of purple and rose and gray pressed down close to the stream. In summer the wind twisted up dust clouds from the flats of baked clay. But as the summer faded to autumn, the days shortened, the nights turned cold, the stars sparkled icily over the rims of the valley. Winter came wailing out of the northwest, driving the dry snow like flakes of steel. Ice spread over the river; the telegraph wires sang shrilly along the right of way.

Eddie didn't much mind the cold. He stamped up and down beside the train while they switched the cars out, with the collar of his sheepskin coat turned up around his ears and his hands in his pockets. When they finished their work and headed for home, Eddie and the flagman sat in the caboose arguing about unions; Eddie kept saying the IWW would come back because workingmen couldn't get anywhere until they learned sense enough to organize into one big union; but the flagman told him the IWW was deader than Grover Cleveland.

At dusk they rumbled across the bridge again into Fort Mason, watered the engine, picked up an empty boxcar from the siding, and then parked the train while they went into the hotel for supper. The old woman who kept the hotel had the table set for them; the stove was red hot and the room was full of the smells of coffee and roasting meat. She sat with them as they ate, joked back and forth with Eddie and the engineer, and kept bringing out more platters of food from the kitchen. When they had eaten all they could hold, they lit up cigars and leaned back in their chairs for a moment before they went out to the train again.

Eddie walked up to the engine to check his running orders with the engineer. Then he opened the switch to the main line and wiggled his lantern up and down. The engine blasted out a great mountain of steam as its wheels slipped on the icy rails. Then the wheels took hold, the engine and cars rolled slowly past. When the caboose had clacked over the switch, Eddie lined the switch back, locked it, and ran for the rear step, spinning his lantern over his head in the highball signal. As he swung aboard, he heard two hoots from the engine and the train gathered speed.

Inside the caboose, the flagman was bending over the stove, stirring the fire. Eddie stood on the platform for a moment, puffed his cigar and listened to the sound of the wheels.

"There's a brake sticking," he called to the flagman. "Hear it?"

Thrusting his head around the corner of the caboose, Eddie saw a few sparks flashing from under the wheels of the boxcars they had picked up in Fort Mason. He stuck the brake club in his belt and swung up the ladder to the roof. The tops of the cars stretched out in front of him swaying unevenly, with the smoke streaming back over them. Overhead, the night was not quite dark yet. A clear greenish twilight hung in the west, against which thrust up the stark ribs of the valley.

Eddie jumped from one roof to another until he found the car he wanted. Climbing down to the brake platform at the end of the car, he slipped the club into the brake wheel and pressed back to release the catch. The brakes seemed to be jammed. As he heaved against the handle of the club, the brake wheel snapped off suddenly from its rusty shaft and Eddie toppled backwards between the cars. He caught at the corner of the boxcar and threw himself sideways, trying to fall clear of the wheels. The roadbed smashed up at him like the blow of a hammer.

When the flagman got the train stopped and ran back, Eddie way lying beside the track, mumbling, "I got clear of the wheel, I did. They couldn't slice me up, by Jesus." But his left arm was stretched across the rail, cut off at the elbow.

1927

IT was 1927 when Eddie at last headed back towards Chicago. The railroad company had given him a job switchtending for a while, and then let him work as crossing watchman. That was a good job for a one-armed man, because all he had to do was keep from falling asleep so he could step out on the highway every couple of hours with a red lantern. But that job petered out when the state built a highway bridge over the tracks; and so Eddie, with the empty left sleeve of his jacket pinned against his side, hit the boxcars eastward.

All across North Dakota and Minnesota the freights gathered more men at each station. The men lay stretched out on the flat cars with the cinders pouring over them, and they squatted along the roofs of the boxcars like crows caucusing on the branches of trees. Eddie, humming to himself, listened to their talk about the farms they had lost and how there were no more jobs in the harvest. He heard them tell about Camp Dix and the trip across the pond, and about Chateau Thierry and Belleau Wood and the little French railroad cars no bigger than wheelbarrows. The stories went on mile after mile; and in some of the towns the railroad cops were waiting for the freight trains. As the men rolled down from the cars, the cops charged, swinging their clubs; the men fled across the fields, taking refuge behind haystacks and under the frames of abandoned jalopies at the edge of the town dumps.

Down in the gullies, under the weeds that grew higher than a man's head, were the jungles where the men slept and cooked and ate. Flies buzzed back and forth between the stems of the weeds; rats scratched dryly in the fallen leaves and suddenly darted across the cleared spaces under the men's feet to snatch up bread crusts and scraps of paper.

Eddie hopped from one jungle to the next across three states. In the early autumn he reached Chicago, and went to look for his old friend Uncle Jennison.

He found Jennison living in style as the proprietor of an old men's flophouse near Halsted and West Madison Street. He had married a square-faced Norwegian woman who was actually the owner and did all the work; but they had painted across the front of the building in red letters, UNCLE JENNISON'S HOTEL. Eddie settled down there with a cot and folding chair in one of the two-by-six board and chicken-wire cages Jennison's Norwegian wife called a private room. Eddie said he couldn't stand the old men slobbering around all the time and coughing and hollering at night; but he stayed because he didn't have enough money to leave. Then he got used to it after a while. At any rate the place was clean. Uncle Jennison's wife scrubbed it every morning from top to bottom with a solution of something that boiled all over the floor like quicklime, and ate the soles off Eddie's shoes. She didn't allow any women in the hotel, and whenever she caught two men in the same bed she threw them both out.

Uncle Jennison was working in the Great Midland coach yard. He told Eddie how he had been chairman of the local Carbuilders' lodge there for the last ten years, and how the old-timers thought he was a top-notch chairman because he could kick like a mule when it came to collecting disputed overtime. "That's the way you got to do it, Eddie. You got to build solid from the bottom. Then you work along to the fancy stuff when the right time comes. I been moving slow because some of the boys had me tagged for an old-time Wobbly. I got to go easy, particularly around those union officials downtown in the vice-president's office. Shame for reactionary bastards like them to be officials in a union, ain't it?"

But though he had always had to watch his step in the union, Jennison told Eddie that here in the hotel he did and said just what he liked. The hotel was his own property—or anyhow his wife's. On the wall of the second-floor landing, he had painted the words, "Speak your mind, brother. No Pinkertons in here." And twice a week, he ran a session down in the room in the basement he called the Workingmen's Forum. A sign over the basement door said *Meetings Wednesday and Saturday. Workingmen Welcome. Pimps, Finks, and Policemen not Welcome.* The old men thought that was a big joke, and Eddie heard them cackling over it as they dribbled into the basement and lined up in the rows of camp chairs like at a revival meeting. There was a pot-bellied stove in one corner, and a platform where Uncle Jennison sat in a carpet-bottom chair with a gavel in his hand and a table to pound it on. His wife settled down in a rocker beside the stove, holding her cauliflower-eared tomcat on her knees. As for the attendance at the Forum, it was the same crew that turned out for every session— Uncle Jennison's boarders from upstairs, and a flock of hoofers off West Madison Street and from the other flophouses round about. Uncle Jennison would start things off with a crack of his gavel, and the old men pitched in, arguing and yelling, shouting Henry George and Karl Marx at each other. Usually the fight narrowed down to the same two or three, who laid it on while the other old men snorted and guffawed. One of these was a sharp-eyed individual whom everybody called the Shoestring because he peddled shoestrings and odds and ends for a living. Eddie got his eye on him from the start and wanted to murder him. The man kept popping out of his chair, lashing his neck back and forth like a snake trying to look two directions at once, and spouting off about how he was an original First International Marxian Socialist. But the only thing he showed much interest in was running down the Wobblies, claiming their leaders had been scabs that sold the working stiffs down the river and then took it on the lam to his nibs in Soviet Moscow.

64

Eddie couldn't stomach that for long. "You old son of a bitch," he yelled. "What do you know about the Wobblies? You're no workingman. You're no better than a pimp yourself—" Everybody started shouting at once. The First International Socialist's voice shrilled up over the others like a cracked dinner bell. Uncle Jennison banged his gavel on the tin ceiling. After the session he told Eddie, "It's no use letting those guys get under your skin." They had sat down on the narrow front stoop of the hotel; Uncle Jennison loaded his pipe, gnawing and spitting at the stem until he got it drawing.

"Don't you ever get tired listening to those calamity howlers?" Eddie asked.

"Why should I? What's wrong with 'em?"

"Not anything's wrong with 'em, except they're all back in 1890. They're old-timers, Unc, still worrying about the Haymarket Riot. All talk and no fight."

"And what do *you* do that's so sharp?"

Eddie shook his head. He stared down at the half-paved street in front of the hotel, at the narrow faces of the buildings stepping away through the shadows toward the intersection of West Madison, from which drifted back snatches of music and shouting. "I guess I'm an old-timer too," he said.

"You're wrong," Jennison told him. "It's the old-timers that show the only fight nowadays. Here I got a labor forum, something I wanted all my life. But none of the young fellows come to it. Why not? They don't give a damn, that's all. They're out selling vacuum cleaners and buying Ford cars on the installment plan. Or else they're laying stiff in the gutters like those bastards over on Madison Street."

Jennison banged out his pipe and stood up.

"How about a couple of bucks till Monday?" Eddie asked.

Growling and swearing under his breath, Uncle Jennison dug into his pants pocket.

After a few days in Chicago, Eddie had reached his last nickel. He scouted around for a job, and stopped in to see his brother Joe at the Great Midland railroad yard. Joe had become a big shot on the Great Midland now; he had built up a lot of seniority and gotten to be secretary of the yard-brakemen's lodge. Joe shook Eddie's hand and looked him over to see how he had made out in the past years; and when Eddie asked if he knew any angles about a job,

Joe nodded and said, "I figured that's the way it would be, Eddie."

Eddie couldn't work braking any more on account of his arm, but Joe helped him get a job switchtending on the stockyards crossover. Joe acted in a big-hearted way which made Eddie want to give him a punch in the nose; but he knew he couldn't afford to do anything like that, particularly having only one arm.

"Stop over to my house whenever you feel like it," Joe told him. "Come over and see my kids."

"Okay, I'll come sometime," Eddie said. But he was afraid to see Ann again, and it was a long time before he went. By accident one day, he met Ann on Halsted Street. She shook hands with him as if they had known each other a long time ago when they were kids, and they talked about the weather for a while. After that he went to the house once or twice, and sometimes she sent her young son, Dave Spaas, to carry him a piece of apple pie or chocolate cake for his lunch.

At the stockyard crossover where Eddie worked the afternoon to midnight shift, he had a shanty with a stove and a chair, and all he had to do was listen for the telephone and keep the switches lined up for the engines that worked in and out. Every afternoon about four o'clock, Paddy Gallagher's animal train chugged over the hill and came hammering down past the shanty. Paddy would have fifteen or twenty stock cars, which swayed and banged over the crossrails, while the hogs squealed and the young steers bellowed in amazement. On the back platform of the caboose would be Paddy himself, cupping his hands around his mouth and mooing like a cow with a full bag. Abeam of the shanty he always yelled, "Here we come, Eddie. Clear the tracks for the animal train!"

Whenever he had a bottle of whiskey, Paddy would jerk open the brake valve and the train would scream to a halt on the crossover, sparks flying from under the wheels, and the engineer leaning out the cab window shaking his fist. One of the young brakemen would take Eddie's place at the crossover while Eddie rode into the stockyards with Paddy. After they had spotted the cars at the unloading pens, they would empty Paddy's bottle and then set out hunting bull rings. Their main equipment was a screw driver and a couple of sticks—one having a sharp point and the other with a hook in the end. The stockyards, by six o'clock in the evening, were quiet and almost deserted, and Eddie and Paddy Gallagher rambled along beside the stock cars until they found a load of likely-looking young bulls. Then Paddy thrust the stick with the hook on it through the slats of the car and hooked one of the bulls by the ring in his nose. Bracing his feet, Paddy yanked and cursed, the bull began to bellow, and the chorus of roars and squeals ran down the line of cattle cars like a grass fire. If the bull kept on acting stubborn, Eddie climbed around to the other side of the car and jabbed the pointed stick into his rear end. Sooner or later, they dragged the bull's snout over against the slats. Then Paddy grabbed hold of the ring in the bull's nose and Eddie went to work on it with a screw driver. Each ring was made of two halves, held together by a pin hinge on one side and a lock screw on the other. When Eddie had removed the lock screw, Paddy opened the ring and slipped it from the bull's nostrils. The rings were brass, and in a good week Eddie and Paddy picked up forty or fifty of them.

But they had trouble finding a place to sell the rings, and Eddie asked his brother Joe's young kid Dave if he knew any good junk dealers. The kid brought over a friend of his, a tough Polack boy named Vic Koviak who said he knew all about that stuff. The Polack didn't look to Eddie any older than fifteen, but he rolled his own cigarettes from Bull Durham and was always spitting out of the corner of his mouth. Sure, he told them, he knew every junkman on the South Side. Then jerking his thumb at the rings, he asked,

"Stuff ain't hot, is it?"

"What do you mean, hot?" Paddy Gallagher demanded. He stamped all over the switch shanty, preaching to the two boys how taking bull rings wasn't anything like stealing. After all, bulls came to the stockyards to get butchered, and a ring wasn't any use in the nose of a dead bull, was it? Most likely the meat companies only threw the rings away anyhow.

The Polack boy spat on the floor. "That trash ain't worth stealing." But he took the rings and sold them for thirty cents a dozen, which they split four ways; and with places you could buy bootleg homebrew at a nickel a glass, Eddie figured that paid him two or three extra glasses of beer a week. In hot weather like this, he explained to his nephew Dave, a man needed plenty of liquid to keep his system working right.

Eddie got along fine with Dave, but he did not like the Polack kid who was always unlining his switches for a joke so Eddie had to run up and down like crazy when an engine hove up. He heard Dave telling the Polack boy to cut it out because his Uncle Eddie had a bad arm.

"What's wrong with his arm?" the Polack asked, as if he didn't know already. A few minutes later, Eddie felt somebody pinching the empty sleeve of his jacket.

"Let go that," he yelled, whirling around.

"Missing something, ain't you?" the Polack kid asked.

"I ain't missing anything. I got it home pickled in brine."

"How'd you lose it?"

"Used to play baseball," Eddie told him. "I threw my arm out."

One day Paddy Gallagher checked with the junkman and found they were paying forty-four cents a dozen for bull rings instead of thirty. The next time the Polack kid came over to split up the cash, Paddy was laying for him. But Paddy made the mistake of grabbing for him before he got inside the shanty. The Polack kid sidestepped him a couple of times, then spit right in Paddy's eye and lit out across the vacant lot, taking the money with him. Paddy Gallagher chased him six blocks down Halsted Street, but never caught him.

Eddie's nephew Dave admitted he had been sucked in too; but when Eddie told him he ought to punch the Polack in the nose, he shrugged his shoulders. "Vic thinks it's funny to outsmart guys. He'll buy me a bunch of hamburgers or something to make up for it."

"Ain't scared of that Polack, are you?"

The kid shook his head. "Me and Vic never had a fight yet. He's not sure he could lick me and I'm not sure I could lick him."

The young Polack never showed up again after that; but Eddie's nephew Dave took to coming over often. Every couple of days after school, he brought Eddie some food or a bottle of homebrew from Ann. He helped Eddie keep the switches lined when a lot of engines were working through the crossover, and during slack periods he sat beside Eddie on the bench in front of the shanty. The kid always had a few spare automobile parts and some odds and ends of junk with him that he picked up crossing the city dump. He tinkered with the spare parts while Eddie talked about the old days and the Wobblies. The kid would listen for hours while he monkeyed with his spare automobile parts. One night after the kid had gone home, Eddie noticed a shiny brass bull ring on the doorstep of the shanty. As he reached down for it, a spark half an inch long jumped out of the ring, and he thought he had lost his other arm. He tracked the wire under the floor of the shanty where he found a Ford sparking coil. He was afraid to touch the coil, so he left it hooked up to the bull ring for the morning-shift switch-tender.

The kid was always fooling around with things to find out how they worked. Eddie would come out of the shanty from answering a telephone call, look around for the kid, and finally spot him forty feet above the tracks scrambling through the girders of the viaduct. When he came down, he would draw diagrams with the poker to show Eddie how all the girders were hitched together. He said he was going to be a civil engineer when he grew up.

"That'll be great," Eddie said. "You'll work for a big corporation and make a million dollars."

"I won't either work for a big corporation. I'll work for the government."

"That's just as bad."

They argued back and forth over what the kid's high-school civics teacher had said about working for the government. As they argued, the kid scratched with the poker, drawing up plans in the dirt for a town with a lake and a railroad tunnel. Eddie slapped his knees laughing, but after a while he pitched right in trying to figure how to get that railroad under the lake. When Paddy Gallagher's animal train roared over the hill, Eddie had forgotten all about the crossover. The train ran through one of the switches, and it took Eddie and the kid and Paddy Gallagher thirty minutes' hard work with a crowbar to get the switch points bent back where they belonged. The engineer walked up from the cab, waving his fists over his head.

"You damn sleeping switchtender," he yelled at Eddie. "I'm going to write you up for this."

Paddy Gallagher dropped the crowbar and went for him. "You'll write who up? If you hadn't been coming twice as fast as you had any business over that hill, you wouldn't got into any trouble. Get back on your engine, you foul-mouthed old hoghead, before I smash you into a jelly."

The two walked back up the train together shouting at each other, while Eddie and the kid stood laughing.

Eddie paid his back rent to Uncle Jennison's wife, and he picked up a second-hand Ford car on the installment plan. "You gone off your noggin?" Uncle Jennison asked him. "You're just like the rest of 'em. J. P. Morgan's got an automobile, so you got to have one. Keep up with the crowd, mortgage your false teeth—"

"You been listening to them calamity Janes again," Eddie said. "I got no family, I'm too old to be chasing skirts; I might as well have a tin lizzy." When he learned how to drive, he took Uncle Jennison for a ride. They bought a quart of snake juice from a speakeasy and stopped for a few sniffs in Garfield Park. It was the kid's birthday, and Eddie had promised to go out and see his football team play Bridgeport High; but the game was half over by the time they got there. Eddie spotted the kid finally from his helmet falling off at each play, and his stubbly yellow head sticking up through the tangle of legs and arms. "There he is," Eddie shouted in Uncle Jennison's ear. "There's the kid, right on the bottom." The kid seemed to be always on the bottom, but each time he got up, yanked his helmet back on, and piled into the next one. After a while the boy opposite him limped off the field, and a few plays later the substitute went off too.

Eddie recognized the Polack kid named Vic Koviak who had spit in Paddy Gallagher's eye. He was at quarterback, trying to play the whole game himself. Neither side scored until the Polack threw some fancy passes and gave the other side a touchdown. Then near the end of the game, he intercepted a pass himself and ran the length of the field, turning and dodging. When he got in the clear, he slowed down to a walk and crossed the goal line, pitching the football up in the air and catching it again. At the final whistle, the two teams were bucking each other in center field, and as soon as the whistle blew, the Polack kid walked over to the opposite quarterback and punched him on the nose. At once the two gangs milled into each other; the referees, acting as if they were scared to get too close, finally called a carload of cops to break it up. Booing each other and hissing, the teams filed into the shower room in the basement of the school.

Eddie and Uncle Jennison waited in the tin lizzy, killing the quart of snake juice. When the kid came out, he already had a purple ring around one eye, and the skin gone from his knuckles. "That's the way Bridgeport High is," he told them with disapproval. "They never play a game but it winds up in a fight."

"I seen who started this fight," Eddie said. "It was that Polack roughneck that spit in Paddy Gallagher's eye. I seen him walk right over and punch that lad on the snoot."

"But Eddie, you saw what they did in the game. They kicked Vic in the crotch. You can't let 'em get away with that."

Eddie and Uncle Jennison began to laugh, and after a moment the kid grinned in embarrassment. Eddie passed him the bottle against the pain in his eyes, but the kid took it like an old head, wiped the neck on his sleeve, and tilted the bottom sky-high.

"That boy must have been weaned on snake juice," Uncle Jennison said.

They dropped Jennison at the car line and Eddie drove the kid home, feeding him peanuts to cover up his breath. Ann Spaas and the boy's older sister Grace had the birthday dinner on the table —chicken and mashed potatoes and black chocolate cake with candles. But Joe called up from somewhere saying he couldn't get home for supper, and Eddie settled down to stay, although Ann Spaas had not invited him. He and the kid stuffed themselves, went into a laughing jag, and almost exploded trying to blow out the candles on the cake. Afterwards, Ann gave Dave and his sister money for a birthday movie, and they went whooping off toward Halsted Street, while she and Eddie sat down on the steps of the front porch.

"How did he get the black eye?" Ann asked.

"They had a little riot after the ball game."

She laughed and nodded. "That always happens." Then she said, "Listen, Eddie, what you been talking to that boy about?"

"Talking to him about? What do you mean?"

"Joe told him if he ever caught him going over to see you any more he'd whip him so he couldn't sit down for a month."

"When did Joe say that?" Eddie asked.

"A week ago."

"He's been over two three times since then."

"I suppose he has. But don't tell Joe."

"I don't tell Joe nothing," Eddie said. "What started all this, Ann?"

"The kid asked Joe if he ever knew Eugene Debs, and Joe began yelling all over the house it was more Wobbly talk of his Uncle Eddie, and he'd better keep away from that switch shanty if he knew what was good for him—"

"I never said nothing to the boy about Debs."

"No? Maybe he heard it in school. He's got some history teacher he's always talking about—"

"Is Joe working tonight?" Eddie asked.

Ann shook her head.

"He might have come home for the kid's birthday."

"I guess it's just as well he didn't," Ann said. Inside the house, the new baby began to wail. She went in, and Eddie heard her through the open window, cooing and singing. He leaned back, looking up at the leafless branches; the night was warm, a faint mist drifted in the moonlight above him. Now the baby's cries dwindled to a quarrelsome gurgling, and a few moments later Ann came out again with a bottle of homebrew under her arm. She filled their glasses and Eddie drank in silence, not knowing what to talk about. They had almost emptied the bottle when Ann Spaas said again, as if they had not been interrupted,

"It's just as well. Things go smoother when he stays away. Maybe all men are like that. Nights he comes home, the kids quarrel, they get under my feet and I get mad; then Joe blows up, trying to act the boss in a lot of things he doesn't know anything about because he's never home enough to find out. And the next day, he says he has to work late again and we're all glad, Eddie. The kids and I have a quiet supper and nobody gets mad at anybody."

She laughed. A streetcar rattled along Halsted in the distance. The trees stirred in the wind. "Maybe all men are like that," she said. She pushed herself up from the step and reached down for the empty beer bottle. "But I got nothing to complain about. He brings me money every payday. He doesn't drink it all up or spend it on women."

Eddie was standing indecisively on the porch step.

"Goodnight, Eddie," she said; and he turned and crossed the yard to his tin lizzy.

Now that he had worked through his three months' probation period, Eddie paid up his dues and was admitted to the yard brakemen's lodge. Paddy Gallagher herded him up to his first meeting, but at the door of the hall Eddie forgot the password for new members and the sergeant-at-arms wouldn't let him in till the meeting passed a special vote to admit him. When the door finally opened, Paddy Gallagher held him by the elbow and hissed into his ear, "Don't forget to make the high-sign over the Bible, you lame brain." They tramped down the center of the hall, waved their hands a couple of times over the book on its fancy wooden stand, then dropped down in chairs against the wall. Ten or fifteen other men were lined up along the wall, and Eddie saw his brother Joe on the Grand Master's throne staring straight in front of him as if he had swallowed a brakeman's club. During the meeting nobody spoke except Joe and the Assistant General Chairman who had come from downtown to report on seventeen overtime claims and five seniority violations left over from the month before. That took an hour and a half, and when he finished, the meeting adjourned. Paddy disappeared around the corner into a speakeasy, but Eddie waited at the door of the hall for his brother. After a while, Joe came out and they walked together up Sixty-Third Street through the smoky fall evening.

"How did you like the lodge meeting?" Joe asked.

"All right. But your boys don't talk much, do they?"

"We get the work done," Joe said. "We take care of grievances, and when any man's got overtime coming, we get it." They both looked up at the same time, their eyes met and broke away. Joe Spaas was beginning to grow fat, Eddie noticed, but his face had a gaunt look and drooped at the corners. Joe said suddenly, "Now listen, Eddie, don't make any trouble for me. We don't want none of that Wobbly stuff around here. The boys in the lodge are good solid union men; we got our seniority, we don't want any trouble. So keep your mouth shut, see?"

"I didn't say a word, did I?"

"Listen, Eddie, I was glad to get you that job. There was a time I thought I'd kill you if I was ever to see you again. But I don't feel that way now."

"What would you want to kill me for?"

"You know what for. But I don't feel that way now. I was a young punk then and I thought a lot of things I didn't have any ground for thinking." He walked along nodding to himself, then said finally, "I guess you got what was coming to you, anyway. How did it happen to you?"

"Brake wheel came off in my hands and I fell between the cars."

"That's tough, Eddie. But I could have told you it was going to happen that way. Always you had to be trying something new. No matter where you might be, you always wanted to take off for someplace else. And always talking that Wobbly talk. It didn't get you anywhere, did it? Look at you—older than me, and you got no seniority at all. Maybe you can work switchtending for a while, but if things turn for the worse, you won't be able to hold the job because you got no seniority."

Eddie shrugged his shoulders.

73

"I guess you thought I was a young punk back in those days," Joe said. "But I could have told you right then, there's only one thing in this railroad business and that's seniority. If you got no seniority, you're not worth a snort in a windstorm. But if you got it, you're somebody. I fought fifteen years for my seniority, and I'm somebody, Eddie. I'm secretary of the lodge, and I can hold one of the best jobs on the turnpike—"

"Quit blowing your horn!" Eddie shouted.

Then suddenly feeling sorry for his brother, he patted him on the arm. "Sure you're somebody, Joe. You couldn't got me the job if you hadn't been somebody. Maybe you were right and I was wrong. Maybe if I could do it all over again, I'd do it different." He peered up for a moment at his brother's face. "And maybe I wouldn't," he said. They stopped at the corner where Eddie had parked the tin lizzy. "Well Joe, if you're going home, I'll drop you off."

Joe shook his head. "I'm going over to Olsen's for a couple hands of poker and a drink maybe."

"Almost suppertime, isn't it?"

"The old lady doesn't expect me, Eddie. She'll most likely be out to a movie." They stood silent, the fallen leaves on the pavement rustling against their ankles. "Women don't know anything about a man's work," Joe said. "You can't talk to them, they got no interest in how hard a man has to plug for his seniority; but god-damn, they're always ready to take your pay check off you at pay-day. I tell you this, Eddie, women nag and fuss at you, and the best way to get along with them is to stay away a good piece of the time."

Eddie did not answer. He climbed into the tin lizzy and Joe walked away up Sixty-Third Street. Softly the evening darkened over the flat-faced buildings, and Eddie remembered the night in the rain when Ann, giggling and whispering, had crept down the wet shingle roof to the dormer window.

The reddish glow from the city reflected against the low clouds. With dusk, a powdering of snow blew across the black earth of the railroad embankment. Wind whistled around the corners of the shanty. When Eddie finished work and walked out to the street, snow lay a couple of inches deep through the dead leaves of the vacant lot, and snow had outlined in white the hood and fenders and roof of his tin lizzy. He saw that someone was sitting on the

74

running board of the car. As he slid down the bank to the sidewalk, the figure stood up to meet him. It was the kid, Dave.

"Listen, Eddie, can you drive me somewhere? Not far, only a couple blocks."

"Don't see why not, if we can get the jalopy started. What's the matter?"

"Not anything's the matter."

Eddie reached out, grabbing him by the shoulder. "What's the matter with you, Dave? What's got into you?"

The boy pulled him towards the car. "Don't ask me no questions now, Eddie. I been waiting an hour for you. I was afraid to leave the car fear I'd miss you crossing the lot. Hurry up, can't you please, Eddie—" Eddie wiped the snow from the windshield and began cranking the old Ford. He spun the crank till he was sweating under his heavy jacket, but the motor never let out a grunt. The two of them, slipping in the snow, pushed the car down to the corner, where the kid jumped out in the street and flagged a truck.

"Please, Mister, will you give us a push?"

Nuzzling its square nose against their tail, like a big dog and a little dog, Eddie thought, the truck bumped them along till the tin lizzy began choking and back-firing. Then the truck roared off down the street, leaving them to putter along on two cylinders while Dave hugged the dashboard, listening anxiously to the uncertain firing.

"Spill it," Eddie said. "What's the matter with you?"

Dave sat up straight. "It's Vic. The cops are out after him."

"I should hope they might be."

"No, Eddie, listen. He can't walk. He got hurt."

"He can't walk? What do you mean, he can't?"

Dave looked up, his eyes wide in his white face. "He fell off a coal car. He didn't fall off, Eddie; the cop knocked him off. I seen it, I was hanging on the train right behind. The cop knocked him off and he fell over the wall and he can't walk now, Eddie—"

"Son of a bitch," Eddie said. The engine sputtered and almost went dead.

"Pull your spark down," Dave told him.

Eddie yanked at the spark and throttle levers until the cylinders began hitting again. "Where is he now?"

"We were looking for coal on the tracks, Eddie, only there wasn't any, and we was going to throw some down from the coal car—" Dave was shaking all over. Eddie saw how he kept straining forward as if he was trying to push the car along faster. "Take it easy," Eddie told him. "Where is he now?"

"He's hid under a shed. Honest, Eddie, you got to help. The cops are looking for him."

"The cops probably forgot all about it by this time."

"No, he didn't forget about it."

"What makes you so sure?"

"I seen who it was, Eddie. There was only one coal car on the train, and he was hid right there waiting for us. Just when Vic jumped on the ladder, he come up out of the top of the coal car in that black coat—" The tin lizzy skidded around a corner and slewed sideways across the street; Eddie straightened it out and kept on going. "I seen it, Eddie," the kid yelled in his ear. "He kept ahold of him till they got over the wall by the bridge and then he pushed him off." Eddie drove southwest following the line of the embankment.

At last the kid pointed to a row of frame houses. Eddie stopped the car and switched out the lights, but left the motor running. The snow stretched unbroken across the sidewalk and the street. Snow was still falling and the night seemed muffled and quiet. Eddie could hear the tiny sifting sound of the dry snow driven by the wind. The kid ducked into the mouth of an alley, leaving a line of purple footprints behind him. Eddie followed. Across the far end of the alley, he saw the snow-covered railroad embankment rising up against the black sky. Now the boy stopped so suddenly that Eddie almost fell over him and they crouched close together against the wall of one of the houses. Voices were coming from somewhere. A couple of flashlights moved into sight up on the embankment and the beams stabbed down into the alley and into the yards on each side.

A voice said, "I don't see no footprints."

"The snow would have covered them. He's down there somewhere. He didn't travel far."

"Well, start at the end of the block and work back, that's all."

The lights moved away. Eddie and the kid ran down the alley to the base of the embankment, where they slipped through a hole in the fence into a back yard. They could see the beams of the flashlights moving in a yard two or three houses down.

The Polish kid had been watching for them. He clawed his way out from under the shed, pulling himself by his hands while his legs trailed sideways behind him. Bending down, Eddie whispered, "Listen, Bud, don't make a sound even if it hurts like hell. The cops are right next to us." He and Dave grabbed the Polish kid under the arms, pushed him through the hole in the fence, and carried him up the alley. Between the lines of their footmarks, his dragging feet cut two long furrows through the snow; but he made no sound all the way back to the car. When they lifted him into the back seat, Eddie looked at his face. He had bit clean through his upper lip, and a line of blood trickled off the end of his chin.

Christ, Eddie thought, he's hurt bad. We shouldn't have moved him. The Polish kid, letting out a thin wail, slumped sideways in the seat. Eddie threw the car into gear, drove around the corner, and doubled back northward. The streets were white and empty. Snow drifted out of the darkness into the pale circles around the streetlamps. Without speaking, Eddie and Dave stared straight ahead through the snow-blurred windshield. Neither of them looked back at the Polish kid lying on the seat behind them.

Following Dave's directions, Eddie drove South on Halsted, then turned again into a small street paralleling the railroad and stopped in front of a row of houses backed against the embankment. There were no lights from any windows and the streetlamp on the corner behind them made only a milky pool in the falling snow. As Eddie stepped out of the car, the snow came up over his ankles. Wind rattled the branches of the trees in the yard, and somewhere near by a dog began to bark.

He hammered on the door of the house. After a long time he thought he heard steps, but nothing happened and he knocked again. A light snapped on, a chain rattled in the door; the door opened a crack and he saw a little girl looking out at him.

"What do you want?" she asked.

"Koviak live here?"

"Yes, he does. What do you want?"

"Aren't your mother or father home? Where are they?"

The little girl stared at him through the crack of the door without answering.

"Get somebody, will you?" Eddie yelled. "What are you waiting for?"

"My father's working and my mother's in bed. What do you want?"

"Get your mother down here. Your brother's been hurt."

Still watching him, the little girl called, "Mamma, you'd better come down. There's a man at the door."

Then suddenly her voice turned shrill, and she ran up the stairs shrieking, "Mamma, Mamma, Mamma."

The 30's

PLEDGER McADAMS had begun to eat most of his meals in the Chile Parlor next door to where he lived. After his wife Sarah died, he didn't have time to cook his own meals at home. Then there were the two young children, the girl Judith and the boy Billy, and who was going to feed them and keep an eye on them while he was at work? The widow woman who ran the Chile Parlor took over that job; so the kids spent more time getting underfoot in her kitchen, or climbing the cottonwood tree in her back yard, than they did up in Pledger's room in the apartment house.

The widow woman, Ruby, was a husky, double-chinned woman with stringy black hair. From her ears she wore a couple of dangling green stones, and she kept jugs of homemade wine under the icebox, which she served to her friends at night after she had closed up the front room of the Chile Parlor. She had a lot of friends, most of them men; but she was good to the kids, and when Pledger felt like talking, she would listen to him after he came home from work at midnight, fix food for him, and bring him coffee or some of her wine if he wanted it. The Chile Parlor was a half basement, low and dark, a couple of steps below street level. It had a front window like a neighborhood grocery store, but Ruby never displayed anything there except billings from the local movie theater and a crop of dead flies which had batted their brains out against the glass. She mopped and scrubbed inside, but she told Pledger that if she kept the front too fancy, that brought her the wrong line of customers.

Pledger had never talked much before, but gradually now he fell into the habit of talking to the widow woman, Ruby. He told her about the Alabama town where he had grown up, and how he first went to work in the roundhouse when he was thirteen years old; how he learned the trade of carman, and came to Chicago; then went to New York to enlist in the army. The woman listened without saying much; but he knew she understood him, and he told her things he had never told Sarah. While he sat clenching and unclenching his fists, he tried by talking to find relief from the bitter and helpless anger inside him. He told her how he had stayed three weeks in bed with his broken ribs after the race riot, and when he went back to work, Jarvis, the yard foreman, threatened to fire him. In the end Jarvis had taken him back, him and Andrew Masters both; but broke them down from carmen to coach cleaners. The chairman of the white union who had promised to go to the office and fight for him had never lifted a finger. Pledger told Ruby how proud he had been of his craft; when they took it away from him, that was the worst thing he'd ever had done to him.

"Old Andrew Masters acted like the Bible says you're supposed to, Ruby. You got to be humble and trust in God, that's what Andrew Masters says. Every time they crack him, he turns his cheek around and says, crack me again. You think that's right, Ruby?"

She shook her head. Pledger leaned towards her across the table. "Even my own wife acted like she agreed with the white men. 'They took you back, didn't they, Pledger? Boss wouldn't hired you back if he hadn't thought good of you.'" He banged his hand down on the table in front of her and shouted, "Maybe if they'd paid me the money I had a right to, she wouldn't have died like she did."

In the empty Chile Parlor, they sat at one of the back tables under a single electric light which swayed slowly at the end of its wire from the ceiling; a criss-cross pattern of shadows stirred over the walls, light winked here and there from the porcelain counter-top and the stacked dishes. Sometimes when Pledger had talked himself dry, the widow woman got out her cards and they played cribbage; but in the morning she was always up to take care of Billy, send the little girl Judith to school, and shine up the Chile Parlor for the day's trade.

On warm summer evenings she moved her business out to the sidewalk, where she set up a stand and sold iced watermelon. Often coming home from work, Pledger found her there beside the empty stand, fanning away mosquitoes with her handkerchief. One night he told her he was thinking about asking her to get married to him;

Ruby said she was thinking about that too, but she hadn't made up her mind yet.

It was not till the Great Midland railroad laid Pledger off in 1933 that she finally did make up her mind. The depression settled over Chicago. All across the city, the yards and roundhouses, shops and factories, ground to a halt; the people were on the streets, bitter and cold and hungry. Ruby insisted that Pledger get married to her then, and she managed to keep him and the two kids fed on what she earned from the Chile Parlor. But that grew steadily smaller because not many people in the neighborhood had enough money to pay for a meal. Pledger applied for relief. A social worker came to see him, and when she learned his wife ran a chile parlor she wrote down a lot of notes, shaking her head gloomily, and went away. Nothing happened after that. He applied to all the other railroads and the steel mills and the foundries; but they were not hiring. Every day he walked over east into the sections near the University where the houses had gardens and the streets were lined with trees. He went from house to house, asking for odd jobs; sometimes he got some rugs to beat or a cellar to clean out. But it was not till he had to keep the kids home from school for lack of cold-weather clothes, that the social worker put him on relief.

The others at the Great Midland were laid off one by one. Pledger watched with angry enjoyment, for by wintertime many of the white carmen were out on the street too. The Negroes stuck together as close as they could. Most of them came Sundays to Andrew Masters' chapel, and they formed themselves a society called the Independent Railway Lodge, to help each other out when they got evicted or had no food. The relief office sent Pledger to a WPA street-repair project on the far west side. Out in the open prairie beyond the airport he worked with a little group of men who picked all day at the frozen earth and moved rocks back and forth in wheelbarrows. Because the project was so far away, Pledger had to allow an hour and a half each way on the streetcar.

Every day now, families were being evicted in the neighborhood. Pledger returned home at night sometimes to find Ruby waiting for him with the address of the eviction; then he went out again to round up the brothers of the Independent Railway Lodge. Word passed from block to block. In the winter dusk, the crowd gathered before the house where the eviction had been; somebody smashed open the door and they carried the furniture back inside. If the police came, the men spread down the street, fighting with clubs and bricks. And often when the eviction was close to the line between the white section and the black, white men crossed the boundary to help them.

One night, returning home from work, Pledger found a white man at the counter of the Chile Parlor talking to his wife. "What you want here?" Pledger asked.

The white man stood up and held his hand out. He was a head shorter than Pledger, but broad and with a square red face and lightish hair. "Take a seat, Honey," Ruby said. "This man's got something to talk to you about." The white man began at once telling Pledger about the unemployed councils that were growing up over Chicago, fighting evictions and fighting for relief. All the while he talked, Pledger kept thinking, mighty queer for a white man to be acting like this; what does this white man want with me? When the other finished, Pledger continued eating and made no answer.

"You don't trust me because I'm white," the man said at last. "You had a bad egg once, so you never going to eat eggs again?" Pledger saw Ruby make signs at him, but still he kept silent. "You used to be a carman," the white man said. "You used to be a carman on the Great Midland and the white union broke you down."

"How come you know so much about me?"

"From Roman Koviak."

"What do you want with me? What you come here talking for?"

"It's times like these men can learn fast," the white man told him. "Only how they going to learn if the people that can teach them sit around on their butt ends? I come from the Unemployed Council across Wentworth Avenue. We want to work with you and hold meetings with you; that's what we want."

Pledger swung around in his seat and stared at him. "What good you think that do?"

"The more people we got working together, the stronger we are," the white man told him; and Ruby said, "He's right, Honey."

Pledger shrugged his shoulders. He wrote on a paper napkin the address of Andrew Masters' chapel. "I can't stop you talking to the members. They want to hold any meetings with you, they can decide that for themselves." After the white man had gone, he bent his head angrily over his plate, thinking, he'll talk sweet till he gets what he wants, then he'll kick you down and spit on you.

But Ruby said, "The white man's all right, Honey. You didn't treat him good."

"How come you know all that?"

"How come I know you was all right?" Ruby asked. "By the way you act, that's all."

"They can come to the chapel," Pledger said softly. "They can come. Maybe I'll stand up and pray for them, like Andrew Masters." Then he rose, furious, from his chair, and shouted into her face, "I'll pray, God strike dead every one of those white men. God strike them dead for what they done to us!"

Ruby met his gaze without dropping her eyes. Then she shook her head slowly and turned away.

To the next meeting of the Negroes in Andrew Masters' chapel came the white man bringing other white men with him. He introduced himself by the name of Dave Spaas, said he had worked as a carman too, but now like everybody else he didn't have any job. He got up and talked to the meeting, and while he spoke, Pledger studied his words suspiciously. But he could see from the faces of the people around him that they believed what the white man was saying; and at the end, they voted to accept his invitation to visit the Unemployed Council across Wentworth Avenue. Pledger did not go. But some of the others went and came back to say they had been well received. They reported that the white men kept their hall open twenty-four hours a day and there was always somebody in the hall to send help when anybody in the neighborhood needed help; the white men were fighting hunger and evictions just like they were.

All through that winter, the Negroes' lodge in Andrew Masters' chapel worked more and more closely with the council of unemployed across Wentworth Avenue. They began to hold joint meetings together, and the white man, Dave Spaas, who seemed to know a lot of people, brought speakers from outside—a union organizer, a Negro lawyer, a spokesman for the Communist Party. Pledger made no objection; if that was what his members wanted, that was up to them. But he kept thinking, pretty soon things will change and those white men will go back where they came from. When they think they need our help they'll be sweet as honey; but when they got no need for us, then they'll push us down and spit on us.

The white man, Dave Spaas, had gotten hold of a mimeograph

machine from somewhere and asked Pledger to help him put out a neighborhood newssheet. Pledger refused. He didn't know what to write, he said, or anything about how to run a newspaper.

"You chairman of this lodge?" Dave Spaas asked him.

Pledger nodded.

"Your members are way out in front of you. You aren't leading them. They're leading you—or trying to."

Pledger walked off without answering. But the white man kept coming back and arguing with him, asking questions and writing up what he said. Before long he had enough for the first issue of his newssheet. He sent a big batch of the mimeographed papers over to the chapel, and Pledger's own members got excited about it. Pledger realized that what the white man had told him was true: the members of his own Lodge were trying to lead him in a different direction from what he wanted to go. At the next meeting, he made up his mind he would stand up and warn them—warn them how the white men would shove them aside as soon as they didn't need any more help from the Negroes. That was how the white men always acted; talked sweet to your face and laughed behind your back. . . .

But all the while, somewhere in the bottom of his mind, Pledger knew that he would not stand up. For when the white man, several months before, had walked out of the Chile Parlor and he had jumped from his chair to shout angrily into Ruby's face, he had known at the time that Ruby was right and he was wrong. But the walls of hatred and stubbornness were slow to crack: it had been many weeks before he had admitted this, and it was months before he could act on the admission.

So he agreed at last to help the white man with the newssheet. They wrote about the evictions and how the police acted; and about the two relief workers from the district office. The paper spread all over the neighborhood. People began hooting the relief workers wherever they went, and before long a couple of new workers took their places in the district. More and more people came to the joint meetings of the Independent Railway Lodge and the Unemployed Council.

When the snow melted off the streets they held outdoor rallies. The April days were cold and miserable, the northeast wind came wailing over the rooftops; but they brought out a couple of thousand people to picket the district relief office. Through the surging crowd in front of the office, the placards marched back and forth. The evening sky darkened, the streetlamps glowed up, lighting the fronts of the buildings. Pledger remembered the red sign of Sam's Restaurant and the crowd under the railway embankment. For a moment he saw again the pack of white men close over the Negro boy, the feet stamping and kicking.

"Ready, Pledger?"

He climbed up into the doorway they were using for a speakers' platform. Before him moved the faces of the men and women, Negro and white, watching him, listening. Amazement filled him and suddenly he found himself talking without worrying what he said, without being frightened for once, and his voice did not shake. When he finished the people cheered for him, and one of the other speakers yelled up the steps, "Nice going, brother." Dave Spaas stood up in the doorway and began talking about social security and decent relief.

It seemed to Pledger only a few moments before he heard the police sirens hooting in the distance. The squad cars wheeled around the corners from both ends of the block; they came butting into the crowd, the cops piled out, elbowing their way toward the steps. Dave Spaas kept on talking as long as he could. "If you want to be friends with the cops," he shouted, "you got to have money in your pocket. You got to be a pimp or racketeer or a big businessman or a city alderman. The cops know where the pay money comes from. They'll gas you and shoot you and crack you over the head if you're only a workman without a job. But, brother, if you're a pimp or a racketeer, the cops say yes-sir no-sir and take their hats off to you; they'll lick your boots and polish your spittoons—"

Down below, the men from the Lodge and the Unemployed Council were blocking the cops away from the steps. Clubs began to swing. The crowd broke and scattered. Bricks sailed through the lamplight, and Pledger saw one of the blue uniforms collapse on the sidewalk. A moment later they came charging up the steps. The first one Pledger caught in the chest with his foot, and sent him rolling down again to the pavement; then they were all jammed together in the entrance, stepping and hitting in the dark. They backed through the doorway into the hall of the house, threw their weight against the door, and forced it shut behind them. Dave Spaas had figured the way out beforehand. They followed him down the hall, crossed a back yard, and doubled back and forth through the alleys until they were clear. Dave Spaas was laughing and spitting, half blinded with blood and trying to wipe his eyes with a blood-soaked handkerchief. Across his forehead was a long gash where the tip of a policeman's club had ripped the skin open. They stopped for a moment and held a council in the alley. Then they split up, the other two speakers heading off in different directions, while Pledger took Dave Spaas home with him.

His wife Ruby washed the cut, poured in iodine, and bound it up. They fixed a mattress for Dave Spaas on the floor of the Chile Parlor. In the morning he said he felt fine, but his eyes were ringed with circles of yellow and lavender. "You ain't going out like that," Pledger said. "The cops will be looking out for a pair of shiners, and man, they couldn't miss you a mile away."

Dave Spaas stayed with them until his eyes faded back to something like normal. Evenings, his girl came over to see him; a thin, dark-haired girl, who told Pledger she was the daughter of the Polish carknocker named Koviak he had worked with in the railroad yard. After the kids went to bed, the four of them played poker in the back room of the Chile Parlor and drank Ruby's homemade wine.

■　■

When, something over a year later, Dave Spaas and the Polish girl got married, they held their wedding supper party at Ruby's Chile Parlor. The girl's father came to the party—old Roman Koviak, whom Pledger had known since he first went to work in the Great Midland coach yard. Pledger could see that Roman Koviak thought his new son-in-law was the most wonderful guy that ever breathed; but not too good for his daughter Stephanie. Roman brought a bottle of whiskey, got himself drunk as an owl on a couple of swigs; hooted and yelled, sang Polish songs, then sat down at the table and began to cry like a baby. There were a lot of Dave's friends at the party too; a CIO organizer named Hanson and a black-skinned, bald-headed Negro, Jackson, whom Pledger knew as the secretary of the South Side section of the Communist Party. And it was that same night that Jackson and Dave Spaas had taken Pledger aside and told him they wanted him to become a member of the Communist Party.

This came as no particular surprise to Pledger. He had known for more than a year that Dave Spaas was a Communist Party member, as were many of the others who had taken active part in the unem-

85

ployed councils and tenants' strikes. Jackson was well known in the Negro community of the South Side; Pledger several times had sat down for discussions with him, and had found himself generally in agreement with what Jackson said.

But actually Pledger paid little attention to things people told him, or to the leaflets and documents they sometimes gave him to read. He had always remembered Ruby's comment on that night when Dave Spaas had first come to visit them: "How come I know he's all right? By the way he acts, that's all." So throughout the bitter and difficult years from 1934 to 1936, Pledger had watched the way Dave Spaas acted. The two had worked together constantly as they struggled to build the Unemployed Council, the tenants' leagues, the Negro Railway Lodge, into a political force in the neighborhood. And for a time these groups *had* become a force: the neighborhood councils had blunted the brutality of the evictions; they had fought for and won improvements of city relief; they had finally brought the machine bosses of the area, their hats in their hands, begging favors. During that time Pledger's first distrust of Dave Spaas as a white man had changed slowly to confidence and to affection.

So now there was not much doubt left in his mind as to the answer he would make to their invitation. But he asked for a week to think it over. At the end of the week, he signed the application card and became a member. He brought in five other Negroes with him from his own Lodge; and these, together with five or six white men scattered throughout various crafts and various yards on the South Side, formed themselves into a railroad branch, of which Dave Spaas was elected the branch organizer. Since all but two of the members were new in the Communist Party, the first meetings of the branch were given over mainly to discussion.

They argued about capitalists and workers and how industries like the railroads made their profits; and why Negroes were always pushed into the worst jobs and jimcrowed into the worst sections of the cities. Dave Spaas, or sometimes Jackson, would get up and report on some book; and then hammer them into reading it. As a matter of fact, Pledger had plenty of time for reading, because he, like most of the other Negro members, was still unemployed. He found the books hard to understand at first; then more and more plain, although he did not agree with everything they said, particularly about religion.

86

Depression and war, the Negro organizer Jackson shouted, hammering the desk in front of him, his bald head gleaming in the light from the open window: depression and war, these were the twin fruits of capitalist economy. At the end of that summer, as if in confirmation, came news of the civil war in Spain. And Pledger, with a cold feeling in the hollow of his chest, said good bye to his new friend Dave Spaas, who went away to fight in Spain, leaving his young wife behind him.

Depression and war: Pledger knew himself to be the child of both; and now he came to see these two like buckets swung over a pulley wheel—when one goes down the other goes up. In the past few years, they had seen the war settle on Ethiopia, China, Spain; and the newspapers carried the daily threats of war in Europe. To Pledger, it seemed these anticipations of war only brightened the lights over Chicago, for now he watched the pulley wheel swing through another half turn. By the summer of 1938, the Great Midland was hiring back again by ones and twos the Negroes whom it had laid off from their jobs during the early thirties.

In the railroad yard, Pledger found things at first much as they had been before. Familiar faces, the same men doing the same jobs. Old Jennison was still union chairman for the white carmen, and Upstairs Jarvis was the same as ever, only a little older and fatter, maybe, and he had moved one step further upstairs with his promotion to General Foreman. But for the Negro coach cleaners, there was one large difference; they had brought back with them something they had not had before—their organization of the unemployed years. This they were careful not to disband, and they continued their regular meetings in Andrew Masters' chapel. Jarvis of course refused in any way to recognize the coach cleaners' Independent Railway Lodge; and a few weeks after Pledger had returned to work, Uncle Jennison, chairman of the white union, came around to see him. Withdrawing his pipe from his horse-shaped face, Jennison worked his jaw up and down as if he were chewing a piece of gristle; then stuck his hand out. "Glad to see you back, Brother McAdams. We been through some tough times." They shook hands and Jennison said, "I hear you got a lodge of your own now?"

Pledger nodded.

"Don't see what good that's going to do you, Brother McAdams.

87

The company won't deal with you, and it just makes it harder for me to speak up for you."

"When was that?" Pledger asked.

"When was what?"

"That you spoke up for us?"

"No use to be digging up old grudges, McAdams. My hands were tied then."

"What do you care if we have a lodge of our own? We can't join yours."

Uncle Jennison mumbled something about dual organization weakening the strength of the men, and Pledger felt a sudden impulse to brain him with his coach cleaner's mop; but he said nothing and turned back to his work.

Later, when the General Foreman, Jarvis, called one of the coach cleaners a troublemaking nigger, all the Negroes walked off the job together. It was just after seven o'clock and the midnight express was standing on the wash track with an hour's work needed on her yet before she could go down to the depot. Jarvis apologized. Within half an hour after the men had gone back to work, the story was all over the yard how the coach cleaners had pinned Upstairs Jarvis's ears back for him. At quitting time, Pledger's old apprentice, Red Brogan, who was working the night shift in the depot, came hunting for him. There was a bunch of men in front of the locker room talking back and forth; and Red began to yell and wave his arms as he always did. If they could make Jarvis knuckle in like that, Red demanded, why the hell didn't the coach cleaners pull a walkout for promotions?

Pledger saw that the others had stopped to listen. Carefully he explained that Jarvis had given in to them only because he knew the big shots downtown would not stand having their trains held up for the luxury of insulting coach cleaners; but if it came to a real issue like promoting Negroes, then the big shots would support Jarvis all the way down the line. Pledger noticed Uncle Jennison standing within hearing, and he added, "And the white union would slip the old knife right into us, wouldn't it?"

"I guess it would," Red said. He glared at the ground, and Pledger waited for him to blow his cork as he did two or three times a week. "Rotten lousy son of a bitch!" Red shouted. "If we aren't all of us getting played for a bunch of suckers! I'd just like to see the CIO come into the yard—" Pledger watched, grinning, while the men standing around laughed and wisecracked.

"There goes Old Faithful."

"Red's got the rag on again."

Red stamped off across the yard to catch a ride to the depot on the midnight express which was just rolling out; and the group broke up.

Through that entire year there came no news from Dave Spaas. Almost every day at work, Roman Koviak stopped Pledger at lunch hour: had he heard anything from Dave? Then Roman would ask how things were going in Spain, and walk away, shaking his head. The months rolled into winter, then spring and summer again. In the summer, Pledger received a queer short note with the postmark of the Panama Canal Zone. "Saw your friend D in France," the note said. "He is out now and wishes to see you soon. Fraternally and with best wishes." After that there was nothing. Every day during that summer, the newsboys were out on the streets whooping their extras. One crisis followed another across the headlines. When the war finally broke in Europe, Pledger felt as if he had already heard the news several months before. Germany invaded Poland; France and England were at war. . . .

Each Sunday, after the meeting of the railroad branch, he and Jackson, the South Side secretary, would stand in front of the large map of Europe that hung on the office wall. There they would trace the possible routes of escape from Spain and mark on the map the places where they had heard were refugee camps in France and North Africa. They guessed that Dave, wherever he was, must have met some seaman and asked him to write to Pledger's address.

The pale autumn skies flamed over the city. Sunflowers covered the embankments and the evening wind carried the smell of burning grass. Twilight faded into the darkness; lights blurred from distant street corners, and the great blue neon sign at the end of South Park Avenue blinked on and off, hazy and indistinct over the rooftops.

Sometimes at midnight, crossing the embankment on his way home from work, Pledger stopped, peering in wonder into the darkness that lay over the city. The night hummed with sounds. Merging one into another, the throb of them replaced the silence; he listened, catching now and then some particular sound out of the others: the clatter of the can factory beyond the tracks, the engines puffing through the yard behind him, the blare of an automobile horn, the tapping of heels along a pavement. All across the city, people were moving, waking, sitting at lunch counters, stepping into the bright lights of crowded street corners. The silence hummed with the stirring of people, and from the embankment, Pledger saw how the glare from the intersections of streets reaching out to the west pulsed up against the base of the sky.

Now once again he thought of his own memories of war: the soldiers loafing in the sunlight by the French roadsides; and the rain, the rain that fell day and night in the trenches, the rumble of guns, the smell of bodies lying in the wet earth. He remembered the lines from the Bible which Andrew Masters always avoided, but which he himself had read over a hundred times. "I come to set brother against brother and father against son." They had driven the people down into oppression and death and now there was only the one answer—out of the darkness, the long battle, for when you shall hear of wars and rumors of wars, be not disturbed, such things must need be.

■ ■

One day in November, Pledger received a phone call from Dave Spaas' old friend Hanson. The CIO had opened its campaign to organize the factory of the Sheet Steel and Can Company, Hanson told him, across the tracks from the Great Midland coach yard. Hanson asked him to stop at the local CIO office on his way home from work that night.

Pledger found the office in a store front a block away from the can factory. It was after midnight when he got there, the rain still drizzling down, chilly and penetrating. But the store front was lighted, a girl was working over a mimeograph turning out handbills, and Hanson, sprawled on the desk drinking coffee from a paper carton, was waiting for him.

Hanson jumped down to the floor, clapped his hands together and shouted, "Hello, McAdams, you old bastard. I thought you must have drowned yourself tonight."

"What's the matter with *you?*" Pledger asked. "You acting like you struck oil."

"Never mind what's the matter with me. Let's get our business done." They sat down and pieced together their plans for making contact with the Negroes who worked in the can factory. Then Hanson pulled a letter from his pocket and flipped it down on the desk. Pledger recognized the handwriting, and a knot of fear tightened suddenly in his throat. He picked up the letter as if he were afraid to open it.

"Don't look like that," the girl called from the mimeograph. "Read it; he's home." The letter was from Dave Spaas. He had been wounded a little bit, he said, and he had caught pneumonia in New York; but now he was all right again. He was coming to Chicago in November and he wanted to try for a job on the Great Midland. Pledger could not speak for a moment; he handed the letter back to Hanson. They all three began to laugh, shook hands and slapped each other on the back.

But as Pledger made his way home through the rain, he discovered under his happiness a small feeling of hurt because Dave Spaas had not written to him too. He stopped for a moment in the dark outer room of the Chile Parlor, bending his head, trying to drive the feeling out of his mind. Ruby heard him come in; she called from the kitchen,

"That you, Pledger?"

"It's me."

"What you waiting for? Come in here."

"Getting my rubbers off," Pledger said.

"Come in here, will you?" Ruby shouted. "I got a letter for you."

Part Three

THE UNIVERSITY

4

STEPHANIE finished her work. She put away her equipment, hung her white gown on its hook, and stood at the sink trying to wash the smell of formaldehyde from her hands and wrists. As she rubbed the yellow soap between her fingers, she looked down through the window to the track and football field, lying green and gold in the summer sunlight. A runner trotted around the track, and on the field three figures were practicing niblick shots. She rinsed her hands and sniffed at them. The smell wouldn't come off.

Stephanie tugged her blouse straight, squinted into the mirror powdering her nose, then went into the menagerie to make sure all the animals had water for over Sunday. The cats in their cages got up as she came in, stretching and rubbing against the wire, while the rabbits regarded her stupidly out of their red eyes. In the last cage, the six new puppies began yiping and scrambling over each other, thrusting their noses through the mesh of the screen. She stopped for a moment to tickle their crumply brown ears with her finger tip. All the water pans were full; she said good night to the puppies and went out.

The afternoon was warm and quiet. Across the lawns and over the walls of the University buildings flooded the summer sunlight, filtering and stirring through the green-gold leaves of the trees. A lawn mower whirred in the distance, and all around Stephanie the swathes of fresh-mowed grass steamed in the sunlight. After the day in the laboratory, she felt almost drunken from the smells of the summer afternoon. She walked slowly across the campus, pleased the week was ended, enjoying the Saturday afternoon luxury of walking without hurrying.

As she turned the corner into the Midway, she recognized the girl ahead of her as Marguerite Strauss, and dropped back so she would not have to walk with her. But the girl glanced over her shoulder at the same time and stopped to wait. "Hello, Marguerite," Stephanie said. "It's a lovely afternoon, isn't it?"

"Yes, I suppose it is. I'd hardly noticed."

"That's what comes of locking yourself in those library stacks all day."

"I suppose I ought to get out more."

"How's the Old French coming?" Stephanie asked. "Is that what keeps you in?"

"That's the reason, Stephanie. It comes so dreadfully slowly. I put in the whole day in the library and I don't seem to accomplish anything. I don't make any progress. Your brother Victor told me if I kept on at this rate I'd be fifteen years finishing my thesis."

"Don't pay any attention to what Victor says."

"I have great respect for your brother, Stephanie."

"Oh, so do I."

They walked a few steps in silence. Across the Midway, people were sitting on the grass reading, or in groups talking together. A Good Humor man on a bicycle pedaled along the street, tinkling his little bell. Now and then when someone waved to him, he propped his bike against a tree and walked across the grass, carrying handfuls of ice-cream bars.

"You're looking wonderful," Marguerite said. Stephanie glanced up apprehensively and Marguerite, shaking her head, told her, "I wish I had your health and vitality."

"Why, you're healthy as a horse, Maggie."

"I wish I were."

Quickening her step, Stephanie hoped they could reach the corner where she turned off before the flood of Marguerite's troubles burst their gates. But she knew it was no use, for the gates hung open most of the time.

"I finally did it, Stephanie. Yes, I suppose it was good advice."

"Did what?"

"I suppose there was no use putting it off." She shrugged her shoulders rapidly four or five times. "Anyway, I've made up my mind I'm not going to be ashamed of it. I'm going to do my best to be perfectly casual about it, just as though it were simply measles or smallpox or something physical."

"Marguerite, what are you talking about?"

"I went to the clinic today. I had a long talk with Doctor Gregory."

"Who's he?"

96

"*She*, Stephanie. A brilliant woman, rising very fast in her profession. We had a long talk about my problems. She's a most sympathetic person."

"Has it helped you, Marguerite?"

"It upset me terribly. But I suppose we can't expect a thing of that sort to be painless. I've been burying it, trying to conceal it even from myself. It's like an infection in a tooth that poisons the whole system—"

Please, I don't want to know about it, Stephanie thought; but she saw Marguerite was determined to give tongue, and finally she asked, "Well, what did the doctor say to you?"

"I don't know whether I could bring myself to tell you, Stephanie. I don't know whether I could talk about it to anyone right now."

"I certainly wouldn't, if you don't feel like it."

"You see the doctor didn't actually tell me in so many words, but there's no mistaking an intimation. I understood very clearly what the doctor had in mind from the questions she asked me. . . ." Stephanie said nothing, and after a moment Marguerite went on. "She asked if I'd ever thought of marrying. I said I had, but I couldn't begin to consider such a thing seriously until I was better established in my field."

"Don't you think you could have a career and get married too?"

"Well, Stephanie, I don't know how it worked out in *your* case. But my career is so important to me I wouldn't care to take any chances with it."

Stephanie smiled. "It wasn't the career that caused difficulties in my case."

"No, perhaps not. I suppose all people have both tendencies, don't they? You understand what I mean?"

"Yes, I know what you mean. That's what the psychologists tell us."

"Do you think it's true?"

"I suppose so."

"Doctor Gregory said it was true. She said I shouldn't worry if I found *that* kind of tendency in myself because all people had them; and basically it was a question of which kind one desired." Marguerite looked at her suddenly and then stared away as if she had seen something over Stephanie's shoulder. "That's what's so terrible, Stephanie," she said in a low voice. "Now I'm not sure what I basically desire—"

97

"Marguerite. You're talking yourself into something."

"Oh, I don't know, Stephanie. I don't know." They had reached the steps of International House. Here Marguerite stopped, but went on talking into Stephanie's ear. "You see, Stephanie, I told Doctor Gregory quite frankly that I had been attracted to several men—not only intellectually, but physically as well. I suppose it was my misfortune that two of them happened to be married and one much older than myself, so our interest in each other could hardly develop into real intimacy— Were you planning to meet someone, Stephanie? Would you care to have supper with me?"

"I was supposed to meet Hawkins and Martin back at the apartment."

"Oh."

Stephanie was touched by the note of disappointment in Marguerite's voice. "Why don't you come and join us for supper?" she asked.

"Oh no, thanks. We'll have our chat some other time." Marguerite started up the steps, but from the open doorway at the top, looked back for a moment. "Give my regards to the star of the Philosophy Department," she called. "I'm sure Monsieur Abelard won't miss my company."

She waved and went through the doorway. For a moment as Stephanie watched her stocky figure in its ill-fitting dress disappear between the groups in the lobby, she felt a tightening of her throat in pity.

Then continuing down the block, she turned south from the Midway toward the apartment house. When she reached the building and started up the stairs to their apartment on the top floor, she heard feet stamping up the flight above her. Martin's and Hawkins' voices burst out suddenly singing a hymn:

> "Glorious things of thee are spoken,
> Zion City of our God!
> He whose word cannot be broken—"

"Hey!" Stephanie called.

The singing ended and they waited till she caught up with them. "Who won the handball game?" she asked.

"I did," Martin told her. "As usual."

Hawkins shrugged his shoulders. "Martin was lucky and somewhat lax about scorekeeping. I anticipated you would have had supper waiting for us, Stephanie."

"You'd best hire a maid servant, Hawkins." They stopped in front of the apartment door while Stephanie fumbled for the keys in her handbag. There was a note thumbtacked to the door which Martin pulled down and read. "Smith's coming over," he told them. "Smith and Leeds. He wants us to read that article she's prepared for the *Quarterly*."

"Ah, *Leeds*," Stephanie said. "Dear old Leeds. I suppose we'll have *them* for supper. Is this the famous article on education?"

Martin nodded. "When did you hear about that, Stephanie?"

"From Smith. Smith stopped me in the library the other day and told me all about it; Leeds was preparing an article on the Marxist approach to education—" She opened the door and they stepped inside. "So I laughed; and I'm afraid Smith was insulted."

"I think you're a bitch," Hawkins told her.

"But I made it up to him, Hawkins. I told him I was glad he was taking a broad-minded view as the new editor of the *Quarterly*. Then I asked him if he agreed with Leeds' analysis, and he fell all over himself. He's going to write a refutation in the same issue."

"I still think you're a bitch," Hawkins said again. He threw off the raincoat he had been wearing over his gym clothes; then tugged quickly at his belt, trying to close the gap between his shirt and trousers. In his sweatshirt and baggy pants, Hawkins seemed to thrust out further than usual, front and back.

"You look awful, both of you," Stephanie said. "And smell, too. Go change your clothes." They disappeared into the bathroom and Stephanie, leaving the front door open for Smith and Leeds, closed the bedroom door and sat down to finish the chapter she had been reading in her book on comparative anatomy. After a time, she heard Smith and Leeds come up the stairs and settle down in the living room; but she did not got out to meet them. The radio snapped on to a news broadcast—Leeds keeping her finger on the pulse of events, Stephanie thought—and when the broadcast ended, Leeds herself carried on. Through the closed door of the bedroom, Stephanie could not make out the words; but the cultivated Bostonian intonations reached her, and she could picture Smith, who came from Aurora, Illinois, listening in rapt concentration. Nodding her head, she returned to her textbook.

The shower was running now in the bathroom, and through the

transom over the door, steam billowed out like clouds of smoke. They were singing again, Hawkins voice lagging a few paces behind as if he were not sure of the words—

> "Zion City of our God!
> He whose word cannot be broken
> Formed thee for his own abode."

"—his own abode," Hawkins repeated in a shrill echo.

Stephanie threw down her book at last and walked out to the living room. There she found Smith studiously regarding a typewritten manuscript and Leeds smoking a cigarette. "Hello, Stephanie," Leeds said. "Martin has quite a good voice, doesn't he?"

"Yes, he used to sing in the choir. Do you sing, Leeds?"

"I never learned any songs like that." Leeds smiled and raised her eyes. She had a button-shaped nose and wide, high cheekbones. She was not a pretty girl, Stephanie thought; yet she always managed to give other people, particularly men, the impression that she was pretty. Now, with an easy gesture, she draped one of her slim, silk-stockinged legs over the arm of her chair.

"Perhaps you'd care to join the duet?" Stephanie asked.

Leeds threw back her head, laughing. "No, really. I don't need a shower. How does Martin learn all those hymns?"

"He comes from a very religious family. Fundamentalists." Stephanie noticed Smith shifting uneasily in his place. Then she turned back to Leeds, whose eyes met hers steadily.

"I was so sorry to hear Martin was resigning from the *Quarterly*," Leeds said. "Why is he giving it up? Of course, I don't agree with the viewpoint of the *Quarterly*, but under Martin's editorship it certainly has improved. He built it almost singlehanded."

"He's taken a job now," Stephanie said. "He has no time for the magazine."

"Oh yes, he's working on Professor Parcher's new book, isn't he? What a shame the research assistants do all the work and the professors collect the money! But that's what turns the wheels of higher education. Why don't you sit down?"

Stephanie shook her head. "I have to put our supper on the stove. Would you and Smith care to stay for supper?"

"No, thanks. We have an engagement."

So Smith and Leeds are dining together, Stephanie thought as she went out to the kitchen. And which one would pay the bill?

Smith had no money from Aurora; but Leeds had plenty of it from her family on the North Shore, enough to keep her mink coat and her Mercury convertible in nice condition. On the other hand, Smith's ego, a tender flower at best, would suffer if he allowed the lady to handle the check. There was a problem to which Smith was very likely now trying to apply the first principles of Ethics.

Stephanie put on the coffee, made salad, got out the corned beef and bologna. Then she returned to the living room, where Martin had built a fire in the fireplace and was leaning against the mantel discoursing, while Leeds urged him on with little exclamations of surprise and admiration. Stephanie sat down beside Hawkins and patted him on the knee. "You smell much better now," she said. Hawkins gave her a cigarette, but did not reply.

"And you mean you broke out of that kind of background!" Leeds exclaimed. "That's quite extraordinary."

"As a matter of fact, I didn't break out. I was thrown out," Martin said. "When I finished high school, the old man sent me away to college—a fundamentalist outfit in Indiana. Redmund Institute—ever hear of it?"

Leeds shook her head.

"Curriculum of Bible history, Bible, and arithmetic—that's the liberal arts course, so to speak. I was top student in the class too. But the end of the year I brought a bottle of whiskey into the dormitory and they expelled me. So I told the old man I wanted to go to the University of Chicago and he washed his hands like Pontius Pilate. He's never spoken to me since."

Leeds shook her head again as if she could find no words to express herself. But then, as Smith looked at his wristwatch and tried to catch her eye, she said, "I've often wondered what impulse starts a young person towards breaking from a reactionary background. I suppose my own case would be somewhat similar. But I believe there must always be some outside influence to start the individual moving in a progressive direction, don't you?"

Stephanie saw Martin wink at her over Leeds' head.

"Perhaps that's true," he said. "The town I came from would be right in your line—a case history for economic determinism."

"Please, I'm not an economic determinist."

"No?" Martin asked. "But I'm not sure that I'm not. You see, I owe my liberty to the fact that the state of Michigan chose to build a highway through that town. Up till then it had been a little religious community where the church elders ruled the roost. My father was head of the school board, and the only school in town was a grammar school; just like Redmund Institute, as a matter of fact—taught Bible history, Bible, and arithmetic. That was my old man's idea of uplifting the younger generation. But after the state built the highway a lot of ungodly folk moved into town and wanted some ordinary high schools for their kids. So as soon as there got to be enough of them, they threw my old man off the school board. He wouldn't let any of us go to the new school at first, until the state police took a hand."

"And did you go?" Leeds asked.

"We went, but I hated it. I'd been cock of the walk in the old church grammar school; but as soon as I went to the new school, I didn't amount to a hill of beans. Until I'd been there for a while, anyway—"

"I bet you were a hot-rock when you were a kid," Hawkins said.

"You bet I was. I had six sisters all older than I: but when I stepped out, I was king of the world because I was the first-born son."

In spite of herself, Stephanie began to laugh, picturing Martin barely able to walk, but already ordering his six elder sisters around the house. "Have you shown Leeds your photographs?" she asked.

"What photographs are those?" Leeds said coldly.

"Why, Martin's pictures. He has a fine picture of his high-school baseball team—"

"It's getting late," Smith said.

"And guess who's sitting right in the middle of the picture?" Stephanie insisted. "Martin was *captain* of the team. Weren't you, Martin?"

The five of them sat for a few moments in silence. Stephanie noticed Martin grinning at her from the fireplace. "Well," she said at last. "I thought you came to discuss an article on education."

"We did discuss it," Leeds told her. "While you were in the kitchen."

"You mean you resolved all the conflicts between Marx and Aristotle in that short time?"

Smith rose from his chair and stumbled around looking for his coat. "We didn't try to resolve the conflicts, Stephanie. This is to be in the nature of a forum."

"But aren't you afraid Leeds may be using the *Quarterly* as a transmission belt for radical ideas, Smith? She might even be using you. That wouldn't sit very well with the Philosophy Department, would it?"

She saw that Smith took her seriously as always. "I feel strongly, Stephanie, that the only way to meet wrong ideas is to bring them out in the open and answer them." Having finally discovered their coats, Smith put on his own, then helped Leeds into hers, trying to thrust her arm through the lining instead of into the sleeve. They called good bye and went out to the stairway. Stephanie, who had crossed over to the window, watched them emerge on the sidewalk down below and get into Leeds' Mercury convertible which was parked at the curb.

When she withdrew her head from the window, Martin was sitting on the back of the sofa, laughing at her. "I thought you were going to throw something at them. What makes you so antipathetic to Leeds?"

"How was the article?" Stephanie asked.

"Well-written. That's about as much as I can say for a Marxist article."

"Are you going to print it?"

"It's none of my business. Smith's the editor."

"Smith does what you tell him."

"I've no objection to his printing the article."

Stephanie waved her hands and wiggled her shoulders. "Dear little Leedsie," she said. "Do you know, back at Radcliffe we had the most progr-r-essive student publications. . . ."

Hawkins, who had not moved from his place, was puffing on his cigarette and blowing smoke rings. "I find women somewhat akin to snakes," he said. "They get from one place to another, yet one never quite sees how they move. Now you and Leeds are rather similar in many ways, Stephanie. I don't understand why you get along so badly."

"Watch what you're saying, Hawkins. You're riding for an injury."

"For example, I observe that both you and Leeds are generally on good terms with men but bad terms with women. That's an interesting phenomenon."

"Maybe that's the answer to the question you just asked," Martin said.

He walked over to the desk, picked up the typewritten manuscript, and dropped it in Stephanie's lap. Skipping from paragraph to paragraph, she glanced through it, then tossed it back to the desk.

"Good or bad?" Martin asked.

"It's all right."

"Do you agree with it or not?"

"I don't particularly agree with it, but there's nothing I disagree with."

"I should think you would agree with Leeds," Martin said. "Aren't you one of those people who believe in progress?"

Stephanie got up from her place. "We'd better go eat before all the coffee boils away."

She understood the question Martin had asked, and its importance to him and to both of them. He had asked the question before in other forms, and she had never been able to answer it precisely; she could not answer it precisely now. In this, Leeds was of no particular importance, except that her article provided a reflection of views which *were* important. As they walked out to the kitchen, Stephanie slipped her hand under Martin's arm. "You want to know if I think there is such a thing as progress? Yes, I think there is. I think progress is the growing understanding of the world we live in. I think science is progress. Sometimes I look at my white rats in the laboratory; I don't know very much about them, nor does anyone else either. But I know they'll make more revolutions than all the committees Leeds will ever organize—or all the dissertations you and Hawkins will ever write."

"What hath God wrought!" Hawkins cried. "Here come those little animals again. Damn your little animals, Stephanie! I'm beginning to see them at night."

They sat down at the kitchen table and Stephanie passed around the plates of salad and sliced meat. Hawkins, who was apparently intrigued by his new phrase, kept repeating "What hath God wrought!" each time he bit into a slice of bologna. That set Martin off singing hymns again and intoning responsive readings from the psalms.

But as soon as they finished supper Martin rose, took Hawkins by the elbow, and clapped his hat on his head. Then he gave him his bundle of gym clothes and escorted him to the door. "See you tomorrow, Hawkeye old pill. I enjoyed the handball game."

After Hawkins had gone, Stephanie followed Martin into the living room, and sat beside him on the sofa. "You told Leedsie your life history," she said. "That was awfully nice of you."

104

"I was treating her civilly. I have no reason to dislike Leeds; except that I disagree with her."

Without his saying it, she read the reversal of the statement in his mind: perhaps she had no reason to dislike Leeds except that she *did* agree with her.

"Leeds was one of the first people I met when I came to the University," Stephanie said. "I was such a *little* girl then, just out of high school. Leeds took me under her wing. I was the daughter of a genuine workingman and Leeds thought that was awfully interesting."

Martin laughed softly.

"I'd been looking forward so long to coming here, Martin. And I'd gone through some tough experiences. But everything was going to be different at the University. I was going to begin a new life for myself. I didn't intend to be a workingman's daughter any longer."

She stared for a moment in silence at the fire, at the orange-colored flames which flowed smoothly and continuously over the bricks at the back of the fireplace. "You know, these campus left-wing groups are made to order for Leeds. With her money and the prestige of her name, she just bowls them over. Men? Why, she can take her pick. If she stayed up in that North Shore society where she belongs, she could never swing half the weight. Brains are a liability up there; and she *is* smart. She has that sexy look, but she's no beauty."

Martin tapped her on the knee. "Just as Hawkins told you, you're being a bitch."

"Leeds always hits me in a raw spot," Stephanie said. "She's like a barker at a side show. Step right this way, folks, for a squint at the wonder woman of the campus. When I first came to the University, I tried to get into a sorority and they turned me down. Leeds was the big shot of the sorority at the time. You know, her daddy's a millionaire, just like all the University trustees. And Leeds resigned from the sorority on my account."

"What was wrong with that?" Martin asked.

"Nothing. Nothing was wrong with it."

"You mean it was not the act, but the manner of acting?"

She nodded her head. "I couldn't possibly tell you how important that sorority was to me. I can hardly reimagine it now myself. But I'd been looking forward so long to things being different at the University, so I was awfully disappointed. And to Leeds, of course, it was wonderful. She resigned; she wrote letters to the *Maroon.* What a gesture! What a dramatic action! But what difference did the sorority make to her? She already had all the sorority could offer and more."

"Why did they turn you down?" Martin asked.

"That's what I couldn't understand." For a moment she sat silent remembering the teas she had gone to in those chintz-draped parlors of the sorority houses, and how she had sat on the edge of her chair, trying desperately to talk to these girls. But she had been too terrified to speak, and while they played the gracious hostess she could only answer their questions in monosyllables. So they passed her from one sorority house to the next, and as she left each parlor, she knew the voices chirped behind her,

"What a *peculiar* dress!"

"Oh my dear! From West Thirty-Sixth Street—"

She had gone home, locked herself in her bedroom, and wept.

"Why did they turn you down?" Martin asked again.

"Oh, I don't know. I suppose I was a mousy-looking little creature."

"What hath God wrought!" Martin said, and laughing, put his arms around her, pulling her down beside him on the sofa. In the dark room they lay watching the fire, which had burned down now to a bed of embers.

5

AS Stephanie rode westward across the city, gray light filtered through the early morning mist and patches of blue began to show over the roofs of the houses. The whole sky was clear by the time she reached Halsted and Thirty-Sixth Street, and the wet pavements smoked in the sunshine. Around her, she heard the factory whistles blowing for eight o'clock. Her father would be home by now, she thought, and Victor already gone. After his night's work, Roman would soon go to bed, and she would not have to stay long. Immediately she felt guilty for not wanting to stay; but Sunday was the only other day she could come, and if she came Sunday, when would she see Martin?

Stephanie turned the last corner before Thirty-Sixth Street reached its dead end in the embankment of the Great Midland Railroad. Here, as the sidewalk dwindled away from the corner, she moved into the center of the street to avoid the wet grass growing where the sidewalk should have been. Beyond the coal yard she came to the row of frame houses, all alike, each with a patch of grass and a few bushes in front of it. By the third house Roman's Chevrolet was parked, and Stephanie found her mother and Roman in the kitchen sitting down to breakfast.

"Ahey, it's Stevie!" Roman jumped up, put his arm around her, and pulled her down into a chair at the table. "You had breakfast, Stevie? You hungry, no? Put some ham and eggs on for her, Mama."

Mrs. Koviak, who was working at the stove, talked steadily over her shoulder. "Why don't you come for Sunday dinner sometime, Stephanie? We don't see you any more. You don't have class and school on Sunday, do you?"

"Let her alone, Mama," Roman said. "She comes when she can."

"She comes when she can! That's never."

"Let her alone, Mama. You doing all right in your school, Stevie?"

But before Stephanie could answer, her mother banged the plate of ham and fried eggs in front of her and filled her coffee cup. "You heard about Johnny's Rosa?" she demanded. "It's her time any minute now. Her mother's over there with her, and I got to go over as soon as the pains come. You never see anything like how big she is! I was waiting for the telephone all last night."

Roman tried again to ask about the University, but Mrs. Koviak cut him off, and Roman did not raise his voice over hers. Rosa had blotches on her face, Mrs. Koviak said, but they would probably go away afterwards and it looked as if she would have plenty of milk for the baby, but the way she carried on smoking all the time, the milk would likely be worse than poison. . . . Stephanie sat in silence, nodding her head sometimes. During the long days her mother spent in the house, Stephanie knew what a pressure of words accumulated, for to her mother talking was like movies or drink with some people.

"Rosa's mother never taught that girl anything about how to get ready for a baby," Mrs. Koviak went on. "I'd feel ashamed if

107

it was my daughter. When we went over there last summer, Rosa didn't have hardly anything to eat on the table, did she, Roman?"

Roman nodded in agreement. Stephanie, watching him, noticed the embarrassed smile, the quick nod of the head—that was what always came first to her mind when she thought of him. He would be trying to tell her something, waving his hands, mumbling disconnected phrases; and finally turn to her with that smile. "You know what I try to say, Stevie?" And she would know and tell him, and they would laugh at the struggles he had made for words. Incoherent, agreeable, always getting pushed around; she wondered how often the yard foreman Jarvis had called him out to work on Christmas Day or New Year's because he was short of men and he knew Roman would come? Yet in some manner, she thought, he seemed to her the most self-sufficient person she had ever known. Nothing that happened to him seemed to infringe upon his personal dignity. People took advantage of him, but at the same time they respected him, and it was almost as if they were afraid of him. Mama ordered him around the house a hundred times a day, but on any matter by which Roman set store, they never came to issue. This seemed to Stephanie a strange relationship; yet apparently it suited them both.

She heard a clatter of feet on the back porch. The door banged open and her brother Johnny stumbled into the kitchen. His suit coat was torn, his hair hung over his eyes, and a deep scratch crossed his cheek and nose.

Mrs. Koviak got up from the table. "Johnny! Johnny, what happened to you? What you been doing, Johnny?"

Giggling, he put his arm around her. "Had to work all night, ma. Had a tough night, all right." He looked down suspiciously at Roman and Stephanie. "Maybe you don't believe that? Well, I'll tell you this, I switched cars all night. Real bitch of a night, pop. Sixteen hours straight." He slapped his mother on the back and dropped into the chair she had just left. Stephanie could smell the whiskey all the way across the table; he must have been switching at Walter's saloon, she thought. Johnny's eyes wavered back and forth from Stephanie to Roman, and finally he said, "Well, I stopped in for a little drink this morning, see, at Walter's. Hit me pretty hard 'cause I hadn't had nothing to eat. Been switching cars all night—no time to eat—"

"You're drunk," Roman told him. "You better go upstairs, go to bed."

"He's not drunk," Mrs. Koviak said. "He hasn't had anything to eat. You sit right there, Johnny. I'll fix you some eggs and coffee."

"Okay, ma. You dish 'em out. Man's got to eat, hasn't he, pop? Can't do a man's work without food, now you know that, pop. Couldn't tell you how many cars we put away last night. Bet if you stacked 'em end to end they'd reach here to Milwaukee." He began counting boxcars on his fingers. "One two three four—cut 'em off, Walter m'lad, cut 'em off. Puff puff puff puff—Blam!" Johnny shrieked with laughter and dropped forward on the table, pressing his head into his arms. By the time Mrs. Koviak brought the eggs from the stove, he had fallen asleep.

"No use, Mama. We put him to bed, that's all," Roman picked Johnny up as though he were a six-year-old child, carried him upstairs and laid him on Stephanie's bed in the attic. Stephanie followed. She spread the old patched quilt over Johnny, who was mumbling in his sleep, ". . . get out of my house, you bitch, you. I didn't get married to no mother-in-law. Drag your fat ass out of my house and let a man have some peace. . . ."

Stephanie and Roman looked at each other and Roman shook his head. "It's no good, Stevie."

They went downstairs. Stephanie said good bye to her mother and promised to come for dinner the next Sunday. As she left, Roman walked out to the street with her; she knew he had something on his mind that he was afraid to say to her. He shifted from one foot to the other, looking all around as if he had never seen the houses in the street before. "Stevie, you hear anything from Dave?"

"No," she said.

"Are you—are you going to stay with Dave?"

"How can I stay with him when he left me?"

"You don't think he come back, Stevie?"

"I don't care whether he comes back or not."

Roman shook his head again.

"You would take Dave's side against me," Stephanie said.

"I always like Dave a lot, Stevie."

"After he walks off and leaves me, you still like him? Victor's been talking to you, hasn't he? Victor's been telling you his dirty little stories."

Roman did not answer.

"Hasn't he? He has, hasn't he?"

"Stevie, I don't listen to what Victor or anybody else says. I want you to be happy, I want you to do right, and now I try to talk to you."

She stared at him angrily. Finally she said, "Well, go ahead and talk." Roman looked down at his hands without speaking and Stephanie asked, "Aren't you going to say anything? What are we standing around for then?"

"Is it true, Stevie?"

"Ah, there it comes out. Is what true?"

"What Victor told me?"

"You say you want me to be happy," she said in a low voice. "You're so generous about it—God, it's wonderful. But the first thing you do is take Dave's side against mine, and listen to Victor's stories behind my back."

"Tell me, Stevie."

"I already told you. I told you over a year ago I was leaving Dave, and I was going to get a divorce from him. I don't consider myself married to Dave now, and it's my business if I want to go with somebody else."

"You going to marry him?"

"Yes, I'm going to marry him."

"Is he good?" Roman stretched out his hand toward her. "Please, I don't want to fight you. Don't make secrets from me, Stevie. If you like him bring him over sometime—you do that?"

"So you can give him the once-over like a prize horse?" She stood with her fists clenched and the fingernails digging into the palms of her hands. The anger flared through her; she did not try to check it now. "I won't bring him over. Damn the whole lot of you anyway!" Her voice rose and she stamped her foot. "Why can't you let me alone? If you like Dave so much, you can have Dave." Turning, she hurried down the street past the coal yard, her heels clicking sharply on the pavement.

The morning was bright now and warm. The little houses, the trees with their yellow leaves, drowsed in the midmorning sunlight. She turned the corner into Thirty-Sixth Street. Flies buzzed up in front of her. As she passed, a cat stretched out in the middle of the street looked at her out of round green eyes, then closed its eyes abruptly and went on sunning its stomach. The sound of children playing came to her from somewhere on the next block. I won't go back, she said to herself; then stopped, glanced around to see that no one was watching, and turned back toward the house.

Roman was waiting for her on the steps of the porch. She sat beside him, dropped her head on his shoulder, and he put his arm around her, making incoherent comforting sounds in his throat. After a long time, she said, "I'm sorry. I didn't mean what I said."

He patted her on the shoulder. They got up, she kissed him good bye and he whispered. "You don't worry. Everything going to be all right." He stood on the porch while she ran down the steps and along the street.

At the corner of Halsted and Thirty-Sixth Street, Stephanie saw by the clock in the jewelry store window that it was barely a quarter of ten. A trolley car was coming, headed not for the University, but for the Loop. It would be too late to get much done in the morning anyway, she thought, and crossed over to take the car downtown.

The picture of Roman waiting on the steps kept coming back to her. She felt sad for what she had said to him, yet at the same time the anger remained gnawing into her mind. She had flown into a rage at Roman—and now she was not sure why. Was it that he had listened to Victor's stories behind her back? But she had known what Victor would tell him, and she had not gone to him first. Or was it because he had taken Dave's side against hers? She remembered how proud he had been of Dave in those months of '34 and how he had boasted to everybody about Stevie's friend Dave. Yet he was ready to give Dave up, if she had made up her mind to leave him; she had no reason for anger. He had never pried into her affairs. He had not forced his advice on her, nor tried to stop her doing the things she wanted.

The streetcar clattered across the Archer Avenue bridge over the river. On the far side, the factory buildings piled up one on top of another in blocks of sunlight and shadow, and the yellow smoke bellied up from their stacks. She felt suddenly like weeping for the way she had treated him. Someday, she thought, she would make it up to him; but she knew that she could never make it up. The gulf between them was too wide. He was old and she was young. The hopes of his life were concentrated on her; but her own hopes swept her forward out of the shadows that surrounded him. There was no part of her life she could share with him. His love had become a burden which she tried to escape. Even now, as she remembered sadly how he had waited on the steps for her, the anger burned through her again that she had had to go back. She had almost come to hate him for the love that bound her to that house and to that street.

Stephanie left the car, walked quickly through the Loop and across Michigan Avenue to the Art Institute. In the entrance hall she stopped for a moment, sniffing the familiar odor of dust and plaster and oil paint. Then she climbed up the wide staircase to the galleries of modern French art, and walked through the almost empty rooms, returning to the paintings she had always liked best. The anger and disquiet of her mind subsided. In one of the galleries, she was overtaken by two little girls who were moving systematically from one painting to the next, reading about each one in their mimeographed notes. Stephanie, smiling as she watched them, followed at a respectful distance while they completed the tour of the modern French art and came around again to the staircase on the far side. Then from the doorway of the last gallery, she watched them patter down the marble steps. They left her feeling strange and old. It seemed a long time ago she had come here for the first time, a little girl herself then, in cotton socks and a coat too big for her. She remembered that she had come doubtfully at the suggestion of one of the junior high-school teachers; and to her amazement, it had been like discovering a new universe. The passion and color of those pictures had struck her like the first warm day of spring, thawing the gray snow, bringing enchantment and life even to those streets and back yards and alleys which marked the boundaries of the world she had lived in.

Other girls she had known in junior high school spent their Saturday mornings in Balknis' candy store, where they whispered and giggled with the boys who hung around the soda fountain. They smoked cigarettes and looked through the spicy story magazines, and always somebody was putting nickels in the nickelodeon so that it kept playing "My Blue Heaven" and "Dream Train." When Stephanie passed the store on her way to the streetcar stop, the girls of course were always watching for her.

"Who you got a date with?" they called.

"Where you going, Miss Stuck-up?"

The shrill voices of the junior high-school girls pursued her up the block; and she lifted her head in the air and hurried towards the corner.

Their voices called down the corridors of the school, "Oh Miss

Stuck-up, Miss Teacher's Pet." The girls giggled in class while Stephanie recited; they never knew the answer to anything the teacher asked them, and Stephanie despised them because they never even wanted to know. She despised them for the way they smeared lipstick on their faces and because the boys fooled around with them after school and took them to movies and sat with them in vacant lots in the evening. . . . But on Saturdays, on those Saturday mornings, she had taken the streetcar to the Art Institute as to a house of her own.

The loneliness of those days lingered beside her. She felt again how it had been, coming Saturday after Saturday, hoping to find friends, but not finding them. In the children's lectures, and later in the sketching classes which she had attended for a time, or down in the cafeteria in the basement, she had watched the people around her, trying to guess which of them those friends might be. She invented excuses to sit beside them and hoped they might speak to her. She learned to know their names from a distance—what they did and where they came from. There were the North Shore girls with their wavy brown permanents and tailored slacks; there were boys in tweed coats with hair long on the backs of their necks. There were the sophisticated young women from the Near North Side who wore bangs over their eyebrows and smoked cigarettes out of green holders. They all seemed to know each other, they called each other by first name, and she felt the more lonely for watching them. But in all the time she waited, none of them ever spoke to her, except to ask, "Is this place taken?" or "Pass the salt, please."

Figures in her mind she had created from the figures around her; she peopled the empty world with fantasies of the friends she might have met on those Saturdays. There had been a girl for whom she imagined half a dozen different names; but who came to her always in the same way, took her home to the North Shore, where the girl's father and mother waited for them in the parlor, which was bright with fresh flowers. And later, she remembered, this much-dreamed-of girl had turned into a young man. He was thin and light-haired, and he too went with her to the symphony and the art exhibits. How often she had come home from the Art Institute in the late afternoon, lost in such dreams! The streetcar would bang westward on the viaduct over the railroad yards. The smoky sky settled over the city, and the little girl, her hand covering her eyes, dreamed of the friends she might have met.

Stephanie shook herself free from the doorway of the gallery. She thought sourly: How's that for a first love affair? and began humming to herself, "I've got a date with a phantom . . ." No wonder she had had her troubles since then. She walked down the marble staircase and crossed Michigan Avenue to the drugstore on the opposite corner. There she had a sandwich and cup of coffee for lunch; then caught the Illinois Central suburban train back to the University.

6

THE leaves fell from the trees and blew back and forth across the lawns of the University. Everybody talked about the war for a while. In the Commons, Stephanie heard people asking, how soon will they really start fighting? Maybe they won't fight each other at all; they'll fight Russia. And she heard people say with a thrill of anticipation, once they start fighting, it won't be long, you'll see; it won't be long before we get in too.

All across the city, kids played football in the vacant lots, bucking and charging at each other, piling themselves in heaps in the gravel and cinders. The blue skies of autumn sparkled over the rooftops. Yellow and white smoke from the steel mills of South Chicago towered into the sky, and at night when Martin and Stephanie walked down to the lakeshore they could see the glow of the furnaces pulsing and throbbing along the horizon. Overhead the stars burned coldly and the scent of winter came with the singing wind. But the first week of November brought clouds rolling in from Lake Michigan. Rain slanted all day against the roofs and windows; the branches of trees danced in the wind, and wet raincoats steamed over the radiators of the University classrooms.

The gray cat grew bigger and bigger, and late one afternoon Stephanie found her under the laboratory sink with a kitten halfway out of her. Stephanie and the professor were the only people in the building. They moved the cat to a nest of straw in one of the cages; and the professor, joking about the money he could have made if only he had gone in for obstetrics instead of physiology, delivered the kittens as carefully as if they had been babies. Stephanie clipped the umbilical cords and cauterized the little round bleeding ends with iodine.

The mother cat looked sunken and emaciated. Her ribs showed and the knobs of her spine protruded through the fur. She washed the four kittens, then lay down wearily and ate up the afterbirths one after another. The professor offered Stephanie a cigar, and in the cage the cat and her kittens, exhausted, fell asleep.

"Well, Miss Koviak," the professor asked, "would you like to have a baby?"

"Is that an offer?"

The professor blushed. "No, I'm too old for that. I was curious to find out what my young students think about such matters these days."

"Of course I'd like to have a baby," Stephanie said. "Most women would."

"I've always called you Miss Koviak. Are you married?"

She nodded. "But I've a good stretch yet before I finish at the University, and it may be a long time after that before I get much of a job. You don't have children right away under those circumstances."

"I suppose not. Not unless you marry a trustee."

Stephanie laughed. "I'd rather be childless."

The professor put on his hat and coat, called good night, and went out. Stephanie stood for a moment longer, looking down into the cage. Rain drummed against the windowpanes, and in the room it was almost dark. The mother cat purred in her sleep.

Stephanie wandered around the laboratory, closing the windows, checking the pans of water. Then she put on her coat and hat and took her umbrella. Outside it seemed to be night already. The lamps at the corners of the buildings made yellow circles through the mist. Rain pattered across the shiny black flagstones. A few people were hurrying towards the Commons for supper, and in the archway to the Commons a figure in a raincoat and slouch hat stood waiting for someone. What a night to be waiting for your girl, Stephanie thought; and she wondered whether she would eat in the Commons or walk through the rain to International House. The cold, earthy smell of the rain was good after the laboratory, and she turned across the campus towards International House. As she turned, she saw the figure in the raincoat move down from the archway. She could not see his face; but she knew who it was.

Her throat tightened. She felt her heart turn cold, and her legs seemed suddenly too weak to carry her. The rain slanted in silver streaks across the glow of the lamps. He was standing in front of her and he said, "Hello, Stephanie."

"Hello, Dave."

They stared at each other in silence. God, he's old, she thought. His face was in shadow, but she could not mistake the sharp angles of shadow across the jaw and under his cheekbones.

"How are you, Stephanie?"

"I'm all right."

"May I walk with you a way?"

"Yes, of course."

They moved between the buildings towards Fifty-Ninth Street. Questions she wanted to ask poured into her mind, but she pressed them back, afraid to ask them. The silence weighed upon her. At last, in a toneless voice, she said,

"And you—are you all right?"

"Sure."

"Were you hurt?"

"Some."

"Oh, Dave—"

He glanced at her sideways and she stopped. She wanted to ask what had happened to him and how he had been hurt and if it had been very bad. But how could she ask those questions without bringing to the minds of both of them a thousand details from the years they had lived together? She was afraid the intonation of her voice might mislead him.

They walked again in silence, turned down Fifty-Ninth Street and went east along the Midway. He seemed to be watching her, waiting for her to make the first move. He was unsure of himself, she realized. He did not know whether she had changed her mind in the two years since he had gone away—and he had come to find out. Certainly it would only be harder for both of them if she prolonged the decision, or left any doubt in his mind as to her own feelings. There was no middle ground. But after a time his silence began to provoke her and she felt reassured by the warmth of her own anger. Why couldn't he have telephoned her and made an appointment if he had wanted to see her? Why should he come all the way out here in the rain and then not say a word?

They reached International House before either of them broke the silence. "Here's where I'll have to leave you," Stephanie said. She turned to face him. "Why did you come here? Did you have something you wanted to say to me?"

"I wanted to let you know I was back."

"I'm glad you came back, Dave. But—"

"But you want a divorce. Maybe we'd better talk about that."

"Who told you I wanted a divorce?" she asked sharply; and wondered immediately why she had asked the question.

"You told me yourself before I went away."

"Yes, that's true, I did. And I haven't changed my mind. Yes, I want a divorce. I'm going to get married."

"Do you have any idea how we go about getting the divorce?"

"I talked to a lawyer about it. I'll probably have to sue you for desertion. Shall I give you the name of the lawyer? Do you want to talk to him?"

He shook his head with a slight smile. "No, thanks. I won't contest it."

Stephanie had the sudden feeling that both of them were moving in a dream, or speaking the parts of a play. Often before, she had pictured this moment of Dave's return, when she would tell him she was going to marry someone else. And she had pictured many different reactions on his part—contempt, or anger, or the plea that they should give themselves one more chance together. She had even imagined that he might try to make her ashamed by waving his service in the Spanish war in front of her. For all of these, she had had answers ready—if not for him, then at least for herself. But she had never imagined that they would stand here in the rain, chatting like two casual acquaintances about the business details of this divorce. The casualness, the contrast with past occasions which she knew must now be close to the surface of both their memories, struck her as so tragic that she felt the tears start to her eyes. What was he thinking? Was he sorry, or glad? He had not even asked her whom she was going to marry. Maybe he didn't care, maybe he didn't want to know.

"My father will be anxious to see you," she told him. "Will you stop at the house?"

"I already did."

"All right, Dave." She paused for a moment, dropping her eyes from his. "I'm very glad you're home safely." Then she turned, and without looking back, walked up the steps and through the doorway of International House.

Inside, the lobby was warm and bright, crowded with students chatting in groups and calling back and forth to each other. Stephanie elbowed her way to the check desk where she left her raincoat, then went downstairs to the women's washroom in the basement. She splashed water against her hot cheeks, dried her face, and powdered her nose. From the mirror her eyes flashed back at her and her wet black hair shone under the lights. Well, she thought, I don't love him any more. I saw him and I don't love him, I don't even hate him. Now the uncertainty which had gnawed so long in her mind was ended. He had returned; he had agreed to the divorce. She remembered how she had been afraid that as soon as she saw him again, everything would turn back to the way it had been. But now she had seen him and nothing had turned back. She neither loved nor hated him; she was free of him.

Stephanie lighted a cigarette and walked back up the stairs to the lobby.

7

HERE comes your agreeable brother," Martin said. They had finished breakfast and Stephanie, following Martin's glance through the window of the drugstore, saw her brother Victor crossing Fifty-Seventh Street. "Has he moved into his new apartment?" Martin asked.

"I suppose that's why he's here. We'll have to find another place to eat our breakfasts." But as soon as Victor entered the drugstore, Stephanie saw that his coming was no coincidence. He looked around until he spotted them, then headed for their table, clattering his steel-shod legs across the tile floor. He said good morning to both of them rather ceremoniously, and sat down beside Martin.

"Are you going to the reception for Jean Peyrel tonight?" he asked. Martin nodded, and Victor began firing a lot of questions at him—whether the visiting French philosopher was a Thomist, and how much Martin was interested in Peyrel's Catholic philosophy. But all the while he talked, Stephanie noticed that he kept glancing up as if he intended speaking to her; then smiled, showing his square white teeth, and said nothing.

"How do you like your new apartment?" she asked.

"Very comfortable. I thought you'd seen it?"

"I'm to go over with Marguerite sometime. Apparently she's fixing some curtains for you."

Victor nodded and smiled again. "Marguerite has some feminine instincts after all. They were aroused by the notion of fixing curtains. Are you supposed to help her? Is that the idea?"

"She insisted I come. I don't know why."

"She's showing off to you," Victor said. "She's discovered she has a feminine instinct and she wants to let you know about it. Here's Marguerite with her curtains, cackling over them like a hen over its first egg."

Stephanie looked out the window again, at the newsboy on the corner who was clapping his hands over his fire of broken boxes.

"Are you going to hear the Man of God, too?" Victor asked.

"Peyrel, you mean? If I finish in time."

"If you finish in time! I should think you'd let nothing keep you away. I can tell you, I'll be there. It's not every day a brother-in-law of mine serves on the reception committee to a Man of God."

Stephanie felt herself flush and raised her eyes sharply. No one spoke for some time, and Victor spread his newspaper out on the table. Finally Stephanie asked, "What did you come to tell me? What pretty story have you brought us today?"

"Nothing. I simply stopped for breakfast." But then, watching Stephanie, he said, "Have you been following the strike at the Sheet Steel and Can Company, Martin?"

"Not particularly. Why should I?"

"I have."

Martin shrugged his shoulders and Victor told him, "I've been treated to all the inside dope. I know all the issues involved." He raised his clenched fist. "Canworkers of the world, unite! You've got nothing to lose but your cans. That's the slogan the canworkers are ready to fight and die for. Look at the headlines." He banged the newspaper with his fist, and asked Stephanie, "Who do you think gave me the inside dope?"

"How should I know?"

"Roman," Victor said. "Roman, who usually doesn't know anything. But he knows all about the can strike."

"Roman?"

"Aha!" Victor cried. "I see you're surprised. I see you're interested in spite of yourself. You're wondering, Who told Roman about the can strike? What firebrand has been filling Roman with working-class solidarity?" He blinked his sharp black eyes at her. "Shall I go on?"

"Who's stopping you?"

"Nobody. I didn't know whether or not you were interested. Roman's union local is going to send a sympathy delegation to march in the picket line."

"You're kidding!"

"No, it's God's truth: signs, placards, everything."

"Well, good for them," Stephanie said. "I didn't know the old bunch had that much life in them." She stopped, feeling suddenly that Victor had trapped her; and she faced him, waiting. He was eating his roll now, breaking the roll into small pieces which he fed into his mouth while his thin blue jaw worked steadily with a rotary motion.

"A friend of yours is in town," he said. "Or maybe you knew that?"

She waited in silence.

"He just got back. I imagine he's the cause of the burst of activity among Roman's cronies. He's working as car repairman on the Great Midland." Victor looked up at her. "That's where Roman got all the dope about the can strike, you see? Your friend seems to be organizing the carmen. Or maybe you had already talked to him?"

"Had I?"

"Had I, she asks. There, Martin, you see how my little efforts to make conversation come to nothing against her sibylline silence. I bring her news of an old school comrade of ours—"

Stephanie pushed her chair back from the table. "I have to go to work. Thanks for your company, Victor." She got up, Martin got up with her, and they went out, while Victor remained at the table sipping his coffee and chewing the fragments of his roll.

The wind slammed the door of the drugstore behind them and they walked west toward the University.

"You should have told me your husband was back, Stephanie."

She noticed the stiffness in his voice. "I know I should. But I didn't want to talk about it."

"Have you seen him?"

"Once."

"And what happened to him? Was he wounded?"

"I think so. Yes, I saw him. We talked about the divorce. I didn't tell you because it's something I'll have to go through alone. I don't want you mixed up in it."

"I'm mixed up in it already, don't you think?" They had reached the building where she worked, and Martin walked up the steps with her. "Is he going to fight the divorce?"

"Oh, no." She stood silent, staring past him through the arched doorway of the building. "I guess I knew it would wind up this way from the beginning," she said at last.

"Why did you marry him?"

"I don't know. He certainly doesn't fit the pattern I had ever imagined for myself. I was seventeen when I first started going with him. Seventeen and just out of high school. He had a job on the railroad then. He was going to night school to study engineering, and we used to go out every Saturday evening—oh, Martin, why should I be telling you all this?"

"Tell me," he said.

"Maybe he's still going to that night school for all I know. He's a stolid, persistent person. Then I came to the University and he lost his job because of the depression. He went away from Chicago, worked on a lake steamer, and bummed around picking up odd jobs, I never did know where. And when he came back, we'd both changed. We knew different things, thought different things; we'd made different friends. We got married anyway—that was in 1936. I guess I knew right then it wouldn't work out. And it never did. It never did. But it took me a long time to see it."

"You see it now," Martin told her. "I'm glad of that." There was no one else in the doorway of the building, and he took her by the shoulders and kissed her. "Don't worry, Stephanie." Leaning against him, she felt the pressure of his arms around her. "When will I see you," he asked. "Will you come to the reception tonight?"

She nodded. "I'll come as soon as I can get finished at the lab." He turned to go, but she drew him back to her for a moment longer. "I'll be there as early as I can. I'll see you there."

At the end of her late afternoon class Stephanie hurried through her work in the laboratory, putting the kittens and puppies and white rats to bed. It was close to nine o'clock then, and without stopping for supper, she crossed the campus to the reception at Professor Parcher's house. Here she found all the familiar faces of the Philosophy Department and the editorial staff of the *Quarterly*. Professor Parcher, in a starched shirt and dinner jacket, was playing the proud host while his guest, the French philosopher Peyrel, discoursed on some complex matter. By stretching up on her tiptoes and peering over the heads of the people in front of her, Stephanie could catch a glimpse now and then of the visiting philosopher. He was a dark-haired little man, also dressed in a dinner jacket, who spoke fluently, but with a slight accent. As he spoke, he balanced a coffee cup in one hand and with the other gesticulated in the air, as if he were catching his ideas between thumb and forefinger, plucking them delicately like worms out of a log.

Stephanie felt hungry and tired. She went into the dining room where an array of cups and spoons sparkled on the black mahogany table; but there was nothing to eat except coffee and small teacakes. Picking up a handful of teacakes, she went back into the other room. The crowd had formed in a half circle around Peyrel, Parcher, Martin, and a few others. People bent forward listening, and when anyone clattered a coffee cup or made a remark to a neighbor, there were indignant hisses for silence. Stephanie heard Parcher's heavy voice, then Martin's voice cutting across it sharply. That idiot Parcher, she thought; head of a philosophy department and he has to keep Martin tagging around after him like a caddy to carry his bag of ideas. She knew it would be hours before she could pry Martin loose from that discussion; they might at least have put out some food for people to eat while they waited. Then she looked for Hawkins in the crowd, found him, and motioned him over.

"Hawkins, will you do something for me? Tell Martin I've got to get some supper and I'll wait for him at home."

"Are you all right, Stephanie?"

"Yes, I'm all right. But I'm tired and I missed supper and I don't feel very well." She left him staring after her doubtfully, put on her hat and coat, and went outside.

At an all-night restaurant on Fifty-Fifth Street, she stopped for a sandwich and a cup of coffee. There was a newspaper on the counter, but she pushed it aside and stared down at the rings on the porcelain counter top. As soon as the counterman set the food before her, she realized that she did not want to eat. She had been kidding herself about being hungry. She had wanted to get out of the reception, that was all. But now she remembered how anxious Martin had been for her to come to the reception. Even Victor had not missed that point. For to Martin, the evening was a great occasion; he had appeared as second in command to Professor Parcher himself; a few moments before, she had watched him acting as spokesman for the entire Philosophy Department in the discussion with Peyrel.

Certainly Martin had wanted her to be there, to see him—just as she would have wanted *him* to be present at her own graduation, for example. She should have waited for him, she should have waited. Stephanie took a swig of coffee that burned her mouth. The pain lighted the anger that was rising inside her. She did not know where the anger came from or why, and her chagrin at its violence made it flare up the more. Those fools, she thought, those fools and their questions, bubbling along like water out of a bottle, each one trying to make his own fingernail of scholarship look like a new field of philosophy. Damn grubstakers! And she sat repeating to herself, bunkshooters, thimble-minded research clerks—how can Martin endure them?

She was ashamed of her anger at the same time that she could not check it. When she went out, she did not go directly home, but walked through the dark streets. What's wrong with me? She kept wondering. Why do I act like this? Sometimes I hate them all—the physiology books, the laboratory, the apartment, the friends we have, the University. The scholars and their questions—the endless fencing with broomstraws. Poor old Hawkins, writing his thesis on some book of Melville's nobody ever heard of. Victor and Marguerite with their medieval French—

Oh Martin, Martin, what are we doing? What's wrong with us? Who are we to lift up our heads as if we were superior to those little bitches from the North Shore with their sororities and their blue Mercury roadsters? What good does that do, when we live here too at the bounty of the North Shore trustees, basking like so many tabby cats in the artificial sunshine?

The anger faded suddenly, leaving her cold and frightened. Overhead the wind hummed against the trolley wires. A few particles of snow whirled through the glow of the streetlamps.

She thought of the rows of little houses stretching out to the west; the mass of factory buildings beside the Great Midland; the two stacks she remembered, thrusting up into the night sky. So he had come back.

She returned to the apartment. There she found Martin in the middle of the living room waiting for her, angry and hurt as she had known that he would be.

"I thought you were so tired," he said. "I expected to find you in bed with an ice pack on your head."

"I *was* tired. I had no supper and I stopped for something to eat." She wanted to explain to him, to talk to him and make him understand why she had not waited. But she stood silent and without moving. It was as if she were watching him from a distance, unable to make a sound or a motion towards him. His face changed and he stepped close to her.

"Stephanie what's the matter with you? What happened?"

She raised her hands suddenly, covering her eyes. "Oh Martin, Martin—"

He asked, "Did you see him tonight, Stephanie? Or have you just been worrying about him?"

"I was walking around," she said. "I didn't know I was so long."

Martin took her by the hands. "It's late, Stephanie. Let's go to bed." His voice was soft, but his fingers pressed hard against hers. He pulled her towards him and kissed her, biting at the tendons of her neck. She drew her head away.

Part Four

THE EMBANKMENT

8

AS the train rolled out of the yard, Dave Spaas and the red-headed carknocker swung aboard the last car. This was a lounge car with the name *Saphira City* in gold letters across the vestibule door. When the door closed behind them, the clanking of wheels faded to a velvet tick; the darkness inside the car smelled of soap, brass polish, lemon peel, and whiskey. Watery patterns floated across the ceiling as the lights of the coach yard slid past outside the windows.

"Sit down, gents," a voice told them. "But don't dirty up my armchairs or they'll hang me sure." Dave and the carknocker, groping their way down the aisle, found the white jacket of the Pullman porter and dropped into the chairs on each side of him. The end of the Pullman car was a curved sheet of glass through which they looked out at the red and green lights, the interwebbed gleaming rails of the yard behind them.

"We'll have frogs legs on toast," Dave said, "with brandy and soda."

"They keep a padlock on the groceries, gents; but I can get you some music. That's one thing that's free." The white jacket drifted away; a light in an alcove at the far end glowed against blue mirrors behind a bar. There was a rustle of dance music and the porter returned, two-stepping down the aisle. Red, pulling a handful of cigars from his overalls pocket, passed them around and they lighted up.

The train rolled out to the embankment and stopped. An old brakeman with a lantern in his hand stamped into the car, glared at them without speaking, then yanked up a panel in the sill of the observation window and began testing the signal and air-brake valves.

"What you waiting on?" Red asked. "The Fourth of July?"

The brakeman let go three shrill whistles on the signal hose, there came three answering hoots from the engine; the train lurched forward, stopped, and then rolled backward towards the depot. The brakeman sat down beside the brake valve. "Mind your own business, you crabby redhead," he said over his shoulder. "And let me have one of those cigars." Setting his lantern between his boots, he turned and stared at Dave. "I ain't seen you around before. Who the hell might you be?"

"You've seen me before, Paddy. You just forgot, that's all."

"Where do you get that Paddy stuff? I don't know you."

"Why, you got Paddy written all over your mug in big green letters," Dave said. "A man's only got to look at you to know your name must be Paddy or Moikel."

"Watch your talk, lad. You're talking too goddamn smart." Red began to laugh and the brakeman shouted, "The quickest way to get in trouble on this railroad is to talk smart. You'll learn that mighty soon. How long you been working?"

"Two weeks."

"Two weeks! And they made you a carknocker already? Mother of God, but they must be hard up for men."

"They're not hard up. I hired out as a carknocker. I knew more about railroad cars when I was ten years old than you'd know if you lived to a hundred and fifty."

"You knew what?" Dave could see Paddy Gallagher fumbling at his feet trying to get hold of his lantern. "I've seen you dynamite the brakes on a freight train," Dave told him, "so you flattened every wheel on the train. And then you tried to blame it on the engineer."

The lantern flashed on, shone in his face, and went out. In a grieved voice, Paddy Gallagher said, "I know who you are. You're Eddie Spaas' young nephew." He patted Dave on the knee. "Glad to see you back, boy. I should have known you were Eddie's nephew from the smart-aleck way you were talking. Eddie told me you was over here too."

"When did you quit the animal train, Paddy?"

"A year ago now, lad. Not so much leg work for an old man on these passenger backups."

"You must be getting on towards ninety, aren't you?"

"You son of a bitch—I'm fifty-five."

"How do you make out for bull rings on this run?"

"God's truth, I don't find any bull rings. But I pick up a little overtime now and then. And I hear you're going to be getting a wage raise for us?" Dave glanced up at the angry shower of sparks from the end of Red's cigar; the rumor mill was running already, he thought. "Yessir," Paddy Gallagher announced. "They're saying Joe Spaas' boy hired out only two weeks back and here he's talking about a wage raise already. Why look at that, the bastard's set me a stop board." Down the main line, a block of signal lights turned red. Paddy Gallagher opened the brake valve, letting the air escape with a thin hiss, and the train slowed to a halt. In front of them, the embankment narrowed and the framework of a bridge thrust up over the roofs of the factories on each side. An engine puffed towards them across the bridge; the smoke from its stack tangled and shredded through the girders, then burst up into a great white cauliflower as the engine emerged from the framework. The engine rattled past them, drawing a couple of boxcars and a caboose. The signal board turned green. Paddy blew his whistle and their own train rolled across the bridge.

"Hell no," Paddy said as he dropped back into his chair. "We won't be getting no raise. The most of these fellows nowadays sit around squawking like a row of hens on a fence, but they never do nothing." Dave saw Paddy Gallagher watching him suspiciously. They were coming into the depot now; the buildings of the Loop rose up in a solid dark wall in front of them. "You're just like your crazy uncle," Paddy said. "First thing you know, you'll be trying to get the CIO in here. And if that's not what they're saying, too. They're saying that no-good Carbuilders' Lodge of yours next to voted itself into the CIO."

"Nobody asked you to stick your nose into our lodge business," Red told him.

"What's that lodge of yours fooling around with the CIO for?"

Red, pulling his cigar from his mouth, ground it out against his boot. "All you lousy brakemen are the same way. Just because you get paid a little more than somebody else, you act like you was half owners in the company."

Paddy drew himself up with dignity. "I'll not be listening to that kind of talk."

For a moment he eyed Red coldly; then he turned back to his brake valve. They were under the train shed, coasting down between the platforms of the station; he eased the train to a halt just short of the bumping post, they took their lanterns and tools and dropped down from the car. Without waiting for them, Red strode off by himself, while Dave walked along for a moment beside Paddy.

"Can't walk so good now, I got a bum leg," Paddy said. "If I was younger, I'd have punched that redhead's teeth out through the back of his head."

"It was your own fault, Paddy."

"It was my own fault? What are you trying to tell me?"

"You haven't got your head cut in, that's all. You let the bunk-shooters fill you so full of crap, it's running out your ears."

"You watch what you're saying."

"It's true, Paddy. Look, you haven't had a raise in years, you don't have a forty-hour week, you don't get vacations. But as soon as somebody tries to tell you anything, you let that bunch of old women throw a scare in you about the CIO. Who were you talking to from our lodge, anyway?"

"Never mind that, lad."

Dave peered at him in the dim light of the train shed. "It wasn't Jennison, was it?"

"I don't want to hear any talk against Uncle Jennison, lad. I've known him since I started to work on this railroad."

So that was what Jennison was doing, Dave thought. He took Paddy by the elbow. "I've known Jennison a long time too—since I was a kid," he said. "And I always liked him. But I begin to think he's taken root in the ground from sitting on his keester too long. Sure, he knows the contract by heart, he's a good grievance man, he fought all his life for seniority and overtime. But you ask him to fight for something a little bit different and he begins to scream about the CIO. Don't rock the boat, he says, don't shake me up—"

Paddy Gallagher was still scowling.

"It's not only Jennison," Dave told him. "It's all over the railroad. It's a disease like measles. My old man was the same way when he was your chairman."

"Don't speak no evil of your poor father. I don't want to hear it."

They reached the head end of the train. Dave dropped down between the engine and the cars to unfasten the steam line and close the air valves. When he crawled back on the platform, Paddy Gallagher asked, "Is it the truth then, what Jennison said, that you're going to help the CIO in that can factory?"

"Sure, it's the truth. The guys walk past that factory every day of the year. They got friends in there and relatives. Why shouldn't we help them? You want to come?"

"No sir, I don't."

Dave yanked the lever uncoupling the engine and waved to the engineer to move ahead. But the engineer, leaning on the sill of his cab window, had dropped asleep. "Wake up, you wart-faced old son of a bitch," Paddy bellowed suddenly. "It's a wonder they don't give you hogheads sleeping compartments." The engineer snapped awake, clawing wildly in front of him, then glared back at Paddy. "What are you waiting for?" Paddy asked. "The lad's got you unhooked and he wants you to get this teakettle out of here. You figure to spend the night in the depot?" The engineer pulled back his throttle, the drive wheels eased forward a half turn; the coupling knuckles parted and the air hose disconnected with a pop like a cork coming out of a bottle.

"Listen to me, lad," Paddy told Dave. "Don't you go fooling around with the CIO. Maybe it's all right for spicks and niggers, but we don't want none of it—"

"Say, Paddy," the engineer called. "You coming back to the yard with us?"

"Sure I'm coming back. Did you think I'd be taking the streetcar?"

"Then run for it," the engineer yelled in a shrill voice. "Run for it, you gandy-dancer." He slammed in his throttle and the engine leaped up the track. Paddy let out a yell and raced after it on his game leg, swinging his lantern over his head. Dave, shaking with laughter, saw him catch the engine up at the far end of the platform.

The depot was quiet after the engine had gone. A blue film of smoke floated up across the lights that hung swaying from the arch of the train shed. Except for the cars the engine had just left, all the tracks were empty. The rails gleamed dully and here and there pools of ice glinted between the ties. On the wall of the station, above the gate to the waiting room, the red neon sign flashed on and off: GREAT MIDLAND RAILROAD—SOUTH SOUTHWEST—FAST FRIENDLY SERVICE—GREAT MIDLAND RAILROAD . . .

Dave, picking up his tools, walked out the open end of the train shed. The stars sparkled in the black sky and the wind whistled shrilly across the unsheltered tracks. At the express platform he found Red working on the baggage cars, which were glazed an inch thick with ice that they had to crack off with their hammers before they could check the coupling irons and air lines. They worked steadily, marking the hours which circled the clock on the station tower. The dividing points of the night came and passed. At two o'clock, an engine from the Milwaukee Road delivered the freezer loads of Wisconsin cream. At three, a coach-yard engine hauled in the string of empty baggage cars to replace the loaded cars Dave and Red were working on. And finally, at four in the morning, Red chalked his okay on the last of the baggage cars and they walked back through the train shed to the buffet in the empty waiting room, slapping their hands and stamping to thaw the cold out.

A sleepy-eyed woman behind the lunch counter brought them coffee and doughnuts and leaned on the counter waiting for them to start talking. Red was still growling about the brakemen and how they thought they owned the turnpike. Emptying his cup, he shouted at the woman who was only two feet away from him, "Fill her up, sister." Then he handed Dave a cigar and lighted it for him. "I tell you, Dave, they're all the same, these brakemen. Remember one time I was lying on my back under a car working on the air line. First thing I know one of those sons of bitches is trying to couple an engine on to me, I see the engine coming from under the car. Well, I kick out of there like I'd straddled a rattlesnake and you know what that brakeman says? He says, what's the idea crawling around under cars like that? That's how guys get hurt. Listen, buddy, I tell him, you see that blue lantern? You know what a blue lantern means? Where's any blue lantern? he says. So I pick it up and clout him over the head with it. Broke the lantern all to hell and they give me ninety days' suspension. That was back in the depression; I was lucky they didn't fire me."

"Don't go getting in a bind about the brakemen," Dave said. "They aren't any worse than anybody else around here."

"Aw, don't hand me that stuff. I've known too many of the bastards."

Dave grinned at the woman behind the counter. "What do you think when you hear guys talk like that?"

She shrugged her shoulders. "I don't pay any attention. I got to listen to all kinds of talk."

They finished their coffee and went back to the train shed. At six o'clock the two sections of the Kansas City Express rolled in, spattered with mud and ice; passengers surged down the platforms to the waiting room. A pair of switch engines, following the trains into the depot, began yanking them apart; set the Pullmans on the far track so the first-class passengers could finish their sleep, lined up the mail cars for the mail gang who went to work heaving canvas sacks out into the hand-trucks; banged all the empty coaches together for the drag back to the coach yard. After that, one on top of another, commuters' specials whistled into the depot. The platforms swarmed with office workers, and Dave, as he moved along tapping his hammer against the wheels of the cars, had to shoulder his way through the crowd.

At seven o'clock, the night shift went off duty. Dave caught a ride to the coach yard on one of the switch engines, changed his clothes in the locker room, and walked home for breakfast. He had been sleepy before, but the first glow of daylight brought him wide awake, and he swung along, whistling and clapping his hands together. At home his mother, Ann Spaas, was getting the little girl Sally off to school. Then she set his breakfast on the table, and while he was eating, told him,

"Jennison called you last night."

"What did he want?"

"I don't know. He sounded mad."

Dave nodded. "I'm going down to see him today." Then he asked, "Did Eddie pay you a visit, Mom?"

"Oh yes, Eddie stopped by. But he left right away. I guess he was afraid you'd catch him here." She fell into a fit of laughter, and Dave watched her while she wiped her eyes on a dish towel; then abruptly she turned serious and stared at him across the kitchen table.

"You going to stay on the railroad?"

"I guess so," he said. "Why shouldn't I?"

"No reason. No reason at all. Your dad was a railroader all his life. Why should you do anything different?" She walked over to the stove, but after a moment returned to the table and stood looking down at him. "What about all the engineering? You going back to that night school?"

"No."

"Why not?"

"I don't see any use to it now."

"You used to."

Dave grinned at her. "There're a lot of things I used to do that I don't do any more."

"I'd like to know what they are." Then she said suddenly,

"There's Joe's insurance money, Dave. If you want to go back to that night school—"

For a moment, thinking she really wanted him to go back to the engineering course, he tried to think how he could refuse the money without making her angry. But then he realized she was hanging over him, hoping he would say no. He shook his head and watched her relax slowly and drop into one of the chairs at the table.

Dave remembered the telegram he had received from her while he was still in the hospital in New York, notifying him of Joe's death from a heart attack. He had thought at the time that she probably was not very sorry. And why should she be? As far back as he could remember, his father had never actually belonged to the house. He had lived there like a rent-paying tenant, his comings and goings being of small concern to the others. Now the only difference was that when Joe did not show up for meals or come home in the evening, it was not because he was hanging around the brakemen's shanties, or playing poker with the boys; but because he was buried over in Westwood Cemetery. That probably made a difference for Joe, he thought, but not much for the rest of them. It was too bad it had been that way, but there was no use pretending it had been different. At least Joe had kept up the insurance policy and had the house almost paid off; but that was all. In the upstairs bedroom, which Dave had taken over, he had found what few other belongings his father had left: a couple of suits, several clean pairs of overalls, a brakeman's lantern, and a stack of paid-up union cards dating back to 1911.

Now as he sat watching his mother across the table, there came into Dave's mind a picture of his father as he had last seen him— the lantern slung over his arm, his face lined and pouchy under the eyes and at the corners of the mouth. He remembered the bitter arguments they had had over politics, and how Joe Spaas had always blamed Eddie for his son's radical ideas. Joe, who read the Chicago *Tribune* every day of his life, believed the country was being driven into the ground by the New Deal, Wall Street, the Jews, the CIO, the Reds. But for all that, Dave thought, he had been an officer in his union, a man ready to fight for the last dot over the last *i* in the contract—and a good brakeman.

The teakettle began to hum and vibrate on the stove. Ann got up from the table. "You better catch some sleep, Dave. It's getting late."

He nodded, but did not move from his place. He wondered what she intended to do next. When he had first come back to Chicago, he had still thought her very little changed from before he went away. She had never talked to him about his marriage before, and she said nothing about it now. She had never been particularly friendly to Stephanie, he remembered, and now she accepted the breaking up of the marriage without question. Although he had not even mentioned the divorce to her, apparently she knew from somewhere. She still showed him the same mixed attitude of impatience and affection as before, the same pestiferous comments with the same school-girl toss of the head. She still played the same crazy games with the little girl Sally. But her hair was gray now, and when she walked, there was a solid thud to her footsteps. He had thought of her as being always about the same age, and the gray hair startled him.

"Well, Mom," he asked, "are you sorry I don't need the money?"

"No," she said. "I'll tell you the truth, Davey—I'm glad. I want that insurance money more than anything. I don't know as I'd really given it to you if you had asked for it." She giggled suddenly. "But I offered it to you anyway, didn't I?" Then she jerked her head towards the door and told him, "You better go to bed. You ought to get your sleep before Sally comes home from school. She'll wake you sure."

Dave finished his breakfast and went upstairs to the bedroom. During the eight-hour shift at the depot, he had grown tired and his shoulder ached sometimes. But that would only help to make the bed feel softer, he thought. Sleeping, eating, working, these still seemed to him a novelty and wonderful pleasure. He stretched and yawned, rolling luxuriously under the covers.

9

THE engineer on the switch engine blew three blasts of his whistle. Dave ran up the platform and swung himself into the engine cab. With a deafening roar of steam, the pop-off valve let go, and the fireman wrestled with his injector to get more water into the boiler. Dave shouted into the engineer's ear, "I want to drop off at Andrews Street. Will you slow down under the viaduct?" The engineer nodded and Dave, stepping across the cab, sat down on the opposite seat box to keep out of the fireman's way. The engine puffed slowly backwards now, while the fireman stoked his boiler against the drag of coaches they were pulling out of the depot. The fireman worked with a steady swing, scooping coal from the bunker behind him, then with a long sweep of his shovel, driving the coal into the roaring fire. The engineer leaned back on his throttle, the engine barked against the load, while the floor plates buckled and crashed under the fireman's feet. At each swing of the shovel and each opening of the butterfly doors, a red glare of heat swirled out into the cab. The fireman wiped his face on his bandanna.

They were rolling along the embankment above the Chicago River. Below them, to the right, Dave could make out the roofs of the warehouses, dotted with patches of snow. The engineer eased up on his throttle, and as the engine slowed, Dave lowered himself from the cab and dropped off, running a few steps over the tie ends to keep his balance.

The coaches rumbled past him and disappeared around the curve of the embankment. He was directly under the viaduct now. It was close to daybreak, and to the east, he noticed the sky fading behind the roofs of the warehouses. He stepped over the rails of the inbound main line. Beyond the tracks he came to a little shanty with a light in the window and a mushroom-shaped water tank looming over it. Water, leaking from the tank, had formed long beards and streamers of ice, and frozen into a great black pool around the stem of the water tank. Dave felt his way cautiously across the ice, then stepped inside the shanty. There was a coal fire smoking in the stove, and Roman Koviak sat on the bench, removing his overalls. Roman jumped up when he saw Dave, tangled his feet in the overall legs, and almost fell on his face. He shook Dave's hand up and down.

"Sit down, Davey. Get yourself warm. Goddamn cold tonight."

Dave pulled off his gloves and held his hands over the stove.

"How is it in the depot? Lot of work?"

"They kept us pretty busy last night, Roman."

"Got terrible up here just before Christmas. All these warehouse cars. Not bad now. You get warm, Davey. I give you a ride home as soon as I put my pants on. We wait for Johnny, too—"

"Johnny?"

"Johnny's on the eleven-o'clock job last night. I give him a ride home too." Roman finally managed to extract his feet from the legs of his overalls. He stood up, the tails of his red- and blue-checked shirt reaching down to the knees of his gray union suit.

"Davey—"

He stopped and Dave turned towards him from the stove.

"Davey, you go and see her, you talk to her?"

"Yes, I saw her," Dave said.

"And it's all right, Davey? Everything's all right? What did she say? You tell me, Davey."

"We're going to get a divorce."

"Oh no!" Roman Koviak stood pressing his hands together. "No, Davey. You don't do that. That's no good for either of you. She don't really want that. I know her. I know—"

Dave, remembering the night when he had talked to Stephanie, smiled slightly and shook his head.

Roman caught him by the sleeve of his jacket. "Listen, Davey. That's not right for either of you. I know you both, both of you like you're my own kids. Here's what you do, Dave. Listen to what I say. You got to talk to her, that's all, and it come out right again."

"It won't make any difference," Dave said.

"Here's what you do, Davey. Mama and I, we ask her over to the house on Sunday. She promise to come a long time ago. Mama and I go out and you wait for her. That way you can talk, you can say what you want—"

"That won't work, Roman. I'm sorry."

Roman dropped down on the bench and lowered his head. His shoulders were shaking and he kept twisting his hands together. Dave watched him for a moment, then sat beside him and put his arm around him. "Don't take it like that, Roman. I guess things happen sometimes; but we'll be all right, both of us."

"No, Davey, it's no good; it makes me hurt in here." He pushed the palm of his hand against his chest. "I feel happy she goes with you, and then she gets married to you, but the other, I don't think it's good—"

"Well, she's going to get married again," Dave said. He hesitated, staring down at the floor boards between his feet. "Who's she going to marry, Roman?"

"We wait all this time for you to come back," Roman said.

"All the time, I'm afraid something happen to you. Then you come back and it's got to be like this—"

"Who's she going to marry?" Dave asked again.

"I don't know."

"She didn't bring him over?"

"No, she won't bring him over. She gets mad when I ask her. You know how she is, Davey. Victor knows him."

"Somebody at the University then," Dave said.

"That's it. Somebody at the University. She don't even tell me his name. You talk to Victor; Victor knows him."

Dave shook his head. "I'll leave Victor alone."

"I guess that's better," Roman said in a dull voice. He pulled on his pants and his sheepskin overcoat and set his tools in his locker.

"Where's Johnny" Dave asked.

"I don't know. Maybe he forget to come. Let's go now, Davey."

They went outside, stepped across the team tracks between the uncoupled boxcars. Roman's Chevrolet was parked beside the roadway beyond the tracks. "I don't know whether we get her started or not," Roman said. "She don't run good in cold weather."

He climbed in and began to kick the starter. From the direction of the warehouses Dave heard a whoop, and turning, saw Johnny Koviak running towards them. Johnny piled into the rear seat of the Chevrolet, kicking the snow from his boots. "Thought you'd ditch me, you old coot. But I was keeping my eye on you. Well, Davey, how does it feel to be back at work?— Know how to fix this Chevvy up, Roman? Push her into the river and get yourself a new one!" But the car started at last, and they sputtered up the ramp to the Andrews Street bridge. "Listen, Roman," Johnny said, "will you let me take the car after you get yourself drove home? I got to pick up some groceries for the old lady."

Roman nodded without answering. He turned west to Halsted Street, then south. When he pulled up in front of the Koviaks' house on the half block by the embankment, he asked Dave to stay for breakfast.

"I guess I better go on home," Dave told him.

Roman tugged at his sleeve. "Then you come up on the porch with me a minute." They climbed out of the car, Dave followed him across the yard and up the steps of the front porch. Roman leaned close to his ear. "You got to talk to her again. You got to go see her. It's no good like this—"

"Lay off it, will you?" Dave answered impatiently. "There's nothing I can do about it. She knows what she wants." He turned away, but from the bottom of the steps called back, "So long, Roman."

"So long, Davey."

In the car, Johnny was waiting for him; and as they drove back towards Halsted Street, he said, "I got some time to kill before the stores open. How about a little drink?"

"All right."

"What did Roman want? Was he talking to you about Stevie?"

Dave nodded.

"Don't think I'm sticking my nose in—but you and Stevie—I mean, are you and Stevie going to get together?"

"No, we're not."

"Aw, that's too bad. I don't know though. Maybe it's better to be single. I tell you straight, I wish I was single again."

"What's wrong, Johnny?"

"Oh—nothing. I guess I'm no worse off than anybody else."

"What are you beefing about then?"

"I'm not beefing. You never seen my little kid, did you? Ought to come over sometime. He looks more like Stevie than Rosa. Almost a year and a half old now. But goddamn, it drives a guy crazy. Every day I come home it's the same old thing. Where you been? How much money you got? What'd you do with the rest of it? If she'd only come right out and say it, I wouldn't mind, but she just looks—that's what drives me goofy. We'll stop in at Walter's, eh Davey? It's right up here. But listen, a guy's not a slave just because he gets married. A guy can't stay home all the time, can he?"

"Why don't you take your wife with you when you go out?"

"Aw, it would be different with Stevie, I know that. But a woman doesn't have no fun going out for a drink. Besides she ain't feeling good and her mother's over to the house. When that son-of-a-bitching mother-in-law shows up, that's when this kid takes a powder." Johnny swung past the corner of the Great Midland coach yard and stopped in front of a tavern which appeared to be still closed for the night. The sign was not lighted and the blinds were drawn across the windows; but when they stepped out of the car they could hear voices from inside, and the sound of a juke box. In the tavern doorway Johnny hesitated, then peered up uneasily at Dave. "Little girl I have a drink with sometimes," he said. "Name of Sue. Met her at the Can Company when

I worked on the job that sets out the cars there. We have a little drink once in a while. You won't get sore?"

"Why should I get sore?"

Johnny pushed open the door and they stepped inside. The neon tubes over the bar glowed dimly in the half-light; the place had a frowzy, tarnished look, the floor was half mopped, the air heavy with tobacco smoke and the smell of stale beer. Behind the bar Walter, with his little red mustache and puffy, circled eyes, was mixing drinks for a couple of customers. He and Johnny yodeled at each other, and the middleaged waitress who had been dozing on one of the bar stools started awake, then dropped her head down and slept again. "Looking for Sue?" Walter shouted. "She's in the corner booth."

Two girls, both dressed in slacks and sweaters, were waiting in the booth. Johnny dropped into the place beside the younger and prettier of the two, while Dave took the seat that was left beside the other. Johnny kept glancing at him as if he were trying to think of something to say, then avoiding his eyes and saying nothing. The girl next him, pointing her finger at Dave, asked, "Who's that?"

"Carknocker from over in the yard. Dave, want you to meet Sue and her girl friend."

"Pleased to know you," Sue told him, and the girl friend nodded her head but said nothing.

From the bar, Walter brought them glasses and a bottle of whiskey which he banged down in the middle of the table. Then he patted Sue on the shoulder, winked each of his small eyes two or three times at Johnny, and dropped an ice cube into the front of Sue's sweater. She screamed and slapped his hand when he offered to help her fish for it. But she seemed to have a lot of trouble finding it, and after a while, Johnny reached in to join her. Dave filled the glasses around. The whiskey tasted good to him after the night in the cold; he held it on the flat of his tongue, pressed it against the roof of his mouth, feeling the burn of it spread down his throat into his chest and shoulders. Across the table, Sue was pulling Johnny's ears now, and rumpling his hair. The girl friend said nothing. When Dave asked if they belonged to the union, the girl friend shrugged her shoulders and Sue said no, they were waiting so they could find out what it was all about. Dave started to tell her what it was about, but he saw they were paying no attention to what he said. Sue and Johnny had refilled their glasses from the bottle. Johnny's first embarrassment had now vanished; he put his arm around Sue's neck and began kissing her while his other hand disappeared under the table.

Dave watched them for a few moments and then got up. But as he reached for his jacket, his eyes met those of the girl who had been sitting beside him and who had not spoken. For a moment they looked at each other, he dropped back into his place and filled their glasses again from the whiskey bottle.

"Which way do you live?" he asked.

"South."

He emptied his glass and she finished hers. "I go the same direction," he said. "If you're ready to leave now, I'll go with you." She nodded, and as they left the booth together, Sue waved to them over the back of the seat, while Walter from behind the bar whistled and clicked his tongue. They walked out to the corner and caught the streetcar south.

The girl lived at the top of a building where children and old women and men carrying garbage pails jostled each other on the stairway. In her single room the bed was unmade, and dirty dishes were piled around the gas ring. She pulled down the windowshade, and while Dave got into bed, she measured water and coffee into a percolator and lighted the gas ring. She had hardly spoken since they left Walter's Tavern, but when she rolled into the bed beside him, she began talking and whispering, more to herself than to him. She was not very pretty and not very young; but she was solid and hungry, smelling of sweat and five-and-dime-store perfume. The smell was good to Dave; he kissed her throat and shoulders and pressed his face into her neck.

When he woke, there was an odor of burned coffee and gas in the room. The percolator had boiled over, putting out the flame. Dave got up, shut off the tap to the gas ring, and opened the window. Cold fresh air swirled against him. It was late afternoon; a dusting of new snow had fallen, and now the roofs and backyards sparkled in the sunlight. He reached out his arms in a sudden flood of pleasure at the precise winter sunlight over the city, the clear stretched feeling of his body in the cold air. He swung his fist down into his hand and turned away from the window. The girl was sitting up in bed staring at him.

In the same instant, as if it had been waiting to catch him off guard, the realization he had been fighting back for weeks jumped into his mind. It confronted him, obvious, undeniable. He felt as if it had trapped him in the moment he relaxed; even the familiar smell of coffee, the tumbled sheets on the bed, made his throat hurt with wishing.

He saw again the way she had looked the first time he had ever noticed her. In the Koviaks' kitchen, he was arguing some point with Victor; he had raised his eyes, and there was Vic's younger sister watching him from across the table. The unsmiling, dark-haired little girl whom he had seen for years around school had changed suddenly from somebody's kid sister into the woman he had talked to, loved, lived with, hated. Stephanie Koviak, he thought, Stephanie Spaas; Stephanie—he did not even know her last name now. The defenses he had built up collapsed. The bitter passion of wishing and jealousy burned through him.

Round-eyed, the girl on the bed watched him. "God," she said. "You look like you'd seen something."

Dave nodded and stepped away from the window. "I did."

"What did you see?"

"You."

"Oh go on, you've seen that before." The girl giggled and scrambled out of bed. "What are you letting that cold air in for?" she asked.

"I'm letting the gas out. Your pot boiled over."

"Oh my God! We might have been asphyxiated right in bed." She had turned her back to him and was wiggling headfirst into her slip.

"Hungry?" Dave whacked her across her pink, shaking buttocks. She yelped and jumped.

"Of course I'm hungry."

When they had dressed, they walked out toward Sixty-Third Street looking for a restaurant. The air was still and clear, the winter twilight faded down the long streets to the west. As they walked, he took her by the arm and began to sing in a low voice.

"What language is that?" she asked.

"Spanish."

"Are you Spanish?"

"No, I'm Dutch."

"You're a wooden-shoe, are you?"

"No, that's the Belgians they call wooden-shoes. They call the Dutch krautheads or anything else they happen to think of."

"What was the song?"
Dave sang for her in English,

> "Those four Insurgent Generals,
> Tis true they did betray you,
> My love, they did betray you,
> One holy Christmas morning,
> One holy Christmas morning,
> Those four will all be hanging . . ."

But while he sang, his mind kept forming the name over and over: Stephanie Koviak, Stephanie Spaas, Stephanie, Stephanie— Inside him, he felt his intestines knotting and twisting like a clothesline. He shrugged his shoulders although he knew he could not brush it away; he would recover from this as he had recovered from all the rest. They stopped at a restaurant on Sixty-Third Street, sat down at a porcelain-topped table, and the girl with caution began to study the menu.

10

SUNDAY morning: the streets were quiet and empty, but he heard the churchbells clanging in the distance. Into the winter sunlight, his breath puffed blue clouds of steam. Dave turned the corner from Wentworth Avenue and walked down the side street toward the two-story wooden building of Ruby's Chile Parlor. Inside, Pledger was waiting for him and they sat at one of the tables over cups of coffee. Ruby, behind the counter, stirred her pots of chile beans and barbecued spareribs, while Pledger's daughter Judith sat reading at the cash register. Proudly, Pledger told Dave how well his girl was doing in her nurse's training course at the city hospital; and the girl, hearing her name, raised her eyes from time to time meeting Dave's glance.

It was warm and dark inside the Chile Parlor. The potbellied stove began to whistle like a teakettle, and a red-hot pulse shimmered up and down the stovepipe. Pledger, who had been talking about the railroad, stopped speaking now and watched Dave across the table. "You looking better," he said.

Dave nodded. "I'm coming around." He took out a cigarette, lighted it, and blew the smoke into his empty coffee cup. "I went to see Jennison the other night, Pledger. You'd think we were traveling like a house afire the way he carries on."

"He don't like our going down to the can factory?"

"No, he's trying to talk the men out of it; but I guess the more he talks, the more they want to go."

"And the union officers downtown, they got wind of it yet?"

"Jennison went to them first thing."

"You'll have to bust him sooner or later," Pledger said. "You and Red will have to do that."

"You think so?"

"Sure you will. You don't much want to fight old Jennison, do you?"

"Well, he practically taught me to walk—him and my real uncle, Eddie. I been hoping maybe he'd go along with us when it comes to a showdown."

"That's just when he don't go along with you. I known Jennison twenty years now." Dave glanced up grinning, and Pledger began to laugh, his eyes and his white teeth flashing.

From behind the counter, Ruby called, "You people want some chile beans?"

"What do you think we're sitting here for?" Pledger asked, and Ruby brought them two steaming bowls of chile and refilled their coffee mugs. A few customers were coming in now for Sunday dinner, and Ruby and the girl Judith waited on them.

Pledger drew his gold railroad watch from his pocket and laid it on the table in front of him. "I got to leave you pretty soon now."

"You still go to church?" Dave asked.

"Still do. You want to come with me today?"

Dave shook his head. "Has Andrew Masters anything to preach you haven't heard already?"

"Don't make any difference what Andrew says any more. We all know he got his heart in the right direction."

"Then it's not to let old Andrew Masters down? Is that why you still go, Pledger?"

"I go because I want to, that's why. You trying to needle me, boy?"

144

"No." Finishing his food, Dave pushed the empty dish aside. "I wasn't trying to needle you, Pledger; and I wasn't trying to be funny, either. It's a long time since I talked to you much, and a lot of things have happened since then. Does it ever bother you being around with people that aren't religious?"

"I had plenty chance to get accustomed to that by now." He looked up and they both smiled. "I tell you," Pledger said, "I always figured if God was big enough to make the world, he was big enough to take care of folks that don't believe in him. You believe in God, Dave?"

"No."

"That's short and sweet. But I do. Who made the world, then? Who started things?"

"I don't know if anybody started them."

"You mean the world just happened? I can't believe that."

"I don't think it's any harder than to believe God just happened."

"It is for me. I got to have a reason for things. What makes people act the way they do? You can't tell me. Why do some people act good and others act bad?"

"If you know the person well enough," Dave said, "you can figure out what made him act the way he did."

Pledger shook his head. "I believe in religion. And I'm glad I do, because some things seem so rotten bad I don't know when they ever get straightened out without a little extra push. You don't believe anything like good and evil then, do you?"

"What do you mean, *believe?* Some things are good and some bad. I can see that."

"I'm not talking about what you can see. I'm talking about the way people act. I known men, Dave, that there was something evil inside them. Something worse than just ignorance or bad upbringing, the way we all like to say now is the cause of men doing bad. I known men, if you was to kill them, I think the evil in them would go right on living."

"You think they had a devil in them?"

"I'm not joking. I tell you something, boy. Something I thought about often, but I don't know if I ever told you. Eight, ten years back, there used to be a house on the corner of this street. It burned down long since, and now there's a gasoline station where it stood. That was back in prohibition and they had a honky-tonk and fake

145

candy store on the corner, and up above was the house where the girls lived. They used to stand out under the street lamp with their purple dresses and gloves as long as their elbows—"

He stopped for a moment, staring down at his watch on the table. "One night I was coming home late from work, I run right into a white man stepping out of this house."

"You think it's worse for a white man to go to a Negro whore house than to a white whore house?"

After a moment of silence, Pledger said, "You know who I'm talking about. It was Morgan. It was the railroad detective Morgan."

Dave nodded his head. He had known for several minutes, without being quite certain why, that Pledger was going to mention Morgan. Now there came into his mind the recollection of the time when he had been sick in New York, the wild nightmares the fever had brought—and the picture, among many others, of the winter night on the embankment when Victor Koviak swung up the ladder of the coal car, and the thin, black-coated figure had risen out of the car above him.

"He come up from Alabama before the last war," Pledger said. "Worked on the Great Midland in Alabama and they moved him up here. I told you how I seen him kill the little boy in the railroad yard? What would make a man act like that."

"I don't know."

"There was one of the coach cleaners," Pledger told him. "Left the yard long ago and went back south, but he come from the same town in Alabama that Morgan come from. He used to talk to me and Andrew Masters—" Pledger leaned forward, peering at his watch again as if he were studying the time.

"What did he say?" Dave asked.

"I often thought, Davey, that town wasn't much different from the town I grew up in when I was a little boy. Maybe all those towns are about the same way: railroad down the middle of the valley, cornfields and cotton fields all around, and along the railroad in both directions the wooden shanties where the colored families live. That coach cleaner told us it was the Morgans ran the general store in the town. You ever been south? You ever pass through one of these little towns, don't have much more to 'em than a store and an old church? I can see the way they look right now, that old store sitting by the dusty road, with big wooden posts to hold the front porch up; and when the farmers drive in

146

from the country they tie their horses to those porch posts—"

"So Morgan's family were the big shots in the town," Dave said.

"That's what he told us. Fat old man in his gallusses, sitting there all day like an old hoptoad too fat and heavy to hop, just waiting for the flies to buzz into his mouth. Before long he owned all the shanties and all the little patches of ground around that town. And all the colored families hated old man Morgan like the devil. But he had a wife with pretty yellow braids—"

"And how about young Morgan?"

"Started out as brakeman on the railroad," Pledger said. "The coach cleaner told us all the hoboes on the line knew him for a killer. He used to knock the bums off the cars with his brake club. Then they switched him over to policeman. You know, the company don't pass up talent when they see it."

"Too bad he didn't stay in Alabama."

"I guess the family kind of broke up. The old lady with the yellow braids died of malaria or something. So the boy come up north to see what he could do for himself."

"And the old man?" Dave asked.

"I don't know. Expect he's still sitting in the general store. Maybe got himself a gas pump in front of the porch now, that's the only difference. But listen, Dave, now listen to me, what would make a man act like that Morgan acted?"

"A devil?"

"You and me ain't talking about the same kind of devil."

"I know what kind of devil I'm talking about. It's good business to breed men like Morgan."

They sat silent for a moment; then Pledger's expression relaxed and he leaned back in his chair. "You got a hard head on you. It's good to talk to you again."

"So you're counting on God to take care of Morgan?" Dave asked.

Pledger stared at him in surprise, and Dave saw that his question had offended Pledger. But the next moment Pledger threw back his head with a roar of laughter so loud the others in the Chile Parlor turned to stare at him. "You're worried about me, Dave. You're thinking how tough it will be for me if all my friends go to hell and I'm all alone up in heaven—"

Dave shook his head. "I guess I *was* trying to needle you. I don't know what's wrong with me."

"Sure you do! You got reason to be out of sorts. But even if you was needling me, it was a fair question. I know what you mean to ask and I thought about it some." Leaning forward, Pledger lowered his voice again. "Here we are: I believe in God, you don't. But we're both of us doing about the same thing, aren't we? I often thought to myself, suppose somebody come along and proved to me without any doubt that there was no God. What would I do? Would I act any different? I guess not; I wouldn't act much different from the way I'm acting now.

"And with you, if some big angel was to stop you on the street and say to you, 'Brother Spaas, God's got his eye on you as sure as you're born,' would you put a sack over your head and crawl in the aisle? No, you'd keep right on doing about the way you're doing now."

"You mean it doesn't make any difference whether a man believes in God or not?"

"Well, God never let me know exactly how he felt about that. Maybe you don't read the Bible, but there's a place where the Lord smites a fig tree because the tree don't give any fruit. Now the book don't say the Lord asked that tree what it believed or didn't believe. The book says, by their fruits you shall know them."

"Then religion doesn't make any problem for you?" Dave asked. "It doesn't get in the way of your working?"

"Why should it?"

"It does for some people."

"Then they got the wrong kind of religion. I wouldn't think much of a religion that got in the way of a man's working."

"Neither would I," Dave said. His eyes met Pledger's, whom he saw watching him steadily. "Or anything else, for that matter."

Pledger nodded his head. He put his watch in his pocket and got up from the table. "I got to go now, unless you want to come with me?"

"No, I'll go home and catch some sleep."

"Judith," Pledger called. "You feel like going to the chapel today?"

The girl looked up through the grillwork above the cash register. "I can't come—now you know that. I got a date at three."

Dave noticed the disappointment in Pledger's voice. "I guess you won't be home for supper?"

The girl shook her head and Ruby yelled suddenly, "Quit pestering that child, Pledger. What do you think, of *course* she got a date for Sunday afternoon! It'd served you right to had an ugly

148

stick of a child no man would look at twice." Judith sidled over, twisted Pledger's ear a couple of times to make up with him, then said she had to dress pretty for her date, and disappeared up the stairs.

Pledger, laughing, pulled on his overcoat.

After Pledger had gone out, Dave stayed a few minutes longer at the table with Ruby, and with Judith who returned all dressed to wait for her friend. She was a dark-skinned, tall girl with black hair drawn straight behind her ears and a big blue flower in the knot of her hair. Ruby, as Pledger had done earlier, immediately began talking with pride about the nurses' training course, and how well Judith was doing; but the girl pouted and shook her head. A group of customers came into the Chile Parlor; when Ruby got up to wait on them, Judith remained at the table, and dropping her voice almost to a whisper, she told Dave she had liked the training course at first, but now, working in the hospital with all the sick people, it was messy and she didn't know if she wanted to go in for that kind of work. She was bound she'd finish the course for her certificate, but after that she wasn't so sure what she would do.

Dave heard a car stop outside. The girl, smiling and twisting her shoulders, said, "Here's my date"; and Dave, glancing behind him, saw a black-skinned, solidly built man in a pin-stripe suit come down through the doorway. The man bowed to Ruby Mc-Adams, telling her good evening in a careful low voice. Then he came over to the table, and when Judith introduced him, Dave stood up and held out his hand. But the other, who was busy fishing a cigarette case from his inside pocket, did not appear to notice. He offered Judith a cigarette, took one himself, and started to put the case away. Then he glanced up at Dave.

"You care for one?"

Dave shook his head. The date helped Judith on with her coat and they went out together. A moment later, Dave heard the car roar off down the street.

1940

PLEDGER McADAMS stopped at the corner of South Park Avenue, and as he watched for the traffic light to change, a big car swung past him with someone waving to him out the window. He saw it was his daughter Judith, but before he could raise his hand to wave back, the car slipped away into the stream of traffic. It had been a Buick, a shiny blue automobile with silver trimmings. Judith's stepping mighty high, he thought. For a moment longer he remained staring down the street, which after twenty years still seemed strange to him. The gray stone houses stepped away endlessly with their towers and gables, their fancy carriage entrances, and in each doorway the signs which said, FLAT FOR RENT—APARTMENT—FURNISHED ROOMS. The sunlight flashed on the icy pavement, crumpled newspapers blew along the sidewalks, the black trees bent their branches under the wind; and in the distance the street came to no ending, but faded from sight into the blue winter haze. A little Negro woman with a woolen cap pulled over her ears hurried past him in the opposite direction.

Pledger turned up his coat collar and walked to the chapel. An arched portico with a cross over it now decorated the doorway and colored glass windows had replaced the old store front; but inside, the chapel appeared the same as always. The congregation, crowded into the wooden benches, clapped their hands and chanted Amen, while Andrew Masters up in the pulpit intoned his sermon.

"We sinned, oh Lord, but heal us with mercy. We transgressed, oh Lord, but it was weakness of flesh, not weakness of spirit. Wash our flesh clean, Lord, though men revile us, to walk in the way of the Lamb of Christ—"

Pledger glanced at the faces of the people around him, some of whom had been here before he first came, while many others were younger and newer. But what Dave had said was true, he thought;

Andrew Masters had not much left to tell that he had not already told them before. And if his people still came to hear him, it was not the letter of the words they listened to; it was something else the old man gave, something different from the meaning of words. The congregation, bending their heads, prayed, stood up and sang, and Andrew Masters, his arms spread in the old gesture, preached again with a tremble to his heavy voice. Afterwards, the people gathered outside to admire the chapel's new entranceway; and Pledger made his way through the group, shaking hands and answering the greetings of his neighbors.

"You feeling good today, Mistah McAdams?"

"How's your wife Ruby today?"

"See your girl pass by, Mistah McAdams. Sure is getting pretty."

It was dark when he returned to the Chile Parlor. Squares of light from the window lay across the pavement on the glittery ice. He went in. Ruby set supper for him at one of the back tables, and he asked her, "Who's that man Judith keeps going out with?"

"Name of Frankie Larkin."

"I never heard that name around here."

"He comes from New York. I don't know anything about him except he's got a big Buick automobile."

"What does he do?"

"I don't know that either," Ruby said.

Pledger ate in silence for a few minutes. Then he asked, "What you think about him, Ruby?"

"He talks pleasant. I guess Judith is big enough to decide who she wants to go out with."

"I guess so," Pledger said. "I guess she is." But when his younger boy Billy came down for supper, Pledger shouted at him, "Where you been all day, boy?"

"Went to sleep—"

"You got plenty of time to sleep but no time to go to the chapel with me." The boy avoided his eyes, and Pledger demanded, "How come you can't even change your shirt when you come to eat? You look like you been rolling in a hog pen."

"Sure, all right, I'll change my shirt." The boy ducked away up the stairs; and Ruby, leaning over the back of Pledger's chair, said in a low voice, "That's not right, Pledger. It ain't Billy's fault who Judith goes out with."

II

OVER the top of his newspaper, as he sat reading at the kitchen table, Dave saw his mother come out of the bedroom. He watched her try on her hat in front of the parlor mirror with the gesture of a schoolgirl getting ready for a party. At the same moment she looked up, stared at him angrily, and went back into her bedroom. Annoyed at the interruption, he continued for a moment turning the pages of the newspaper. Then he threw the paper down, walked over to the bedroom door, knocked and called, "Can I come in, Mom?"

She was sitting on the bed, writing a letter. Without looking up, she said, "You make me awful mad sometimes, Dave. If I'd had a brick in my hand, I'd have busted your head with it."

"What for?"

"I can't even try on a hat without you staring at me like I'm crazy. I'm not so old. I'm not a hundred and eighty yet."

"I was just surprised at how good the hat looked."

"Oh, is that so? You know what it is makes me sore, Dave. It's because you been acting as if I was a stick of furniture around the house. You come back here like you owned the place. How did you know I wanted you back? You never asked. How did you know I didn't aim to sell the house? This place don't belong to you. It belongs to me—me and the mortgage company."

"I figured you had a tongue, Mom, you'd tell me what you wanted to do."

"You mean you never figured anything about it. No wonder Stephanie couldn't put up with you. You think a woman's something that grows in the kitchen like a sink or a garbage pail. But you're always ready to yell a person's head off about how many equal rights women got. You and your Uncle Eddie are just alike."

"No, we're not."

"Oh, I know that."

He sat down on the window sill, and for a time neither of them spoke. He began to laugh finally. "I don't see why I should let myself be made out a heel. Of course I came back; why shouldn't I? And who's paid for the food and the coal ever since I been here?"

"Don't get up on your ear, Davey. I didn't really mean that."

"I'm no mindreader. If you want to get rid of the house, tell me so."

"Do you think it would be good to sell the house?"

"It's all right, if that's what you want to do."

"Well, Davey, Joe's dead, your older sister's married, you'll be moving in with somebody else before long, or tying out for Alaska. There's only me and the kid, and we don't need a house to ourselves. I guess we'll sell it. I can't see any reason not to."

"Only Eddie," Dave said. "Where would he spend his evenings?"

"Oh, I don't care where he spends his evenings. . . . Poor old Eddie. It will hit him right between the teeth, won't it? No place for a free meal; no place to find beer in the icebox. Do you know why he comes over so often?"

"Yes, he told me."

She turned red suddenly and began to laugh. "Poor old Eddie. I don't know why I should feel sorry for him. It ought to be the other way around. But things get switched backwards somehow. What did he say to you?"

"Wanted to know if I had any objections."

"If *you* had any objections? That mangy skunk. He went to you before he asked me. He's never said a word to me yet. But I know what's on his mind—it's Joe's life insurance and the house more than anything else."

"That's only part of it, Mom."

"That's a big part of it. You know how Eddie can kid himself. He can think one thing on one side of his face and something different on the other without even knowing he's doing it." She got up from the bed, straightening her hair, and waved toward the half-finished letter she had been writing. "You know who I'm writing to?"

"Who?"

"I got a cousin named Julie Tirenne up in Ludington, Michigan. That's who." With a triumphant air she shook the letter as if she were daring him to stop her sending it.

"That's all right with me," Dave said. "But what for?"

"Didn't you know I lived in Ludington when I was a kid? Didn't

I ever tell you about that? Back before my mother came here to run that boardinghouse on Halsted Street. Listen, Davey. The kid and I are going back to Ludington after we sell the house." She giggled at the surprised look on his face. "That's what we're going to do; I made up my mind last night. And anybody that wants to see us will have to come to Ludington because we're not coming back here any more."

Still laughing and glancing back at him defiantly, she went into the kitchen to get supper ready.

Dave's ten-year-old sister Sally came home from one of the neighbor's back yards and called for him to pull her rubbers off. She clung to the kitchen table, lifting her feet one at a time while Dave tugged at the muddy rubbers. The shoes came off along with them, and in her stocking feet Sally hopped around the kitchen until Dave grabbed her, sat her in a chair, and laced the shoes back on again. As she wiggled her legs to provoke him, she asked questions in a steady stream, "What's for supper, Mom? What's for dessert? Why doesn't Dave take me to a movie on Saturday? Is my face clean enough to eat supper in, or do I got to wash?"

"Quit asking those questions," Ann Spaas said, "or there won't be any dessert. I'll tell you something if you want to know. You and me are going to Ludington, Michigan."

"We are, Mom? To live? Did you decide for sure?" Dave saw the look of wonder and delight on the little girl's face. He knew she had never been to Ludington, and for a moment could not understand why she seemed so happy to be going. As he looked across at her again, he found her regarding him solemnly. "You're *not* going to Ludington," she told him. "Mom said so."

"No, but I'll come up and see you. What makes you think you'll like Ludington? You never been there?"

"I'll like it. It's different from Chicago."

"Don't you like Chicago?"

"No, I *hate* Chicago."

He started to laugh, but stopped abruptly. Sally could only be telling him what Ann had told her. He had never heard his mother talk much about Ludington. As he watched her working over the stove, he wondered why she had suddenly set so much store by the place.

Supper was ready. Steam from the pots boiling on the stove frosted over the windows. Ann Spaas dished up the food.

"Listen, you two," she told them as she pulled her chair to the table. "If Eddie comes over tonight—"

"Don't worry, he'll be over."

"I said *if* he comes, I don't want you to tell him about the house or about Ludington."

"Why not, Mom?" Sally asked.

"Just because I don't, that's all. Now you pay attention to that, Sally."

Eddie did come over, about the time Ann was pouring coffee for herself and Dave, and along with Eddie was Uncle Jennison. Dave brought in chairs while Ann set two extra cups on the table. As Eddie instead of sitting down strayed over toward the icebox, she called to him, "Where you going, Eddie?"

"Just taking a look—"

"What do you want in that icebox?"

"Thought there might be a bottle of beer there."

"There isn't. Dave drank the last one this morning."

"But there was a couple of quarts, Ann."

"You keep out of the icebox, Eddie. If you want beer, you run down to the corner and buy it."

Eddie returned gloomily to the table. Uncle Jennison was making some remarks to Ann Spaas about how happy she must feel to have her boy home again. Dave waited, smiling, until the formalities had run their course, and Uncle Jennison turned towards him asking, "Well, my lad, how do you like that depot job?"

"Not a bad job," Dave said.

"Not bad at all, I remember I held that job five years in a stretch. And Red's a fine man to work with; a square guy Red is, a square guy."

There was something out of style about Uncle Jennison tonight, Dave thought. He sounded like an Irish politician. "What's wrong with you?" he asked.

"I came to talk to you about the Lodge, Dave. I guess you got no hard feelings from the meeting the other night?"

"Why should I?"

"Things got a little bit hot that night. Maybe we both said some things we'd been better off not to—"

"I'm not holding any grudges, Unc. I hope you aren't."

"I been chairman of that Lodge a long time, boy. I know everybody in it, the oldtimers and the young stiffs. A good bunch of men, Dave, but once in a while they get excited and decide something in a rush—"

Dave could see Eddie stirring uneasily in his place. Ann Spaas got up and began clearing away the dishes, while the little girl Sally wandered around the kitchen, picking up one thing and then another. After circling the table several times, she climbed suddenly up the back of Eddie's chair, grabbed hold of his collar and chanted into his ear,

"I know something you don't know, I know something you don't—"

"Sally!" Ann Spaas caught her by the wrist, led her out of the kitchen and upstairs.

"Regular little devil, ain't she?" Uncle Jennison said.

Dave refilled the coffee cups. "So you think the boys made a mistake, Unc?"

"I damn sure do. It was bum union policy."

"The guys downtown don't like it either, do they? I bet the vice-president's office put the heat on you, Unc."

"They didn't like it, that's a fact. And I told them I'd been against it from the start."

"But did you stand up for us, Unc?" Dave asked. "Did you tell them some of our guys had relatives and friends working in that Can Company for thirty-five cents an hour, and if we got a chance to help 'em out, we were glad to do it?"

"They know all about that. If it was a question of wages only—"

"You mean they're scared of the CIO?"

Uncle Jennison's face turned red and he leaned forward over the table. "We'll not be scared by any CIO."

"Talk English, Unc. You know what I mean."

"Are you off your noggin, boy?" Jennison shouted. "Do you want the CIO coming in here organizing the niggers and Mexican gandy dancers to take our jobs away from us? Do you want to see every shop in the industry split wide open by a jurisdictional fight?" He dropped back into his chair. "Hell, I didn't mean to start shouting; I forgot the kid up there. But when our own Lodge votes to join a CIO picket line, we might sooner send them an engraved invitation."

"You counted the hands in the Lodge meeting, Unc. The members want to go over there and help out in that can strike."

"I know what happened, boy. You and Red Brogan packed the

156

meeting with these young stiffs that hadn't never seen fit to attend a meeting before in their lives."

Dave turned to Eddie. "And what do *you* think about it?"

"I don't think we want the CIO in the railroad, Dave. It's maybe all right for some of these other industries—"

"Maybe yes, maybe no, you mean. Here's the old IWW boys speaking. Bill Haywood would roll over in his grave. Well, I tell you something: I don't want the CIO in the railroad either. The CIO's supposed to be organizing the unorganized, and we're *supposed* to be organized already."

"That's just what I was trying to tell you, boy. What are you shooting up all this stink for?"

"Let me finish, will you? Why do you think the guys are talking about the CIO, Unc? It's not because they'd rather have the CIO than the independent union we already got. But they see the CIO out fighting for wage boosts and vacations with pay and the forty-hour week. And they want to know what the hell are our own officials down in the vice-president's office doing all this time?"

"They haven't let any grass grow under their feet."

Dave began to laugh. Eddie was loading his corncob pipe, and Uncle Jennison sat tapping his fingers on the table. He opened his mouth as if to say something, then glanced from Dave to Eddie and pushed himself up from his chair. As Dave helped him into his overcoat, he said in a low voice, "Step outside for a minute with me"; and he called to Eddie, "Good night, you old son of a bitch."

Outside, they walked toward the trolley stop at the corner. The ice-covered pavement made a metallic ring under their heels and the wind hummed over the roofs of the houses. "I didn't want to talk any more inside, my boy. That thimble-brained uncle of yours sometimes gets careless what he repeats."

"What's the story, Unc?"

"I agreed with most of that stuff you said just now. But God damn it, this CIO picket line is bad business. It's going to make us a lot of trouble; you could see that if you'd only get your head cut in. I figured some of the boys have thought it over since last week, and we maybe better have it up again at the Sunday meeting."

"Bring it up, Unc. You're chairman. We'll fight it out again."

"That's just it. I don't want any more fights on it."

"What *do* you want?"

157

"They don't need us in that can factory. It's only going to make a big smell over nothing. If I had a chance to talk quiet and easy with the boys they'd see that too, and we wouldn't need any fights over it. What do you want to do, boy, tear the Lodge apart?" He hesitated, then said quickly, "Suppose you and Red just happened to miss a Lodge meeting, hey?"

"How much are you paying, Unc?"

"I'm not paying a damn cent, if you want to be funny. I'm asking you to consider the interest of the Lodge you're a member of."

Dave shook his head. "I'm not missing any Lodge meetings. But talk to Red, maybe he'll feel different about it."

"I was figuring to ask you to talk to Red," Uncle Jennison said gloomily.

"Don't worry. I'll talk to him."

"Thanks, boy. You're doing me a big favor by this. I'll remember it." He did not sound angry now, but his voice had lost its ring; it sounded old and tired.

"What did you expect me to do?" Dave asked.

"I might have known I'd be wasting my breath. Now you'll think I'm against you and you'll be laying for me at every Lodge meeting." He walked along shaking his head. "I thought when you came back, you was going to work with me, boy, and things would go easier in the Lodge, and I was glad to see you. I know what makes you act the way you do, and I say goddamn the whole bunch of you. I was giving my pay for Sacco and Vanzetti when you weren't born yet, and Tom Mooney before you ever heard of a union—"

They were close to the corner. In the glow from the streetlamp, Dave could see Uncle Jennison's face working as he chewed at his lips. "Aw, listen," Dave said. "You're a good guy, Unc. Why do you let these old women in the vice-president's office kick you around?"

"I don't let anybody kick me around. If I thought they were wrong, I'd not be listening to them."

"Listen to the men on the job. Those are the guys to listen to."

They waited at the corner, taking shelter from the wind in the doorway of the corner drugstore. "You keep talking about how everything's slow in the railroads, Unc; but the guys are ready to move now, and you're acting like you were afraid of it. I tell you, the vice-president's office won't be able to stop them. Think what our Lodge could do. We could be a fighting Lodge—"

Uncle Jennison gave him a strange look, but turned away without answering. When his streetcar came in sight, he dropped his hand on Dave's shoulder for a moment; then walked out to the car stop.

1940

SIX months, Eddie thought, as he sat at the kitchen table after the other two had gone out; six months was long enough. Joe Spaas had been dead six months, and now every time Eddie came over, he kept hoping Ann might say something to him, because he could not work out how to say it for himself. He knew sooner or later she would say something if he waited long enough. For since Joe's death, it had seemed to Eddie that Ann Spaas was glad to see him whenever he came to the house. At first, he remembered, she had been very quiet; she would sit whole evenings without talking, as if she were figuring in her mind. Then she began to giggle and joke like a young girl, and Eddie thought she was trying to push out of her memory the years in between. She had made him bring his guitar, and he plucked it with one hand while they sat in the kitchen drinking beer and remembering the old songs. But she never said anything special to him and whenever he headed in that direction, she began to laugh at him. Eddie wondered how the kid Dave felt about his coming over all the time. The kid seemed different now; they could not talk together the way they had once talked. When the kid was around, Eddie grew jittery and uneasy as if he felt he'd done something wrong and couldn't figure out what. He had thought it might be his coming to call on Ann, although she acted just as pleased to see him after the kid came home as she had before. Eddie finally made up his mind to talk to the kid about it, but Dave had only grinned and said it was all right with him if it was all right with Ann.

Upstairs now, Eddie could hear Ann Spaas moving back and forth, and the piping voice of the little girl. At last Ann called good night; then a door closed, and he heard her feet creaking down the stairs. She came into the kitchen and sat down.

"All right, Eddie," she told him. "Get the beer out."

"I thought there wasn't any?"

"There wasn't enough to take care of the whole railroad. I don't run a saloon in here." Eddie found the quart bottle in the icebox as he remembered it from the night before. Ann seemed in a queer mood. She peered at him, then turned away giggling as if there were something funny about the way he looked. She asked him questions and laughed at the answers he gave.

"What's the matter with you, Eddie?" she said. "You're acting like you were touched in the head tonight."

"It's not me, Ann. It's you is acting funny."

"Not him, he says." She leaned towards him across the table, tapping her forehead. "Are you all right upstairs, Eddie?" Then, shrieking with laughter, she pressed her hands over her face.

The kid came back, glanced in at them from the kitchen doorway, said he had some work to do, and went upstairs. "Save a glass of that beer for me, Eddie," he called from the top of the flight.

Ann had stopped laughing now and her face turned serious. "Eddie," she said softly, "I've something to tell you."

He stiffened and set his glass down.

"The neighbors have been talking, Eddie. I heard some of them in at the butcher store today. They're saying, what does that fellow come over all the time to see Ann Spaas for? You don't suppose, do you . . . ?" Eddie looked into her face to see if she were going to laugh at him again. "Of course I don't care what the neighbors say," Ann told him. "I guess I've got the right to see anybody I want, haven't I?"

Eddie felt frightened. He knew she was not telling him about the neighbors because she cared anything for the neighbors. He kept glancing down at the corners of the table. His fingers turned cold and he gripped the bottom of his chair. Now he had to say something to her; she was sitting silent, watching him.

"Ann." He stopped, cleared his throat, and looked away from her. "Ann, we've known each other a lot of years. Here we are now. Why don't we get together?"

"What do you mean, Eddie?"

"You know what I mean. Don't go and laugh at me, Ann. Why don't you and me get married? What's to stop us, anyhow?"

She did not speak for a long time. Her eyes closed and her face looked older and more lined than he had ever seen it; but she did not laugh. "Oh no, Eddie," she said at last. "You should have thought of that a long time ago. Joe's insurance isn't worth that much, anyway."

He pushed himself up from the table. "You don't mean that, Ann. It's not the insurance—"

"No? Well, it doesn't matter. I wouldn't care if it was the insurance." She opened her eyes, looked at him for a moment, and closed them again. "I'm going away. I'm going to sell the house. Sally and I are going to Ludington and we're not coming back."

His eyes fixed on the top of her head, on the white line through the center part of the hair, Eddie leaned heavily on the table. He was not quite sure what she had said to him; he wanted to ask her, but she did not look up again or speak to him. Putting on his jacket, he sidled out of the kitchen, expecting her to call him back, which she did not do. He met the kid coming down the stairs into the parlor. Eddie was afraid the kid would laugh at him, and he kept his eyes on the floor so as not to see the kid's face. "She turned me down, Davey." Then he almost shouted, "Tell her it wasn't the insurance, Davey. Jesus Christ, I know I thought of the insurance sometimes, but it wasn't that."

Eddie left the house and rode the streetcar back to West Madison. He thought it was late at night, but when he climbed down from the car at the crowded intersection the clock in the cigar store said only ten o'clock. If he went right away to Uncle Jennison's, he would find the old men still hanging around the Workingmen's Forum. Better get a drink, he said to himself, better look for a little drink. He joined the crowd that drifted west on Madison Street, past the taverns and ten-cent hotels.

In one of the taverns, he bought himself a shot of whiskey with a beer chaser and dropped down at a table. At other tables men were sleeping with their heads on their hands. A few men stood along the bar and two oldish women moved back and forth bumming drinks. The blare of the juke box drowned all other sounds. Eddie stared down at the small glass in his hand. He felt as if part of his life was ended, and now he had to start all over again. It was far and cold to the west, a long time since he had headed that direction, the tracks reaching out over the prairie, the wind humming through the telegraph wires—

He heard a thud and a shrill squeal of laughter. One of the women had fallen from her stool at the bar, and struggled drunkenly on the floor trying to roll over to her hands and knees. No one moved to help her. Her skirt slid up above her thighs while the men stared down at her open legs. The bartender leaned across the bar.

"Get her up on her feet," he yelled. "Get her up on her feet, or I got to throw her out."

One of the men took the woman under the arms and dragged her to a table, where she sat with her eyes open and her head rocking from side to side.

12

ROMAN KOVIAK parked his Chevrolet several blocks from the hall. Stiff-legged, the five men scrambled out to the sidewalk. The night was bitter cold with no sign yet of daybreak. Overhead were the clear, countless stars, and into the sky fingers of silver light pulsed up out of the north. Dave and Pledger dragged the signs from the back seat, and the five men set off with their heels clacking on the sidewalk like a small parade down the empty street. The rows of workers' houses stretched ahead of them, fragile and tiny under the glow of the stars.

On the corner, two cops who had been dancing and clapping their hands against the cold, now waited hostilely with arms folded. The five turned the corner, laughing, and headed north. Before them over the roofs of the houses, Dave saw the factory with its smokeless stacks thrusting up against the luminous sky. Police were at all the corners and there were squad cars parked in the alleys.

But at the triangular intersection where Cleveland Avenue crossed Forty-First Street, no police were in sight. Trolley cars banged through the intersection every two or three minutes and each car let down a group of men who moved towards the hall. Stewards with CIO buttons hurried the groups along, calling, "Let's get inside, brothers. Let's get inside out of the cold." The hall was an old building with a curved roof like a car barn, and the name "Zeiger Auditorium" painted across the front. Beside the doorway, Dave and Pledger McAdams and the other three waited, waving their placards to collect the rest of their people.

By half past five, some fifteen had come. The white carmen looked surprised at seeing the Negroes and stuck close together, glancing back and forth among themselves. Dave took Pledger McAdams by the arm, stepped into the center of the group, and began to talk about wages and working conditions. Pledger, in his booming voice, announced that the men in the colored coach-cleaners' lodge were ready to pitch into a fight for better conditions, just like the workers in the Can Company were now doing. Dave saw the others watch and listen; then after a few moments they, too, chimed into the conversation. Roman Koviak began talking excitedly in Polish. Red Brogan passed out handfuls of his nickel cigars. Everyone lighted up and all together they moved into the crowd around the doorway of the hall.

It was cold inside the auditorium and the men kept their hats and coats on. Cigarette smoke hung in blue clouds under the ceiling. The hall was packed and quiet; from the platform one of the union officials was speaking. Dave, making his way around the hall, found Hanson by the corner of the platform.

"How's it going, butch?"

"Look at the crowd, will you." Hanson shoved his hat to the back of his head and wiped his sweat-streaked face on his sleeve. "What a workout! I haven't slept in two nights. But look at it, Dave; it's wonderful." He flung out his arms, including all the people in the hall; then leaning close to Dave's ear, he said quickly, "They're going to try to open the plant at seven o'clock. We can't move for another half hour yet. No use telling the cops where we're going ahead of time, is there? They'll find out quick enough anyhow."

"Stool pigeons?"

Hanson shrugged his shoulders. "How can you keep 'em out, Dave? Not even the shop stewards know all their guys by sight. Couple of minutes ago I saw a guy I recognized for a company fink. I was just getting ready to bust him in the nose when I thought, take it easy Hanson; we'll catch up with those guys later on."

"It's a good crowd," Dave said.

"Good! For five-thirty in the morning, it's wonderful. I'm jumpy as a kid at my first strike. Look at those delegations, will you, Dave. And railroad workers! Whoever heard of railroad workers sending a delegation? You should have heard the boys yell when those railroad workers rolled in—" Hanson quieted suddenly and glanced at his watch. "Fifteen minutes to go. I want you up on the platform, Dave, after McAdams gets through. How did those cops look out there?"

"Cold."

"Cold, were they? I hope the bastards freeze stiff. Plenty of them, aren't there?"

"Hundreds. Look like they expected an invasion." Hanson smiled slowly, and as the two glanced at each other, they both nodded. Dave suddenly felt his heart pounding, and the blood drummed through the veins of his arms. Over the noise of the crowd, he said into Hanson's ear, "It's good. You can feel it. You can always tell." The light in Hanson's eyes met his, and he knew Hanson felt the same flood of love and hate, the same upsurging of the crowd. On the platform, Pledger McAdams was speaking. His voice rolled out, filling the hall.

"Who gains by it, brothers, who gains by it? You and me don't gain by it, nor our wives and kids don't either. But the big shots, the big mouths, the labor baiters and union busters, they keep coming back to race hatred like a dog comes back to a rotten carcass. . . ."

Dave climbed up on the platform. The crowd was shouting and clapping for Pledger McAdams, and Dave leaned on the speaker's table, looking out over the sea of faces. All across the hall were the signs and banners of the delegations: STEEL WORKERS, FARM EQUIPMENT WORKERS, AMERICAN STUDENT UNION, AUTO WORKERS, RAILROAD WORKERS, UNITED OFFICE AND PROFESSIONAL. They quieted and he felt their attention gather on him. He began to talk while his eyes moved from one face to another—an old man at the back, a woman close to him, a bunch of boys perched on a window sill— and he watched their expressions to make sure they followed him. ". . . more than wages and working conditions, we're fighting for the recognition of our unions. We're fighting for the right to organize for our own protection." As he talked he tried to hold his voice quiet. "We got a job to do today. We've got to be orderly and disciplined when we do it. The cops are out there waiting for us. They want trouble, but don't give it to them—"

Somebody yelled up from the crowd, "How about Memorial Day?"

"Those are the same cops, brother." Dave's voice rose now in spite of himself. He stepped around the speaker's table. "I know they murdered the steelworkers in South Chicago and they got medals for it. Now they're out there waiting for us. We'll catch up with them someday. But right now, we only want one thing and that's to win this strike."

Hanson jumped up to the platform with a sheet of paper in his hand, and Dave spread his arms for quiet.

"We're ready to go now, boys," Hanson said. "The executive committee's been in session all night and we doped out our moves. They'll work right if we do 'em right.

"Now listen. The company's going to open the plant at seven o'clock. The scabs are supposed to collect at the company union office on Forty-Second Street and then the cops are going to take them into the plant. Now our job is to keep the scabs away from the company union office in the first place. You understand?"

The men shouted and Hanson, holding up his hand, went on. "I'm going to divide you guys into three groups. One group goes to the company union office. Get as close as you can and make it tough for any scabs to get in. There'll be plenty cops there, but like the railroad brother just told you, don't get in trouble with those cops. That goes for all of us, all the time."

He pointed suddenly to the door at the rear of the hall. "Watch that door, you stewards back there. Don't let anybody go out till I finish talking." Two men moved in front of the door, and Hanson shouted, "Now listen, brothers, all you men from the platform to the first window are in group one. First window to the third window, group two. Third window to the back, group three. You get it? Group three raise your hands." The hands went up solid across the end of the hall. "Group three moves out first. Scatter as soon as you get outside, like you'd got tired and was going home. Then get together again three blocks west on Cleveland Avenue. Lie down on the tracks if you have to, *but stop those cars*. We don't want one single car through here until seven-thirty. After seven-thirty, come back and join the picket line. All right, brothers, get going."

The men at the back of the hall poured down the stairs, and Hanson said over his shoulder, "Go with them, will you, Dave?"

It was a few minutes after six. The chimneys and water tanks to the east sharpened into silhouette. The stars faded quickly and the windows of the old buildings along Cleveland Avenue reflected the first pale light from the sky. To the east, where the Great Midland crossed Cleveland Avenue, Dave saw an engine puff over the viaduct, and when the engine disappeared, the boxcars rolled after it endlessly. He could hear through the silence the rumble and squall of the wheels.

From different directions now the men gathered at the streetcar stop. The round yellow eye of the next approaching car looked watery in the growing daylight. As the men spread across the tracks, the motorman clanged his bell, then pulled to a stop. The car was loaded with men. In front, beside the motorman, were two policemen, and when the motorman opened the door, these jumped out bawling, "Get off the tracks. Clear the way!"

The crowd gave ground before them. But when they had advanced a short distance ahead of the streetcar, the crowd closed in behind. The two blue uniforms turned quickly and made their way back towards the car. Dave saw that they were afraid to use their clubs because of being so heavily outnumbered. At the same moment, he heard the sirens of squad cars in the distance: by this time, he thought, they must be sending reinforcements in both directions out Cleveland Avenue to break the streetcar blocks.

Dave nudged the men around him, asking, "Any of you guys got a jackknife?" One of the men pulled a jackknife from his pocket, and Dave, taking him by the elbow, drew him out of the crowd and they circled around to the rear end of the streetcar. The man, who was wearing a shop steward's button, pointed up Cleveland Avenue. A block away, Dave saw the headlight of a second car approaching. In a few minutes, he thought, there would be half a dozen cars lined up; and half a dozen loads of strikebreakers—if they let them get through. He took the jackknife from the shop steward's hand and said into his ear, "Pull the trolley rod down."

From the roof of the car, the trolley rod reached up at an angle, pressing its small wheel against the overhead wire. A control rope from the rod ran down to a coil box under the rear window. The shop steward hauled on the rope, and as the trolley rod came down from the wire, the lights went out inside the car. Dave reached up as high as he could and began sawing at the control rope. But the knife was dull and he had to chew his way through it strand by strand. He heard shouts and the sound of stamping feet; then the shop steward yelled, "Hurry up, for Christ's sake, here come the squad cars." The shop steward let go the rope and ducked sideways; at the same time, the last fiber parted, the trolley rod shot up into the air, where it flopped uselessly, with the short end of rope dangling high out of reach.

Dave dropped the knife and jumped away. A blow in the back

knocked him flat on the pavement. As he rolled over and came up on his hands and knees, he saw a pair of blue-uniformed legs above him. He dove for them, heard the club whistle over his head, and he struggled to his feet with his arms around the cop's middle. For a moment he and the cop strained against each other; the square red face, smelling of whiskey and tobacco, was three inches in front of his own. Then Dave wrenched one arm free, rolled his shoulder back, and struck. As the cop stumbled sideways, Dave broke and ran.

He ducked into the crowd that was forming again around the two streetcars which had pulled up behind the first. These were under siege now. Rocks crashed through the windows, the men inside were trying to hold the front door closed against the crowd. As Dave elbowed his way towards the car, he saw the door cave in; there was a fight on the steps and then a man with a CIO button was standing in the doorway shouting down at the men on the street, "Give way, brothers, give way. These guys are going home. Keep your mitts in your pockets."

The strikebreakers came down from the car in bunches of four and five, and followed the stewards who shepherded them through the crowd. At first the men watched in silence. Then someone began to chant, "Shame, shame, shame—" At the fringes, there were a few fist fights, and a bunch of men trailed the strikebreakers up Cleveland Avenue to make sure they did not return.

Behind the three streetcars, other cars were lining up one after another west on Cleveland Avenue. People got down to find out what the trouble was, and the tie-up grew steadily at the corner. The police moved in with their clubs to break up one group; another group gathered a few yards away.

Dave slipped out of the crowd, knowing the cop with the red face would probably be looking for him. He heard the sirens of more squad cars of reinforcements racing up Cleveland Avenue. But he noticed that no streetcars were moving from below; the boys must have done all right down there too. Through a side street, he cut east toward the factory and the embankment of the Great Midland, whistling because they had done the job well.

■ ▨

By eight o'clock, the gate of the factory had not yet opened. The picket line was a solid mass three blocks long, spilling into the side streets and alleys as far as Cleveland Avenue. Across from the plant,

167

the line moved like an endless chain, up the inside of the sidewalk and back on the outside, while the marchers waved and shouted passing each other in opposite directions. Four girls with Student Union placards marched link-armed, singing. Behind them feet began to stamp in rhythm and other voices took up the chant:

> "We shall not be moved,
> Just like a tree that's standing by the water,
> We shall not be moved—"

Dave, stepping into a doorway, waited until the railroad delegation passed. The men were swinging along arm in arm, all of them puffing cigars; Red, who still had a pocketful, slipped Dave a couple, and Pledger McAdams struck a light for him, shielding it in the palms of his big hands against the wind.

Along the street, between the factory and the picket line, squad cars cruised back and forth to keep the pickets away from the gates. But it was almost half past eight before the factory whistle blew. The cops elbowed into the crowd, breaking a passageway from the company union office, and some fifty strikebreakers hurried through. A few walked with their heads up, but most of them covered their faces with their hands while the pickets, driven back on both side by lines of police, shouted, "Scab, scab, scab!" The gates swung shut behind the strikebreakers and the picket line resumed its march. All down the line now, people laughed. Voices called out to the cops who were swinging their arms against the cold:

"How many cans they going to turn out today, copper?"

"When you're out of a job, brother, come to us."

A press car nosed its way around the corner into the crowd, and someone sang out, "Get your facts straight, boys. Five thousand loyal workers went into the plant." Some of the pickets, producing doughnuts and bottles of coffee, ate breakfast as they marched. The coffee steamed in the cold air, and the scent of it drifted back over the heads of those behind. The railroad workers began telling each other how hungry they were, and when they reached the top of the picket line, they broke up, half of them heading over to Cleveland Avenue for breakfast, while the others went on marching.

Dave stepped out of the crowd for a moment to point Roman Koviak to the nearest restaurant. As he turned back, he raised his eyes suddenly; directly in front of him was the red-faced policeman he had fought at the streetcar stop. They stared at each other, then Dave eased into his place in the picket line. But from behind, the cop caught him by the collar and dragged him into the street. Dave wrenched loose, turned, trying to duck into the crowd again. Out of the corner of his eye, he saw another cop behind him, and swung up his arm to shield himself. Light burst across his eyes. For an instant he felt as if blood were raining over his forehead while his knees buckled slowly beneath him. The pavement rolled up to meet him. Then he was being dragged by the arms, and when his head cleared, he found himself propped against a wall with the two cops standing over him. He raised his hand, moved his finger tips cautiously over his head; he could feel the goose egg and the hair around it, sticky with drops of blood.

One of the cops asked in a friendly voice, "How do you feel, bud? Can you stand up?"

Dave pushed himself to his feet. Facing him was the red-faced policeman. A fist banged against Dave's cheek, and he slumped down against the wall again. The sunlit pavement rocked itself back to an even keel; he lay still, licking the cuts on the inner side of his lips. Between the legs of the cops, he saw figures moving out in the street. People were running, and he watched the blue backs of the police and the clubs swinging up and down. The placards of the picket line swayed like corn in a summer wind. The crowd broke and scattered, leaving a few knots of struggling figures. Dave's head cleared with the anger that surged into his throat. He saw the pickets who had been clubbed sprawled across the curbs, and the winter sunlight flickering over the long empty pavements. The cops, returning from the side streets, grinned at each other and hefted their clubs. Over Dave, the policeman with the friendly voice asked again,

"How do you feel, bud? Can you stand up?"

Dave did not move, and the one with the red face said, "The bastard's faking. Stand up, will you?" Taking him under the armpits, they pulled him to his feet; Dave hung limply between them. "Where the hell's the wagon?"

"Must be busy," the first cop said, and laughed.

But now from the side streets, Dave saw the pickets coming back. Hanson was with them. One of the shop stewards carried an American flag, and the men fell in behind him two by two as if they were marching at a firemen's parade. Dave felt his heart beat solidly in his throat. He wanted to hear them singing and to call out to them, but he only groaned and shook his head drunkenly.

"Look at the bastards," the red-faced cop said. "They got an American flag."

Dave, moving his feet carefully, braced them on the pavement. He flung his arms out and spun sideways. The cops lost their hold, Dave jumped free and raced down the sidewalk under the wall of the factory. The police in the center of the street were all looking the other direction, watching the pickets with the American flag. Dave saw them turning one after another at the sound of his feet and the shouts behind him. But he reached the corner of the factory. Ahead of him, a squad car swerved across the avenue and bumped up over the sidewalk. Doubling back, he plunged into the alley that ran under the end of the factory. The shouts of the crowd faded and his footsteps rang out sharply on the concrete pavement. Blocking the end of the alley, the retaining wall and steep cinder embankment of the Great Midland reared in front of him. He went at it on the dead run, jumped, reached the ledge at the top of the concrete with his finger tips, lost his hold and fell. He crouched again and jumped. As he hung struggling for a foothold, the loose sand over the ledge slipped under his fingers and again he dropped back. His hands were bleeding; he leaned against the base of the wall gasping for breath. Behind him, he saw the cops pour into the mouth of the alley. He flattened into the corner where the wall of the factory joined the retaining wall. Between the two walls he found a crack wide enough for his fingers, braced his feet sideways against the walls, and using the crack for a handhold, inched his way up. Then he got his elbows on the ledge of the retaining wall and rolled his body over.

The corner of the factory sheltered him from the men below and he lay still for a moment to catch his breath. Then, wondering whether the cops would have reached the embankment yet, and whether the railroad dicks had heard the shouts and police whistles, he crawled up the cinder slope. Cautiously he lifted his head over the crest. The tracks stretched out wide and empty in the winter sunshine. He rose to his feet and started across at an angle towards the Great Midland coach yard. One of the commuters' specials roared down the main line in front of him, and after it passed, he saw three railroad detectives moving towards him along the siding that swung around the car corner of the can factory. Dave walked as if to meet them. He recognized one of the three—the thin, black-coated figure of the detective, Morgan. While they were still too far away to hear, Dave began shouting questions and pointing towards the factory building; to himself he kept saying half out loud, "Keep together, you damn scum. Just don't spread out—" He clenched his fists against his sides to keep from running.

The wind flicked tears out of his eyes and froze them on his cheeks. Up here, the wind swept unbroken out of the sky, rushed like a gigantic stream over the roofs of the low houses in the west. In the distance now, beyond the houses, he saw a column of smoke whipped back low by the wind; another commuters' special swung around the curve of the embankment.

He heard shouts behind him; the cops were coming up over the wall from the alley. The railroad detectives caught on at last and broke into a run, Morgan struggling in the pocket of his black overcoat to unlimber his gun. Dave swerved sideways towards the factory, and the three detectives turned with him to trap him against the wall of the building. The commuters' special was close now; its whistle wailed shrilly, the steam and smoke streaked back over the coaches. This is it—turn now, turn! The engine thundered over the nearest viaduct. Dave pivoted and raced back across the embankment. Morgan turned also, and for a moment they ran parallel to each other; then Dave plunged across the main line so close under the wheels of the locomotive that he smelled the hot oily wind and the gas from the firebox.

He did not look back. As he reached the edge of the embankment where it dropped into the coach yard he lost his footing and shot down the slope in an avalanche of gravel and cinders. In front of him stretched a line of Pullmans and he rolled beneath them. The coach yard was crowded with the day's trains ready to go out. He counted four tracks as he crawled across them, then got to his feet, opened the door of a car, climbed inside, and ran down the aisles of the empty coaches. When he stepped out at the far end, he was directly across from the carknockers' locker room.

There was no one in the locker room. He hung his street clothes in the locker, pulled on his overalls, his grease-smeared canvas jacket, and put on his cap, covering the scar from the policeman's club. After setting out his lantern and carman's hammer on the bench, he went into the washroom to see how his face looked in the mirror. Dark purple bruises showed across his lips and cheekbones. Wiping his face on the sleeve of his jacket, he left a smear of grease across the marks.

When the railroad detective Morgan came into the locker room, Dave was sitting on the bench putting his lantern together.

"What are you doing?" Morgan asked.

"Fixing my lantern."

"What shift you work on?"

Dave looked up. "You the General Foreman now?" he asked. "Or still a gumshoe like you used to be?"

Morgan watched him for a moment in silence. When he spoke again, the tone of his voice had changed. "I asked you a civil question. What shift you work on?"

"I work on the twelve to eight. I just finished breakfast and now I'm here fixing my lantern. All right?"

"How long you been here?"

"Half an hour."

"Half an hour?" Morgan's hand moved down toward the pocket of his overcoat. "You come in just now. You come in across the tracks."

"I been here half an hour," Dave said. "And I came on the street-car." He got up from the bench, swinging the carman's hammer lightly against his thigh. "What are you trying to do, kid me?" The two stood facing each other in the empty locker room. "You trying to throw a scare into me?" Dave asked. "I work on this railroad just like you do, Morgan. This is my locker room—I belong here. There's a sign on the door says 'Carknockers' Locker Room'; it don't say 'Gumshoes' either." The shaft of the hammer was smooth and supple under his fingers. He wondered whether Morgan would reach his hand into the coat pocket. Their eyes met and he stared into the protruding blue eyes of Morgan's face. Dave dropped his eyes first. He looked down at Morgan's hands again, and Morgan, turning abruptly, walked out of the room.

After he had gone, Dave began to sweat under his armpits and across the back. The bluff had been a thin one; but for those few moments he had been ready to back it up by splitting Morgan's skull. Probably Morgan had known that too, he thought, and that was why he had not called the bluff. Dave sat down on the bench for a moment and lighted a cigarette. Then he put his hammer and lantern away, locked the locker, and went outside. Morgan was nowhere in sight, and Dave hurried down the steps of the embankment to the street. As he walked towards the Wentworth car line, he passed a couple of policemen coming up from the corner, but they did not even glance at him.

13

HALF awake, Dave pulled the blankets up over his ears and felt his toes emerge into the cold air. The strokes of a sledge hammer clanged monotonously from the back yard. He woke, sat up rubbing his eyes, stretched and yawned. Through the bedroom window he saw the gable of the house next door, blinding white with sunlight, and the black angle of shadow which slanted across the tarpaper roof behind it. A lopsided chimney thrust out of the roof, and the sunshine sparkled from frost crystals frozen like white moss over the bricks. He rolled out of bed, jumping and slapping himself against the cold. As he pulled on his clothes, he heard kids on their way home from school, shouting at each other through the alley. A dog was barking. The strokes of the sledge hammer began again, and Dave, looking down from the window, saw the old man next door out in his yard splitting up a batch of railroad ties.

Dave washed his face and went downstairs. His mother and Sally had gone out to a movie, but there was a note on the kitchen table saying they would be home by five; and out of the oven drifted the odor of roasting meat. Opening the door, he found a pan of pork chops and Spanish rice, turned the chops over, added salt and pepper, and took a bite of the rice, which burned his mouth. From under the mail slot in the front door, he picked up the paper, put on his jacket, and went outside.

The afternoon was still and cold. Smoke from the chimneys of the houses rose straight up into the blue sunlight. Dave vaulted the porch railing and ran up the street, chasing a couple of kids who were tossing a football. One of the kids threw him a pass and Dave raced to the corner as if he were making a broken-field run. From the corner, he waved the kids back and tried a drop kick; the football spiraled up end over end, but struck a branch on the way down, bounced off a porch roof, and the kids, chasing it, piled through somebody's shrubbery and disappeared around the end of a garage. Dave stepped into the corner drugstore, laughing.

The girl behind the counter served him his coffee. "What are you so happy about?" she asked.

"Just happy, that's all. It's a nice day, why shouldn't I be?"

Shrugging her shoulders, she went to wait on a couple of high-school girls at the end of the counter, and Dave, opening his newspaper, worked through it page by page while he drank his coffee. From time to him, he was half-aware of the familiar movements around him—the Negro bus boy dragging a crate of empty milk bottles out to the sidewalk; the druggist in his white jacket checking the shelves of patent medicines; the girl behind the counter who was making chocolate milkshakes, scooping up ice cream, shooting in syrup, setting the shiny chromium containers on the mixing machines which hummed like a row of small dynamos. An oldish woman leafed through the heartbreakers at the rental library; while in one of the booths, a boy and girl were slapping each other's hands and giggling as they sucked at their ice-cream sodas. Through the door to the street, the school girls and the mothers with children moved constantly in and out. Dave, who had finished the last editorial, folded the newspaper and swung around on his stool. The sounds, smells, movements of the drugstore, all so well known he had scarcely noticed them, now took on a sharpness and precision as if he had just returned. He remembered describing these things to himself on certain bitter nights when they had wished for home. Thirty-First Street and Halsted, Chicago, the United States of America; to read the newspaper over a cup of coffee in the corner drugstore: the syrupy smells, the colored globes over the soda fountain, the plate-glass windows coated with ice, the smiling cardboard faces of the Coca-Cola girls. He remembered how these things, now once again a daily matter of course, had then seemed to him a symbol of the America they had left behind—as remote and valuable as life itself.

The waitress, who was washing dishes in the sink behind the counter, glanced up at him. "What are you so happy about?" she asked again. She had red-brownish hair and a pimpled face. Around her neck, on a thin chain, she wore a crucifix which kept popping out from under her apron as she bent over. At last, straightening up angrily, she slipped the crucifix inside her sweater. Dave made a clicking sound with his tongue.

The girl glared up at him. Then she took his cup and filled

it again from the pot over the gas ring. "Say, what do you always come in just the same time every day for?"

"That's when I wake up."

"What's the matter, you work in a night club or honky-tonk or like that?"

"Railroad."

"Oh, the railroad." She nodded her head as if that explained something. "You like the coffee? I just put it on fresh."

"Tastes fine," Dave told her. "You'll make somebody a good sister."

"A good sister! I got a husband and two kids already—"

Through the side door, a deliveryman dragged a case of bread and rolls, kicked the case behind the counter, and sat down. "Service up here," he yelled. The girl winked at Dave and went to wait on the deliveryman. As she turned away, Dave followed with his eyes the up and down motion of her hips, and when she leaned sideways, the sagging curve of her breast under the sweater and apron. Not a bad deal for her husband, he thought; he buttoned his jacket and went outside.

Along the street to the house he walked whistling, his steps rang out with a sharp brittle sound, and his breath made a cloud of steam that drifted up over his head. On the porch, he stopped for a moment to look back at the street, the lights coming on in the windows, the dusk filtering down through the branches of the trees. He thought again of the girl; suddenly banged his fist against the porch railing and went into the house, rubbing his knuckles and swearing under his breath.

In the kitchen his mother and Sally bustled about getting supper on the table. When they sat down to eat, Sally counted up the number of days before they would be eating in Ludington; she brought a pencil and paper and made Dave multiply the days into hours, minutes, and seconds. After supper, she wanted him to install electric lights in her dollhouse; it was not till she had gone to bed that he finally settled down at the kitchen table with his figures and clippings on railroad wages.

His mother was cleaning out the cupboards. She made two piles of all the material she pulled down from the shelves, one pile for rubbish, the other for packing. "What do you want with all this stuff?" she asked, bringing over to the kitchen table a drawing board, triangles, and a sheaf of drawings. She watched over his shoulder while he turned through the sheets; they were ink-drawn, neatly lettered details of machine parts and structural sections. Dave studied the last sheet for a moment, rolled them all together, and tossed them into the pile for rubbish.

"You don't want them?"

"No." He put the drawing board and triangles on the floor beside his chair.

"You aren't going to throw those away?"

"No, I'll keep them or sell them. I don't know."

"That's silly, Dave. Why did you ever take up that engineering if you don't aim to go on with it?" She glared down at him angrily. "Oh, I know, the depression come along and we didn't have no money. But you could have gone back later. Or what's to stop you going to night school now? You haven't even got a wife to take up your time."

"I learned another job," Dave told her. "And I like it better than engineering."

She started to say something, then turned abruptly, went back to the cupboard and began packing her dishes in a barrel from the butcher store. The house was quiet, but outside, Dave heard the wind rising; the branches creaked, and somewhere near by a door banged monotonously.

Towards eleven o'clock, Dave put on his jacket and slipped his bag of sandwiches into his pocket. The old thermometer which he glanced at as he crossed the porch said five below zero. He walked up the street, staring at the sky. The stars seemed to be winking on and off as the wind-driven branches lashed across them. The wind came from northwest, which meant it would be even colder before morning. At the corner, he waited for the streetcar, and behind him a few others waiting huddled out of the wind in the doorway of the drugstore. The car, when it came, was almost empty. Dave dropped into one of the seats and took out his newspaper; the bell clanged, the car swayed along the uneven tracks.

Over the top of his newspaper, he stared up suddenly at the forward window which reproduced a distorted image of the car behind him.

He swung around. Between the empty straw-backed seats, moving towards him down the aisle, he saw Stephanie Koviak. She wore a scarf tied under her chin, which outlined the triangle of her face. From under the scarf, wisps of black hair straggled across her forehead and cheekbones. She seemed to him strangely thin and small, steadying herself now against the jolting of the car. A knot of fear tightened in Dave's throat, the lights darkened before his eyes, he half rose out of his place. She sat down beside him, and without looking up, folded and unfolded her hands on her lap. She must have been waiting for him on the corner in the door of the drugstore, he thought. Her face was white and her lips cracked and swollen from the cold. Though he watched her, she would not raise her eyes, and he understood she was like a little girl who has returned home, yet sits stubbornly outside on the steps, waiting till she should be invited to come in. Not until he touched his hand against hers, did she look up at him. They leaned close together staring into each other's eyes. She got down from the car with him, and they walked together towards the coach yard.

"Well," she asked, "do you want me back?"

"I want you, Stephanie. Do you want to come?"

She nodded her head, and they stopped under the shadow of the embankment. "Where are you staying?" he said.

"Nowhere particular."

"Do you remember our hotel, Stephanie? Will you go there and get a room? I'll come in the morning."

"All right." She caught him suddenly by the collar of his jacket. "I don't know whether I love you or hate you, Dave. But half of me is inside you; that's why I came back."

He pulled her against him and pressed his mouth against hers; but after a moment she broke away and hurried up the street.

That night on the job they found a lot of broken steam lines, exploded by the ice inside them. Red swore steadily at the cold as they worked, but Dave did not notice it much. He felt himself sweating inside his jacket; his legs ached and sometimes the blood pounded in his forehead. When he pulled off his gloves to pick up a bolt or small tool, he saw his hands shaking.

"What's the matter with you?" Red asked. "You must have had a stiff one."

Dave shook his head and grinned, but did not answer. He threw his sandwiches away and at supper hour only drank a couple of cups of coffee.

The suburban trains began rolling into the depot while it was yet dark. Dave and Red worked up and down the lines of coaches, checking the wheels and brakeshoes. At last, in the high arch of the train shed, the electric lights faded to rusty orange; out the open end of the shed, Dave saw the darkness disintegrate, the freight houses, the square bulk of the power house across the river, the skeleton framework of the Andrews Street Bridge take shape in the gray light. The last half hour before seven o'clock was longer than all the rest of the night. Yet when he had finished, caught a switch engine back to the coach yard, and hurried into the locker room, Dave did not change his clothes at once. He sat down on the bench, lit a cigarette and then another one, while he stared vacantly at his hands. Then he pushed himself up, took off his overalls, put on his jacket and hat.

The Halsted car carried him to Sixty-Third Street; then he transferred and rode east to the end of the line, where he dropped off by the lakeshore park at the edge of the city. The sun had risen high enough now to gild the top branches of the trees, and their swaying shadows appeared in the light that flooded the fronts of the buildings along Stony Island Avenue. The blaze of light gave a false appearance of warmth, but the wind, cold as ever, wailed out of the ice-blue sky. Men at the car stop huddled into their jackets and coats—the South Chicago steelworkers on their way home after the night shift. Dave elbowed through the crowd and walked down Stony Island Avenue towards the hotel.

After the glare of the street, the narrow lobby of the hotel seemed to him dark as a basement. He blinked and rubbed his eyes until he made out a desk where an old man wearing a green eyeshade watched him between the bars of a wooden cage. The old man ran his finger down the columns of a ledger book looking for the number of the room in which Mrs. David Spaas had registered; then he crawled through a trap door in his cage and hobbled over to the elevator. They rode to the third floor, where the elevator jerked to a halt half a foot below the landing. Down the long corridor, Dave made his way from one door to another, peering at the numbers in the faint glow of the bulbs overhead. A strong odor from the toilet drifted through the hallway along with the smells of wet plaster and musty linen. He found the number he was looking for, glanced over his shoulder at the old man in the green eyeshade who was still watching from the gate of the elevator. Then he tapped on the panel, stepped inside, and closed the door behind him.

Stephanie sat up in bed, holding the covers to her shoulder. Her hair seemed very black against her white skin and the white sheets. She was biting her lower lip, holding her lip between her

178

teeth, and her eyes followed him in every move as he kicked off his shoes and hung up his jacket and hat. Then she threw the covers aside and stretched up her arms to him. Supple and warm, he felt her body lock against his, her sharp fingers fasten into his thighs.

Against his ear, she was saying, "Oh Davey, Davey, Davey . . ."

Part Five

RICHMOND COURT

1940

TWO weeks after the mass picket line in front of the can factory, Hanson and a committee of CIO members visited the meeting of the coach-cleaners' lodge in Andrew Masters' chapel. They thanked the railroad workers for their support in the strike, and Hanson announced that the union had reached an agreement and the men had all gone back to work. Afterwards, Hanson told Pledger that they had not won a complete victory by a long shot; but the company had agreed to bargain with the union, which was one of the main points they had been fighting for. "You never win the whole pot on a single draw," Hanson said. "We got one foot in the door this time. Next time we'll shove the other foot in. You guys helped out."

Pledger grinned and shook his head. "We didn't go in there to help you, Hanson. We got a door of our own we're trying to squeeze a foot into."

"Well, maybe you inched that door open a crack, Pledger. I was over to the white carmen's meeting the other night with Dave. I thanked them for their support and got a big hand. A big hand."

The can company reopened its factory, and the men in the coach yard heard again the familiar clatter of the machinery from across the tracks. At first there was a certain amount of talk about the strike; then this died down and the men seemed to forget all about it. But Pledger was not surprised one day at work when Uncle Jennison came to see him accompanied by a gray-headed gentleman in a tweed overcoat whom Jennison introduced as Vice-President Donohue of the Carbuilders' Union of North America. Jennison seemed uneasy and left most of the conversation to the nimble tongue of the vice-president, who told Pledger that the Carbuilders' Union was starting a campaign to drive race prejudice out of the industry. In order to lead off on the right foot in

Chicago, the union had decided to offer a charter to the men in the Independent Railway Lodge—the colored coach-cleaners' lodge. "With no strings attached," the vice-president repeated. "How does that strike you, Brother McAdams?"

Pledger turned away for a moment to keep from smiling. He knew it was the appearance of the white carbuilders' delegation in the CIO picket line that had brought him this visit. The boys downtown were getting frightened. "Let's talk right out in the open," he said, "and I think we get along better, Mr. Vice-President. Some of us Negroes used to work as carmen and some of us been working as coach cleaners fifteen, twenty years without ever a chance at a promotion—"

"I know that, Brother McAdams. That's what we're out to change."

"Now the white union, like Chairman Jennison here can tell you, never did much to help us out. Fact is, it got its own members boosted right into the jobs we should have had by seniority and experience. Why, I believe I could point out to you half a dozen men around here that I myself taught all they know about carman's work—and then seen those men get promoted over my head—"

"We couldn't help it," Uncle Jennison said. "You weren't members."

"I guess I only tried to join about fifty times, didn't I, Chairman Jennison?"

"It wasn't in the union constitution."

The vice-president interrupted in his soothing voice to explain that the last convention of the Carbuilders' Union had amended the constitution, enabling brothers to join regardless of what might be the color of their skin. "Times are changing, Brother McAdams. We know that. Now haven't we all of us made mistakes in the past? But let's let bygones be bygones and consider this offer in the spirit it was made in."

"Why don't you give the Negroes an invite into the Carbuilders' Lodge that's already established in this yard?" Pledger asked. "What's the idea of the new charter?"

"We felt your men would prefer to have their own organization," the vice-president said. "Autonomous, but affiliated as it were."

Pledger stared at him for a moment, then glanced at Uncle Jennison. "I guess you better let me see that amendment you were talking about." The vice-president, after ransacking his brief case, finally found a copy of the union constitution, and as he gave it to Pledger said, "That's the only one I got. I'd like it back."

Pledger slipped the copy into his shirt pocket. "That's all right. You'll be able to get another one easier than me." He buttoned the straps of his overalls and they walked out to the yard together. The starting whistle had not yet blown for the afternoon shift; Pledger listened a few moments longer to the vice-president, who had begun talking about how necessary it was to go slow at the start and how it wasn't right sense to crack eggs with a sledge hammer.

At lunch hour, Pledger carried his sandwiches across the yard to the roundhouse and settled down to eat them in the warm little room behind the boiler. When he opened the carbuilders' constitution, he understood what the vice-president had on his mind about not cracking eggs with a sledge hammer. He read the amendment over to himself.

Auxiliary Lodges

Whenever non-white Coach Cleaners, Helpers, or Carbuilders are employed in sufficient numbers in any yard or shop, they shall form an Auxiliary Lodge. Members of Auxiliary Lodges shall be deemed full and equal members of the Carbuilders' Union of North America. They shall be represented in district and national conventions through the delegates elected by the nearest regular Lodge and they shall be represented in all disputes with the employer by the Grievance Committee Chairman of the nearest regular Lodge.

Finishing his lunch slowly, Pledger sat staring at the dusty brick floor of the boiler room. "Auxiliary Lodge" could mean nothing other than Jim Crow lodge. The amendment gave them no rights in the union, except apparently the right to pay dues. They could not vote for delegates to the union conventions; they could not even vote for their own grievance committee to represent them before the company. Who would represent them? The chairman of the nearest "regular" lodge—the nearest white lodge, in other words. That meant they would have Jennison to represent them. And if Jennison did not feel like defending the seniority of the Negroes, they would be as bad off with the charter as they had ever been without it.

Then what was the next move, he wondered—take it or turn it down? It would be easy to tear up the charter and laugh in their faces. Maybe that was the only way to do with a Jim Crow charter.

185

He knew his own men would be angry and hurt; but some of them would want to take the charter because they had been fighting twenty years for membership in the Carbuilders' Union. And because he was chairman of the Negroes' Independent Lodge, they would listen twice to what he said; maybe they would agree with him and maybe they wouldn't.

But he had to have a position to recommend them, and he had to have the right position, because he was a Communist and they all knew it. Certainly the big boys downtown had offered the charter because they were frightened, and so there must be something in it worth having. But at the same time they must be figuring the charter would pry the Negroes loose from the rank and file discontent in the white unions, and so there was something in it to watch out for also. But the only real question was, where could they fight better? From an independent lodge outside, or from a Jim Crow lodge inside?

Pledger finished his lunch and went back to work. He talked it over with the coach cleaners on the evening shift, and when he went home, he argued it back and forth in his own mind until he fell asleep. In the morning, he telephoned Jackson at the office on State Street to call an emergency meeting of the railroad branch.

The men met at noontime, Pledger and four other Negroes from the coach yard and roundhouse; a couple of Pullman porters just off the streamliner from the South; a white switchman and a retired engineer; and Dave Spaas from the Carbuilders' Lodge, bringing Red Brogan along as a visitor. As soon as Pledger led off the discussion with, "Well, comrades . . ." Red interrupted him.

"How many times I got to tell you, McAdams, I ain't no comrade?"

Grinning, Pledger began over again, adding the words: ". . . and visitor." He told them about the offer of the charter, and then sat back listening to the others talk. Red said the Negroes ought to join the CIO and let the Carbuilders' Lodge go to hell. One of the Negro coach cleaners wanted to remain independent; Dave and the two Pullman porters favored accepting the charter.

At last, as the discussion died down, Pledger broke in. "Let me tell you the ideas I figured in my mind listening to you people talk. I come to think now we should take the charter. We should take it and turn in our bids for promotions just like our seniority entitles us to. That'll put it square up to Jennison—is he going to defend our seniority rights, or is he going to welch on his promise?"

"You know how the white Lodge stands?" Dave asked.

"How do you mean?"

"Let's not kid ourselves. If I was to go to the next meeting and ask the Lodge to support promotions for Negroes, I wouldn't carry four votes."

Pledger nodded his head. "If you was to do that," he said, "you'd belong in the booby hatch. Like you told me once yourself, Dave, men learn from working together. We seen to do it five years ago with the unemployed councils, we can do it again. A man can't support his family on no forty-one cents an hour. That's the same for white men as it is for Negroes—except the Negroes got mostly the lowest-pay jobs. I guess we aim to be boosting for a wage movement right soon, don't we? And that's the time we'll fight for Negroes and whites to join together, just like we done in the can company strike." For a moment Pledger studied Dave Spaas' face. He knew that Dave must be thinking on the same line as himself; for it was largely through Dave that the white carmen had agreed to march in the CIO picket line; and largely through Dave that white men in the yard had already begun talking about the need for a wage increase.

"Then how about it?" he asked the others. "You agree with me? Is that how I should recommend it to my Lodge?" As he glanced from one to another, the men nodded in agreement—even Red nodded his head. "I been working with some of these fellows fifteen, twenty years," Pledger told them, "and here's something I see over and over again. Often I done a job with a man, laughing and joking while we worked, talking about our families; then fifteen minutes after we quit and he'd forgot I was around, I'd hear him shoot his mouth off to another white man about all the damn niggers in the yard. What do you make of that? I used to ask myself, are all these white men liars and hypocrites that they hate us behind our backs but they don't tell us to our faces?"

"Some of them," Dave said.

"Maybe so. But I tell you what I learned about most of them. No, they don't like Negroes; but when they come to working with one particular Negro, mostly they get along all right. Then he isn't a nigger any more, see, he's just the guy they work with. I remember once, I went after one of those fellows, I picked up a hammer and grabbed him by the strap of his overalls. 'You bastard,' I said to him, 'I don't care if you hate me, but when you laugh with me one minute and then call me a nigger behind my back, I don't know why I don't kill you.' I guess he was scared because it was a mighty big hammer. But he was ashamed too. He told me, 'I didn't mean you when I said that.' "

Laughing, Pledger took up his overcoat from the corner of the desk. "We got any more business? Move we adjourn."

They broke up the meeting, and Pledger waited while Dave Spaas locked the office. Then as they walked down the stairs to the street, he said, "Maybe my men won't go for taking a Jim Crow charter. And I wouldn't blame them. Well, I'll tell 'em from the best I can figure out, that's what I recommend."

"Don't worry, they'll see it."

He and Dave parted at the corner of State Street, Pledger going back to the Chile Parlor for some food before he started work. The settling of this problem relieved his mind, and he swung along feeling free and light-stepping. He realized suddenly that here had come a day he had waited twenty years to see. Those twenty years had given him at last a friend in the white men's Lodge he could trust as if he had been there himself. Between them now, they could do what neither one could do alone—throw their two Lodges together into the coming fight for wages. That meant they were on the road, he thought; they were on the road again. And somewhere up ahead, he saw his own men from the Lodge climbing down into those same wheel pits the last Negroes had come up from twenty years before.

Twenty years was a long time to wait—a long and bitter time to wait; but one lodge could make the key to a whole railroad, a whole city. Certainly that was worth waiting for.

14

STEPHANIE KOVIAK had wondered often at the dulling of the aspects of the world which seemed to have overtaken her. She had thought this due to some physiological change, some clouding of the senses as she grew from adolescence to maturity. For the sharp enjoyment of sunlight and sound, the movement of her own arms and legs, or the taste and smell of food, seemed to have crusted over with habit. She had regretted their loss because the world turned sullen without them.

But now to her surprise as the winter drew to an end, she felt again the stirring of something she had thought lost. She began to find pleasure in the simple processes of living. She and Dave rented the attic of a carriage house behind an empty mansion on Richmond Court. The mansion stood at the far corner of the court on the slope above the Illinois Central tracks, which here skirted the lakeshore. Every morning Dave came home from work at daybreak, and as they ate breakfast they watched the sun glowing through the spirals of mist which floated over the surface of the water. Slowly the packed ice melted from the streets, the smell of grass and wet earth met her each morning as she came from the carriage house. Sunlight was filtering through the mist, while the sharp black branches of the trees blurred under the spreading green haze of buds. Or in the evening, riding home from work, she watched the twilight darken behind the chimneys in the west. The spring took on a quality which she had thought was not part of spring, but rather part of herself as she had been five years before. When she reached the carriage house, Dave would be awake and working on the ceiling of the second room of their unfinished apartment. But she knew it was not only because of Dave that the aspects of the world she lived in seemed to have changed.

One night after he had gone to work, she crossed the footbridge over the Illinois Central tracks, and sitting on the rocks by the lakeshore, tried to figure in her mind what had happened to her. Living again with Dave, she knew, and the brightening aspects of the world, were not cause and effect; but both were symptoms of some shifting of forces within herself—some "dubious battle" in her own mind, as Martin, with his delight in paraphrasing Milton, would have told her. Towards Martin, whom she had left on the second day following his triumph at the reception for the philosopher Peyrel, she felt affection, but no regret. She had left him after battling the issue for two days in her own mind. And now she noticed with surprise how quickly the present flowed into the past, joining Richmond Court to the years when she had lived with Dave before as if there had been no gap of time between.

Stephanie lighted a cigarette. A thin haze veiled the lake. The silver moonlight poured through the emptiness of the night like a silent chiming of bells. But to the south, against the base of the sky, lay banks of artificial cloud which throbbed with the red

189

pulse of the steel mills. She pushed herself up at last, crossed the bridge again over the railroad. The footbridge led up at an angle to the crest of the embankment overhanging the tracks. An iron fence rimmed the embankment, and beyond stretched the weedy expanse of Richmond Court, surrounded on three sides by buildings whose windows stared back vacantly across the tracks of the Illinois Central, over the strip of park, out to the lake under the moonlight. Richmond Court, Stephanie thought, was like an island the city had forgotten. The rumbling busses from the Greyhound Company garage, the hollow thunder of Diesel engines on the railroad, beat like surf against the silence. Factories, warehouses, breweries, car barns, pressed up to the sagging grillwork fences of Richmond Court. But inside, the weeds grew undisturbed, the soot blackened over the granite obelisk to Civil War dead, slates scaled down from the gables of the mansions, while the tenants and roomers strung their wash on lines across the front yards. Faded gentility hung in the air of Richmond Court like the decaying odor of an empty house.

Stephanie and Dave, from their windows, commanded the whole sweep of Lake Michigan; but one of their two rooms had no ceiling, and their only heat came from a potbellied coal stove. They bought lumber and paint and spent their Sundays rebuilding the attic.

Dave's mother, Ann Spaas, took a sudden interest in their house and came over sometimes to help them, or to cook dinner while they worked. She had sold her own house, cashed in on her husband's life insurance, and now was packing up to move to Ludington. Stephanie found her in a curious mood about leaving. Sometimes she giggled like a little girl, and sometimes she would stop suddenly, staring as if there were something other in front of her than the blank wall of the attic. Whenever she came to see them, she went out of her way to provoke Dave. She would ask him how he expected to support a family when he had given up his engineering course; or how he thought Stephanie would like it, after working her way through the University, now to spend her life as a carknocker's wife.

"Stephanie's a carknocker's daughter after all," Ann Spaas told him. "Do you think she wants to be a carknocker's wife too?" Dave tried to answer her seriously sometimes, but she only giggled at what he said.

On the Sunday when she left for Ludington, Ann Spaas came to spend the afternoon with them, bringing the little girl Sally. Dave, who had worked all night, was still sleeping and Stephanie took them outside so Sally would not wake him. The spring sunlight flooded over the grass; all around Richmond Court, people were reading the funny papers on their doorsteps, while from the embankment, kids were flying red kites. Stephanie and Dave's mother crossed the footbridge and sat by the lakeshore; Sally ran ahead of them, scrambling over the sunlit rocks, throwing pebbles into the water.

"Are you going to stay in Ludington?" Stephanie asked. Ann Spaas nodded, and Stephanie wondered what vision she expected to find there.

"Dave's Uncle Eddie asked to come over this afternoon," Ann said. "I told him he could come. Is that all right?"

"Of course it's all right."

Ann glanced up sharply at Stephanie. "If you don't mind my asking you a question," she said, "are you always sure that you *like* Dave?"

"Sure that I like him?"

"That's what I asked."

Stephanie puzzled over the question for a moment. "Yes, I guess so, Ann."

"I don't think I ever liked him very much," Ann said. "I think I was disappointed when he came back from Spain." Stephanie turned in surprise with the sudden feeling that the stocky, dark-haired woman beside her was some stranger she had never seen before. "I began to take to you when you left him," Ann said. "Are you sure you know what you're doing coming back? Or is it any of my business?"

"Why don't you like him?" Stephanie asked.

"I don't know for sure. Things like that are complicated, Stephanie. I can think of a million reasons for not liking him, but I don't think any of them is the real one. Don't have babies until you're sure you want them, that's all I can say to you."

"You didn't want Dave then?"

Ann Spaas laughed and shook her head. "I didn't even want his older sister Grace, for that matter. But I hadn't more than got through with the first one, when the next comes along. That was too much. I spent all my money at the drugstore trying to get rid of that kid, but none of the damn stuff worked. Then I made up my mind I'd be mean to him, but I never was. You can't be mean to a baby, even when you'd like to wring its neck."

The little girl Sally scrambled back across the rocks and squatted in front of them. "What shall I do now, Mummy?"

"Throw some pebbles in the water."

"That's what I been doing. Could I go wake Dave?"

"No, you let Dave alone." Ann took a quarter from her handbag. "Run up to the corner and get us a newspaper."

"Can I buy an ice-cream cone, Mummy?"

Ann nodded, and they watched the little girl climb the stairs of the footbridge over the railroad. In the afternoon sunlight, they watched her spry and gangly-legged shadow hop up the steps behind her. "Don't get the wrong idea," Ann said. "Dave was legitimate and all that. It wasn't for that I didn't want him."

"You were very young, weren't you?"

"Oh, I was nineteen. That's not a bad age to have kids; they come easy. But I guess the trouble was I was so crazy when I got married. I married Joe because I couldn't stand living alone, and he happened along at the right time. Or the wrong time, you might say. I suppose I knew what it was going to be like, but I kept on kidding myself. I thought I wanted the moon, and I wanted to see mountains and bananas growing on trees, and to live in hotel rooms in all different cities. So Dave's father, Joe, bought a house on the installment plan in a new subdivision and I been there ever since. Yes, ever since." Stephanie, staring across the water, saw a column of smoke smudge up over the horizon—an ore boat, most likely heading in towards South Chicago. Why is she telling me all this? Stephanie wondered. Apparently it was on purpose that Ann Spaas had come early, being lonely at leaving, or perhaps wishing to convey something to Dave at second-hand. Stephanie felt in Dave's mother a remoteness, as if one part of the woman held very little concern for what the second part might be doing. This remoteness Stephanie liked; but she realized that, being haughty and self-contained herself, she had never made much effort to know Dave's mother. Even now that Ann Spaas had for some reason decided to speak intimately, there was no intimacy between them.

"Tell me," Stephanie said at last. "Why are you going to Ludington?"

"That's the same thing Dave asked me about a hundred times. I don't know for certain, how should I know? Are you and Dave going to have any kids?"

192

"Sure we are."

Ann pushed herself to her feet and they stood at the edge of the rocks looking down into the water. From the cloudy depths, sunlight came dazzling back to the surface in long green spokes like the blades of a palm frond. "If you don't shock easy, I'll tell you something."

"I don't," Stephanie said.

"You know how I felt when Dave's father died? I felt glad. I guess he'd been a good husband to me too. But you know, it's one thing for a young kid to go traveling and all that, but for an old woman, that's a joke, isn't it? So I said to myself, I'll go back to Ludington, Michigan, where things were free and happy when I was a kid."

Turning, they climbed the steps of the footbridge. The Illinois Central tracks stretched out beneath them, sweeping in a long curve towards the towers of the Loop, far down the lakeshore. "I grew up in Ludington before I ever came to Chicago," Ann said. "Now I got nothing much else to do but go back. I always been depending on other people and they always let me down. Now I'm going to Ludington and I won't be depending on anybody but myself. I don't want to make any mistake this time."

Across the stretch of Richmond Court, they saw Sally running toward them with an ice-cream cone in one hand and a newspaper under her arm.

"And why don't you like Dave?" Stephanie asked again. "Does he take after his father?"

"No, he doesn't take after his father or me either. I don't know where he came from. I guess I feel like the chicken that laid a duck's egg. Oh, I don't really dislike him, Stephanie. But I always fancied people that were a little bit screwy and wild, maybe because I feel that way myself sometimes. Eddie was screwy and wild like that when he was a young fellow; but Dave's father was always stiff and dull as an old broom handle. Now Dave, he does some of the screwiest things in the world, but he does them all so hard and sensible I always get mad at him."

They both laughed. Sally came up to them, and they followed the weed-grown drive to the rear of the mansion, where Dave and Eddie were sitting on the doorstep in front of the carriage house. Dave was drinking a cup of coffee while Eddie plucked at the strings of his guitar.

"He's awake," Sally cried. "Oh Eddie, you woke him up!"

193

Dave, leaning forward, took a bite from the little girl's ice-cream cone. Then he put on his shirt which had been lying on the door-step, and he and Sally and Eddie set off to get some beer from the saloon at the corner. Stephanie and Ann, climbing up to the attic, started cooking dinner. Dave brought back lemon pop for Sally and beer for the rest of them. On the sill of the open window, Eddie settled down with his guitar and began singing. To Stephanie, who had never heard Eddie sing before, his voice sounded shrill and tuneless; yet the songs brought a tightening of her throat and she stopped beside him to listen. The bald-headed little man plucking at his guitar, the reedy sound of his voice, filled her with a heavy consciousness of the passage of years. Stephanie lost track of the dinner, and Ann Spaas did most of the cooking.

Ann had turned gay and noisy. Now, beating a spoon against a frying pan, she kept time for Eddie and repeated after him in a deep voice the last line of each verse. When they had finished dinner they went outside, taking the beer and the guitar with them, and lay on the grass between the carriage house and the edge of the embankment. The young leaves of the bushes danced in the spring sunlight, and across the railroad tracks, beyond the strip of park, the lake sparkled silver and blue under the blue sky. Ann Spaas was joking with Eddie about all the women he must have tagging after him on West Madison Street. Then she asked softly,

"You remember the carnival we went to, Eddie? It was a day like this. We rode on the ferris wheel, and we could see over the tops of all the houses. Remember?" Stephanie noticed the tone of cruelty under the melancholy of Ann's voice; but when she glanced at Eddie, she saw that he had drunk too much beer to be paying any heed to what Ann Spaas said. The strings of the guitar chirped, and Eddie sang shrilly,

> "And the starvation army they play,
> And they sing and they clap and they pray.
> Till they get all your coin on the drum."

Beyond the corner of the mansion, Sally was trying to borrow a ride on a little boy's velocipede. The little boy shoved her away, Sally grabbed for his hair, and the two of them rolled over and over in the weeds.

194

That evening, they rode downtown to the Pere Marquette railroad station. Sally, who had been half asleep with her head on Eddie's lap, woke up and began chanting, "I'm going to Ludington, but Dave can't go, Dave can't go."

Ann had already checked her luggage. They walked through the station and stood together on the platform waiting till the train should be ready to leave. Stephanie shifted her feet uneasily; in the last few moments, no one knew what to say; they kept glancing back at the station clock, then peering up towards the engine. Eddie repeated three or four times, "You'll soon be wishing you was back in Chicago." Ann stared past him, smiling faintly, while the little girl Sally hung against her knees, wailing, "Why don't the train start, Mummy?"

At last air hissed under the cars, the conductor shouted "All aboard!" Dave boosted Sally into the coach and Ann stepped after her. For a moment Stephanie saw the little girl's face at one of the windows, with her nose flattened against the glass like a lump of white putty. Then the train rolled out from between the platforms, the red lights dwindled into the darkness beyond the train shed.

Stephanie, Eddie, and Dave returned through the station. As they reached the front entrance Eddie, without a word to them, set off by himself, heading with his long, bow-legged stride in the direction of West Madison Street.

"Poor old Eddie," Dave said. Stephanie shook her head, puzzled and tired. Dave had forty minutes yet before he was due at work, and they walked together from the Pere Marquette station to the station of the Great Midland, where they stopped for a cup of coffee at the lunch counter in the waiting room.

When they finished, Dave kissed her good night, crossed the waiting room, and disappeared through the gate to the tracks. Stephanie remained for a moment looking around the empty station. Under the arch that loomed over the gates to the train shed, she watched the red neon sign blink on and off: CHICAGO GREAT MIDLAND RAILROAD—FAST COURTEOUS SERVICE.

She thought again of Ann Spaas who wanted to see palm trees and live in the hotel rooms of strange cities. SOUTH—SOUTHWEST—WEST the sign blinked; but Ann Spaas had stayed in the subdivision east of Cleveland Avenue.

15

At quarter past eight, Stephanie gulped down the last swallow of coffee, kissed her husband good bye, ran downstairs and across Richmond Court to Lake Park Avenue. Having timed the streetcar schedule to the final minute, she reached the car stop approximately four paces ahead of the streetcar; by a quarter of nine she was opening her laboratory with time enough to glance through her lecture notes and set out on the table the equipment she would need for the demonstration. A few students drifted in, settling in the corners, where some began to study while others opened their newspapers. Stephanie skimmed over her notes, then pulled down from the roller on the blackboard the bloody figure of Mr. Gallagher, the anatomy chart, disemboweled to expose the mysteries of the circulatory system.

"Charming," said a voice behind her. She glanced around and found Martin sitting on the corner of the laboratory table. "Can you spare a minute?" he asked.

"Sure, if you can spare a cigarette." They stepped outside to the concrete stair well, and she said, "What's on your mind, Martin?" She knew he had come purposely at ten minutes before her morning lecture so their session would be short. He was watching her in silence, tapping his fingers together.

"I feel unsettled in my mind about you," he told her after a moment. "I don't like that. We keep meeting around campus; it seems silly to be nonchalant, yet I don't know what else to do."

"Do you feel angry towards me?" Stephanie asked.

"No, I guess not. You're taking your Master's degree, aren't you? Is your husband coming to convocation?"

"I think so."

"Maybe I'll come too. I'd like to see him. Unless you'll invite me over to dinner sometime?"

She shook her head.

"How does your husband feel towards me? Not too friendly, I suppose?"

"I don't know. He's never asked anything about you."

Martin made a half-humorous grimace. "Perhaps he thinks of me not as an individual, but as an embodiment of some trend of economic corruption." Stephanie did not answer, and Martin nodded. "I know, that's the kind of stuff I shouldn't say. But to be frank—" He made a gesture of twisting something between his hands. "Aren't you tired yet, Stephanie? I'm tired—"

"Let's not go through that again," she said.

His expression changed and he glanced down quickly at the toes of his shoes. "No, by all means, let's not. I didn't enjoy that session any more than you— I've been trying to say something to you, but I don't seem to know how to express myself any more. That other time I got angry, and that wasn't what I meant. This time I suppose I sound very flippant to you; but that's not what I mean either." Raising his eyes, he looked directly at her. "Well, what I wanted to say was that I liked things better the way they were before. I wish you'd change your mind—"

She shook her head again without speaking.

"Anyway, I owe you congratulations on your degree. I know how hard you worked for it."

"Thanks, Martin."

"The things I said that day—" He stopped and watched her, smiling.

"What about them?" she asked.

"Do you think they were true?"

"They were shrewd comments. Some of them were true. But not all, I don't believe."

"I was going to say to you that I didn't mean them, but that's not strictly true either; I did mean them. I've thought it over, and discovered that wounded vanity was a considerable factor in all that righteous indignation."

"Was that the first time a girl ever walked out on you, Martin?"

He nodded and tapped his heart. "Vanity of vanities, saith the preacher. I guess I'd gotten the idea it couldn't be anything but the other way around." The buzzer sounded from inside the laboratory. "There, your undergraduates are ready for you. I'll see you later."

"Thanks, Martin." Stephanie reached out for his hand, then turning away, stepped through the fire door into the laboratory, where the undergraduates were creaking into their chairs, getting their notebooks ready. She felt sympathy for the undergraduates, because the lectures were undoubtedly very dull. Now and then she saw their faces waken as she traced some artery down towards the midrift of the bloody Mr. Gallagher; there would be a rustling of skirts, a slight scraping of chairs. But each time she had to disappoint them. Her professor had outlined the material, leaving no opportunity for transgressions. She scratched on the blackboard lists of vessels and veins, and the faces shuddered back into half-consciousness.

At ten o'clock the buzzer sounded again; the undergraduates pushed themselves up from their chairs and milled towards the exit. Stephanie released Mr. Gallagher from his agony with a tweak at the button which sent him whistling back onto his roller. A few earnest students gathered around her with questions. These she disposed of on the way downstairs; paused for a moment to watch a couple of boys playing tennis on one of the University courts, then crossed the quadrangle to the library.

Her brother Victor was just emerging from the elevator. He swung himself to one side of the hall, and balancing between his crutches, lighted a cigarette. With a jerk of his head he motioned her over, then offered her a cigarette and lighted it for her. "How are you?" he asked.

"All right, thanks."

"Everything going well? Are you happy?"

"Thank you, yes, Victor. Thank you."

"And Dave?"

"He's all right too."

"I'm awfully glad. No wait, don't be angry. I'm not trying to provoke you. I thought you were coming to see my new apartment? Didn't Marguerite say something about it?"

"She said something about it, but nothing specific."

"Do you need a specific invitation to come to my house?"

"I guess I do."

"Why don't you drop by this evening?"

"No thanks, not tonight."

"As you please. Marguerite's been looking for you. She's up in the Modern Language reading room. You'll see her when you pass through." He took a final puff from his cigarette, dropped it on the stone floor, and pressed it out with the point of his crutch. "Do you know where I'm going now, Stephanie?" She shook her head, and

198

he told her, "I'm going out for a whiff of sunshine. That's a luxury I never used to enjoy when I worked at the library desk. But now I can call myself master of my own time—wonderful what a few pennies will do. And I'm making progress on my thesis now—real progress."

"Will you finish soon?"

"In the autumn I expect. But I may take time out for another article if I need a bit more cash."

Victor took a hitch on his crutches and swung himself toward the doorway. "Good bye," he called over his shoulder. "Perhaps I'll even stop for a cup of coffee. It helps in the middle of the morning."

Stephanie, as she rode the elevator up to the library, wondered just how her brother could have earned enough money from a few scholarly articles to quit his job and rent an apartment. Previously he had lived at home, commuting to the University at Roman's expense; now he seemed to be coming up in the world. But she felt no great interest in Victor's successes and dropped the matter from her mind. In the card catalogue she looked up the books she wanted, put in slips for them at the call desk, and went into the reading room to wait. As she was glancing through some notes, Marguerite Strauss sat down beside her.

"I've been wanting to talk to you," Marguerite said gloomily. "Where have you been keeping yourself? But I suppose you had things on your mind—" There was an indignant stirring at near-by tables and someone hissed for silence. "My voice carries so," Marguerite said. "Have you time to step outside for a moment?" Stephanie followed her out to the stairway, where they stood by the window looking down at the quadrangle intersected into geometric patterns by the criss-crossing paths. "I asked you a long time ago to come and see Victor's apartment. Now I've finally got the curtains finished, I'd like you to look at them."

"I'll come this afternoon if you want. I'd have to be back in the laboratory by five-thirty."

"Oh, not this afternoon. That would be impossible, I'm afraid."

"All right. Next week then. What's the book you've got?" She reached out for it, and Marguerite did not prevent her taking it. As Stephanie leafed through the pages, Marguerite said, "It's a history of the cult of the *Danse Macabre* in medieval Europe. Do you read French, Stephanie?"

"No."

"That means Dance of Death." Marguerite struck a match. Her

hand shook and she sucked too hard at the flame, which flared up, blackening the paper of her cigarette.

"Well, I do know that much," Stephanie said. Towards the center of the book, she found a series of engravings which seemed to represent a parade of figures from all stations of life. There were the pope and the emperor, a queen in a peaked hat, then men-at-arms, monks, priests, fishwives, burghers, and peasants. Intertwined with these figures in gestures of intimate affection, she saw the grinning and emaciated dead.

"The quick and the dead," Marguerite explained.

"According to these pictures," Stephanie said, "the dead seem a lot quicker than the quick."

Marguerite scowled, then smiled faintly. "I'll remember that, Stephanie. In your flippant way, perhaps you've expressed the core of the whole idea."

"If I said anything smart, it was accidental. What is the core of the idea anyway?"

"Why, the dance of the quick and the dead. It's symbolic that for all walks of life there can be only one dancing partner—in the final dance, that is."

Stephanie started to close the book, but reopening it, stared again at the engravings. The live figures appeared sedate and full of dignity; while the dead cavorted like mannequins on strings. As badges of their condition, they carried shrouds or coffin covers; some had worms wiggling from their eyes and mouths, while others had bellies bloated with corruption, split open to expose the entrails. Like my friend Mr. Gallagher, Stephanie thought, on the anatomy chart. She looked at Marguerite without smiling. "And the captions under the figures, what do they mean?"

"Each figure has its own verse," Marguerite said. "I wish you could read Old French."

"So do I. But can't you translate them? Here, under the king, what does that say?"

In a gloomy voice, Marguerite chanted:

> "The art of dance I did not learn
> To any dance and note so rude.
> Alas, alas, how little worth,
> Are power, force, and royal birth!"

"But you're translating them into verse, Marguerite. Can you do that extemporaneously?"

"No, I've been working on them for several days. Victor asked me to translate them for one of his articles. Now what are you laughing at? Is there some joke I've missed?"

"I wasn't laughing." Marguerite glared past her angrily, and after a moment Stephanie asked, "Who wrote the verses? Were they widely read?"

"Yes, they were." Marguerite moved away as if she intended to say nothing more, but she turned back. "They were, Stephanie. I think the cult of the Dance of Death grew out of the terrible plagues and famines that swept Europe in the fifteenth century. Do you know what a charnel house is?"

"Why, that's where they keep the stiffs, I suppose."

"Yes, a house for the dead. In medieval times, every cemetery had a charnel house. The originals of those engravings, Stephanie, were painted in the court yard of the great charnel house of the Innocents in Paris. And the strange thing is, it became a favorite place for people to stroll in the evening, looking at the paintings and stepping over the bones that they say were scattered around the yard. Isn't that strange?"

"Very strange," Stephanie said. "Look—I must get some books and go back to my laboratory."

"Perhaps I *could* arrange to be free this afternoon, Stephanie, if you'd care to see Victor's apartment?"

"All right. Four o'clock. Where shall I meet you?"

"Why don't you stop at the Modern Languages tea? I could meet you there."

They walked back through the reading room, and Stephanie picked up her books at the call desk.

That afternoon she saw a crowd of students gather in the quadrangle beside the Commons. She finished work a few minutes before the time she had agreed to meet Marguerite and went downstairs to find out what was happening. It was a demonstration by the University Student Union; someone was speaking from a stepladder beneath a cardboard placard which read: CHICAGO STUDENT UNION WELCOMES PEACE DELEGATE BACK FROM WASHINGTON.

As Stephanie reached the fringe of the crowd, she saw that the speaker was a thin, grave-looking boy whom she remembered from her own brief days in the Student Union; but she had forgotten his name. He was talking about a visit to the Senate, and how certain senators had pledged to fight against American entry into the war.

Then he described the peace vigil in front of the White House, where he had marched in the same line with other student delegates, labor unionists, and people from the American Peace Mobilization. There were a few boos and a few cheers in the crowd.

After the boy stepped down from the ladder, Stephanie saw her old friend Leeds, suave and smiling, take his place. Leeds proceeded to explain how England and France had made war inevitable when they sold Czechoslovakia to the Nazis at Munich. The crowd was mostly on her side, except for one or two determined hecklers who kept yelling questions about Joe Stalin in Moscow. But Leeds, poised graciously on her stepladder, bending her slim wrists and ankles as if she were lounging on a davenport, ignored these interruptions; the war, she announced, was one of imperialist aggression on both sides; the only hope of peace was if the United States—and the Soviet Union—could both stay neutral. When one of the hecklers shouted so loud she could not make herself heard, Leeds turned her head in an attitude of attentive listening and waited till the heckler had shouted himself out. Then she made him an old-fashioned curtsy. Stephanie admitted to herself that this was quite a tour de force from a rickety stepladder. The curtsy brought a wave of applause and whistles from the audience; and Leeds proceeded with her talk.

Now the bells of the University chapel struck four o'clock. Stephanie slid out of the crowd and returned to the library. In the corridor outside the Modern Language Department's common room, she found Marguerite, and together they crossed the quadrangle, circling the knot of students who had gathered about the stepladder. The voices faded behind them. A lawnmower whirred in the distance, and over the gray towers of the University, little puffy clouds floated through the spring sky.

Marguerite broke the silence, returning at once to what Stephanie recognized as an echo of their conversation of the morning. "How I envy people with faith," Marguerite declared. "I understand why a T. S. Eliot would join the Church—I understand fully. But you can't have faith just by wanting it. Not everyone can travel the road to Damascus, I suppose."

"Why not?" Stephanie said. "It pays some people very well."

Marguerite shook her head, not deigning to answer, and Stephanie asked, "Don't you suppose T. S. Eliot got faith by wanting it?

And Paul too, for that matter? God helps those who help themselves, doesn't he?"

"No, that's a lie!" Marguerite cried. "Those who are *able* to help themselves are the ones God has already blessed."

Stephanie glanced up, startled. She remembered a long time ago, Hawkins insisting that Marguerite Strauss was not stupid. "Oh, I understand why people conceived the Dance of Death," Marguerite said suddenly. "What an attraction the mind finds in the idea of death. . . ."

"Not for me. I've cut up too many of them."

"I suppose you have." They crossed Fifty-Seventh Street and walked under the trees of Woodlawn Avenue, in front of the rows of small apartment houses. "But what I mean is, Stephanie, I understand why those people went to the charnel houses and all that. They were making a mockery of life, and they found some reposefulness that way. They had lost faith, the Church had become a broken reed. And after all, it's got to be one or the other. How else could the human mind endure it . . . ?"

"Endure what?"

"Why, life, I mean. The things that happen to people, the obscenities of the flesh. I suppose I seem very pessimistic—"

"You don't sound cheerful."

"But I don't feel gloomy," Marguerite said. "I feel I've learned a greater acceptance of things than I ever knew before. Perhaps once I did hope for a faith, Stephanie, but we're really too intellectual and sophisticated; we've gone beyond that. Of course there might be what Victor calls the scientific dogmas; but I think they require greater naïveté even than the Church."

"What's a scientific dogma?"

"Communism," Marguerite said. "Fascism. Utopias based on a faulty understanding of science, as Victor put it."

Stephanie stopped abruptly. "If I thought you were planning these remarks for my benefit, Marguerite, I'd be angry."

"Oh pardon *me*. I forgot that kind of thing would sit so badly with you these days."

Stephanie laughed and walked on again. "As a matter of fact," she said, "I'm considering seriously joining the Communist Party. And I'll match my understanding of science against yours—or Victor's either—any day of the week."

Marguerite shrugged her shoulders. "It's because your husband wants you to."

"You would say that."

"But isn't it true? Turn here, Stephanie." They entered the lobby of one of the small apartment buildings and Marguerite rang for the lift. "Isn't it true?" she asked again.

"Maybe so. But that wouldn't tell me why I married him in the first place. Or why I went back to him."

"You're sure it wasn't just for—?"

"Just for somebody to sleep with? No, I guess there's more to it than that. This looks like an expensive joint. I was thinking this morning, those must have been powerful articles Victor sold."

"Was that what he told your family?"

"I don't know what he told my family. But he told me he sold some articles to the *Yale Review* or some magazine. Was there another story? What did he tell you?"

"The same thing, Stephanie." They stepped into the automatic lift and rode up to the third floor, where Marguerite fumbled in her handbag for a key and opened the door of an apartment. In the entrance way they stumbled over a couple of large paper parcels. These, Marguerite explained, were the curtains; and dragging them into the living room, she began to tear off the wrapping. Stephanie meanwhile peered around at the apartment, which still smelled strongly of paint. The walls were gray, almost black, and the ceiling dark rose color. There was no furniture except for a gigantic day bed under a red cover, bookshelves, and a desk painted black. On the bookshelf, Stephanie recognized a picture from Victor's room at home—a Dürer engraving of a knight on horseback riding in company with death and the devil.

She laughed uncertainly, and Marguerite glanced up from the pile of curtains, which were also dark red. "I know what this room is," Stephanie said. "It's the regular furnished, light-housekeeping two-by-six, that's all." She pulled open a door. "Here's the kitchenette, stove, and icebox. And if you open that door behind you, the folding bed comes down on your skull. Oh, I've lived in half a dozen of these."

"I don't doubt it."

"But why the color? And where's all the furniture?"

"Victor had it moved out. Could you help me with these?"

Marguerite climbed on a chair in front of the window and Stephanie handed her the rod with the curtains. When Marguerite had fixed the rod to its brackets, she descended rather painfully and began to make tea in the kitchenette. Stephanie wondered why

Victor, whom she had never seen drink a cup of tea in his life, should now have provided the makings in his apartment. But all the equipment seemed ready at hand and after a few moments Marguerite emerged from the kitchenette with teapot, cups, and a plate of cookies.

As they sat on the day bed, sipping the tea, Stephanie began to grow uneasy at the silence. This surprised her because she had never felt uncertain of herself with Marguerite; it had always been the other way around. But now there seemed an air of triumph in the assurance with which Marguerite accepted the silence, leaving it for Stephanie to break. At last Stephanie emptied her teacup and stood up. Now Marguerite's look changed at once and she reached out to hold her back.

"Oh no, Stephanie, stay a few minutes longer. We'll have another cup of tea." Her hand shook as she filled the cups, and when she had set the pot down, she asked, "Well, Stephanie, do you like the curtains?"

"They're fine. But you won't get much light through them."

Marguerite giggled ponderously. "I wonder you weren't frightened to come here after the things I told you last summer."

"I didn't believe what you told me."

"I know. You did me a lot of good then. I really was upset. One of the things I wanted to tell you is that I'm better now. I'm working my way out of it step by step."

"I'm glad." Stephanie stirred the spoon in her teacup, watching how quickly the lump of sugar melted. She thought again of the morning Victor had found her with Martin in the drugstore, when he told them about his new apartment and the curtains Marguerite was going to fix for him. "She's showing off to you," Victor had said. "She discovered she has a feminine instinct after all, and she wants to let you know about it." Stephanie recognized now the brutality of the words, which she had only half perceived at the time. She moved uneasily, glancing again at the curtains. The room was hot and terribly small, and in it there was a strange odor, now that the curtains were drawn across the window. On the crimson day bed, Marguerite sat cross-legged, balancing her teacup cn one knee. So the curtains are a symbol of triumph, Stephanie thought; that's why she wanted me to see them. After a long silence, she said, "This is your apartment too, isn't it, Marguerite? You live here too?"

"Yes, that's right."

Stephanie finished her tea and got up from the day bed. "I must go. I have a gang of undergraduates coming into the laboratory at five-thirty. And you paid for the apartment, didn't you? Victor couldn't have made enough from those articles."

But Marguerite jumped up, shaking her head, saying over and over, "Oh, no! No, I didn't. No, Stephanie—Victor paid for the apartment. I don't want you to think I paid for it. It's *our* apartment and Victor paid for it. It's his money."

Stephanie opened the door to the hallway and they shook hands. "All right," she said. "I'll think that then."

It was almost half past seven before she closed up the laboratory and started home. The Lake Park streetcar banged north along the darkening street, past the rooming houses and apartment buildings, and the old gabled mansions behind their weed-grown yards. Couples were strolling in the spring twilight, and the neon signs of the bars and drugstores glowed at the intersections. Stephanie felt hungry and hoped Dave had remembered this was his night to cook the dinner. The attic window of the carriage house was lighted, and when she climbed the stairs she found him at the table in his underdrawers, working over his batches of papers and clippings. Laughing, she shoved the papers aside and sat on his knee, plucking at the hairs of his chest.

"Sure I remembered," he said. "You saw me bring the food in this morning."

"I was too sleepy to notice."

The attic was full of the vinegary smell of spareribs and sauerkraut. Dave dished it up while Stephanie set the table.

1940

PLEDGER McADAMS' boy Billy finished high school in June and went out hunting a job. Despite the list of employment offices he copied each morning from the newspaper, Pledger suspected he did not hunt very hard and probably spent most of his time over on the ball field behind the high-school building. He was surprised when Billy came home, his eyes shining, and announced he was to start work at the steel mills the next morning. Together with his surprise, Pledger felt a strange wave of anger, half towards himself and half towards the boy. He knew it had always been this way—most of everything going to Judith, and when the boy did something right, everybody acted as if it must have been an accident. Sometimes he had talked this over with Ruby, but no matter what they did, they never seemed to make it come out any different. The next day, Pledger got up at six o'clock to see the boy off, and walked down to the car stop with him. As the streetcar banged away into the smoky half-light of the early morning, Pledger remained on the corner, examining, as he had done often before, the way he felt towards his boy Billy. He knew the boy's mind had taken after his mother, Sarah. Maybe Judith took after Sarah in looks, but the boy had taken after her in the way he acted—good-natured and yielding, accepting things as they came. He had been impatient and sharp to him; often he had been un-just, and it hurt him now to see the boy grow disturbed when they were alone together.

The following morning again he got up at six and sat at the table while Ruby gave the boy breakfast. Then he stepped outside into the street with him. "Look, Billy, you're working now. A man needs something to keep the time by when he's working." Pledger held out his railroad watch on its square-linked gold chain. For a moment the boy stared at him, then raised his hand slowly to take the watch. He looked at it in the palm of his hand, hefted it, held it up to his ear, listening to the tick. But after the boy had gone, the picture remained in Pledger's mind of the embarrassed, un-willing manner of his taking the gift.

Now that Billy had gone to work and Judith was getting close to the end of her training course, Pledger jokingly told Ruby he would have to quit his own job so he could get his real work done. The Lodge took a lot of his time; the wage movement was shaping up; and in the early spring the Education Committee had assigned him to teach a course at the People's School. Pledger shifted from afternoon to a daylight job—a change which his seniority entitled him to anyway; and he went down to the People's School two eve-nings a week. Although he grumbled to Dave that the class was taking his time from more important work, he came to like it and would not have wished to give it up. The subject assigned him

207

was the American Labor Movement since the Civil War, and he told his students he was certainly learning more about it than they were.

At the start of the summer term, the Education Committee asked Dave Spaas' wife Stephanie to teach a class also. The night her class was scheduled to begin, Pledger found her waiting for him in the lobby of the office building on Randolph Street where the People's School had its rooms. She told him she was scared and wanted some advice on how to start off.

"How long you been teaching at the University?" he asked.

"Four years," she said, and Pledger began to laugh at her.

"You asking me how to run a class? I never run one before in my life. I tell you what *I* do, but it won't work for you. I got an outline from the Education Committee with each week's reading assignment in it. So every class I assign some reading, and then I go read it myself. Mostly the students don't have time to do the reading, so I'm that much ahead of 'em. I tell 'em what was in the assignment, and of course they think I knew it all along." He winked at her, but saw she was very serious about her question. As they rode up in the elevator, he told her to start off by asking everybody where they came from and what kind of work they did. "That gets people to knowing each other, and maybe gives you a notion what they need to learn." Taking her into the office, he showed her where to pick up her list of students, and he introduced her to the school secretary, Rita Hanson, who was the wife of Dave's friend Hanson. Then they smoked a cigarette in the corridor, and Stephanie went off to meet her class.

Pledger had scarcely known Stephanie, except for seeing her sometimes with Dave. But now they met quite often; they found a cafeteria on Washington Street that made no objection to serving a Negro, and they usually ate supper together before class. He started out by distrusting her because of the trouble she had made for Dave; but within a few days, found himself changing his mind. She was friendly and open with him, and he talked to her about the school, the problems of teaching, the subjects they were trying to teach. Her class was on race and racial discrimination, and he asked her many questions: Where did races come from? If two men had different colored skins or odd-shaped noses, did that mean one had better brainwork than the other? How much was a child made when he was born, and how much was he made by growing up? Questions he had known the answers to only because he believed they were right, he found now she could explain to him in fact and understanding. He saw that education, which he himself had never had, and which he had considered only as a pastime for the white people and the rich people, might be a weapon also. And because she had studied this weapon and handled it sharply, he decided she was a person of great value.

But although he watched her closely, he found her not easy to understand. Sometimes when they talked, she threw herself into the enthusiasm of the subject; her eyes lighted, she marked her points with taps of her knuckles, her voice came light and quick. Then he had the feeling that this science she had studied, this knowledge of the bodies and minds of people, the workings of these bodies and minds, was something more important to her than any other could ever be. He came to love her enthusiasm and her large pleasure in work. That person who had faith in what he did, Pledger believed, was one to be trusted. Yet at other times she seemed lost inside herself, sat moody and silent, answering his questions with single words. She worked hard on her class, and Pledger, from talking to some of her students, knew they thought well of her. They brought their friends, and before long the secretary, Rita Hanson, had to move Stephanie's class into a larger room.

But Stephanie had not been at the People's School two weeks before Pledger saw that she had a feud on with Rita Hanson. Pledger admitted to himself that he had never liked Rita very well even though she was the wife of his friend Hanson. She had an aggravating way about her, as if she had just received personal instructions from God Almighty on any question one might think up to ask her. And when she came busting into the classrooms, taking half the class period for a sales talk on the latest literature in the bookstore, regardless of whether it had anything to do with the subject of the class or not, that was too much for anybody. He knew that Rita liked having a good record for the bookstore in literature sales; but the classes were more important than the literature, and there was no use slapping the fly so hard you killed the baby. Most of the other teachers agreed with him, Pledger found out; but of course it had to be Stephanie, the newest teacher in the school, on her trial run so to speak, who was the first to tell Rita off.

"You got no diplomacy," Pledger said when he met Stephanie in the cafeteria.

"Well, she made me mad. I couldn't help it."

Pledger was careful not to let her know how he felt about Rita himself. He refilled their cups of coffee which cost only four cents on the refill. "You lay off Rita Hanson," he told her, "or we'll have you two scrapping like a couple of cats in a bag. That's not likely to do anybody any good, is it?" Pledger reached for his watch, which was no longer in his pocket, and shook his head angrily. "I guess that's the hundredth time I've reached for my ticker this week. If that boy busts it . . ."

They finished their coffee, and as they got up from the table, Pledger tapped her on the shoulder and told her again, "You keep clear of Rita. I'll wait a few days and then I'll have a talk with her myself. But I don't want you getting in any more fights with her, you hear?"

■ ■

By the first of June, Pledger began to think the Carbuilders' Union had forgotten all about the coach cleaners and their application for a charter. But there arrived at last by mail a parchment scroll bearing the representation of a Pullman car that had sprouted wings, and the text of their charter with all the capital letters in different colors. Along with the parchment came stationery, carrying the same flying Pullman at its crest; union buttons, an official seal, and a gigantic shipment of dues books. The coach cleaners held their inaugural meeting in Andrew Masters' chapel. Everybody shook hands and congratulated each other, and Andrew Masters gave one of his prayers. The vice-president of the union, Donohue, came from downtown to make them a speech of welcome. Uncle Jennison, champing his long jaw and glaring into the farthest corner of the chapel as if he saw a company man hiding behind a trap door, explained how the grievance committee was going to collect all their overtime claims. Then Pledger introduced Dave Spaas as a rank and file carman and a leader in the neighborhood whom many of them would remember from the old days. Dave got up and demanded unity of Negro and white railroad workers to fight for a wage raise. That brought the members to their feet, yelling, "Amen, brother. That's what we need."

Pledger, glancing at Vice-President Donohue by his side, saw him looking solemn and dignified. Dave Spaas had already moved on to his next point. "Why do the railroad companies succeed in splitting the workers against each other?" he demanded. "Because the white unions help them do it, that's all. When the white unions exclude Negro workers from union protection they help the companies build up a reservoir of cheap labor. That drives down the wage levels for everybody in the industry. And there's the stupidest union policy that ever came down the drain!" Dave had leaned forward, pounding his fist on the top of Andrew Masters' pulpit. Again the Lodge members jumped to their feet, whistling and calling,

"You said it, brother. . . ."

When the noise subsided, Dave told them, "Now your Lodge is coming into the Carbuilders' Union of North America. I hope this indicates a change of policy on the part of the official leaders of this union. I hope it does."

Jennison and Vice-President Donohue left as soon as the meeting was over. After they had gone, the coach cleaners placed their new charter in a frame and hung it on the chapel wall. They regarded it half with pride and half as a joke. "She's got wings just like an angel," one of the men told Pledger. "Now old Brother Andrew ought to fix her up just like they do in a Catholic church— put a couple of candles in front of her and a place to drop your money." Laughter ran through the crowd, and somebody sang out, "Don't you forget to tip your hat and spit over your shoulder when you pass them angel's wings."

Pledger made out a list of the seniority of all the men in the yard, including the Negroes. From then on, he watched the company bulletin board and sat back waiting for the next vacancy. But he expected that when the vacancy occurred, the company would do what they had always done in the past—skip over any eligible Negroes despite their years of seniority and promote a white man with less seniority or no seniority. Then it would be up to Uncle Jennison to defend their rights as union members. That would be the test case.

In June, Pledger and Dave Spaas called together a small conference of railroad workers in the Chicago area. They had not expected many and not many came—only twenty-five, and all but two or three of these Communists. They met in the "banquet room" of a hotel on the South Side, where through all of a Sunday morning and afternoon they discussed the question of railroad wages. Everybody agreed that railroad workers needed a wage increase and that the men were ready to fight for one. But the officers of the various unions seemed afraid or unwilling to move.

"So what can we do about it?" Dave Spaas asked them. And the conference decided they could at least begin to organize pressure from below, from the workers in the yards and shops, to force the officers of the unions into action. Pledger called for a show of hands on this. Then he went the rounds of the twenty-five, assigning to each man a group of yards and roundhouses to cover. After the meeting broke up, he stood by the window of the "banquet room," watched the other twenty-four come out through the doorway below and drift away into the Sunday evening crowd on Cottage Grove Avenue. There were so few of them, he thought, after all these years of work, still so few of them. Twenty-five men among the endlessly reaching railroad yards which spread west and north from Gary and Michigan City to Desplaines and Waukegan: they were like a few grains of salt scattered across an ocean beach. And if the salt shall lose his flavor, wherewith shall it be salted . . . ?

He went to work in accordance with the decisions of the conference. Many evenings, when he was not teaching at the People's School, he spent touring the city on streetcars, banging through the twilight streets from one railroad to another, making contact with the Negro coach cleaners and roundhouse workers. Now and then, coming to a roundhouse, he found that one of the other twenty-four had been there before him. That always gave him a warm feeling under the collarbone.

Whenever he could, Pledger took some of the younger men from his own Lodge along with him. After they had covered the roundhouses and yards, they went to the meeting rooms of the Negro railroad lodges. Like his own Lodge, these seldom could afford rent for a hall; they met wherever they could find space—in chapels, or the back rooms of taverns, or the sitting rooms of funeral parlors. But most often, it seemed to Pledger, he found their meetings in the funeral parlors, which always occupied the fanciest store front of any South Side district. In these parlors with their waxy odors, their dimmed lights and funereal rubber plants, he talked, watching the men's faces, noticing how they nodded their heads when they came to agree with him. It gave him a strange feeling to meet these men who lived the same life he lived, worked at the same jobs, walked the same streets, slept in the same houses, biting at their anger and hatred under the same injustice. And as he talked, he believed he was talking for something greater than a few nickels of wage increase; he was talking for the unity of Negro and white to build a new world.

One afternoon as Pledger came home from work he found Jackson, the South Side Section Organizer, waiting for him in the Chile Parlor. Jackson shoved a card at him.

"You feel like putting your autograph on this, Pledger?"

Taking the card, Pledger saw that it was Stephanie Koviak's application for membership in the Communist Party. The application required the names of two members as sponsors, and one of the lines already carried the signature of Dave Spaas. Pledger took out his pen and signed the other line.

"Did you talk to Rita Hanson about Stephanie?" he asked.

Jackson shook his head.

"Why not?"

"Her husband told me to come to you instead."

Pledger leaned back, laughing. Then he told Jackson: "I think Stephanie's sharp and smart, Jackson, and I think she's done a good job at the People's School. She's got a bad disposition some of the time. That's why she picked that fight with Rita—or let Rita pick the fight with her—however you want to look at it. And maybe she's got some problems I don't know much about. But I'm glad I got the privilege of signing her card."

16

DOWN at the end of the weedy stretch of Richmond Court, Dave was showing one of the little boys how to hold the football. Dave drew back, swung his foot, and the football sailed end over end into the air. Stephanie saw it coming straight towards her; she held out her hands, knowing she would not catch it. But fortunately one of the twelve-year-olds on her own team cut in front of her, scooped the ball neatly under his arm as it descended. From the far end of the court, Dave ran towards them with his team of kids hooting in his wake. On her side, the boy with the ball began to dodge and zigzag, thrusting his arm out first on one side, then on the other, like the photographs in the sports sections; but as soon as Dave bore down on him, he threw the ball away in a panic. It landed in Stephanie's hands, she caught it, fumbled, and while she struggled for a grip on the slippery leather, Dave charged towards her, laughing and waving his arms.

"Hold on to it, Stephanie! Run now!" She started to run, and he tagged her, planting his hand with a thump between her shoulder blades.

"First down!"

Now the little boys surrounded her in the huddle, arguing the next play. They decided that Stephanie, being the tallest, would take the ball and throw a forward pass. The twelve-year-old who had caught Dave's kick appointed himself quarterback; no one raised any objections, and he explained carefully to Stephanie that he would call a lot of numbers and she would receive the ball on number sixteen.

"Formation," he cried. "Signals: six, nine, five, four . . ."

Ahead of her, Stephanie saw the row of upturned bottoms of the little boys in the scrimmage line. The center had an unusually large bottom, and his round excited face peered back at her upside down between his legs.

"Eight, eleven, sixty-two . . ." The quarterback apparently intended to reel off all the numbers he could think of before he came to sixteen. But the center couldn't hold it any longer. He let the ball go and fell on his face, while Stephanie, who had not yet heard the magic signal, was taken by surprise; the ball thudded into her stomach and she wrapped her arms around it. Again Dave came bounding towards her, waving his hands in the air. But he slowed down to let her throw the ball. Down the field, she could hear her team-mates yelling like banshees,

"Here I am. Throw it to *me*."

They had all run farther than Stephanie could throw. She ducked around Dave and ran towards them, beckoning them closer. Dave let her go, and the little boys on his team raced along behind, unable to catch her, while her own team-mates changed their tune to "Run, run! Touchdown play!"

Halfway down Richmond Court, Stephanie slipped in the wet grass and skidded to a halt on the seat of her slacks. The twelve-year-old quarterback was very disappointed. He told her she would have to get shoes with spikes before she would be much good at football.

"Second down," Dave called. "Two to go."

As they went into their huddle again, Stephanie's team developed bitter factionalism over the question of the center. The center insisted he had heard number sixteen even if nobody else had; the rest of the team charged him with crossing his signals and spoiling the play.

At last the quarterback hissed, "Shut up, you guys. You want 'em to call time penalty on us? I'll throw the pass myself. Formation! Signals! Hike! One, two, three . . ." He threw the pass, which Dave intercepted. He loped off for a touchdown in the opposite direction. The noise of the game attracted other players. Some big kids joined and the game grew faster and trickier. After a time, Stephanie dropped out and sat on the steps of one of the old mansions reading a book; she glanced up now and then to watch Dave. In speed, at least, the big kids were a match for him, and by mid-afternoon he had stripped off his shirt, and his shoulders glistened with sweat. When he finally quit, the whole swarm of kids beseiged him.

"Come on, mister. Play some more."

"Don't be a quitter."

"Hey, mister, choose up sides again?"

Laughing, Dave walked over to the steps and pulled her to her feet. He shooed the kids aside and they went back to work in their attic. Dave was constructing shelves for the kitchen, while Stephanie stood on a stepladder and painted the ceiling. She found that the paint dripped into her eyes and gobs of it ran off the handle of the brush down her wrist. Dave, who was hammering and sawing below her, said it was like working in a rainstorm. When they knocked off late in the afternoon they were both speckled as if they had caught smallpox. Stephanie scrubbed their arms and faces and Dave's back with a turpentine-soaked rag.

At suppertime she scrambled a batch of eggs, and for dessert, they walked down to the corner and bought a couple of double-dip ice-cream cones. Then they strolled westward through streets which were crowded with people enjoying the spring evening. Stephanie, as she licked her ice-cream cone, expected the precariously balanced top scoop to fall off. She tried to eat it quickly, but the cold made her teeth ache. Dave beside her whistled snatches

215

of a tune, and explained to her how he was going to build a shower bath out of a couple of packing cases he had found in an empty boxcar.

They crossed Cottage Grove Avenue into the Negro section and walked on to the Chile Parlor, where Pledger and Ruby were waiting for them. Pledger was busy sorting the chips for their Sunday evening poker game.

■ ■

A few days after Stephanie's initiation into the Communist Party,, she received an assignment to her neighborhood branch. During most of the years she had known Dave, she had moved at the fringes of the Party, but she had never attended the meeting of a Party branch. She knew the branch was the modern name for the old-time cell and she had always believed there was something mysterious and exciting about this unit of revolutionary activity. Without thinking very much about it, she had connected it with the picture in her mind of European-style conspiracy: bearded men meeting in the back rooms of cafés while the Czarist police scoured the city for them. But now that she had actually joined, Stephanie found that the other members of the organization held no such romantic illusions.

Her branch met every second week in an apartment on Lake Park Avenue, not far from Richmond Court. The apartment belonged to the branch organizer, a housewife named Minnie Gardiner, who had two children, one in kindergarten and one in the second grade. According to the schedule, branch meetings were supposed to start at eight o'clock; but generally by eight o'clock, Minnie was still in the bedroom reciting *Jack and the Beanstalk* to her two children while her husband washed the supper dishes. So the other branch members pitched in to help with the dishes, or sat around in the living room gossiping until Minnie reached the climax of her story. Then they would hear her voice through the closed door:

". . . so Jack chopped so hard and fast that the chips flew like snowdrops, and then he took one terrific chop and *down came the beanstalk—*"

"And the giant, Mummy? Did the giant fall on Jack?"

"No! Jack jumped out of the way and the giant made a hole in the ground as *big as a basement.*"

"Mummy, tell us the story again."

"Tomorrow night. Good night now, both of you."

Minnie, emerging from the bedroom, would close the door firmly behind her. The branch then convened around the dining room table and Minnie proposed an agenda: education, circulation of the *Daily Worker,* fund drive, literature sales. But before they could start on point number one, the door from the bedroom would open a crack and two voices cry in chorus:

"Mummy, we've got to go pee-pee."

"All right, go ahead."

The two children raced across the dining room, with the trap doors of their pajamas flapping open behind. From the bathroom came the sound of two short spurts of water, then the children padded back to the bedroom. Again, Minnie closed the door after them. "It's all a gag," she explained. "They want an excuse to stay up a little longer. Now for the agenda."

They did not bother with motions and amendments. If anybody had anything to add to the agenda, they added it. The branch was a small one, consisting of half a dozen housewives and five men, one of them Minnie's husband. All the men worked in offices downtown. After the first meeting, Minnie took Stephanie aside and told her. "This is a middle-class white collar group, Stephanie, and we find it hard doing real work in the neighborhood. I hope you can help us." In spite of her protests, the branch immediately appointed Stephanie educational director, with the duty of making reports on such subjects as "The Problem of India" or "Wage Labor and Capital" or "The Position of Women under Capitalist Society." But most of the time of each meeting was spent on the two ever-recurring problems—circulation of the party newspaper and the raising of funds.

Minnie advised Stephanie to tie these into her educational reports as much as possible. So they would discuss a dozen different methods for coping with the problem. They would argue the whole matter back and forth, reach complete agreement on the necessity for maintaining finance and circulating their press. How else could they counter the propaganda of the commercial newspapers and the radio? The only question that remained was what to do about it. So they ordered a big bundle of newspapers and set a day for the mobilization of the entire branch to sell them across Forty-Seventh Street. But Stephanie, reporting to the mobilization point, found only two others besides herself. They had more papers than they could possibly sell; so they sold fifteen or twenty and left the others on doorsteps. Even Minnie had been among the missing; her youngest child had come down with tonsillitis the day before.

At the next meeting of the branch, the members one after another reviewed their excuses. Stephanie at first looked askance at the excusemakers; this was a fine kind of revolutionary unit, she thought, where they couldn't even bring eleven people out to sell a bundle of newspapers. But within a few weeks she found herself making excuses also, and was grateful to Minnie for understanding that her excuses were valid. She taught two nights a week at the People's School, helped Dave one or two nights a week on his material for the railroad wage movement. In addition to that, she was trying to hold down a job and complete her courses at the University. She learned that most of the others were at least as busy as she. It was easy to make lighthearted promises about what one would do two weeks hence, but when the time came, that was quite different.

Minnie told her it was always this way; there were more jobs than people to do them. To build the circulation of a newspaper, in a sizable section of Chicago, they needed a high-pressure publicity office, delivery trucks, and newsboys. But instead they had six housewives and five men who worked all day downtown.

It was the same with the fund drive. Members of the organization were always contributing cash in one emergency or another, so the purpose of the fund drive was to scare up a few greenbacks from outside sources. They planned a bazaar to raise money, and Stephanie volunteered the use of the attic in Richmond Court. Dave, although he was not a member of the same branch, pitched in as bartender and brought some railroad workers along with him. A lot of people came, danced and drank and went swimming off the rocks. When they counted up afterwards, they found they had cleared forty dollars; but to Stephanie, since most of the people who came to the bazaar were members from their own or from other branches, it seemed they had accomplished very little except to move the greenbacks out of one pocket and into another.

However, the success of the bazaar buoyed up the spirits of the branch. When Minnie came in with her next fistful of bulletins from the state office warning them that the nation was facing the most critical days in its history, they were ready to tackle the twin problems of fund-raising and press circulation all over again. And they solved the problems on paper by assigning themselves a new set of quotas, which they all knew privately they could not meet.

Theoretically they were supposed to have established contact with a lot of rich and friendly sympathizers who would kick in at decent intervals. But the facts were quite different; and at the end of this drive—as at the end of all their other drives—the branch members dug down into their own meager pockets.

Stephanie saw that this did not dampen their optimism. They were always ready to set themselves a new quota, saddle their steeds, and have a whack at it—knowing like Don Quixote that they would be unhorsed by the blades of this windmill as they had been by the last one.

This, Minnie told her, was the life of a neighborhood branch—a continual slugging match against the minor problems of the organization. Stephanie enjoyed talking to Minnie. On Sunday mornings, while she waited for Dave to wake up, she would stop at Minnie's for a cup of coffee. Minnie had been working in the Communist Party for ten years, and Stephanie realized that there was some geometric power in the efforts of people like Minnie who labored so hard to raise a dollar or sell one issue of the *Daily Worker*. For the name of their organization echoed in the halls of Congress and was denounced by every god-fearing newspaper across the land.

17

"Out of the rolling ocean the crowd, came a drop
Gently to me whispering . . ."

DAVE, who had just stepped out of the press of people on Randolph Street, stood beside her in the shelter of the doorway. The signs of the bars and restaurants winked red and green and blue in the many-colored darkness; the flood moved past, the faces, faces, faces, caught in fixed expressions between the bands of light and shadow. From the next doorway a voice reached them monotonously, "You too can learn to dance. Tango, foxtrot, samba, and the latest thing in swing. Beautiful partners are waiting for you inside, my friend—"

"Where were you tonight, Dave?" Stephanie asked.

"Blue Island. I talked to a lodge on the Baltimore and Ohio. Been here long?"

"I just came down. My class was late."

He peered at her in the reflected glow of the doorway. "And what was all that you were saying about a rolling ocean?"

"That was a poem I learned a long time ago when I was in high school. Listen, I'll recite you the part I remember:

"Out of the rolling ocean the crowd, came a drop gently to me
Whispering, I love you, before long I die,
I have traveled a long way merely to look on you, to touch you,
Now we have met, we have looked, we are safe,
Return in peace to the ocean, my love,
I too am part of that ocean, we are not so much separated. . . ."

"That's all I remember," she said. "Do you like poetry?"

"When I understand it."

"And did you understand that?"

"Yes, I guess so. Is Pledger coming down?"

"No. He's having a session with Rita."

They moved out of the doorway into the stream of people. "How are you and Rita getting along?" Dave asked.

"Amiably."

"Hanson wants us to go to the Dunes with them on Saturday."

"Oh, Dave, that's the day I graduate."

"I know. I told him we'd let him know later. They're driving out Saturday in the evening and staying over Sunday. We won't go unless you want."

"Can you get Saturday off?"

"If I put in for it right away."

"That would be fun if it weren't for Rita." She thought of the scrubby sand dunes and the white beach in the sunlight. "Oh the hell with Rita. Let's go with them. I'll be very sweet to Rita."

"All right. I'll tell Hanson."

From Randolph Street they turned along the empty and darker blocks towards the Great Midland depot. The unlighted buildings loomed above them, leaving only a narrow chasm of sky. Stephanie pinched his arm as they walked. "That poem," she said. "How did you understand it? What do you think it was supposed to mean?"

"It was talking about death, I guess. Return in peace to the ocean and all that."

"Sometimes I envy Pledger McAdams," Stephanie said. "He doesn't believe in death."

"What got you off on this track?"

"I don't know. That poem came into my mind. If you look at it the way that poem does, then we're all part of the ocean of matter— aren't we?—and in that sense we don't die, but go on living—living together. How does that strike you?"

"I'm not looking forward to it."

"Neither am I," Stephanie said. "I don't mind being part of the matter of the universe. But I—I like the shape we have right now. It won't be in peace when I go back." Then she added, "But isn't death a stage in the dialectical process? How can we as Marxists struggle against it?"

He laughed and they walked a few steps in silence; when she glanced at him, he was staring down at the pavement as if he were giving serious attention to what she had meant for a joke. "It isn't part of any dialectical process to go in peace," he said. "People fight to stay alive."

"To cram into themselves enough living to last for eternity, you mean?"

"No, that's not what I meant." She knew that her phrase had irritated him. "People fight to stay alive," he said again. "To live better and live longer. I guess that's what people have always been fighting for."

They stopped at the entrance to the Great Midland depot. She pressed her lips hard against his and told him, "All right, then, hurry home in the morning. I'll be waiting for you." As Stephanie rode back to Richmond Court on the streetcar, she kept thinking of what he had said to her and how precisely their few words had reflected the responses of each to the same idea.

She realized that if she were to examine more closely those different responses, they would lead her to the heart and center of her relations with Dave; and perhaps her relations with herself also, she thought. But after a moment the sequence of thought eluded her, and she was too sleepy to pursue it.

In the morning the alarm clock woke her before seven. She shuddered, stretched, pressed her head into the pillow, then forcing herself up, pulled on her bathrobe and groped for her slippers. The room felt damp and cool. Gray streamers of mist trailed through the open windows. After washing her face at the sink, Stephanie fixed breakfast; she made coffee, put on bacon to fry and toast in the oven. The oily, sharp smell of coffee filled the room, but Stephanie slid back into bed and lay stretching luxuriously under the covers, which were still warm. Every few minutes she turned to look at the alarm clock on the table beside her. At twenty past seven she heard his feet on the gravel, the sound of his feet creaking up the steps to the attic; then he was sitting on the bed, laughing and kissing her, leaving a sooty splotch where the seat of his trousers touched the sheets.

"That's why the sheets are always dirty," she told him.

"Who cares?" Dave asked. "Do you?"

"No."

He pulled off his clothes and crawled into the bed beside her. When they had made love, they lay with their arms around each other until the alarm clock rang for the second time. "Damn the clock," Stephanie said. "Damn that clock!" She hung on to him, pressing against him, although she knew the extra moments would cost her breakfast. Then at last she got out of bed, scalded her tongue with coffee while she was dressing, and hurried across Richmond Court to the streetcar line, eating a toast and bacon sandwich on the way.

After several years of teaching, Stephanie no longer felt timid about standing up to deliver a lecture in her classroom. But when Dave asked her to go to South Chicago with him to talk to some railroad workers, she knew she would be frightened into speechlessness and refused to go.

At the same time, she wanted to go with him. She had watched with fascination how he and Pledger McAdams moved ahead step by step on the wage drive. Now they were making plans for a monthly newspaper; Dave had mobilized a corps of speakers and was sending them to the various railroad lodges, and going out himself to speak almost every night. He told her he needed someone with him who could talk Polish when he covered South Chicago. He ignored her refusal and assumed she would come. She did.

Hanson drove them out in his car in which Dave had installed his homemade loudspeaker equipment. Stephanie, staring through the window as they drove into South Chicago, noticed the details about her with uneasy precision because she was frightened. All the streets swung to the east where the city came to an end against

222

the black and gray structures of the steel mills. Columns of smoke and dust towered into the sky. The round yellow sun baked down over the tarpaper roofs of South Chicago.

"I'm not going to do it, Dave," Stephanie said.

"Sure you are."

"I won't be any good."

"That's the way everybody feels the first time. You'll be all right."

"I won't, Dave."

The car swung rapidly around several corners. She saw rows of frame houses which seemed to stand at a level lower than the streets, so that their second-story windows came even with the sidewalks, to which they were joined by narrow footbridges. Sometimes at the street corners fire hydrants were spouting water, while Mexican and Polish kids splashed through the flooded gutters. The car nosed across a main intersection where crowds of shoppers swarmed in and out of a Sears Roebuck department store, then turned again and jolted over an endless series of railroad tracks. In the distance she saw a roundhouse with floods of black smoke boiling up from its stacks.

"You speak Polish?" Hanson asked.

"Some."

"You're a natural out here."

He turned parallel to the tracks. Opposite the roundhouse, they bumped over the sidewalk into a vacant lot and stopped. A couple of men were waiting for them, whom Dave introduced as the officials of some railway lodge. While the two men hung an oilcloth sign against the side of the car, Dave dragged coils of wire and a microphone from inside. He blew into the phone which produced a barking noise out of the speaker, grinned at her and asked,

"Nice tone, hasn't it?"

From many directions across the rail yard and the low roofs of the city, whistles began to sound the end of afternoon shift. The whistle of the roundhouse blasted out suddenly, and men came hurrying through the gates. Dave had started a record playing. The men glanced up at the noise, and drifted across the street, gathering in a semicircle around the automobile. One of the two lodge officials climbed up to the roof, Dave passed him the microphone and said, "Up you go, Stephanie. I'll give you a boost."

He held out his hands with the fingers locked, she set one foot in the stirrup and scrambled to the roof, barking her knee on the way up. Dave followed her. The lodge official was already speaking into the microphone, and his voice came blaring back from the wall of the roundhouse across the street. Stephanie felt Dave's hand on her elbow. Before her, the upturned faces of the men in their blue-cloth caps pressed closely around the car. She tried to think what she would say to them, but her mind had turned numb and she could only stare off into the shimmering sunlight, beyond the roundhouse and railroad yards where the tall white chimney of the Sears Roebuck department store rose over the plain of trees and flat roofs.

"And now, brothers," the loudspeaker roared, "our next speaker, a young lady . . ." He's forgotten my name, Stephanie thought. ". . . a great pleasure, this young lady . . ." Dave reached out for the microphone, adjusted it to Stephanie's height, and put it into her hands. When she spoke, a shrill howl answered her from the opposite wall of the roundhouse.

"Too close," Dave said.

He forced her hands, which were clenched around the throat of the microphone, farther from her face, and she heard her own voice chatter senselessly back at her. It sounded frightened and angry; her knees tapped together under her skirt, and for several minutes she had no idea what she was saying. Then, out of the haze which had covered them, the faces of the men in the crowd took shape again. She felt they were pleased at seeing a woman talking to them from the roof of an automobile, and she began to hear her own words.

"Anybody here speak Polish?" Dave called.

Hands went up all over the crowd, and Stephanie said into the microphone in Polish: "Listen, brothers, get behind this committee and make your unions fight for a wage increase. That's what you got unions for!" There was a wave of clapping and whistling from the crowd. Taking her by the wrists, Dave swung her down from the roof of the car; Hanson, who tried to help her, lost his balance, and they both sprawled backwards into the weeds. When they picked themselves up, laughing and brushing each other off, Dave had already begun to speak. The car creaked on its springs as he stepped from corner to corner of the roof. Stephanie looked up at him. The crowd was on the far side of the car and he faced away from her; but she saw the angle of his head when he turned, his sleeves rolled up to the elbows, the channel of sweat down the back of his blue shirt. He was working carefully through the facts on railroad wages. Stephanie knew from the silence of the crowd that they were following him. Beside her, Hanson clicked his tongue, winked at her, and raising his hand, made a circle with thumb and forefinger.

"What does that mean?" she asked.

"It means you picked a right guy."

She stared at Hanson for a moment in surprise. Then, as she looked up at Dave again, there came to her a sudden perception of Dave, not as she had ever seen him or known him before, but as others must see him. Now it struck her that other men must regard him with very intense feelings—of hatred or loyalty, admiration or fear.

Over the scuffling of the loudspeaker, Dave's voice boomed out: "Support the Independent Committee for a Living Wage. Roll your own lodge into this drive!" Then he cried, "Thanks, brothers," and jumped down from the car. Men pressed around him, asking questions while Hanson stowed the loudspeaker equipment in the back seat. To Stephanie, now that her speech was over, came a light-footed feeling of relief; as for the meeting in the evening, she knew that she would be frightened again, but she did not worry about it. She and Dave and the two lodge officers climbed into the car. Hanson called, "Hop aboard, gents," and a dozen others scrambled on the bumpers and running boards for a lift to the streetcar line.

They drove back to the main intersection by the Sears Roebuck store. Overflowing the sidewalk now were the homebound crowds of workers—men and women from the steel mills with identification tags pinned to their shirts; switchmen from the rail yards carrying their lunch pails and lanterns—all blocking traffic as they swarmed out to the safety islands to board the streetcars which stopped one after another. Hanson parked the car, the five of them pushed along single file towards the department store, where the lodge officials said there was a place to eat. Inside, in the crowded aisles between the merchandise counters, Dave squeezed up beside her.

"You were good," he said into her ear. "You put on a regular stump speech."

"No, I didn't."

"You were all right. They liked you."

"I was awful glad I didn't drop the microphone, Dave, or forget how to talk. But I didn't say much." She glanced up at him. "You're grinning as if you'd eaten a canary. What's the matter with you?"

"I guess I was scareder watching you than the first time I ever got on a stump myself, Stephanie. But you were good. They liked you." She slipped her hand into his, realizing that this was the first time they had ever worked together on anything. He put his arm around her suddenly and kissed her on the lips; and she felt her cheeks flush crimson with embarrassment and pleasure.

After supper they came out to the street again. The leaves of the small trees stirred faintly in the wind. At the intersection the crowd had thinned, the clatter of streetcars came at longer intervals, colored lights blinked on in the window of the department store. Stephanie felt the coolness flow down against the heat of the pavements; shadows veiled the angles of streets, while the twilight darkened across the summer sky. Something strange and bewitching drifted with the evening, the stirring of leaves, the intertwining of lights and shadows. Hanson went off with the two lodge officials for a drink, but she and Dave wandered arm in arm along Commercial Avenue. A few blocks carried them beyond the shopping section to the rows of frame houses built on a lower level than the street. Now the windows showed squares of light, the clatter of dishes came from inside, voices and the smell of cooking food. Eastward, towering over the low roofs, the shapes of the steel mills stood in silhouette against the red glow they cast into the sky. Stephanie and Dave walked a long way before they turned back towards the main intersection. In front of a grocery store, they stopped to watch a farm truck unloading vegetables whose white stems were still spattered with mud from the market gardens beyond the city. The proprietor appeared. Stephanie bought spinach and green peas and baskets of strawberries which they carried back to Hanson's car.

By eight o'clock it was almost dark. They timed their second meeting for the supper hour of the late shift at the roundhouse. The men drifted across the street, bringing their lunch pails; one after another, Stephanie watched the blue caps and overalls pass through the beam of the headlamps, the long shadows sprawl out behind the men across the cobblestone street. When the lodge official, who remembered her name this time, put the microphone into her hands, she felt paralyzed as she had before, and her knees shook; but she found the words she wanted. She talked a few minutes in English, ended in Polish while the men hooted and clapped for her.

Afterwards, Hanson drove Dave downtown for his job at the depot, and Stephanie, with her arms full of fruit and vegetables, dropped off at Richmond Court. She woke in the morning, feeling bright as a new dime, and Dave, when he came in, joked with her about being an accomplished stump speaker. They breakfasted on the strawberries they had bought the night before; then Stephanie hurried off to work. She wondered why a few minutes of speaking from the roof of an automobile should have made her feel so pleased with herself. The answer was easy, she thought; she had been frightened, but she had gone ahead and done it anyway—

That evening, at the People's School, Stephanie finally wound up her class at quarter after ten (fifteen minutes late). This, she thought, was the only class of all those she could remember where the final buzzer had not emptied the classroom as if by magic: that was a compliment for the teacher—or more likely, for the subject. She shooed the last students out into the corridor, turned off the light, and locked the door. The students, who included Negro, Irish, Jewish, and Scandinavian (and a teacher one generation out of Poland, Stephanie added to herself) had gathered in front of the elevator door, still continuing the discussion. The old Irishman was trying to get started on one of his endless harangues about the British Empire. Stephanie called good night to them, and stopped in the bookstore for a moment to glance through the latest books and pamphlets. When she came out into the corridor again on her way to the office with her class attendance list, the corridor was empty except for a woman standing alone at the elevator gate. This figure seemed familiar to Stephanie, and at the same moment the woman turned towards her. It was Genevieve Leeds.

"Hello, Stephanie," Leeds said. She held out her hand and they shook hands. Stephanie glanced down at the dark flowered skirt Leeds was wearing, the silk blouse, the heavy silver chain. As usual, she thought, Leeds looked very sleek.

"What are you doing down here?" she asked.

"Getting some material from the bookstore." Leeds pressed the bell for the elevator, smiled and said, "I'll probably see you at convocation on Saturday, Stephanie. We'll both be graduating at the same time, won't we?"

"I didn't know you were finishing your doctor's degree so soon," Stephanie said.

"I speeded it up a semester. I've been in one university or another for eight years. That's enough for anybody, don't you think?"

The light flashed over the elevator door. "Where are you going afterwards?" Stephanie asked. "Back to Winnetka?"

"Hardly back to Winnetka. I'm going to New York."

"You are?"

"I've gotten a job as economic analyst for a newspaper."

"Good for you," Stephanie said. They looked at each other in silence. Stephanie wondered suddenly whether Leeds was taking her so-called convictions with her, or leaving them behind on campus, along with her slacks and her college textbooks. In a low voice she asked, "And where will you be two years from now?"

The other did not appear startled at the question. "I'll give you my address if you like," she said. "Where will *you* be, Stephanie?"

The elevator gate opened, Leeds waved and stepped into the elevator; the gate closed again. In the five or six years she had known Leeds, Stephanie realized this was the first time it had ever occurred to her that Leeds' phrases might be anything other than hypocritical. Now all at once there seemed ground enough for either judgment; this left her somewhat shaken in her own opinion of herself. She turned rather hesitantly and went on down the corridor to the office. The office door was half open and Stephanie saw that Rita Hanson had been waiting for her.

"I talked to an old acquaintance of yours just now," Rita said.

"Is that so?"

"Genevieve Leeds. She was here in connection with some educational work on the South Side."

"Yes, I just passed her at the elevator. Who was she planning to educate—herself or somebody else?"

"I take it you and Leeds didn't get along very well?"

"I never liked her and as far as I know she never liked me."

"You resented my coming into your class last week, didn't you?"

So that's it after all, Stephanie thought; she's angry at what Pledger told her. "I didn't resent it," she said. "But I understand that each class elects someone to take charge of bringing in books and reading material. What do you think? Is it necessary for another person to come in too?"

"Sometimes a particular issue must be emphasized, Stephanie."

"What's the use having people come down here to teach courses if you're going to take all the class time yourself?" As soon as she spoke, Stephanie was sorry for speaking so sharply. Rita did not look up from the desk, and Stephanie turned to go.

"Your friend Leeds," Rita said; "she told me she didn't remember you as being very active at the University. I'd have thought you would at least have belonged to the Student Union."

"I did join the Student Union. Leeds was one of the main reasons why I dropped out."

"I've never heard any question of Leeds' reliability," Rita said. "That strikes me as rather an irresponsible attitude." Stephanie felt the anger flare up into her throat, but she did not want a fight with Rita; she nodded her head, making no answer, and again turned towards the door. "Your friend Leeds," Rita said; "when she saw your name on the teaching list, she wanted to know if you were teaching a course on Aristotle."

Stephanie swung back. "She asked that, did she?"

"Yes, she wondered if the People's School was sponsoring Aristotle or Saint Thomas this semester."

"Why, that lousy little bitch! I wish I'd been here. And you, Rita, what business was all this of yours?"

"I'm held responsible for the school, Stephanie."

"Since when?"

"I can't help wondering why the Education Committee would have asked such an inexperienced member as yourself to teach a course here."

"Why don't you take that up with the Education Committee? And you're not responsible for the school, Rita. Don't kid yourself. What you amount to here is the bookkeeper." Stephanie left the office, slamming the door behind her.

18

HAWKINS had become involved in a dissertation on the return of Odysseus, and Stephanie sat idly, paying little attention to what he said. It was hot in the basement of the chapel, full of the limy smell of new concrete. All around her, the M.A.'s and Ph.D's were struggling into their gowns, adjusting the colored stoles and tassels which accorded with their rank. Hawkins, whose gown covered his stomach tight as a drum hide, was standing up because he was afraid to sit down. She heard him say that her husband bore the legendary character of Odysseus himself, and she looked up frowning.

"I haven't been listening, Hawkins. Are you making more witticisms?"

"I was saying that all of us here have heard of your husband, but no one yet has seen him. When you step outside, I fancy you'll find everyone you know encircling him ogle-eyed."

"How will they know whom to ogle at?" she asked. "They haven't seen him yet."

"Why, the same way the soldiers recognized Christ in the garden. After the ceremony, the first person you kiss, Stephanie—"

"I shan't kiss anyone."

"No, no," Hawkins cried. "I've mixed my metaphors. In fact, Smith told me himself he'd arranged with the lame swineherd, your brother Victor, to play the role of finger-man. You aren't apprehensive of violence, Stephanie? You know, I can't help remembering what a vengeance Odysseus wreaked on the suitors, even though poor Penelope never sewed anything more serious than her own web—" Hawkins stopped with his mouth open as if he had heard something that startled him. Stephanie, who had been studying the cracks in the concrete pavement, raised her eyes. Then she realized what he had said and jumped to her feet.

"That wasn't very funny." His eyes dropped away from hers.

Even as she spoke, her anger faded and she felt sorry for him. She turned away without speaking; the marshals were forming up the procession and she took her place in the line.

Organ music rumbled down from the chapel above them. Slowly the procession mounted the stairs, then moved down the central aisle between the crowded pews, the Ph.D.'s leading the way with the M.A.'s at their heels, while the unsashed hordes of bachelors trod humbly at the rear. The organ shuddered into the alcoves of the church; the bobbing black mortar boards poured endlessly through the shafts of sunlight which slanted down from the windows. Stephanie took her place in the choir stall reserved for the masters' candidates and leaned back, looking up at the pointed arches above her head. Through an open window behind the choir, puffs of the June morning scented with lilac drifted past. She felt sleepy and tired and wondered if her hat would fall off when she got up to take her diploma. It seemed to her strange that this milestone in a span of many years should call forth no unusual sensations. The organ ceased abruptly as if its bellows had collapsed, and a mosquito remained humming shrilly in the silence. Hidden by a gothic buttress, some officer of the University began to address the multitude, telling them of the pricelessness of knowledge and the duty of young folk in an unscholarly world. The graduate candidates nodded drowsily in the choir stall while the address dragged on and came to an end at last. The doctors and masters and bachelors marched up single file for their diplomas. In the nave of the chapel, the great doors were thrown open and the crowd poured out to the lawn, black gowns mingling now with the light-colored suits and summer dresses. As Stephanie made her way towards one of the side doors, she found Hawkins close behind her. "Am I forgiven?" he asked.

"You've been unbearable the last few weeks. What's the matter with you?"

"No doubt I did it deliberately," he said. "Good friends are the rarest of vintages. One feels sad at seeing the bottle emptied."

"Why, you sound like an old man."

"I'm close to forty."

From the steps she stared across the crowded lawn, looking for Dave and Roman. "Like J. Alfred Prufrock of immortal memory," Hawkins said, "one takes refuge in small talk." He brandished his roll of parchment. "This is my key to a cozy berth in some small and worthless college equipped with modern plumbing, but lacking any divine justification. One takes refuge in a witticism; from the Puritans one defends oneself somewhat uneasily—"

"What Puritans?"

"You, Stephanie. People like yourself and your husband—and many others, I presume—"

"There they are. Now quit weeping for yourself, Hawkins." But she saw that he had been right about the oglers. Dave and Roman stood near the corner of the chapel. Between them, balancing on his crutches, Victor was making elaborate gestures—like a patent-medicine salesman, she thought; while near by, half the people she knew at the University had assembled, chatting in pairs and looking carefully in other directions. "That bunch of sheep," she said to Hawkins. But when she glanced around, Hawkins had disappeared.

Roman spotted her, began to wave his arms, shouting, "There she is, there's Stevie! Here we are, we're here, Stevie." He made her unroll her diploma and regarded it from top to bottom as though he were deciphering very fine print. Stephanie returned the stares of the spectators, but only two or three of the people she knew came over to them. These she introduced coldly, leaving them to flounder between Dave who was not talking and Roman who was speechless with enthusiasm. But Victor filled the breach, chattering along with no one to interrupt him. Stephanie felt Roman tugging at the sleeve of her gown. "You get your friends, Stevie," he whispered. "We all have a drink together."

She shook her head. "Let's go for a drink, but we'll leave the friends here." Then she turned quickly to Dave, put her hand in his, and they walked away from the chapel, with Victor and Roman following behind.

Stephanie returned her gown to the rental office; and as they left the campus, she noticed that Dave, who had scarcely spoken, began to limber up. They went to a restaurant on Sixty-Third Street where they ate lunch and sat most of the afternoon getting drunk; Roman was giggling like a kid, telling Dave how he had recognized Stephanie in the procession and what he had felt like when he saw her step right up to collect her paper. He told them two or three times how he had made up his mind before Victor was born that his kids were going to have a real education—and now look at it, look at it! The whiskey had carried Roman into a talking jag which seemed to release the whole accumulation, the speechless days and nights of many years. Dave and Stephanie drank and listened, while Victor smoked one cigarette after another.

It was four o'clock before they paid their bill and went out into the blistering afternoon sunlight. Roman said good bye half a dozen times, then finally boarded a streetcar home to catch some sleep before work. Victor walked off without saying where he was going, while Stephanie and Dave caught the suburban train downtown to meet Hanson and Rita.

But Hanson was tied up at a conference of shop stewards, and it was almost dusk when they finally started for the Dunes. They drove out through South Chicago again, crossed into Indiana, and stopped for supper at a cafeteria on the main street of Gary. After her last session with Rita, Stephanie was primed for another fight; but she found Rita curiously humble now that her husband was with her. As they sat down at the table, Rita leaned towards her. "I'm sorry we had that argument the other day. It wasn't any business of mine about the Student Union." She blushed all over her wide freckled face. "Hanson straightened me out."

"Sure I did," Hanson said. "I told her because she was secretary of the school didn't give her any business taking over the functions of the State Educational Committee." Hanson grinned suddenly. "And if it's okay with you, Dave, I'm going to straighten Stephanie out a little bit too."

"Has he got your permission?" Stephanie asked. Dave nodded.

"I don't know anything about this gal Leeds," Hanson told her, "and I don't care. But to say that you couldn't work in the Student Union because you disliked Leeds, that was ridiculous now, wasn't it?"

"I suppose so."

"It's almost an occupational disease with some of our people," Hanson told her. "They can't work with this person, can't get along with somebody else. The fact is, you can work with anybody if you're determined to do it. And we've got to work with people; that's what makes us tick. I'll say ninety per cent of the cases where somebody says he can't work with somebody else, he's only covering up that for some reason he doesn't want to work. I don't believe it was because of Leeds that you dropped out of the Student Union."

"Maybe it wasn't, Hanson." She understood he was not talking so much about Leeds in the Student Union as about Rita at the People's School.

"Well, that's ancient history. I was using it for an example. But here's the point. Anybody we can't work with, we've got to fight; there's no such thing as being neutral. But we can't afford to fight anybody for personal reasons; we've got enough to do fighting the genuine wreckers and enemies of the working class. You see what I mean?"

Hanson, his graying blond hair straggling over his forehead, looked at her anxiously. She knew he was trying to say what he had on his mind without offending her, and she nodded her head. What a pity he'd had to marry that Rita, she thought; but she noticed again that Rita acted very differently with Hanson; the overbearing executive tone of the other night was gone, she had become quiet and as if unsure of herself.

"We ready to go?" Hanson asked.

They got up from the cafeteria table and went back to the car. The neon lights were blinking on down the main street of Gary; but the summer twilight lingered in the sky, fading from blue to gray, infinitely high over the flat fronts of the buildings. Hanson drove while Stephanie and Dave sat in the back seat. He put his arm around her and she dropped her head on his shoulder; as the car swung out to the highway, the evening wind poured across their faces.

Off to the left, against the darkening horizon, Stephanie saw the stacks of the steel mills, out of which jets of flame flickered up now and then into the blanket of smoke which hung over them. Barometer of war, she thought; as London burns, the sky reddens over Lake Michigan, the housewives buy food once more in the stores of Gary and South Chicago. She stared out the side window, watching how the tongues licked up red and yellow into the sky, while the shadows danced fantastically for miles across the flat, marshy ground.

"Dave," she asked, "have you ever been in the steel mills?"

He nodded.

"When?"

"When I worked on the ore boat."

"I'd almost forgotten about the ore boat. That was a long time ago."

"Seven years," he said.

234

She turned, clutching at the lapels of his jacket, pressing her face against his chin. She remembered the summer morning when he had come to the house and she had refused to see him; but she had watched from the window how he walked slowly down the street past the coal yard and disappeared around the corner towards the streetcar line. That middle summer of the depression there were no jobs in Chicago, he was going away to work on the ore boat, and she had let him go without speaking to him. That was the spring she had started at the University and she had thought she would never see him again. How long ago that seemed—and then as if only a moment had passed, a month or a week. When Dave had returned from the ore boat and wherever else he had wandered during that year, she had known in spite of herself that somehow they were joined closely together; as if during the spring, when they had first gone together, they had built up a common language, each one growing so meshed into the memories and understandings of the other that they were linked irrevocably whichever way she turned, living together or living apart, whether they loved or whether they hated. Only a short while ago, she remembered, she had told Martin how from the very beginning she had doubted that her marriage to Dave could last. And that had been true, that was how she had felt; but the other was true also. These conflicting ideas, these opposite feelings had existed simultaneously in her own mind.

She thought suddenly that all her life she had been divided in some such manner as this. All her life that she could remember, part of herself had nourished hatred against the other parts. Among the struggling factions she had never known which side to choose, uncertain what the factions were, or to which side adhered the shifting center of consciousness she called her self. Yet why? Why had it always been this way?

Dave's arm was around her. The highway hummed solidly against the wheels of the car. As she glanced over her shoulder, she saw that the steel mills had dropped from sight, leaving only a glow on the horizon. Around them now, the fields of the market-garden country lay misty and flat in the twilight. Always Dave had seemed to her very different from herself; he had seemed to possess a monolithic quality, she thought, as if there were no division of opinion within him between what he desired and what he determined. She remembered she had felt sometimes that Dave was undivided only because he was stupid and insensitive; she had

235

tried to feel contemptuous towards him because he lacked the imagination to be torn apart by conflicting impulses. But now she understood that all the time they had lived together before he went to Spain, she had tried deliberately to nourish in him the civil war of her own mind. She had wanted to see him torn apart as she was torn, between the longing for prestige and safety on the one hand, and the hunger to fight on the other.

This sharp insight startled her. She shivered uneasily. It was not what she had done that frightened her; but that she had done it without knowing what she was doing. For all the while another part of herself had counted on Dave to remain unshakable. When she had sought refuge in the University at the bounty of the North Shore trustees—if Dave had done the same, she would have despised him for it.

She straightened up in her seat. The moon was rising. At the side of the highway, telegraph poles ticked past monotonously, and now the flat country was ruffling up into dunes and hillocks where slopes of white sand gleamed between the jet black shoulders of scrub oak. Off towards the lakeshore, a line of sand dunes sparkled like surf in the moonlight.

"It's a lucky thing you're consistent," she said.

"Why?"

"Because I'm not."

Hanson put on the brakes suddenly. Ahead of them a lighted gas station and café stood at a crossroad. Slowing down, they waited while three trailer trucks, lit up with red and green Christmas tree lights, roared past them in the direction of Michigan; the car swung across the highway, bumped over some tracks, and rolled down a country road between hedges of alder whose leaves hung silver gray in the beam of the headlamps. Hanson stopped in front of a farmhouse, and he and Dave went inside to find if the land-lady had room for them. While she waited, Stephanie climbed out of the back seat and walked up and down in the grass which yielded pleasantly beneath her feet. Across the lawn, in the glare of the headlights, stood a cast-iron carriage boy on a block of white-washed concrete. He was holding out his crooked finger to receive the reins, and behind him his shadow, making the same gesture, sprawled across the white clapboard front of the farmhouse.

Hanson and Dave came out after a time. They drove the car around to the back of the farmhouse, where the landlady showed them into a double cabin. The cabin smelled of fresh-sawed pine board, and drops of resin had exuded from knots in the unpainted walls; a partition down the center divided the cabin into two rooms, each of which was almost completely filled by a four-posted double bed.

"Looks like tourists have got only one idea," Hanson said.

"To sleep?" Stephanie asked.

"That's not my idea," Hanson told her.

They went outside laughing, circled the farmhouse, and followed the road between the alder hedges towards the lakeshore. They could hear the rumble of motor trucks on the highway behind them, while close at hand, the night rang shrilly with the sound of crickets. Clouds piling up, darkened the moon; but as Stephanie's eyes grew accustomed to the darkness, she saw again the dunes rising in front of her. The road turned, climbed sharply under the scrub oaks. Their feet sank into the loose sand and their breath came short as they climbed; beyond the crest of each dune, they found another crest mounting higher yet. But they reached the divide at last; before them, like sparsely-covered ribs, the dunes fell away towards the beach, the line of surf, and the black expanse of lake. Joining hands, the four of them raced down, slipping and stumbling, shooting feet first in an avalanche of sand down the steep bluff to the beach. They picked themselves up, shaking the sand from their clothes, and walked along the hard-packed rim where a ribbon of froth bubbled towards their feet and fell back again as each wave rolled up and receded. Rita pulled off her shoes and stockings and splashed up to her knees in the water, laughing like a two-year-old.

After a time, when they had walked for a short distance up the beach and returned, they sat down beside a timber which they found half buried in the sand. Rita began pestering Dave to talk about Spain. Dave had opened his jackknife and was building a small fire of splinters that he whittled from the beam. He looked up at Rita with a grin. "Ever tell you about the time I rode in a boxcar with a stiff?"

Asking Dave to talk about Spain was time wasted, Stephanie knew; now he would put Rita off with one of his endless yarns about the railroad. Stephanie punched him in the ribs and dropped her head down as if she were going to sleep. "Are you making this up?" she asked.

"Of course not. This was just after the ore boat we were talking about, Stephanie. They laid off the crew in Duluth, so I hired out

for a couple of months firing an engine on the Northern Pacific—"
Stephanie saw the moonlight flood suddenly across the beach as
the moon rode through a chasm of the clouds. But above the lake,
the clouds were massing higher, and after a moment the moon
plunged behind them again, leaving a milky glow over the crests.
"—I got stranded in Winslowe, Montana," Dave was saying. "It
turned cold as Greenland and we were trying to get across the
Rockies before we froze to death—"

"Who's *we?*" Stephanie asked.

"Some guy. I never did know his name. He was already in the
boxcar when I got in. I remember I climbed into the car outside
the depot just as the freight was pulling out. It was close to zero
and I was hopping and dancing around trying to keep limber. Just
then a voice sings out, 'You better not dance in that direction, bud,
there's a stiff up there.'

" 'What do you mean, a stiff?' I asked.

" 'Go take a look if you don't believe me,' the voice says. So I
eased myself up the car and struck a match. There was a man sitting with his back against the forward wall, his hat pulled over
his eyes as if he was sleeping. I stared at him until the match burned
my fingers, and then in the dark, I reached down and touched him.
He wasn't only a stiff; he was froze solid—"

"Oh my God!" Rita said. "What did you do?"

"Went down to the far end of the car, and the other fellow and
I spent the night jumping up and down slapping ourselves. We
pulled into Butte just before daybreak, and the only thing we
could think of was to go someplace where it was warm and drink
a cup of coffee. But we didn't have any money. Except for two
dollars in my undershirt I didn't tell that fellow about, because I
was saving it till I really hit the end of the rope. 'Well,' I said to
him, 'did you frisk the stiff?'

" 'No,' he says, 'I didn't.'

" 'Here are the matches then. Go take a look.'

" 'Guess you better go,' he says. So I went up forward, only I
didn't strike any match because I didn't want to see anything.
I got down on the floor beside it, and the sweat was dripping off
me when I finally shoved my hand into its pocket—"

"Empty," Hanson said.

"No, I found a dollar bill and some change. We thought we'd
struck it rich. But when we went to get down from the car, we
saw the flashlights working along the train from both ends—the

company dicks shaking the bums out. We were afraid to make a break for it because we were so cold we didn't think we could run fast enough. So I grabbed the stiff by the feet, pulled it across the car, and left it sitting in the doorway. After a while a light flashed in and a voice yelled, 'Get up out of there, you son of a bitch.' But the stiff didn't say anything and the cop cracked it across the ankle with his club. That stiff's ankle made a noise like a dinner gong, Rita, like when you hit a pipe with a rock. The cop let out a howl and dropped his lantern. Then we heard the other cops talking it over; they were telling each other the stiff would be too heavy to carry, and they'd just ask the switchmen to drop the car off beside the depot when they busted the train up. So the cops went away, and after a while we crawled out and hobbled up to the town."

"That's a pretty story," Stephanie said. "Do you believe it, Hanson?"

"Is it true, Dave?"

"Of course it's true. I just told you, didn't I?"

"So did you get to the coast?" Hanson asked.

"No, we got in jail." Stephanie felt Dave's hand on her shoulder. "Sometime I'll tell you about the jails I been in," he said. "The dirtiest one of the lot was right here in Chicago. But after that night in the boxcar, we didn't feel like riding the freights for a while. We went down and got in a passenger train. Of course we didn't have any tickets, so a couple of miles out of town, before the conductor comes through, the other guy went into the men's room and pulled the emergency stop cord. Then I walked down from the other end of the coach shouting, 'Everybody out of this car please!' Those people piled out like crazy, leaving their baggage and ticket stubs and everything else. I picked up a couple of stubs that would have carried us all the way to Seattle, only—"

"Only what?"

"The cops come aboard in Spokane, and we spent the rest of the winter in the state penitentiary."

"What a maniac," Stephanie said. "You know, Hanson, Dave looks like a slow, stolid kind of fellow, and yet he does things like that as if it were a matter of course."

"But I never get away with anything," Dave said. "It always winds up with me getting cracked over the bean or carted off to jail. But the Washington State penitentiary was the best berth I hit all that year. They made me a trusty and I used to hoe the warden's vegetable garden outside the fence and run errands for him. I'd have been willing to pay rent there, if I'd had any money."

Stephanie fed more shavings into the fire. She turned sideways, resting her head on Dave's lap, and stared up at his face, which appeared as though caricatured by the fragmentary glow of the burning splinters. "You should have seen Dave when he was a kid," she said. "He looked just like a little Dutch boy—stubbly yellow hair and pinky cheeks—"

"Have you been going together since you were kids?" Rita asked.

"We used to go to the same school, but I wouldn't say we went together. I always felt pretty snooty about Dave because he played football and necked the high-school girls in the basement."

"Didn't you go for that?" Rita asked.

"No, I had my mind on higher things." She laughed, and they sat silent for a moment, listening to the hush and fall of the waves against the beach. Lightning flickered in the distance, and a few raindrops splattered over their faces. Rita pushed herself up from the beam where she had been sitting.

"We'd better start back or we'll get wet."

"We might stay and go for a swim," Dave said. "How about it?"

"We're too old for that," Hanson told him. "Rita and I are heading back to that four-poster bed. You two stay if you feel like it."

"Let's stay," Stephanie said. She felt Dave's hand tighten on her shoulder. They sat without moving while Hanson and Rita stumbled away across the beach, their voices fading into the darkness. The raindrops had stopped, but lightning still flashed under the clouds. "You remember the spring we first went out together?" she asked.

He nodded, and she said, "This is sort of a high point for me. I've been working seven years for this masters' degree. . . ." Then, as if there were some connection, she added, "I remember you came to talk to Victor one night, and all of a sudden I found you staring at me across the kitchen table as if you'd never seen me before. You asked me for a date and I didn't want to go."

"But you went."

"Yes, I was very lonely. I had you classed as a hot-rock because you played football and hung out with the high-school girls in that damn candy store. I decided you weren't my type. But I went anyway." As she looked up at his face above her, she thought of the Saturday nights when they had gone to the movies that spring

240

and then sat by the lakeshore because they had not enough money to do anything else. Each time he brought her home, she had told herself, "I won't go out with him again, because he's not my type and I'm only giving him a wrong idea." But on the following Saturday he came for her and she would be waiting. Always it made her angry that he did not talk to her about the important things, as she considered them—art and painting. She was not interested in engineering, she explained to him very often; but that was what they always talked about—buildings and engineering and how they could reconstruct the city of Chicago. Sometimes she would forget herself enough to join his enthusiasm while he talked, yet afterwards she would be angry for it. "That's the one thing you can figure as sure,"—she could almost hear him again, the stubbly-headed Dutch boy telling her in his matter-of-fact tone: "That's the one thing that's sure, Stephanie, if you can build things. Because no matter what happens, they'll always need somebody to build bridges and houses—" So he had laid out the city for her in parks and playgrounds, boulevards, industrial zones, residential sections. And all the while he was doing it, she kept thinking they ought to be talking about music or painting or something important. But she opened her arms to him at last and they made love in the park; a miserable few moments, and afterwards she walked home with her head down, refusing to look at him. That had been their farewell date before he went away on the ore boat. He had come to the house the following morning, but she locked herself in her room and would not speak to him. From the upstairs window, she had watched him walk away down the street. And although she had enjoyed this tragic gesture, she had felt very miserable; she was eighteen in that spring of 1933, and he was twenty.

Roman, for all his years of seniority, had been laid off most of that year, she remembered; while Dave lost his job on the railroad, had to give up the course in engineering, and went away on the ore boat. And that was the end of the Dutch boy with the fat and pinky cheeks. For when she had seen him again a year and a half later, the fat cheeks had grown straight and tough, the quality of enthusiasm which once had set him bubbling over with ideas about parks and buildings had toughened into a hard and silent drive. While she was a sophomore at the University, Dave was fighting the police on the street corners, acting as organizer in the tenants' league, leader in the Unemployed Councils. . . .

"Dave," she said. He was running his fingers through her hair. "You liked that engineering, didn't you?"

"Sure I did."

"Do you ever want to go back to it?"

"I wouldn't mind going back—if certain things happened first."

"But don't they always need people to build things?" she asked. "Houses and bridges and things?"

She saw that he remembered the phrase.

"You're kidding me now. But I'm not building any bridges for somebody to make a million bucks out of."

"You'll be all your life on the foundation. Someone else will build the bridge."

"That's all right. Somebody else will fly the first rocket to the moon, but I'm not eating my heart out over that."

"I suppose not. But to have worked so hard on something—" And then he had let it drop as if it had been nothing, she thought; didn't that ever worry him? Had she been in his position, the choice would have torn her apart.

"And if it was me," she said, "if it was me that got in the way of—of building the foundation, you'd drop me just as painlessly, wouldn't you? But there's no need to ask. You've done it once already."

"Are you jealous because of that, Stephanie?"

"Sometimes. Why shouldn't I be?"

"It wasn't painless," he said.

"But you'd do it again?"

She stared at him and he looked down at her, smiling. "Of course I'd do it again. What's the use being jealous of that? It's like being jealous of the food a man eats. If he ate different food, he'd be a different person, that's all."

She started to answer him, then checking herself, turned away, peering across the lake. But she felt him watching her, and at last she said, "I love you so much that I hurt inside, Dave." The sound of her own voice surprised her because it was distant and impersonal, as though she were discussing a railroad fare with a ticket agent. "Now I'll tell you something maybe you know already."

"What?"

"I *have* tried quite often to change you into a different person. And if I'd succeeded, I suppose I would have hated you."

He took her by the shoulders, drawing her backwards across his knees. Her hair was in the sand, and he bent down, kissing her ears and throat. As she tightened her arms around him, she felt pressing uneasily inside her the things she had never spoken of, that now she wanted to tell him, to explain to him so that he would understand. But he jumped up and pulled her to her feet. Raindrops pattered towards them across the sand. The lightning, ripping suddenly through the clouds, showed her the endless succession of white headlands stretching away to the north. "We'll get wet anyhow, Stephanie. Let's go swimming."

"Mightn't we be struck by lightning?"

"Sure we might," he agreed.

She pulled off her clothes and followed him across the beach. The rain came pelting against her body in small drops, hard and cold now, driven by gusts of cold wind. But the water of the lake was warm. They swam out until the water reached up to their chins, while only the tips of their toes touched the sandy bottom. Behind them the blinding white sand dunes leaped again and again out of the darkness and shivered away through a blue afterglow into the darkness again. Thunder followed instantly on the lightning flashes. From the lukewarm water of the lake, wreaths of steam drifted up as the raindrops drummed across the surface.

"Think how wet our clothes will be," Stephanie said. "We'll have to stay in bed all day tomorrow while they're drying out."

"I won't mind that."

She pressed her face against his, trying to focus in her mind the things she had wanted to explain to him. "We've had kind of a remembering jag on tonight," she said. "You don't like remembering jags, do you?"

"I guess they don't do any harm once in a while."

"Was that story true about the boxcar?"

"More or less."

"I never heard you say much about that winter."

"No." She felt him hesitate, and then as if he were asking a question he had held for a long time in his mind, he said, "Tell me something. Why were you so mad at me that night before I went on the ore boat?"

"Have you been wondering about that ever since?" He seemed to have picked up the question where they had dropped it that night seven years before.

"Off and on," he said.

"Almost, Dave, you asked me what I was just trying to figure out in my mind how to tell you. Why was I mad at you after that night? I was a girl with a lot of romantic notions. It came as a shock, you know, to find myself making love with a guy under a bush in the park."

"To find yourself? You did as much of the work getting us there as I did."

"Perhaps that's why I was angry. It's not easy to explain, Dave. When I first knew you, I was living in a kind of dream world which I had built around the Art Institute and the pictures there—I used to go to look at them every Saturday. I don't know whether I can make you understand or not, you're so different in some ways. I was really very lonely, and I made up for myself the friends I needed just by imagining them. The kind of guy I thought I wanted to fall in love with, I dreamed about until I actually fell in love with the dreams. I used to make myself half sick with thinking about it.

"Then you came along, and while I wanted to see you, I kept telling myself you weren't at all like the guy I had dreamed for myself." She stopped. The rain was slackening, the lightning flashed into the distance beyond the dunes. "You taught me things about myself I didn't want to know. Those high-school girls who used to hang out at Balknis' Candy Store, I thought I hated them more than anybody in the world, and I was determined I wouldn't be like them. But I couldn't understand any difference between what I did with you in the park that night, and what they did in the back yards and alleys. I hated myself and you and everybody else."

"If we'd had a little more money," Dave said, "we'd have gone to a hotel. Then it would have seemed different."

"You say bitter things sometimes. That's more *my* style."

"Well, I didn't feel very happy after that night either. Or in the morning when you wouldn't see me."

"But do you understand what I was trying to say to you? When your mother asked me once how I felt about the railroad and I said I hated it—that wasn't any joke. All my life I've felt the shadow of that thing hanging over me. If it was only what I saw looking out the window when I was a little girl, Dave; the embankment and the tracks and the coal yard and the smoke over the houses. But there was the way we lived, the way they drove Roman day after day; there was what happened to my brother Johnny and my brother Victor—and what happened to me. That's why I made up those dreams about the Art Institute. And when I first went to the

University, I thought everything was going to be different. I was going to break through into a new world."

"Stephanie . . ."

"No wait. This is what I want to tell you. Often, as far back as I can remember, I've had the feeling that I was trapped in some strange, gloomy world like a nightmare, and I've wanted to break my way out into a new, bright, sharp world—"

"There aren't any nightmares, Stephanie, and no place to run to when you're awake."

"I knew you'd say that. That's what you've always been saying to me. Half of me knows that and half of me doesn't. That's why I hate you sometimes."

She stared at him, trying to make out the expression of his face. She wanted to ask him, do you understand me? Do you see what I'm trying to tell you? But she did not ask. Instead, she turned, struck off through the water and he swam beside her. Smooth and black, the water flowed past. After a time, as the thought of the silent depths beneath entered her mind, she swung back towards shore and they splashed up through the shallows to the beach. The night was clearing after the storm, the air had turned cold, and their teeth chattered as they ran along looking for their clothes. They found them soaking wet, flattened into the sand by the rain, and they had to rinse them in the lake before they dressed. The wet clothes made the air seem even colder than before.

Slapping themselves, trying to keep warm, they scrambled up the bluffs to the road that led back towards the farmhouse. From the highest crest they looked out for a moment over the flat Indiana prairies, black and silver in the moonlight, streaked with mist which spiraled up from the rain-soaked ground. The red and green lights of a trailer truck bored northwards on the highway. She reached out for his hand, and they ran down the slope under the oak thickets.

In the cabin, Dave pulled her clothes off and rubbed her with one of the thin towels provided by the landlady. Stephanie stopped him, and with teeth chattering, said,

"Dave, listen . . ."

"What, Stephanie?"

"Did it make sense what I said out there? Did you understand me?"

"I think I did."

With the towel, they rubbed each other until their arms ached. When they crawled into bed, she pulled herself against him, whispering, "Do you love me?"

"I do, Stephanie."

"Thank God, you're consistent."

She heard Hanson and Rita snoring from the other half of the double cabin; and in the distance, she heard the rumble of the trucks on the highway.

1940

IN midsummer Pledger's daughter Judith finished her course at the nurses' training school. A few weeks later she got married and went away to New York. Pledger had foreseen that this would happen, but he had not known how to stop it. And he had not been sure in his own mind whether it would be right to stop it even if he could. Judith was grown up; she had the right to choose her own husband. And who was he to feel that she had chosen wrongly because she had not chosen the man he would have picked for her?

But he felt in his heart that the cards had been stacked against her, that she had never had a fair choice. He understood that the South Side neighborhood they lived in, the chapel, the Chile Parlor, must have seemed to Judith like a treadmill where she could run out her whole life for nothing—just as she probably believed Pledger and Ruby had spent their lives for nothing. She had never talked to him much about the nurses' training course; but Pledger knew most of the girls in the course were white and very likely did not make friends with her. And after she finished the course, how many jobs would she find open to Negro nurses? About that, they had never talked either; but he had often thought of it, and he was certain that she had thought about it too.

She was tall and pretty to look at and he was glad of that. During the summer, in the last few months of her training course, she had come home often for week ends. Then Ruby cooked a big dinner and they held a celebration. But Judith always had a date for the evening; she disappeared after dinner to go dancing some-place, came home late, and slept most of Sunday. And always it was the same man who called for her—the man with the blue Buick automobile. He was a pleasant-acting, easy-talking man, but he never bothered to sit down and say much to Pledger or Ruby. He had some money and came from New York, and that was all they knew about him. They learned nothing from Judith, either; when Pledger asked her any questions, she got angry and complained everybody was bossing her around.

Evenings when Pledger found the man waiting for Judith in the Chile Parlor, he checked his desire to knock him through the store front window. He told himself again that he had no business to stick his neck in. Judith was grown up and she had the right to do what she wanted for herself. And he tried once more to understand from Judith's point of view the value of things he himself had set no value by: money to dance and drink with and a shiny automobile. Here these were if she wanted them, waiting at the corner, hers for the taking. New York had bright lights, things always came out right in New York, so the stories and the movies said. He tried to tell her different, but why should she believe him? And so one afternoon when Pledger came home from work Ruby showed him the note from Judith saying she had gone off to get married.

The next week the couple stopped on their way to New York. They ate a meal with Ruby and Pledger in the Chile Parlor and all talked very friendly together. Judith packed her suitcases and Billy carried them down to the automobile for her. As they said good bye on the sidewalk, she began to cry a little; then she got into the automobile with her new husband and they drove off up the street.

She wrote a few gay-sounding letters from New York and Pledger made up his mind there was no use worrying about her. He was working harder than he could ever remember, with his class at the People's School and the campaign for the wage movement. During the summer and fall he saw the wage drive grow until everyone knew about it and everybody was asking how long the union officials could hold out against the demands of their own membership.

As they had anticipated at the conference of the twenty-five rail-road workers in June, there were bitter attacks against the wage movement. Pledger heard the word going around that the whole thing was only a wedge to bring the CIO into the railroad industry. And he heard that Communists were swarming into the industry (he wished he could locate a few more of them) and the Communists didn't give a damn for the rank and file or the wage movement either; all they cared about was to drag in a lot of politics and radical slogans and break up the established unions to make room for the CIO. He felt the confusion and division pour down among the men as if someone had opened a sluice gate. He knew where it came from and he fought against it, explaining, arguing, and explaining.

To give themselves a better weapon, he and Dave Spaas started a little mimeographed newspaper. In every issue, they emphasized that the wage movement had been started by railroad workers who were members of the established unions; that it was not a rival union; that it had no connections with the CIO. They wrote that certain union officers, gone soft in their pie-card jobs, had lost the guts for a fight with the railroad companies, and were trying to cover up by labeling everybody who spoke for decent wages a Communist. One way or another, the little sheet got around to most of the yards and roundhouses, the shanties and locker rooms, the lunchcounters and the taverns where the men stopped for a beer after work. It grew into a kind of official organ for the wage movement, and by mid-autumn it was carrying the names of eighteen sponsoring railroad lodges. These became the framework for the whole drive. The eighteen lodges agreed to call a city-wide conference in December for the purpose of setting up a Wage Movement Committee and planning a series of mass meetings immediately after.

Throughout the entire summer, Pledger and the other coach cleaners had watched the company bulletin board, waiting for Upstairs Jarvis to post the opening of a new job. But when the job came, it was Red who heard about it first. He grabbed Pledger one morning at the door of the roundhouse. "Come here, you son of a bitch. I got some news for you."

"That so, man?"

"They're putting on an extra gang in the wheel pit the first of the month. There'll be two carmen's jobs open."

Pledger went up to the office and watched Jarvis' clerk post the two jobs on the bulletin board. At lunch hour that day, he called his Lodge members together in the Negroes' locker room and they went over their seniority list. Andrew Masters had the highest seniority, but he said he was too old to go back into the wheel pit. That left only Pledger and one other who had worked as regular carmen; they went to the office together to put their bids in.

"You can't bid for those jobs," the clerk told them.

"How come?" Pledger asked.

"You're coach cleaners. You're not eligible."

"How come that?"

"All right, leave the bids. It don't make any difference to me."

As they turned away, Pledger saw the clerk get up and head for Jarvis' private room. He knew what Jarvis would say; but in the end it would be up to Jennison and the vice-president, Donohue. For they could enforce the seniority if they made up their minds to do it. This was the test of the new charter. The coach cleaners waited, watching the bulletin board. At the end of the week, the jobs were assigned—to two white men who had hired out on the Great Midland only six months before.

Pledger hunted all over the yard until he found Uncle Jennison on his back under a Pullman car, working at the air brakes. Pledger sat down on the ties beside Jennison's upturned feet. "What about those jobs?" he asked.

"I know, McAdams. I heard about 'em."

"What are you going to do about 'em? That's what I want to know."

"I'll see those fellows today. I'll put it to 'em straight out."

"You'll put it to *them*? What you figure to do, ask them not to take the jobs?" Uncle Jennison crawled out from under the car, wiping the sweat from his bald head. "Aren't our seniority rights written into that contract?" Pledger demanded. "I and my partner got twenty years seniority over both those men put together. Who you going to ask to do anything? You're going over to Upstairs Jarvis' office and tell him—I said *tell* him—that job belongs to us."

"Now take it easy—"

"Take it easy nothing. If Jarvis says no, you call the vice-president and take the case to the adjustment board."

Uncle Jennison's long jaw champed up and down. He fished out a plug of tobacco, broke off a chew, and shoved it into his mouth. "I can't do it that way, McAdams. The union won't back me."

"They took our dues money right smart, didn't they? What you mean, they won't back you?"

"I don't mean they ain't really going to back me. Honest to

Christ, they won't let you men down. You heard what the vice-president himself said when he came to your meeting last spring, McAdams. But they put it to me like this: you got to do things easy, Jennison, by diplomacy, you might say; you can't go bulling in and antagonize a lot of people. And I don't even know if we got the legal ground. You ain't on the Carbuilder seniority roster, McAdams—"

"Those white men, were they on the Carbuilders' roster?"

"No, but they'd done that work before."

Pledger suddenly felt sorry for Uncle Jennison. He got to his feet, and as he turned away, said,

"I wouldn't want to be in your shoes."

Jennison ran after him, catching him by the arm. "Listen to me, McAdams. I'd get you that job in a minute if I had it in my power. But how can I move if they ain't going to back me down at the headquarters?"

The next day Pledger heard from Red how Uncle Jennison went to the depot at eleven o'clock to speak to Dave Spaas. "We were at that lunchcounter knocking off a cup of coffee before we went to work," Red said. "Jennison comes up, grabs hold of Dave, and begins crying in his ear."

"What did Dave say?"

"Dave says, 'How soon they goin' to make you a foreman, Jennison?' Then he walks off like he hadn't even seen him."

19

THEY did not go again to the lakeshore that summer. But Stephanie thought often of the sand dunes, and how when you looked out from the crest of one, the next appeared almost within arm's reach. Or seemed so until you started towards it. Then you found the long hollow in between, where your feet slipped in loose sand and the underbrush cut off your view. The going became more difficult; each new step required an effort of will. And with the end of summer, Stephanie felt herself coming down from the crest, where for a brief period the other crests had seemed to her so close at hand.

From the time of her graduation in June, she had hoped for a research job at the University or a place in the laboratory of one of the city hospitals. When no such job turned up, she went back to the long grind towards her doctor's degree. She held on to her half-time job typing lecture notes for her professor, because she and Dave needed the extra money. Her afternoons she set aside to study in the library, and decided that when fall came, if she still had no regular job, she would start taking courses again. But the afternoons slipped past her with little accomplished. She seemed to have reached a sticking point in her ability to work. Sometimes for an hour on end she sat staring at a page, listening to the liquid summer sounds that floated through the windows. Then the days of her long years at the University drifted back across her eyes, the winter evenings and spring evenings, the rooftops against the sky, the students streaming across the Midway under the blurring lights of a rainy autumn dusk; the nights when they had talked themselves dry in little cold rooms of the dormitories; the nights they had thrown down their books and gone out to get drunk on beer, using up their week's funds in a rush because they could not help it; the books, classes, laboratories; the ache and will that had carried them through on no money, no clothes, no time. She pushed her book aside and let her head drop into her folded arms. Now the people she remembered came back one by one, those she had loved and hated, despised and respected, some who had vanished, others who lingered on like herself, ensnared by some charm of the years behind them.

As she raised her head and went back to reading the page, she thought of the diploma in her bureau drawer, seven years tied up in a roll of parchment. And what pot of gold had this procured her? A part-time job that any high-school girl with a ninety-day secretarial course could fill more effectively than she. Sometimes when the library grew unendurable to her, Stephanie walked down to the lakeshore to watch the kids swimming off the rocks. And sometimes an exhaustion came over her, she went to the woman's clubhouse and slept. With the autumn, she still had no new job, but she postponed starting any courses once again until winter.

She felt an urgent need to forget all about the University for a few days. So she persuaded Dave he needed a rest from his railroad and his wage movement; and they took the Saturday morning train to Milwaukee. Here they tramped around the city like a pair of tourists, inspected one of the breweries, and drank gallons of beer. They went to a movie in the evening, which for some reason would never have occurred to either of them to do in Chicago. After that they drank beer again till the beer gardens closed, then returned to their hotel through the empty streets of the city, walking hand in hand at arm's length as if they were performing a tight-rope act. On Sunday they slept till midday, woke heavy-headed and wobbly in the knees. After a breakfast of black coffee and toast, they caught an afternoon train to Chicago.

In October Stephanie heard that Martin had won his appointment as assistant professor of philosophy at an eastern college. Hawkins invited her to the dinner which the *Philosophical Quarterly* gave in his honor. She refused at first, then changed her mind and accepted the invitation. The dinner was held in the side room of one of the University dining halls—the usual creamed chicken on biscuit, and kelly-green peas which she and Hawkins pursued back and forth across their plates in silence. Professor Parcher himself, she observed, was at the speakers' table; and there were the other professors also, and the cream of the graduate students—all the old windbags she had listened to so often, she thought.

Smith, as editor of the *Philosophical Quarterly,* was presiding. He spoke through several quarter hours on the acute dangers of nihilism, then turned over the floor to Professor Parcher. The Professor also held forth for a decent interval, tugging all the while at the points of his tuxedo vest which kept working up over his round stomach. Stephanie smoked and drank coffee. It was Martin she had come to hear.

Parcher's rhetoric ran dry at last and Smith introduced the guest of honor, Martin, who stepped around the central table, looking like a small boy, she thought, whose face had been scrubbed till it was red and shiny. There was something about Martin which always appealed to her, a quality that aroused amusement and respect at the same time. Through all the years she had known him, she could not remember having ever seen him in doubt for a moment about anything. So now, he had come with something to say and he plunged into it directly, omitting the customary "humorous anecdote" with which all the others had prefaced their speeches. He spoke in a sharp, dry voice, standing straight up with his hands behind him. After a few moments she realized she had been noticing how he looked, rather than listening to what he said. When she paid attention, she found him in the midst of one of his usual head-on collisions.

"A leveler is a person who tries to put everyone on the same ignominious level with himself," he announced. "The levelers tell us that education exists only to serve the community. But I do not agree with that. I believe the community exists to serve education. . . ." Stephanie saw that Hawkins, while pretending to study the dregs in his coffee cup, was watching her sideways; his eyes jumped away from hers when she looked at him.

". . . Rather than an adherent of democracy, I prefer to call myself a believer in aristocracy," Martin continued, through a muffled clatter of dishes. "When I use the word *aristocracy,* I use it in the same sense by which Plato's Republic was an aristocracy. Aristocracy denotes rule by the best. But who are the best? The best simply are those who have the best brains.

"True education therefore should select good brains. It should select them without regard for family or money. It should place them in positions of power in the community. Of course and obviously, our present system of education does none of these. . . ."

That she would disagree intensely with much of what Martin said, Stephanie had known beforehand. But now, as always, the disagreement was overshadowed somehow by the fascination of his arrogance—his conviction of the universal excellence of his own kind, the aristocracy of scholars. She heard him working around again to a point she knew well, a kind of divine justification for philosophy. "It is typical of the levelers in education that they attempt to separate science from philosophy. They ask, what can the philosopher nowadays add to the information of the scientist and the specialist? Yes, the specialist has translated the information of the scientist into steam engines and steel mills. He has built an industrial society. Yet he has only exchanged one brand of paper money for another. For what good is an industrial society if we do not know the purposes of society itself?" Here he stopped, beckoned across the dining room to a waitress with a pot of coffee. There was complete silence while the waitress advanced, blushing down to the collar of her dress, filled his cup and vanished hastily. He drank, then went on.

"That, my dearly beloved brethren, is the realm of philosophy.

Its realm includes the human mind and the human society; it defines the purpose of society as the perfection of that particular set of organs which make men human rather than animals—the brain. Essentially its realm is education. And because education is the process in which we shape the minds and souls of citizens, the building of a system of true education is at the same time the reconstruction of the very society we live in.

"That is the task of philosophy."

The people at the tables applauded. The speeches were over, the guests got to their feet. Martin was shaking hands with Parcher and the professors. Stephanie started pushing her way through the crowd to congratulate him on his speech and his appointment; but once again she changed her mind, said good night to Hawkins, and went outside. The orange autumn moon floated behind the top branches of the trees, which already were losing their leaves.

She now half-regretted she had not spoken to him. She could not avoid liking the buoyancy of his arrogance, because at least he was consistent. Certainly he *too* was consistent. His contempt applied not only to the humble ignorant, but to the pompous ignorant—to the professors and trustees, she thought, as well as to those unlettered mechanics and artisans with whom he was required to share the sidewalks. He set himself apart as if the hand of God were his special pedestal. And while he separated himself from levelers and plutocrats, from humble and from pompous both, still she had no doubt where he had staked out his own career. For she knew that with his conviction of his own excellence, he felt himself entitled to all the plutocrats could give and more besides. Already he had captured the first emblazoned toga, the first consuldom, and now the *cursus honorum* of scholarship stretched before him—assistant professor, full professor, department head, university president. She saw him again walking around the table to make his speech, as if the bright light into which he stepped were not a matter of lamps in the ceiling, but a quality of mind, a reflection of his own fortune.

The contrast threw her into a mood of angry discontent, because fortune had seemed so sparing of its gifts with her. If only she had turned back, she thought, if only she had waited for Martin just now in the dining room, congratulate him in a certain tone of voice, with a certain quick glance, she would have found herself accompanying him once more. The *cursus honorum* would have been hers also: wife of an assistant professor, full professor, department head. Her doctor's degree would come easily then, the right job would come with a little waiting. Tomorrow would be bright noonday, fruitful with hard work—*and with success.* For in the safe world of scholars, the quiet libraries, well-furnished apartments, conversation over dinner tables, in those safe and sunlit islands, she had no doubt of her success. And in that success, would not the dreams of the little girl at the Art Institute have found complete fulfillment? Sometimes she wondered if she had not turned her back on fulfillment of any kind.

The moon rose higher. Stephanie heard the wind rustling the fallen leaves along the pavement; a dog barked in the distance. As she walked through the streets towards Richmond Court, she felt that each step carried her more deeply under the banked shadows.

Autumn into winter, her old friend the winter again; the ice heaped like mountains against the sea wall of Lake Michigan, wind rattling the windows, the smoke-filled sky over the rooftops, streets and pavements sheathed in black ice. She felt herself struggling against a perpetual weariness; when her job ended at noon, she was tired, her bones ached, she sat in the library trying to hold her eyes open. She thought she was pregnant and began to hope she might be, but it was not so. Each afternoon as she rode home to Richmond Court with her brief case on her knees, she wished she and Dave could spend the evening at home together, eat supper slowly, and then just sit down. But the few evenings they had were for her overcast by the clock ticking away the minutes till he put on his jacket, took his lunch and went out, leaving her alone. On other evenings, Dave was off to a meeting, or people arrived for a conference, or to plan the next week's newspaper. Then there were the nights she went downtown to her class at the People's School. She liked the class, and she liked going with Dave or Pledger to the wage drive rallies; she still shivered with the same excitement as she climbed the platforms of the meeting halls, reaching for her first words, hearing her own voice begin to speak. Yet when the meeting had ended, she felt too weary to move. More and more often she avoided the meetings and stayed home to go to bed early, believing she was exhausted; and then could not sleep.

Her whole life seemed to center on that hour in the morning when Dave came home. They lay in bed together and then ate breakfast, while Dave talked to her between mouthfuls. He never appeared discouraged about the wage drive, yet to her it was incredible how slowly they moved. She knew that he and the car-knocker named Red worked all summer simply to persuade their own union Lodge to endorse the drive and support the committee.

Dave told her how Jennison and a few of the old-timers had shifted the regular Lodge meeting from Sunday afternoon to Sunday evening; how at every meeting they followed the same tactic of stalling until Dave and Red and the younger men who held the night jobs had to leave. Then they voted down all proposals connected with the wage movement. The younger men fell out of the habit of going to meetings because it seemed so little use. But Dave and Red finally rounded up enough of them to catch Uncle Jennison by surprise for once. They slammed through an endorsement of the wage drive and shifted the meetings back to Sunday afternoon.

But that seemed to her only a small step. For next came the job of swinging the rest of the Great Midland yard—the switchmen, brakemen, machinists, boilermakers, and electricians, into the drive. And the Great Midland, after all, was only one railroad in dozens. She watched Dave and Pledger and the small committee they had built, working to spread the wage movement to other lines across the city. When she had time she helped them put out their weekly newspaper. Each week brought a crisis to pay for the mimeographing; and each week brought a crisis to get the paper distributed to the yards and taverns and lodges. Usually Dave resolved the crisis by taking his afternoon and evening to tour the city with a bundle of papers under each arm.

But halting and slow as the early steps had been, Stephanie realized that they were leading into something. The meetings of six or seven in their attic had grown to sessions of twenty and thirty people. The mimeographed newspaper blossomed out with illustrations and a list of official sponsors. When in December, the paper published the call for a city-wide wage conference of railroad unions, Dave was jumping around as excited as a schoolgirl at her first dance. And the enthusiasm was contagious, she observed; for on Dave's night off, Roman invited them all out to dinner to celebrate. Dave's working partner, Red, came along, and Stephanie's brother Johnny and his wife Rosa. Roman took them to the Polish restaurant on Milwaukee Avenue where Johnny had got married. They drank and danced, and for once

Johnny was no drunker than anyone else. Stephanie taught Dave the polka again, which he had forgotten since the last time.

But sometimes when she lay waiting for him in the mornings she thought, this struggle for a few pennies—good God, what's the use?

1940

ON the piano in Walter's Tavern, Eddie plunked at the keys with one finger. The frowsy-haired waitress came over from the juke box.

"You play the piano good."

"No," Eddie told her. "But I can play the guitar." And he transferred his hand from the keys down to her thigh.

She giggled and slapped. "That's no guitar. That's me. Can't you play no song?"

Eddie shook his head. Then, glancing up at her, he asked, "You ever hear the song about the roosters and the goose?"

"No, I never did."

Picking out a few notes, he began to chant,

> "The roosters the goose,
> The roosters the goose,
> The roosters are hopping all over the goose."

"What's the rest of it?" the waitress asked.

"That's all there is. You want me to sing it again?"

"No. Sing something else." He put his hand on her leg again and she said, "Why don't you sit in a booth. I'll bring you a glass of beer."

Eddie moved into the corner booth and waited for the waitress; but before she returned, he heard the front door bang open, and then Uncle Jennison's voice shouted at Walter to know if Eddie Spaas had come in. A moment later Jennison sat down opposite him.

"What do you want?" Eddie asked.

"Have a little drink with you. Got any objections?"

"Here I almost had this waitress lined up. Go drink somewhere else."

"Aw, you can line her up any day of the week." The waitress appeared with Eddie's glass of beer, and Uncle Jennison bawled at her, "Well, sit down beside the man. What's the matter with you?"

"Nothing's the matter with me, mister. But three's a crowd, I always say."

"That ain't what you used to say. You're getting mighty particular."

"Don't pay any attention to him," Eddie told her. "He's drunk."

"Sure I am. Bring me a glass of whiskey, will you, sister?"

The waitress walked away, wiggling her shoulders disdainfully. Uncle Jennison glanced at Eddie. "You ain't making a play for that are you? You want me to take off?"

"No, Unc, stay where you are. I was only killing time."

"You're too old, Eddie."

When the waitress came back with the glass of whiskey, she had her coat on. "You can wait on yourselves after this," she told them. "It's after midnight and tomorrow's my day off."

"See you next year," Uncle Jennison called after her.

"Not if I see you first."

The door slammed behind her, and Jennison said, "Quick, ain't she?" He emptied the whiskey at a gulp, then took a swig of Eddie's beer for a chaser.

"What's on your mind, Unc?"

"I feel bad, Eddie. My gut's bothering me."

"You're drinking too much of that liquor. Ought to stick to beer, like me."

"You got no worries, Eddie. But I got too much to worry about and my gut's bothering me."

"You're getting old, that's what's wrong with you, Unc. You got your burial insurance up to date?"

"Don't kid around with me, Eddie. I'm in no mood for it."

"Go have a drink with somebody else then," Eddie said angrily. "I could have had more fun playing post office with that waitress than listening to you bellyache."

"I'm sick of the whole mess, Eddie. I'd get the hell out of here if I was a few years younger."

"Suits me. Let's take off for Tallefer."

Uncle Jennison shook his head and stared down into his empty glass.

"It makes me sick, Eddie," he said after a long time. "When I think how many years I been building up the organization here, it makes me sick. And I knew what I was aiming at all the way along, but you can't tell these guys anything, they won't listen. Took me twenty years to set myself in solid with the union and win the confidence of the men. You know that. You been here with me from the beginning. Right now, if things had worked like I planned 'em, I could be doing a rock-bottom job around this yard. It makes me sick, Eddie, I tell you."

"I don't know what you're talking about. You're drunk as a hoot owl."

"You know what I'm talking about."

"Don't know and I don't care, Unc. It ain't any business of mine."

Jennison banged his fist on the table. "Damn well is your business, you one-legged hyena. I'm talking about that nephew of yours. He wouldn't listen to me, goddamn him. I told him, but he wouldn't pay me no heed. He thinks he knows it all and he ain't going to listen to nobody. And now he's broke down what I been twenty years building up. Walter, bring me another shot of this snake juice." Jennison sat with his head in his hands until Walter came over from the bar and filled his glass. Then he said, "He don't leave me no choice, Eddie. I known the boy since he was weaned and it makes me feel bad things got to be like this."

"Like what?"

"No, you're right, Eddie. Keep your nose out of it. You'll be better off. The boy's riding for a fall, that's all. I'm fed up. My gut's bothering me."

"Well, why don't you tell him?" Eddie asked.

"I already told him. I told him you can't do things that way on the railroad. You got to work slow from the bottom. But he don't listen to me."

Uncle Jennison shook his head, studying the glass of whiskey in front of him. "When he first come back, Eddie, if I'd felt like it I could have kept him from ever getting hired on this turnpike. I didn't do that. Wish I had now, it would have been better for both of us. But I was glad to see the kid. I thought he'd help me, thought he'd take some of the load off my shoulders. That ain't the way

259

it worked out." Jennison reached suddenly across the table, clamping his hand on Eddie's wrist. "You know what he done to me few weeks back? I went all the way down to the depot to see him, and he won't even speak to me. He walks around me like I was so much dirt. I could have told him some things, Eddie. But I won't tell him nothing now in a million years after the way he acted to me. . . ."

Eddie got up from the table and Uncle Jennison jumped up, leaning close to him. "Listen, Eddie, you ever see the kid to talk to?"

"Not very often."

Jennison's long jaw champed up and down while Eddie could see that he was arguing something in his own mind. Then he yelled in Eddie's face, "I don't care how much you talk to him. Tell him anything you want. I wouldn't tell him nothing in a million years. He asked for it, he give me no choice. . . ."

Mumbling to himself now, Jennison slumped down at the table again. "You want another drink, Eddie?"

"No, I'm going home."

"That's a good idea. It's one o'clock, ain't it? I'll come along with you."

Eddie waited while Uncle Jennison drained the whiskey, holding the glass to his mouth and moving his head backwards in a series of small jerks. As he set the glass down and pushed himself up from his seat, the door from the street opened, letting in a gust of the November wind. Through the open door came the railroad detective Morgan. He pulled the door shut behind him and stepped over to the bar.

"Yessir," Walter greeted him. "It's the right night for a short snort. The colder the weather, the better she slides. Same as usual?"

Morgan nodded. Motioning with his finger to the table where Eddie and Jennison were standing, he said, "Set those boys up if they want it." Walter poured Morgan his drink at the bar, then came over to the table with the whiskey bottle.

"I don't want none," Eddie told him. But Jennison held out his empty glass and Walter filled it. Weaving over to the bar, Jennison stood beside Morgan, raised his glass and called "Here's how!"

Morgan lifted his own glass about an inch off the bar in acknowledgment.

"Cold as Greenland tonight, ain't it?" Jennison said.

Morgan nodded his head. For a moment Eddie stared at the backs of the two men who were standing side by side at the bar.

Then he turned towards the door. But he heard Jennison yell out behind him, "Hold your water there, Eddie. I'm coming with you. Got to catch a little shut-eye," he explained to Morgan. "Thanks for the drink."

Morgan nodded again without speaking. Eddie kicked open the front door and Jennison followed him into the street.

In silence they walked all the way to the corner before Eddie demanded, "How come you didn't ask if you could wipe his boots for him, Unc?"

"What's eating you now? The man bought me a drink and I thanked him for it."

"I wouldn't take a drink from him if it was the last drink in Chicago."

"Who gives a goddamn for your opinion?"

They boarded the Halsted streetcar, and as they sat down inside, Jennison said, "I know what you mean, Eddie. I don't like no company flatfeet either. But when you're in an official position like me, you got to keep up good relations with these bastards." Jennison was wobbling in his seat and his voice mumbled down so Eddie could scarcely hear it. "Play it smart, Eddie, that's the way. Keep good relations with these bastards until the right time comes, then you give 'em the old one-two. . . . Steps in about every night and I buy him a drink sometimes. What's wrong with that? . . . Some of the boys see him over in niggertown at night. What do you think of that, Eddie? . . . He's buddy-buddy with Jarvis. Play it easy and before long these bastards spill their guts to you. String up the both of them when the right time comes, Eddie. . . ."

"You're drunk," Eddie said. "Why don't you take a nap for yourself?" But Jennison rode all the way to Madison Street, rocking backwards and forwards with the swaying of the car, chewing his lips and twisting his hands together. When they got down at the corner of Madison and Halsted, he whispered into Eddie's ear,

"I got part of a pint left, let's finish it off." They stopped in the shelter of a doorway and emptied what remained of the pint. Now Jennison's mood changed suddenly. He let out a whoop and punched Eddie on the arm. "Listen, you hyena. You got any vinegar left in you?"

"More than you got."

Uncle Jennison leaned down, thrust his face close, blowing his whiskey breath into Eddie's nose. "You got it in you to hit the road again, boy? I'm sick to death of this mess around here. My gut's bothering me. I'm sick of it."

"You're drunk," Eddie told him. "You wouldn't move if they was to plant a load of dynamite under you."

"You know what I seen in the paper?" Jennison shouted. "An ad for the Southern Pacific line. They're hiring men right here in Chicago and they pay your transportation out to California. You got any vinegar left in you, Eddie?"

"Your old lady wouldn't leave you go, Unc."

"My old lady don't give me no orders, boy. I tell her we'll be back in a couple months so she feels good. She won't mind; good money in it. . . ." Jennison smashed the empty bottle on the doorstep, and as they walked back to the old men's hotel, he put his arm around Eddie's shoulders, singing and howling till his voice cracked.

In the morning Eddie woke as usual just before his alarm clock went off. He sat up in bed, shut off the alarm, and reached for his pants. From down the row of chicken-wire cells he could hear the old men coughing themselves awake, hawking and clearing their throats. He pulled his clothes on and walked downstairs to the second floor. It was only six o'clock, but already half a dozen old hoofers had perched on the bench to read their newspapers. Eddie glared at them in sudden hatred.

"What you trying to do? Learn those sheets by heart?" A chorus of shrill profanity followed him as he pushed past them, knocking their papers aside. At the end of the landing, he rapped on the door marked, 'Private.' After a long silence, Uncle Jennison's voice called, "We're eating breakfast. I'll be out pretty soon."

But Eddie opened the door and thrust his head in. Uncle Jennison's Norwegian wife was cooking flapjacks on the gas ring while Jennison sat at the table eating.

"We going down to the SP office today?" Eddie asked.

Uncle Jennison shook his head without looking up.

"I didn't think so," Eddie said. "I didn't think so."

Uncle Jennison jerked his thumb towards an empty chair. "Sit down, Eddie. Have a cup of coffee."

"Thanks," Eddie told him. "I'll eat outside." He slammed the door behind him and knocked the old hoofers' papers out of his way again as he stamped across the narrow landing.

20

THE day of the city-wide wage conference, Stephanie did not
return home because Dave was not coming for supper. She
left the library early, and on her way downtown stopped off at her
mother's house to see Rosa, who had just brought her new baby
home from the hospital.

Snow had fallen during the morning and the street leading to
the embankment stretched ahead of her, white and unbroken. On
each side the roofs of the little houses were blanketed in snow,
white cuffs rested on the chimney tops; doorsteps and the sills
of windows were outlined in white. Over the snow-covered embankment of the Great Midland, which blocked the end of the
street, hung the cloudy and smoke-filled sky, incredibly black.
She turned the corner by the coal yard, passed the empty machine
shop, and came to the row of houses against the embankment. In
front of the last house, Roman's Chevrolet squatted lopsided
under a bonnet of snow. The car almost never started on cold
days, she remembered; Roman must have gone to work by streetcar.

In the kitchen she found her mother boiling diapers for Rosa's
new baby. There was a pot of coffee left from lunch; they sat at
the table while her mother grumbled about the diapers, and how
Rosa's little boy, a year and a half old now, kept tracking snow
into the house and Rosa stayed up in bed with the new baby as if
she had a servant to wait on her.

"And her own mother don't come over to help. I think she'd be
ashamed to look herself in the face. How come Rosa didn't go to
her own folks' house instead of coming here?" Stephanie smiled,
knowing that her mother actually regarded it a sort of triumph
over her in-laws that Rosa had gone not to their house but to hers
with her second baby.

"And Johnny?" Stephanie asked.

263

"He's working such long hours," Mrs. Koviak said. "He don't get home much."

Stephanie finished her coffee and rose from the table. Through the kitchen window she saw the little boy, in his red stocking cap, tumbling over the snowdrifts in the back yard. She went upstairs to the bedroom where Rosa lay propped on pillows nursing her baby. Rosa had slipped down one strap of her nightdress and the heavy breast drooped sideways. As Stephanie came in, the baby twisted away, contorted its wrinkled face, and began to wail; from its open mouth a blue stream of milk ran down the crease on one side of its chin. Rosa guided her nipple back into the mouth and the baby began to suck with a smacking sound, until having taken its fill, it relaxed suddenly, sound asleep. Stephanie watched with a sense of envy the long brown-nippled breast and how Rosa, gathering it in one hand, slipped it beneath her nightdress. Rosa straightened up for a moment, drawing the strap over her shoulder. Then she dropped back into the pillows as if the movement had exhausted her; the glow faded from her face, the flesh of her cheeks appeared suddenly gray and sagging.

"How do you feel?" Stephanie asked.

"I feel all right."

As Stephanie leaned forward to look at the sleeping baby, Rosa told her, "It's another boy." The baby, nuzzling against her side in its sleep, was opening and closing the fingers of its half-formed hands. "Another boy," Rosa repeated, "another boy."

Another switchman for the Great Midland, Stephanie thought. "Would you rather have had a girl?" she asked.

"Yes, I guess so." Rosa closed her eyes. The creaking of the rafters of the house grew loud in the silent room; Stephanie heard the soft thud of snow falling from the eaves, and as if from a distance, the laughter of the little boy who was playing in the back yard. Rosa seemed to have dropped asleep. Stephanie turned out the light, stepped down the stairway to the parlor where her mother was waiting for her, trying as usual to persuade her to stay for supper. Three or four times on her way out the door Stephanie promised to come Sunday bringing Dave; it was only at the far side of the yard that she finally broke away, waved, and walked down the street.

The afternoon already had darkened to evening. The shadows converged, the light from the street lamps lay in blue patterns across the snow. Downtown in the Loop, she stopped for a sandwich at the cafeteria. Then she went on to the People's School where she took Pledger's class along with her own, since Pledger had gone with Dave to the wage conference. But the two classes joined together made a confused, noisy session; she was glad when the ten o'clock buzzer finally sounded.

After the class, Stephanie exchanged greetings with Rita Hanson in the corridor and rode down to the lobby. She waited at the door, hoping Pledger McAdams or Dave might finish the conference and stop by to meet her. She knew the conference could not have ended yet, but she felt herself growing angry and hurt that Dave did not come. She began to remember the many nights she had slept alone, the mornings and evenings she had waited for him. Now, standing alone, she was waiting again. A few snowflakes drifted through the colored lights of Randolph Street. People moved single file along the sidewalk, shuffling past one after another in the snow. The endless stream, the faces half glimpsed in the shifting light, collars turned up, heads bent, hats pulled down, as if some common purpose gripped them all, she thought, bringing a people out into the winter streets, marching with this strange determination, this fixed stare. But the snow fell quietly; and as she watched, the stream resolved once more into the series of lonely figures moving in that endless, hopeless search which stirred the crowds on Randolph Street. Of all the movie palaces, which one would each select tonight? Which bar, which soda fountain, which seller of chocolate-covered doughnuts? She heard her old friend the barker crying from the next doorway, "You too can learn to dance. Beautiful partners await you inside, my friend." But out of the rolling ocean neither Dave nor Pledger McAdams came to her. She slipped into the crowd, but broke away from it to the empty white streets leading west towards the Great Midland depot. In the middle of the second block she stopped.

Why should I look for him? she thought. He never called or came to look for me. Instead of going to wait for Dave in the depot, Stephanie turned back to catch the State Street car, which appeared at last under the blue spark of its overhead trolley, flashing like lightning through the falling snow.

The alarm clock waked her in the morning. She jumped out on the icy floor, pulled on her bathrobe, started the coffee and bacon. Then she crawled into bed again, wide awake, watching the hand of the clock, the small jerks with which it moved across the dial. Each minute meant that much less time afterwards; she listened for the crunch of his feet in the snow, but there was no sound. The feeling came to her as sometimes in dreams that she had lived through this all before. It was as if she had anticipated each tick of the clock, each bleak and empty day, each climbing notch of resentment. She thought how much she had abandoned for him, but he had abandoned nothing. As in the months before he went to Spain, she felt again the sick, heavy certainty they could not go on together. He would leave her standing at a crossroad as he had left her then, because some fantastic responsibility had taken precedence.

The coffee boiled on the stove. She climbed out of bed, lowered the flame, dressed, and sat alone to eat her breakfast. And suppose he had been hurt tonight, she thought. She pushed her chair back from the table. Suppose he had been hurt in the train yard; surely they would have called her? Crossing the room to the telephone, she reached out for it indecisively. Would they think to phone her here, or would they be trying now to telephone Ann Spaas in the house Ann Spaas had left? And if she called and he had not been hurt? She could hear the yardmaster into the phone, I couldn't say ma'am, he left a couple hours back; the men laughing in the yard office, don't these women ever learn not to ask? If only it were as simple as that, she thought, some little girl he went to see, it would be easy then to fight him back. But to be widowed by a committee meeting, abandoned for a cause, a dream, a fantasy— No, there was no use calling, he had not been hurt. Almost she wished he might have been; then she would go to him and, for a brief space, life would become simple and direct.

The door banged down below.

His feet came up the stairs, he was in the kitchen stamping the snow from his boots, laughing and slapping his hands, whole, uninjured, hungry. He put his arms around her, lifted her up and dumped her on the bed. Between kisses he shouted into her ear, "We did it, Stevie! We got a regular committee set up, and by God I'm chairman of it. Listen to me, honey, we're on the road, we got the bastards by the ears now."

Breaking away, she jumped up, smoothing her dress. "Your breakfast is on the table," she said. "I'm going to work."

"Couldn't you be a little bit late today?"

"No, I couldn't." While she put on her coat, she felt him watch-

266

ing her, and from the doorway she turned back for a moment. "Why should I be late? Do you think the jobs I have don't make any difference? I'd like to see the day you're late to one of your damn committees." She ran down the stairs and outside where the line of Dave's boot tracks marched across the unbroken snow. She was laughing at the look of disappointment she had seen on his face; then suddenly found herself choking and biting her lips to hold the tears back.

From the windows of the library that afternoon, she watched the wind rocking the trees, tearing to shreds the gray curtain of cloud and smoke that had lain over the city. By sunset the panes of the library windows had frosted over, and when she went outside, the wind was singing shrilly under the winter stars. Across the new snow of the day before a crust had frozen which cracked and tinkled beneath her feet. She had worked hard during the day; her anger had swept her mood clean as the wind had swept the sky; she felt quiet now, for the first time since summer satisfied with the work she had done. She hurried home, going over in her mind the things she would say to Dave and how they would understand each other. He was not at the house, but a few moments after she came in, the telephone rang. He was calling from downtown; she smiled at the apprehensive sound of his voice and then the note of reassurance when he understood she was no longer angry. She agreed to meet him for supper in an hour, and changed her dress and washed her face, whistling as she moved back and forth in the cold attic.

Leaving the carriage house, she saw a car turn in at the gate of Richmond Court. The lights swept in a wide arc over the snow, the car moved towards her, pausing at each house as if the driver were trying to read the numbers on the doors. By the last house the car stopped. The driver thrust his head out the window, watching her as she came up.

"Pardon me, ma'am."

"Who are you looking for?" Stephanie asked.

"I'm looking for a party named Koviak." The driver had a thin face, and protruding eyes which caught the sparkle of the car's headlights on the snow as if they were made of glass. "Which house does this party named Koviak live in? Or might that be you, ma'am?"

"Yes, that's me. What do you want?"

The man looked at her in silence. Finally he asked, "You the daughter of Roman Koviak?"

She stepped forward into the deep snow at the roadside. "Where is he? What happened to him?"

"He's down in the express yard." The round eyes stared back at her without blinking. "He got hurt, Miss."

"He's dead you mean?"

"He ain't dead. You'd best come with me, Miss. He asked after you." She got in beside him, the car circled Richmond Court and turned north along Lake Park Avenue, skidding sometimes at the icy intersections. They swung down Michigan Avenue, turned west and bumped up the viaduct leading to the Andrews Street bridge. But before they reached the bridge, they cut off at right angles into a ramp which slanted down steeply to the river bank. The driver without speaking stopped the car at the bottom and Stephanie got out. Five or six tracks here skirted the river with only the blue lines of the rails showing through the snow. She stood still, twisting her hands together, fighting the horror in the pit of her stomach at what she was afraid to see. Beyond the tracks was an ambulance, its two back doors gaping open. She thought suddenly, she had never before been under the Andrews Street viaduct, though she had ridden across it hundreds of times. Close to the parked ambulance was a switch shanty with snow on its roof, smoke rising out of a stovepipe, and in the window, a single electric light bulb casting the pattern of the window frame in a lopsided oblong across the snow. Beyond the shanty, she saw the gray mist over the river, while high overhead, mist and the ribbon of smoke from the stovepipe spiraled between the criss-crossing girders of the viaduct.

The man who had driven the car said, "He's down there where you see all them lights."

They set out together along the tracks. Beyond the viaduct they passed an engine which was standing still, humming and wheezing to itself. The engineer opened the window of his cab and peered down at her, but when she raised her eyes, he jerked his head back and slammed the window. Behind the engine stretched a row of boxcars. Some of the cars were spattered with ice and on some of them, the ladders and cross braces appeared etched in white by thin white lines of snow. In the faint glow of the streetlamps from the roadway of the viaduct behind them, Stephanie made out the names on the cars—Great Midland, Northwestern, Union Pacific, Central of New Jersey. The shadow of the boxcars fell sideways on the snow and her own shadow glided in front of her, while the thin cast of the man at her side seemed at each step to shoot farther ahead, outdistancing her own. She glanced at his face, then looked in the other direction, towards the wall of boxcars, the names one after another—Great Midland, Great Midland, Great Midland—their white roofs curving away towards a mass of warehouses in the distance. And beyond the warehouses, she saw the towers of Chicago rising up like a sparkling precipice against the starry sky.

Halfway to the warehouses was a cluster of moving lanterns. She stopped; the man stopped beside her, and she looked back for a moment at the engine hunched like a sleeping cat, the great vague shape of the viaduct, the veil of mist over the river. Then they walked on again. The snow creaked under the man's boots. The moving lanterns, the dark figures in the snow, drew closer and larger. How will I find him, she wondered, what will it be like to see? She wanted to ask the man beside her what had happened, but she was afraid to ask. One moment she wished he would not be badly hurt, and the next she wished him dead. Fear tightened inside her throat, she forced each foot in front of the other. Someone moved forward from the group of figures to meet her—a priest, she saw by his white collar, who spoke to her in a low voice, but she did not hear what he said.

The men made way for her. Roman was standing between the cars as if he were about to step out and join the others. A switchman raised his lantern, and she saw that Roman's face was flushed and laughing. He recognized her; and when she came close, he said, "Hello, Stevie. I'm glad you come."

The clear tone of his voice made her hope for a moment. But looking down, she saw that his feet did not touch the ground. His weight hung on the knuckles of the two cars which had locked through his body. "They going to get me out of this damn spot in a minute. You got a cigarette, Stevie?" She lit one and put it in his mouth, but after a few puffs he shook his head and she took it back. "Should have known better than walk between the cars, shouldn't I, Stevie—an old head like me? Brakemen feel bad, but they couldn't help it." He paused, his head drooped for a moment. Then he told her, "Doctor says I got to go to the hospital a while. You come and see me, eh Stevie? And bring Dave?"

"Sure we will." Did he not know, she wondered, or was he only trying to make it easy for her? She wanted to speak to him, but could think of nothing to say. The fear was gone now, but when she tried to talk, her lips felt stiff and her tongue seemed to have swollen in her mouth. "Sure we'll come," she said again. "We'll bring you anything you want."

At once she felt ashamed for the forced and artificial sound of her own voice, and could not speak again. In silence they stared at each other until Roman told her, "You go now, Stevie. They get me out of this damn spot."

She turned away. An old switchman, taking her arm, guided her along the tracks back towards the Andrews Street viaduct. "Would you be remembering me, Miss?" the old man asked. "Used to see you often when you was a little one. Used to see your brother, too, and Dave Spaas. For it's Dave's father old Joe Spaas I'd be calling one of the best friends I ever had. Name's Paddy Gallagher if you remember." He tugged at her arm. "No need to be waiting. These doctors will take good care of him. They'll get him to the hospital and he'll be as good a man as ever he was. Don't be looking back now, it'll do no good, no don't be turning."

She stopped and turned back. Roman was there yet in the gap between the cars, his head up, spotted in the lantern beam. A switchman stepped apart from the others, raised his signal lamp. She heard the distant grunt of the engine and then, traveling towards her down the line of boxcars, the intermittent crash of coupling irons as the cars one after another lurched forward. The car ahead moved, the car abreast of her; the gap where Roman was pinned widened suddenly; she saw the flushed color drain out of his face as if the blood had poured down through a trap. His hands thrashed wildly at the dark hollow where the coupling iron had been, and the doctors caught him as he toppled forward.

She turned and walked quickly away beside the boxcars with the old switchman puffing behind her. Under the viaduct, she waited at the shanty until the men brought the stretcher out. She did not ask them or step close to see. Blood had soaked through the canvas stretcher and made a trail in the snow behind. They tilted the stretcher in, closed the doors, and the ambulance rumbled away up the ramp to Andrews Street. He must have known, Stephanie thought, otherwise he would not have sent for me. From the shanty, she remained staring at the corner where the ambulance had disappeared, until with a start she found the priest talking to her, his hand on her shoulder, and the switchmen in a half-circle watching uneasily. She smiled at the priest and thanked him. The thin black-coated man who had driven her from Richmond Court offered to drive her back, but she shook her head and set off up the ramp on foot. At the top she stopped for a moment and leaned on the railing of the viaduct, looking out over the snow-gray yards, the rows of amber and green signal lights, the warehouses, the ice drifting on the river, the trails of mist above the water, which veiled the buildings on the other bank.

Downtown, she thought, Dave must have given up waiting for her. She wanted to go look for him but hesitated, thinking of her mother when she heard; and at last she turned west across the viaduct, going to her mother's. Her mother was in the kitchen, tending a gigantic pot of coffee on the stove. She glanced up, nodded coldly and said, "Run up to the corner, Stephanie, and buy some cakes and rolls."

"Cakes and rolls?"

"You heard me. Johnny and Victor are coming soon."

Stephanie saw Rosa motioning to her. Rosa pulled her into the parlor and whispered, "She's gone out of her head."

"Aren't they coming?"

"How could they be coming? They don't know it happened."

"Where's Johnny?"

For a moment Rosa stared at her, then her mouth fell open and she began to cry.

Stephanie shook her angrily by the shoulder. "Isn't he at work?"

"No. . . . I don't know. I don't know where he is."

"And Victor?"

"I don't know. She talks about them coming, but how could they be coming when they don't know what happened? If you can tell where Victor lives, go find him, Stephanie. She'll go out of her head if they don't come."

With the feeling of having fallen into a trance, Stephanie put on her coat and walked out of the house. Halfway to the car line she stopped, afraid to leave her mother and Rosa alone; but without making up her mind whether to turn back or continue, she walked forward again. Dave would be waiting for her downtown, he would not know where she had gone, he would call the empty carriage house on Richmond Court. Should she go there to listen for the call? Or hurry downtown? But it was three hours since she was to have met him; he surely would have left by now.

271

From the corner drugstore she telephoned Pledger McAdams and asked him to look for Dave. As she came out of the store, the streetcar clattered up to the corner. She climbed aboard, saying over to herself, Now to find Victor, that's the thing. If she wants her sons, at least she can have Victor, the clatter of those steel braces, if that makes it easier—

Marguerite, in a pink-flowered kimono, confronted her in the door of the apartment. Marguerite shook her head. Stephanie heard the automatic lift behind her clang its gate and creak away to a lower floor. "He's not here," Marguerite said. She made a gesture as if to shut the door, then caught Stephanie by the wrist and pulled her inside. "I want you to meet my friend. Come in, Stephanie."

Marguerite's friend was standing in the middle of the room; a thin little girl with mouse-colored hair bobbed across the back of her neck, and wearing a blouse and tweed skirt. Stephanie stared around the room at the dark walls and crimson curtains. "I want you to meet my friend Jackie," Marguerite said. However, the friend turned abruptly and disappeared into the bathroom, slamming the door behind her.

"Sit down," Marguerite said. "I'll make some tea for us." Stephanie shook her head, but Marguerite was already setting out cups and saucers. As Stephanie did not speak, Marguerite whirled back suddenly, her eyes shining with anger. "Well, why don't you ask about him? You came looking for him, didn't you?"

Stephanie nodded. "I wanted him to come home with me." She watched Marguerite, who was standing in front of her, feet planted squarely as if she expected the floor to start rolling beneath her, heavy and shapeless in her pink kimono. Then she saw the anger fade from Marguerite's face.

"He went away, Stephanie. I truly feel we've got the right to split up if we want. It's my apartment, so he went away and I stayed."

"Where is he now?"

"I don't know where. He thinks he's coming up in the world. He eats dinner at the faculty club, and he thinks he'll be a member of the faculty himself soon. Like your friend Martin, he thinks he'll get a fine appointment as professor of Old French at some university. Oh, I'm not stupid, Stephanie. Your brother thinks I'm too fat and frowsy to go along with him when he comes up in the world—"

"You footed the bill, and then he left you, Marguerite?"

She shrugged her shoulders. "I don't know that it's any business of yours. We've got the right to split up if we want. But I'm keeping the apartment. My friend Jackie didn't have any place to stay, so I let her stop here temporarily. Jackie," she called, "I'm making tea." There was no answer from the bathroom and Marguerite turned back to Stephanie. "Don't you want to take your coat off? The water will be boiling in a minute."

"I can't stay," Stephanie said. As she walked down the corridor, she heard Marguerite calling after her, "You might have told me before I started tea." She rang for the automatic lift and rode downstairs. When she stepped into the lobby, she came face to face with Marguerite's friend Jackie, who was breathing fast as if she had run downstairs to beat the elevator. A spot of color showed in each of the girl's flat cheeks. Stephanie walked out into the street, but she heard the other pattering after her through the snow. She turned back, and the girl asked, "Is your name Stephanie?"

"Yes."

"You're Stephanie, then, aren't you? You're the one she talks about?" The girl thrust up close to her. "What do you want with her? You leave her alone, you hear me? You keep away from her." The girl's face contorted suddenly. Stephanie dropped back a step and the other jumped after her, scratching and pulling at her hair. She caught the girl's wrists and held them, staring down with amazement into the twisted face, the sharp black eyes fixed on hers in a frenzy of hatred and fear. In the same instant, the girl ducked her head, grinding her teeth into Stephanie's thumb. Then she broke away and ran into the building.

Stephanie stood for a moment watching the gout of blood that swelled up where the teeth had broken the skin. A dull pain rose through the muscles of her arm, throbbing as she walked back to the car line. In the streetcar, she wrapped a handkerchief around her thumb. With wide eyes she looked at the straw-backed seats ahead of her, the people slouching half asleep. She thought of Marguerite, remembering the summer day when they had walked to International House; and she paused for a moment to be sorry. She was aware of her own mind ticking off thoughts with regularity, as if she regarded it outside herself, like a machine standing on a distant table. But why should she waste time feeling sorry for Marguerite, she wondered; she had enough besides to feel sorry for. For Rosa, Roman, Johnny and her mother—yet she knew that for all of them it was small sorrow she had felt. Inside herself she found only a numb barrier, as if the nerves had atrophied. Now trying deliberately to produce some tinge of feeling, she closed her eyes to see the pictures she knew were waiting in the dark: the spot of lantern light, the flushed and laughing face. But she felt nothing—only a sickness close to nausea—and quickly she opened her eyes.

She understood how utter and complete it was to die. Already even the memory of Roman seemed to lose reality, melting like a shadow with the object which had cast it gone. She had known him, he had been distinct and separate. Surely to him his own self had been the focus of the universe, as her own self to her. He died and there was nothing left. Would it be the same with her? How could the universe exist if her own self should cease? How could she endure that emptiness? There was no need to endure it, she thought, for there was nothing to endure. There was nothing, that was all; hell itself was merciful compared to that.

She remembered now the priest's voice, the careful words she had not listened to. Pray for us, oh holy Mother of God, our life, our sweetness, and our hope. The words of spring; the bitter perfume rising at the morning Mass; the endless aching hope of resurrection. And beside the steps the plaster figure with lilies at its breast smiled out of sightless plaster eyes. There was a step beyond which came no further steps, and for those who like herself believed in nothing but the strength and courage of the human mind, there were no words of comfort. The last step was with open eyes, a long look into the vast emptiness— Nothing, nothing, she repeated to herself; how utter and complete that nothing was.

Unwilling to close her eyes again, she held them open, staring out the window at the white streets in the lamplight. The wheels clattered beneath her. The car stopped at an intersection, then plunged into the black passage under a line of tracks. Surely she had been here before, she thought, this all had happened to her once before. A mist of recollections floated up before her eyes. She found no strength to fight them off, and relaxing, drifted where the mist carried her, backwards into the twilight, the melancholy and consoling past, until she found beside her on the seat a dark-haired, lonely little girl who sat dreaming of friends she would never meet; and dreaming of the years ahead, which for her then were still unlived and wonderful.

The car came out beyond the underpass. Stephanie saw the black, star-sprinkled sky between the angles of the roofs, and silently she watched herself seek refuge from this point of time.

Part Six

THE WHEEL PIT

2 1

WHEN Dave finally reached the Koviak's house that night, he thought the three women had gone out of their minds. Mrs. Koviak was setting food on the kitchen table as if in preparation for a party; Rosa, with tears streaming down her face, followed Mrs. Koviak back and forth, alternately trying to help her, and then to convince her that there would be no one to eat the food. In the unlighted parlor, Stephanie sat by the window staring into the street. Dave got on the telephone, called Rosa's mother, and when the old lady finally arrived, he left her in charge and took Stephanie home to the carriage house. She told him in a few dry words what had happened, then crawled into bed and fell asleep, exhausted. Dave dropped down beside her. For the first time since he had heard the news three hours before, the sharpness of this sorrow came home to him. What he had not felt for his own father, he felt now for Roman Koviak.

During the weeks that followed, Stephanie seemed to him to come out of it quickly enough. They continued the routine of their living, one working at night, the other in the day, meeting at breakfast and at suppertime. Stephanie helped him, as she had before, in putting together the wage-movement newspaper; she went regularly to the University and to her classes downtown. Yet Dave, in the back of his mind, felt that something was wrong. He heard from Paddy Gallagher the details of Roman's death; it was not Stephanie who had told him. After the night when he brought her home from her mother's house, she had never mentioned the subject again. She seemed to have lost the desire to talk about that, or much of anything else. He tried several times to persuade her to talk, with no success. Then he gave up the effort, for weighing on him was the constant pressure of time. He never had time enough. The work of the newly established wage committee and the preparation of the mass meeting which they were planning for the first week in March fell mainly on him. These demands, and his own enthusiasm at the success of the movement, drove him harder each day. But he knew the enthusiasm no longer reached to Stephanie, and he found himself coming to resent her unwillingness to share it with him.

In the first week of March—just before the time set for the mass meeting—Stephanie came down with a cough and high fever. Dave, afraid she had caught pneumonia, telephoned a doctor. But the doctor when he came found no sign of infection in her chest. She had a bad cold, he said, and ought to stay in bed. So that morning Dave called a taxi, wrapped her in a blanket, and took her to her mother's house where Rosa and Mrs. Koviak could keep an eye on her while he was at work. She protested all the way, and when he carried her upstairs to the little room under the gable, she burst suddenly into tears, crying, "Oh Dave, why did you bring me here? I never wanted to come back to this room."

Dave sat on the bed beside her. "I can't leave you alone with a fever like this. It won't be but a couple of nights."

"I know, but even for a night, I hate it. And my class downtown— if Rita takes it, she'll drive them all away."

"You'll be back again next week. I'll ask Hanson to take it for you tomorrow."

"Just so it's not Rita." She laughed a little, then closed her eyes and fell asleep. Dave was out most of the day making the final preparations for the mass meeting that night. When he came back, Stephanie was half sleeping, half waking, while Mrs. Koviak sat beside the bed with her hands folded in her lap. He saw that the bureau top was covered with glasses of water and orange juice, bottles of aspirin and dishes of partly eaten applesauce. Every time Stephanie opened her eyes, Mrs. Koviak said, "Wouldn't you like some orange juice now? Or an aspirin to make you sleep?" Dave asked about supper, but Mrs. Koviak told him she had not fixed any because of taking care of her daughter.

"You don't need to sit up here all the time," Stephanie said.

Mrs. Koviak shook her head. "It's good for somebody to be close if you need anything. Your husband's been out all day," and she added, "He's going out tonight, too."

"Are you, Dave?"

"Tonight's the big show."

"Oh. The mass meeting." In silence, she lay staring at the roof

280

which slanted over the bed, and Dave knew she was thinking, Anyone else would stay home if his wife were sick. At the same moment, Mrs. Koviak said, "It's too bad all this business you got wasn't some other time."

"Too bad," Dave agreed, and as he left the room he heard her telling Stephanie, "But it can't be helped, I suppose it can't."

In the kitchen, Rosa made him a pot of coffee, and they opened a can of beans for themselves.

The mass meeting that night packed the old Turnverein Auditorium on the west side. They had a uniformed band from a labor post of the American Legion which played the "Star Spangled Banner," and afterwards Dave, as chairman of the committee, opened the meeting with a bang of his gavel. Behind him, sitting on the platform, were the heads of eighteen railroad lodges, a state senator, and a city alderman. "We've come a long way since this committee started a year ago," Dave told the crowd. "When we can put on a show like this, there isn't anybody in the industry doesn't know how the men stand on the wage movement. We're about ready to call the showdown, and I think we got the cards to win."

The crowd yelled and the American Legion boys beat their drums. Dave introduced the speakers one after another, rolling out their titles as they came up to the stand.

Some reporters stopped after the meeting and Dave talked for them, giving them facts on wages and conditions of railroad workers, although he did not believe their papers would print what he said. One of the reporters seemed chiefly concerned about Dave himself, wanted to know his full name, his address, where he worked and how long he had worked there. Dave nodded to Red as the reporter walked away. "Now he'll be off looking through the back files to see what he can find on me."

"They got anything?"

"Sure, they'll find something. That paper runs a sort of little Gestapo. That's why they cover these meetings."

Next day, the paper whose reporter had asked the questions, carried a story on Dave Spaas the Red agitator, with a picture of him taken in 1935 haranguing a crowd from the roof of an automobile. As Dave changed his clothes in the locker room after work, he found the men passing the paper around, laughing over it. Someone had clipped out ten or twelve copies of the story and posted them on bulletin boards all over the Great Midland yard. But the paper printed none of the facts on wages Dave had given their reporter; and when he checked the other papers, he found they had not even mentioned the mass meeting or the wage movement.

Red stamped up and down swearing, but Dave told him there was not much more you could expect from the newspapers, and bad publicity was the best kind sometimes.

He showed the story to Stephanie, but she laid the paper aside; he was not sure she had even read it, and she said nothing more about it. He watched her uneasily, for as her cold dwindled off, it seemed to leave her without interest or energy. She got out of bed and moved around the house, letting her mother follow her about to run errands, bring her books and magazines, orange juice and dishes of ice cream; while Rosa took care of the house in addition to her own two kids. In the mornings when Dave came back from work, Stephanie stayed in bed until he finished breakfast, but as he came up to bed himself, she moved down to Roman's old leather chair in the parlor. There he found her every afternoon when he woke, sitting with a book open on her lap, staring out the window at the black ice over the street and the sagging board fence around the corner of the coal yard. Dave felt his uneasiness turn slowly to anger. The tag end of her fever hung on although the cold seemed to have disappeared, and he thought the fever was mostly inside her own head. She did not come into the kitchen when he ate lunch; usually it was Rosa who fixed lunch for him.

Rosa, he noticed in the few days he had stayed at the house, learned how he liked his coffee, what kind of cheese and bread and pickles he preferred. Sometimes as he glanced up, he found her staring hungrily at him across the table. He knew that her own husband Johnny came home only when he ran out of cash or got hungry, every second or third day. Then she washed him and put him to bed, mended his clothes while he slept, gave him food when he was sober enough to eat, took care of him until he went off again, singing and waving and shouting over his shoulder that he would be home for supper.

"Why do you let him do that to you?" Dave asked.

She shook her head.

Rosa's hopelessness seemed to him like a disease. He wanted to tell her she was a fool to put up with it. But the thought suddenly came to him that maybe she had not the power to do anything else—any more than Johnny had the power to quit drinking, or Eddie to put the other half of his arm back on, or Stephanie— or Stephanie or himself to act differently from the way they acted. Dave shook himself angrily. Always it came back to Stephanie. She was the real carrier of this mood of hopelessness and defeat. It had infected him; he knew that. At the very time when they were fighting for the Lodge and the wage movement, with a good chance of winning, he found himself feeling as if he had been beaten already.

Dave finished his coffee and dried the dishes for Rosa. Then, going into the parlor, he sat down beside Stephanie to find if she felt like talking. But she straightened the book on her lap and dropped her eyes at once as if to read. Having reduced his time for sleep because each day required more hours than he could spare, Dave felt too tired and too cross to cajole her. He got up abruptly. As he was putting on his jacket and hat in the hallway, he heard Mrs. Koviak come into the room behind him. "Is he going out again? . . . It's a wonder he couldn't stay home with you one afternoon." Dave's anger broke suddenly out of his grip. He stepped back into the parlor.

"Why don't you mind your own business if you got any?" Mrs. Koviak retreated hastily towards the kitchen door; she was afraid of him, he knew she would say nothing more where he could hear her, but also he knew what she would be saying after he had left the house.

Stephanie continued to read as if no one else were in the room.

It was the second day after the mass meeting that Dave found on the rack in the locker room a letter from the General Foreman's office. Ripping open the envelope, he drew out a printed form with his name typed in the blank spaces:

> The Chicago Great Midland Railroad Company no longer requires the services of Mr: ___David Spaas___ as ___carbuilder.___ Mr: ___Spaas___ will report to the General Foreman's office at once to surrender his keys.

Dave glanced around him to see if anyone were watching. He crumpled the slip in his fist; then carefully opened and read it again. For a moment he could not think what to do next. He had expected many kinds of attacks, but he had not expected this.

Groping back in his mind, he tried to remember if he had made any slips on the job that could have given them an excuse, even a thin one, to fire him. He could think of nothing. He put the letter in his pocket and, instead of going back to Mrs. Koviak's, walked over to Halsted Street for breakfast. After he had eaten, he lighted a cigarette and sat staring through the gray plate glass of the cafeteria at the line of trucks outside.

It was not yet eight o'clock. Streetcars stopped at the intersection to let down crowds of workmen. Horns blared, the streetcar motormen clanged their bells. Dave felt a sudden desire to pack his bag and get out. He could throw his gear into his sea bag, take off for the coast, and there would be an end of the whole mess. That was an easy answer, he thought; a year ago he had come running home like a stray dog, and now already he was remembering what the little Englishman Ardwick, his shipmate on the trip back from Europe, had said to him: "I'll be seeing you soon enough, Da-vey." Maybe it was hard to live without her, but it was a damn sight harder living with her. And maybe it would be better for her if he did go.

He pushed himself up slowly from the table and headed back towards the yard office. He wondered now if Uncle Jennison had known about the letter beforehand. It would cost the company plenty for firing a man without cause—unless they had a deal rigged up with the union. Anyhow, he thought, they had given him his full time when he needed it most for the wage movement. How kind they were! And how long would it be? Two months, three months, all that at no pay, and with Stephanie not working they would have to quit the attic in Richmond Court. But she seemed happy enough at her mother's—until she found she had no choice; then she would want to leave. Dave shrugged his shoulders.

The yard office was a square brick building on a mound of cinders overlooking the coach yard. He climbed the stairs to the second floor and the clerk nodded him into the inner room. The railroad detective Morgan, who had been waiting by the stove, rose and followed him inside, where Upstairs Jarvis, in vest and shirtsleeves, cigar and gray felt hat, sat backwards to his desk, shouting into a telephone, "What's the matter with you, I want to know; you blind or crippled?" Jarvis was a small man with white stubble over his chin, and rimless octagonal glasses, like an old woman. All the time, he kept buttoning his vest, then yanking it open so the wings flapped sideways from his round belly. ". . . Why the

hell didn't you send the cars up here if they need brakeshoes?"
He slammed the phone down and stared up at Dave.

"What do you want?"

Dave tossed his keys on the desk. "I want to know what grounds
you're firing me on."

"Firing you? What's your name?"

"David Spaas."

"We don't need your services any more. That's what grounds."

"I thought you laid men off in accordance with seniority," Dave
said.

"You got no seniority on this road, mister. We don't allow no
seniority to criminals."

"Criminals?" Dave turned to look at Morgan, but the railroad
detective was staring out the window, his back to them as if he
had no concern in what was going on. Upstairs Jarvis pulled a
sheet from a folder in front of him. "Says you willfully destroyed
property belonging to the Chicago Streetcar Corporation, resisted
arrest, trespassed on the right of way of the Great Midland Railroad Company, and threatened violence to a railroad police officer
who tried to question you."

"Who made that report?"

"That don't concern you."

"If you got all that stuff," Dave asked, "why don't you turn
it over to the city police?"

"We protect the railroad company, mister. The city police want
to run you in, that's their business."

"You mean you got nothing but a lot of gossip on that sheet."

"I damn well mean what I say." Upstairs Jarvis shoved back
his chair and the detective Morgan swung around from the
window.

"When did all this happen?" Dave asked. "What's the date on
that dope sheet?"

"That'll do, mister." Upstairs Jarvis jerked his thumb toward
the door. "You can stop for your pay on Saturday." Then he
rocked forward out of his chair, propping himself with his bristly
forearms on the desk. "I got nothing against you, mister. You can
contest the case if you want. That's what you got a union griever
for, ain't it?"

"Thanks," Dave said.

Jarvis laughed briefly and dropped back in his place. As Dave
left the room, he saw the thin head and protruding blue eyes of

the railroad detective turn slowly, following him step by step. When he had crossed the outer office, the detective came after him and stood at the top of the stairs to watch him go down.

Outside, Dave stopped for a moment at the crest of the cinder slope. All across the yard, which stretched below him, the morning shift was beginning work. He saw Paddy Gallagher's back-up engine shove in from the main line with one section of the Daybreak Express. Up and down the wash tracks, bunches of coach-cleaners followed each other single file, the first man squirting his hose over the sides of the cars, the others scrubbing off the streaked mud with their long-handled brushes. The engine stopped its puffing, and in the moment of silence he heard the clang of hammers from the wheel-pit house. The story would be all over the system, he knew, in a few hours; they would have to decide what to do about this, and fast. He must see Pledger McAdams, and then make sure Red did not pull some wild stunt on his own. And again he thought, What about Uncle Jennison? Had he known beforehand about the letter? Was this a deal between the company and the union? That was the first thing to find out, before he tried to figure what to do next.

Dave crossed the yard to the shanty by the lead-in from the main line. There he found the switchtender on the end of a broom, swooshing clouds of dust and cinders out the front door. Inside the shanty, Paddy Gallagher was brewing a pot of coffee. "You working daylight shift now, Paddy?" Dave asked.

"No, lad, I ran into a little overtime this morning and just now got my engine tied up." Dave grinned at the celluloid collar and old black chesterfield Paddy Gallagher was wearing instead of overalls, now he was a passenger back-up conductor. "Yessir," Paddy said, pulling out his watch. "Had my fingers in their pockets for a whole hour this morning."

While Dave sat down to read the switchtender's newspaper, Paddy told him that Uncle Jennison was working on Number Three track and he'd most likely soon be stopping by for a cup of java.

Dave waited. The switchtender, when he finished sweeping, went outside to line the switches for a freight train that came puffing through the crossover; but the freight got stuck on the grade, and right away the depot began ringing the phone off the wall. Paddy Gallagher shouted into the phone, "Hold your water!" and hobbled outside, leaving the earpiece swinging at the end of its wire. All the way across the shanty, Dave could hear the angry voice squeaking out of the telephone: "Your damn monkeys better get that main line clear for the express—" He watched through the window the switchtender and Paddy and half a dozen brakemen chasing up and down, shouting and throwing wild signals at each other. A coach-yard engine at last hitched on to the rear end of the freight, shoved it over the hump, and a moment later the passenger train which had been held up at the red block came whistling through the crossing.

When Uncle Jennison stopped for his coffee with Paddy Gallagher and the switchtender, Dave was sitting in the corner holding the newspaper in front of him. He waited while they filled their cups, then folded the paper and stood up. Uncle Jennison stared at him, his cup half raised to his mouth. "I got something for you," Dave said. "Maybe you seen it already?" He held out the letter.

"They sent you this?" Jennison asked.

"Sure they sent it. That surprise you?"

"No, boy. I expected it. I seen it coming."

"You got good eyesight. I didn't."

"I tried to tell you," Uncle Jennison said. "But you was bound you'd be shooting off all these goddamned fireworks and now it caught up with you."

"Give me the letter back. I might need it. Suppose you come over to the office with me now, Jennison, and tell Upstairs Jarvis you're going to fight my case. I think maybe he's got the idea you don't intend to."

Shaking his head, Uncle Jennison backed away.

"I can't do it. I can't do it, Davey." No one spoke in the shanty. The coals sputtered and dropped from the grate. Jennison shifted his feet and the boards creaked beneath him. "I guess you don't know then," he said at last. "They should have told you."

"Told me what?"

"The vice-president's office suspended you from membership in the union, boy. You're not a member of this union. I can't defend you."

Dave lunged forward. He caught Jennison by the collar and held him, staring into his face, slowly lifting his hand. The other men in the shanty watched in silence, but no one of them moved. Then Dave dropped his raised fist and turned away. "What are the charges they made against me?"

"You shouldn't have done that, Davey. It's not me that did you any harm."

"So it was a deal just like I thought," Dave said. "A sweetheart deal between Donohue and Upstairs Jarvis. What are the charges they made against me?"

"Starting a dual union."

"Anything else?"

"Belonging to the Communist Party."

"And asking for a wage increase, eh? Didn't they put that in?" Dave bent his head, then asked in a soft voice, "Why didn't you tell me sooner? I might have had a chance to defend myself."

"They wouldn't have give you the chance, boy. They say you can appeal it later if you're so minded."

Dave raised his eyes now to Jennison's face. "That's just what I wanted to know, Unc. You knew all about it before, didn't you? You were in on the deal. You knew about it and you went along with them, you never let on in the Lodge, you never raised a squawk." He turned to the other men. "What do you think about that?"

For a long time no one answered. It was Paddy Gallagher who spoke at last. "It's no use to be fooling myself. Even if you are a communist, and I'll not be speaking in their defense, but it's a raw deal they give you, lad." Paddy Gallagher picked up his brakeman's lantern and left the shanty; Dave followed him out.

The day was windy and cold. Iron gray clouds swept over the low rooftops. He had been looking for the wind to change, for the first thaw to come booming out of the southwest. But the winter hung on. The ice remained unmelting on the streets, patches of sooty snow still clung to the frozen ground. At lunchtime, Dave talked to Pledger McAdams, and it was midafternoon when he returned to Mrs. Koviak's house. In the parlor, Johnny Koviak sprawled in the leather armchair.

Johnny blinked and grinned, trying to see out of eyes which were half-swollen shut. "Don't you worry," he yelled at Dave. "Don't you worry, Roman old coot. I guess a man's got a right to take a squat when he get's tired, don't he? Been switching boxcars bitch of a stretch today. But soon as you want this chair, Pop, just lemme know and I'll wiggle my duff right out of it—" As Dave climbed the stairs, he heard Johnny calling behind him, "Lemme tell you the news. Dave Spaas got the sack. It's the Jesus truth, Pop—" He found Stephanie sitting on the bed waiting for him.

"Well," she asked, "is it?"

He nodded and she said, "Why, Dave? Why did you do that?"

"Why did *I* do it? Do you think I fired myself?"

"Because of the wage movement, wasn't it? You could have seen that coming, couldn't you? What are you going to do now? We've got no money."

"We'll make out."

"Sure, we'll make out! A fat lot you care whether you have any job or not. Do you suppose you'll even look for one?"

He watched her face, set and bitter, noticing how question by question she was working around to make it his fault, to justify the burst of anger that would come in a moment. With a sudden feeling of helplessness, he wondered if she were not blaming him for everything that had happened; for her inability to get a job at the University, for her sickness, for having no place to go except her mother's house—even for Roman's death, maybe even for that. "I won't be looking for a while," he said, and turned away. She jumped up from the bed, following him. "And what are we supposed to eat and pay the rent with? I'm to get well right this afternoon and go back to work, is that it?"

"It wouldn't do any harm. It wouldn't do *you* any harm either." Through the open door, Dave saw that Mrs. Koviak had come up the stairs and was peering at them from the stairway, afraid to come in. Stephanie's voice sounded close behind him, but he did not turn to look back at her. "I know you very well, Dave," she said. "You'll be a third-rate hack organizer the rest of your life. If you're a good boy and do what they tell you, maybe they'll transfer you to New York someday at twenty-five dollars a week. You couldn't hold a decent job if you had one—" Her voice rose shrilly in his ear. "I hate you. You won't live off me." She drummed her fists against his shoulders and neck. He disengaged himself, turned around and struck her across the mouth with the flat of his hand. He heard a series of little shrieks from Mrs. Koviak. Stephanie dropped down on the bed, the mark of his hand showing red across her face. He remembered the only other time he had hit her, four, five years ago. She was looking up at him now with a kind of triumph; that was what she had wanted, she had pushed him until he did it.

Mrs. Koviak flattened herself out of his way and he walked down the stairs. Rosa, her arms crusted with pie dough, was staring up from the bottom step. "It's all right," he told her. "We had a fight, that was all." In the parlor, Johnny had fallen asleep across the arm of the leather chair.

Leaving the house that night at his usual time, Dave went down to the depot. He found all the carmen, both from the afternoon shift which was going off and from the night shift coming on, gathered at the lunch counter. They were not talking, and no one was even drinking coffee; they were waiting for him.

"We're going to strike the depot," Red told him.

Dave nodded and sat down.

"Well," Red said, "What do you think? What's the matter; you forgot how to talk?"

"I think it's a bum idea."

"You think what?"

"I said I think it's a bum idea, Red. The union won't back you up. That means you got to fight the union as well as the company. But if you want to fight the union, you got to have an issue every yard in the city will walk out on. Now I know good and well there aren't any other yards would walk out just to put me back to work. We wouldn't even get our own men out solid. Would we?"

"We might."

"Sure, and for every man that walked off, the vice-president's office of our own union would send in a scab to take his place. All of you guys would be out of your jobs and your seniority, and I wouldn't be any better off than I was before."

"Goddamn you, you're talking like Jennison now."

Dave shook his head. "It's up to you guys. If you think I'm wrong, say so. I know what you're trying to do for me and I'm grateful for it." One of the men began to swear under his breath, and Dave looked at the circle of faces around him. "What do you think they pulled this for? It's a booby trap, isn't it? They figured we'd walk in with some wild stunt like this, and they'd get rid of the whole bunch of us. The whole bunch of us at once, you understand? We'd be sticking our necks out so they could chop our heads off; and don't think they wouldn't do it. Where would the

290

wage movement be then? Shot to hell, wouldn't it? And the Lodge right back under Jennison's thumb again."

"What are we supposed to do?" Red shouted. "Lie down and let 'em kick us in the face?"

"Plenty of things we can do. Talk to the other guys. Make sure they all get to the next Lodge meeting. But let's not walk into a booby trap." Dave turned to the other men. "What do you guys think?"

"He's right, Red." The others nodded; but Red shook his head and stamped away without answering. It was close to eleven o'clock. The group broke up, the men who were off duty going home while the others straggled across the empty waiting room towards the tracks. Dave sat a few moments longer, smoking a cigarette, knowing that Red was angry and trying to figure the best way to straighten it out with him. But all the while, his mind kept turning back to Stephanie. A tangle of conflicting angers blocked out all other thoughts. As he stared down at the knuckles of his hand, he wished he had struck with his fist closed instead of open, that would have given her something real to stay in bed for. At the same moment, he wished he had never hit her at all. An ache came into his throat when he remembered the expression of her face and how easily she had fallen. Regret and anger rocked back and forth, and an impatient voice repeating, There's no time to be sitting around. You got Red yet to straighten out tonight.

He saw the waitress watching him from behind the counter. She set a cup of coffee in front of him, and when he reached in his pocket, said, "That's on the house, mister."

He thanked her, then glanced up at the clock, allowing himself five minutes longer. He did not believe Stephanie had intended to say what she said, any more than he had intended to hit her. But months of irritation and disappointment on both sides had flared out. Even now, he kept meeting glimpses of himself turning back instead of walking down the stairs, pulling her up from the bed, and beating her until she collapsed. Yet he knew it was not what she had said that so much angered him. It was the indecision, the unsolved problem she forced on him when he had no time for unsolved problems; the feeling of having been licked already when all they needed was to get out and fight. Maybe it *was* his fault, not hers. But that didn't make much difference. Somehow they would have to find a way to cut through this thing. And he knew it would be up to him.

291

His five minutes were ended. He got up from the counter, and as he crossed the waiting room and walked through the train shed, he pressed back the resentment, shame, regret that had filled him. By the baggage cars on the express track he found Red, who was still too angry to speak to him.

"I got a lot of things to talk to you about," Dave said. He took Red by the arm and pulled him around. "Listen to me, you lame brain. If you'll start using your head, Jennison won't be chairman any more after next week. Maybe it costs one man's job—it's damn cheap at that."

22

"LAY a little bet if you feel like it?"

The man behind the cigar counter jerked his head towards the doorway in the back of his shop. At the same moment a customer emerged and Dave saw through the angle of the door a couple of card tables under green shaded lamps, and a knot of men before a blackboard. He opened the package of cigarettes he had bought, gave one to the clerk and took one himself. There was a lighter on the counter which snapped an electric spark as he pressed it, then flaring into a smoky flame, filled the shop with the odor of benzine. "I'm waiting for somebody," Dave said. "Mind if I stand in out of the rain?"

"Suit yourself." The cigar clerk tuned a new station on his midget radio, while Dave through the window watched the doorway to the meeting rooms across the street. The men were coming alone and in pairs, heads bent, collars turned up. The March thaw rain drizzled into the snow, then came sweeping in gusts from the corner. Dave, as he watched the men slog through the streams and puddles in the hollows of melting ice, counted them off—some for Red, some for Jennison, some in between. He saw that both sides had turned out in spite of the rain; this was the showdown and everybody knew it.

Just before the meeting time, a car drew up at the curb. Uncle Jennison climbed out followed by Vice-President Donohue from downtown. Then that was the scheme, Dave thought: let Donohue loose on the platform, banking on the prestige of the vice-president's office to keep the men from interrupting him. Donohue could spill out high-sounding bilge for twenty-four hours at a stretch—the old stalling game, stock-in-trade for hard-pressed officials. That made their own side of the showdown simple; they would call for a time limit and win or lose on the first vote. Stepping out into the rain, Dave crossed the street and mounted the staircase to the meeting room.

The room was crowded, steamy with the smell of rubbers and wet overcoats. The vice-president was already on the platform and Jennison had his head in the switch box in the far corner, trying to light a few of the dead bulbs which dangled from the ceiling. When Dave stepped through the doorway there came an abrupt silence, a shifting of feet and squeaking of chairs as the men turned to look at him. He stopped, waiting for someone to challenge his entrance, but no one spoke. Then he walked down the center aisle to the place Red was holding for him.

A few minutes after the hour, Uncle Jennison opened the meeting. He explained that Vice-President Donohue had come to talk over with them certain very important questions of grievance procedure, they were certainly mighty grateful to Brother Donohue for traveling to the South Side in all this rain; now he was going to yield the floor to the vice-president of their union, Brother Jim Donohue. Uncle Jennison spoke in a low voice and held his eyes fixed on the table in front of him. Dave noticed that he jerked his hands back and forth as if he had never spoken from a platform before. Beside Dave, Red got to his feet and Jennison, leaning forward over the table, stared down at him.

"Point of order," Red said. "What's your agenda?"

Uncle Jennison shook his head slowly without speaking.

"Point of order," Red shouted up at him. "What's on your agenda? We got a right to know that. We're members of this union, ain't we?"

"On the agenda? You know what's on the agenda. It's just like always—chairman's report, old business, new business, good and welfare, adjournment. Never been any different from that as long as I can remember." Jennison hesitated as if waiting for Red to start shouting again, then he repeated, "I'm going to turn over my chairman's report to the remarks of Jim Donohue, our vice-president."

Red cut him off. "We got to vote on the agenda first. I call for a vote on the agenda and I want to put up an amendment."

"You're out of order, ain't you?"

Dave felt Jennison's fear and confusion from the fact that he had apparently lost the nerve even to make a statement; he asked a question— You're out of order, ain't you? For a moment, Dave felt sorry for him, but in the silence that followed he called, "You making your own rules of order now, chairman?"

"He's in order. Give him the floor."

"Rule him down. Rule him down!"

The members yelled back and forth at each other. Red, with one foot on the seat of his chair, was shouting and pounding his fist into his open palm. His voice bellowed out over the others: "Me and some of the brothers here have got business we want to have up under new business, and we want to make good and goddamn sure we get to new business before day after tomorrow. So I make this amendment that goes like this . . . If we haven't finished the other items one half hour from now, we move right into new business anyhow; and every speaker be limited to five minutes from then on."

The shouting burst out again. Voices yelled, "Second!" and others, "Out of order! Rule him down."

There was a rising swell of laughter, and at the rear someone began to stamp his heels, chanting, "Question, question, call the question. . . . Question, question, call the question."

The rest took up the chant and their voices drowned out the voices protesting. When Jennison counted the show of hands, the amendment had carried, twenty-one to fourteen.

Dave patted Red on the arm and said in his ear, "That does it." He had been sure how the men felt, but he had not been certain they would hold together against Jennison and the vice-president. Now there was only the question of keeping them together until the finish.

Up on the platform, the vice-president was going to work. A big man with wavy gray hair, he strode up and down, delivering his flowery phrases as if he had never a doubt that he would carry the meeting with him.

". . . And a fair time it is we've been marching along together, brothers, fighting for the rights of railroad workers, fighting for the future of our wives and little ones. . . ." The clock jerked slowly through its half hour. Dave's eyes wandered around the hall—the green tin ceiling with a rusty splotch at one side; the stand-up piano, the American flag over the platform. When the clock passed the twenty-five-minute mark, Donohue was still swinging through his warm-up. "A source of pride, believe me, to every man among us, yes, you'll be guessing whom I refer to, the man for twenty years we've given the loving nickname of 'Uncle' because he was always ready with a friendly word and a strong hand. God's truth, brothers . . ."

As the clock reached the half hour, Red started out of his chair. Dave yanked him down again. But five minutes later, the vice-president had still mentioned no important matters of grievance procedure. The men were stirring and shuffling their feet. Someone began to hiss, and Red and Dave jumped up together.

"If the brothers will be doing me the favor to allow me to conclude my remarks . . ."

"You heard the vote of the meeting. You're over your time now."

"I'd not have been coming out here, brothers, if I had not had important matters to take up with you."

"You're taking up for a quick trip down the stairs," Red shouted, and that brought the whole meeting on its feet, yelling and knocking over chairs. The majority of twenty surged up to the front, while the others hung back indecisively. Smiling down from the platform, the vice-president faced them. He tried to make himself heard, laughed, waited a moment and tried again. Plenty of guts, Dave thought; fists were waving around the man's knees as he leaned forward over the speakers' table.

Dave shouldered through, climbed the platform and, pushing past Jennison, took his place beside the vice-president at the table. In the sudden hush, he said, "Now let's get organized, brothers. We can't go on shouting each other down all night. Why doesn't somebody make a motion to move into new business? All right, the motion is on the floor. I hear it seconded. Brother Chairman, would you care to take the count?" He swung around. Light glinted from the top of the bald head bent towards him, and as Uncle Jennison looked up slowly, Dave remembered the night when they had parted at the streetcar stop. But Jennison wrenched the handle off the gavel, let the pieces fall from his hand. He turned, walked down the steps, down the side aisle of the hall and out, forgetting his hat and overcoat. One of the men took them down from the coat rack and ran after him.

"The chairman has left the chair," Dave said. "Thanks to the chairman and to the vice-president here beside me, I am no longer a member of this Lodge. I guess I've got no business on this platform, and I suggest somebody nominate a new chairman so I can step down."

"You'll do. Stay there."

Dave shook his head, and then the men began calling, "Red! Up you go, Red Brogan."

As Dave jumped down to the floor, Red took over the speakers' table. In a quick series of resolutions, they called for the resignation of Jennison from the Lodge chairmanship and turned over in the meantime to Red, as acting chairman, all grievances and dealings with the railroad company. Dave noticed that Jennison's men did not leave the hall, but none of them opposed the resolutions. Up on the platform, the vice-president remained sitting on one of the straight chairs, his hands folded across his knees. At the final vote, which condemned his office and demanded Dave's reinstatement, he looked up with a smile. The meeting adjourned. Donohue said good night to Red and walked out through the groups of men, belly pulled in, shoulders back, his gray tweed overcoat slung over his left arm.

After the meeting, the men piled down the stairs into the street. Stretches of black, wet pavement showed through the melting ice. Everywhere water splashed and gurgled, curtains of fog floated across the streetlamps. The majority section of the meeting reconvened in the tavern on the corner, where everybody took turns standing the drinks to celebrate the victory. They shook hands and banged each other on the back, and only broke up close to nine o'clock, when Red and the others on night shift had to get some supper before they went to work.

The men took off in different directions, yelling and whistling after each other. Dave boarded the streetcar. The beer had made him sleepy, and as the car banged along Wentworth Avenue, he leaned his head against the windowpane and did not know he had dozed off until the waking jolted him as if he had fallen down a flight of steps. He had ridden past his stop. Half-blind with sleep, laughing and swearing at the same time, he stumbled out into the rain again. He walked back a couple of blocks to Thirty-Sixth Street, climbed the embankment, crossed the tracks, and slid down through the mud and melting snow into the back yard of Mrs. Koviak's house.

The rear windows were lighted, and Dave was surprised to find Victor Koviak at the kitchen table drinking a glass of milk.

"Long time no see," Victor said. His crutches stood propped against the table with a new-looking brown homburg balanced on the top of one. He was wearing a gabardine overcoat without a wrinkle, and the hollows of his jaw had a blue shine to them as if he had only finished shaving. "Good day, brother-in-law," he said. "You're looking sturdy as usual."

Dave picked up the homburg, grinning when he noticed the label inside. "Fancy, isn't it, Vic?"

"Yes, a nice toppiece, brother-in-law, but too small for you. And if you're wondering what's come over old Vic Koviak, the rag-bag Polack, I'll confess I've had a little windfall. No doubt Stephanie told you?"

"No."

"No, eh? No doubt she had reasons for not telling you, then. But I'll tell you myself without embarrassment. I am now a member of the faculty of the great University."

"Damn good."

"A humble position," Victor went on. "But the first one is the hardest, they say, and I don't expect to remain an instructor for the rest of my days. As for the fine feathers—" He brushed his finger tips across the lapel of his coat—"As for the fine feathers, brother-in-law, they are not so much in keeping with my present situation as with the one I aspire to. For it is one of the curious facts of the academic world that an instructor has the duty to dress as if he were a professor, whereas the professor has the privilege of dressing any way he pleases. *Ignoblesse oblige,* as they say. But you have your mind on something else."

Dave was listening to the sound of voices from the parlor. He heard Stephanie talking, and then a man's voice he did not recognize. He looked down at Victor. "Who's in there?"

"A school friend of your wife's. Sit down, brother-in-law. Give them a moment to talk over old times. Meanwhile, I'll be delighted to chat with you. Do you think there is any essential difference between the Nazi and Soviet forms of government?"

But Dave, pushing open the door, stepped into the room beyond. Who the friend was, he knew at once, although he had never seen him before. Stephanie introduced them, and the other took up his hat and coat to leave.

"When are you going East?" Stephanie asked.

"Tuesday."

"Good luck to you, Martin. You'll call me before you go?"
She turned away to the window, leaving Dave and the visitor
facing each other at the center of the room.

"I've been wanting to talk to you," Martin said. "Perhaps you'd
care to walk up to the corner with me?"

Dave nodded and they went outside together. "I came to say
goodbye to your wife," Martin told him. "I'm leaving next week
for the East." In the narrow track between the melting snowdrifts,
they had to walk single file, and Martin looked back at Dave as
he spoke. "I might as well tell you that I asked your wife to go
along with me." Dave felt his breathing miss a count and the knot
of anger tighten in his throat. "I have a fair job," the other said.
"One I've been working towards a long while. Stephanie could
continue in her own field at Columbia or New York University."

"Who do you think I am," Dave asked. "Her father?"

"No, but I think you're a reasonable human being."

It would cost you plenty if I wasn't, Dave thought. His hands
had come out of his jacket pocket; as he thrust them back, he saw
that the other noticed the gesture and understood it, but neither
stopped nor quickened his step.

"I believe you're a reasonable human being," Martin said again.
"What do you think is wrong with Stephanie?"

"I don't know."

"No? And is she happy? Does she feel good about the world?
Is she in one piece in her own mind?"

Dave did not reply to the question. "What answer did she give
you today?" he asked.

"None. She hadn't answered when you came in."

"You're afraid she won't leave me? You're trying to persuade *me*
to leave her?"

They turned the corner beyond the coal yard and walked west
toward Halsted Street, side by side here because the path between
the drifts was wider. The little houses with their roofs wet and
shiny in the lamplight stretched in two straight rows ahead of
them. "I feel as if I'd known you a long time," Martin said,
"although I never saw you before today. I've known you vicariously,
so to speak. I watched you fighting inside Stephanie's head for
two years. And you won, but I think she lost. . . ."

"How did you happen to come here today?" Dave asked.

"Her brother Victor told me she was sick and so I came. I

298

respect you. Maybe I even envy you in some ways. Certainly I'm not going to judge what your life is to you. But to me, it would be a waste of time. Perhaps I don't really understand what you're driving at—revenge, or the millennium, or armageddon—I don't know. If we had time I'd ask you to tell me."

"What do you do for a living?" Dave asked.

"Teach."

"What?"

"Philosophy. On your side you consider that a waste of time too, I don't doubt."

"That depends on what philosophy."

"I don't teach Marxism."

They reached the corner, the brightly lighted intersection where the rain slanted many-colored through the neon lights. Behind them in the window of the jeweler's store, a man squatted among the trays of watches, rings, and heaps of tarnished silver. He was locking an iron grill in place against the glass; below the window, the shadow of the grillwork fell across the pavement, and the man's shadow also, stooped and distorted like an ape in a cage.

"I've about three minutes left," Martin said. The blue spark of a streetcar had come in sight down Halsted Street. "Maybe you think Stephanie is cut out to be a fighter and a stump speaker and a meeting-girl. I don't. I think she was cut out to be a scholar and a scientist. Maybe you think the two can go together. I don't. I think it will break her if she stays with you; she'll fight inside her own mind until it breaks her. Maybe she'll decide to leave you, but it will be too late."

"Too late for what? To go with you?"

"That's not what I meant. I think you know what I meant."

Dave felt inside himself an acknowledgment of what the other said. Again his breathing skipped a count, and there was a cold, frightened feeling in his stomach because he had admitted what the other said. "She's free to go where she wants. She always has been."

"I don't think she's in a position to make the choice. You say yourself you don't know what's wrong with her. I've known her five years—a decisive person, quick to make up her mind and act on it. I tell you I've never seen her the way she is now. She acts as if she hadn't the energy to get out of her own chair, much less decide what kind of life she wants to lead. I can't make the decision for her. And if she can't make it herself, you're the only one who can make it. You've got the courage, I know that. Whether you have the understanding or not, I don't know."

Dave stepped sideways so that the light from the jeweler's window fell across the other's face. The eyes met his gravely. "Then if I don't agree with you," he said, "I haven't the understanding. Is that it? Are you so sure you know it all?"

"You'll have to make up your own mind as to that."

Dave turned away. He walked back along Thirty-Sixth Street towards the embankment, splashing through the deep water between the drifts.

1941

PLEDGER McADAMS changed back to afternoon shift. He pulled on his overalls in the Negroes' locker room, he and his partner crossed the yard, past the roundhouse, past the tracks where the coach cleaners swabbed the sides of the cars with their long-handled brushes. All along the way, people stopped work, and by the time Pledger and his partner reached the wheel-pit house, they had picked up a couple of dozen escorts. Two coaches stood over the pits; the day-shift men climbed out from under and Pledger and his partner climbed down. For a moment Pledger looked out from between the wheels at the men who had come to watch him start work. He grinned and waved. The four o'clock whistle blew; the men moved off towards the locker room, and Pledger swung around to the axle, which crossed the pit on the level of his eyes and which was marked with chalk to indicate the repairs it needed.

He was afraid he might have forgotten this trade in the twenty years since he had worked as carbuilder. To catch himself up, he had spent several nights with Red in the depot. Now beginning work on his own, he watched himself at every move, because he knew Upstairs Jarvis would be waiting for the first slip. Within a few hours, however, he felt the work coming back to him: the equipment and tools were almost the same as he remembered.

But he knew that most important of all was the attitude of the white carmen; and this seemed friendly. Most of them, he thought, would help him if he needed help. When Red had taken over as chairman of the white Lodge, he had asked Pledger to go along with him to see Upstairs Jarvis. Some of the other white Lodge members came too. They all waited in the outer office until Jarvis stepped out to meet them—with the railroad cop, Morgan, ambling along behind him. For once Red had kept his temper; he talked fairly quietly to Jarvis, telling him the Lodge intended to enforce its seniority rules. Then Red said Jarvis would have to assign the two new wheel-pit jobs in accordance with the seniority of the bidders. Otherwise the Lodge would start collecting carbuilder's pay for the two men whose seniority had been violated.

Jarvis had shrugged his shoulders. "All right. They can go to work. You better make sure they can handle the job."

At the end of his first day, Pledger was stiff from head to foot. His back ached from swinging the hammer and bending under the axles. But he had made certain to himself that he *could* handle the job. On his way home at midnight, crossing the embankment, he stopped for a moment to look at the glow of the city, and the sky overhead, filled with spring stars. He heard the can factory clattering beyond the embankment, and the puffing of an engine from the coach yard behind him. So after twenty years, he thought, he had come back to the job he had set so much store by; and he realized that it held very little importance for him. At one time he had valued the prestige of being a regular carbuilder; now there were many other honors he valued more. Once he had needed the extra money, but now he had not much use for it. The two kids were grown up—Judith married, not even bothering any longer to write them letters; Billy going away to camp with the first group of draftees from the neighborhood. But if the job was not important to him, he knew how important it was to all the others. For to them it was a mark of victory. They had fought together and won—the first time they had ever won anything against the railroad. It was a symbol to them that Negro and white men could work together; a symbol that one day Negroes would have an even break in all the yards on all the railroads.

Pledger, hungry and tired, happy and singing to himself under his breath, walked home to the Chile Parlor where Ruby and Dave Spaas were waiting for him. Ruby had some food ready and brought a bottle of wine out from behind the counter. While Pledger ate, Dave asked him how the afternoon had gone, what

kind of repair jobs they had given him, and about the attitude of
the various white workers. After Pledger had answered his questions, Dave nodded his head, and then they looked at each other
across the table.

"And how about you?" Pledger asked. "What you going to do
now?"

"I got to do something pretty quick," Dave told him. "I'm down
to the bottom of the funds."

"You going to fight your case, aren't you?"

"Sure I will. But it may take a long time. I'll have to get another
job if I want to eat." And after a moment he said, "Stephanie's
not working now either."

"How about the other railroads—you tried them?"

"I might do that, Pledger, unless they got me blacklisted. Or I
could go out to the steel mills. They're hiring men—" He stopped
for a moment and Pledger watched him in silence. Then Dave
told him, "Or I might go to sea again. I wrote one of my old ship-
mates the other day."

"No, Dave," Ruby said. "What for?"

Dave glanced up at her with a quick smile. "I don't know, I
haven't figured it out yet." He got up from the table, slapped
Pledger on the shoulder, and said he was going home to bed.

■　■

The months of the spring passed quickly for Pledger. The wage
movement, on which he and Dave both had worked so long, had
now become almost respectable in the yard. The attacks against
it had ended abruptly; the weekly newspaper was posted on all
the bulletin boards and tacked to the doors of the locker rooms.
The union officials down in the vice-president's office were keeping
their mouths shut and staying a good distance away from the
yard. Pledger saw that the revolt of the Great Midland Carbuilders'
Lodge, following Dave's expulsion from the union, had finally
convinced them that their own necks were in danger, that they were
only a few steps short of a general revolt of the membership. So
they had holed in till the weather cleared, and now were saying
nothing and doing nothing—just waiting.

But the wage movement was succeeding despite them. Early in
the summer, four of the big railroad brotherhoods suddenly swung
into the drive. They opened up negotiations on all roads in the
country for higher wages and better working conditions. When

four of the brotherhoods began to move, Pledger told his own lodge it was only a matter of weeks before the other unions in the industry, including their own union, would be obliged to join the line. This, he thought, was what they had been hoping and fighting towards ever since the conference of the twenty-five almost a year before.

As for his own job, Pledger found it going smoothly, and he settled into the new routine. He worked steadily and easily with his partner, and was glad Andrew Masters had decided not to come back to the wheel pit. Andrew Masters was too old. And that was the next problem, Pledger realized; that they had so few young men who knew carbuilder's work. He asked some of the young Negro coach cleaners from the day shift to hang around the wheel-pit house in the afternoons so they could learn the trade. And he began figuring ways of bringing a few Negroes into the regular apprenticeship system.

When supper hour came, Pledger or his partner would fetch a bottle of coffee from one of the diners parked in the coach yard. Usually old Andrew Masters, who worked the same shift on the wash track, would join them for supper, and they sat on the bench in the spring evenings, eating their sandwiches. At midnight, after they finished work, Pledger and Andrew Masters walked home together across the embankment. They said good night in front of Andrew's chapel, and Pledger strolled on up the street to the Chile Parlor. Ruby would be serving a few late customers, and Pledger would sit down at the counter for his second supper.

He slept late in the mornings. When he woke, Ruby would be up already, preparing the beans and barbecued spareribs for the day's business. If the day was bright, as most of these June days were, Pledger carried his breakfast coffee into the back yard and sat under the patchy shade of the cottonwood tree, reading the war reports in the morning paper. Every day the reports were the same: the steady advance of the Nazi divisions rolling over Yugoslavia and Greece.

One morning Ruby shook him awake earlier than usual. She gave him the newspaper and Pledger sat up, rubbing the sleep out of his eyes. The paper carried the first bulletins of the German invasion of Soviet Russia.

23

"WHAT'S wrong with you commies anyhow?" Red Brogan demanded. "Back at the last wage-movement rally, you boys come sporting buttons as big as silver dollars: *No convoys— no AEF*. I seen it with my own eyes. But now I guess we'll all be out beating the drums because Joe Stalin got his ass in the hot water."

Dave unbuttoned his shirt across his chest, and where sweat had glued the shirt to his skin, he peeled the cloth loose to let some air circulate. Through the door of the tavern, propped open by a brick, he could see people moving past on the sidewalk, and the glare of sunlight over the street. But inside, it remained fairly cool. Fans buzzed; the smell of spilt beer and the odors of a damp basement drifted out from the rear of the tavern. By the juke box, sat the same frowsy-haired waitress feeding slugs into the machine whenever the music ran slack. *"Oh Johnny,"* the juke box played, and kept returning to that as if there were no other records in the rack. *"Oh Johnny, oh Johnny, how you can love—"*

Walter brought their glasses from the bar, set them down and leaned on the table, blinking his red-rimmed eyes. "Either of you guys ever taste a stingeroo?" he asked. "No sir, I bet you didn't. I was mixing some for Johnny in here last night. Boy, did he go for those, him and that gal of his, Sally. Guess you remember her? She's some looker, eh?" He grinned and showed a couple of teeth missing under the pink mustache. "Built for business, eh? But that gal you had, haven't seen her in two, three months, Spaas old man—"

Red suddenly rose out of his chair. "For the Christ's sake get back behind your bar where you belong!"

Walter jumped clear of the table and sidled away, glancing at them over his shoulder. For a moment the juke box fell silent while the waitress, forgetting to put in another slug, stared with her hand half raised to the slot. But she shrugged her shoulders, banked in the slug, and the machine wailed off again. "That poisonous son of a bitch," Red said. "You need a gas mask when he comes spitting around."

Dave took a drink of his beer, then glanced up. "You got it off your chest now? You ready to settle down and talk?"

"Well, who's stopping you? Go ahead and talk."

"You ask me how come the communists change their position about the war," Dave said. "Because the war changed, that's why. I'm not going to argue with you what day it changed or what made it change—"

"Then maybe you boys were off base when you come around with those *no-convoy* buttons?"

"Maybe."

"And you could be wrong right now?"

"Sure we could."

"That's the first time I ever heard one of you guys admit you can be wrong."

"A position that's right today may be wrong tomorrow," Dave said. "But you never heard me say we couldn't be wrong. So long as we can make mistakes and correct 'em, we'll get along good enough." Red had emptied his glass. He banged it upside down on the table, and Dave asked him, "Listen, Red, who you been fighting all through this wage movement?"

"I been fighting the railroad."

"And who owns it?"

"Son-of-a-bitching bank, I guess."

"The Western States Bank and Trust Company in New York owns it. So who do you think you're fighting when you fight the Great Midland? You're fighting Wall Street and American capital. And American capital doesn't smell any different from any other kind. England, France, America, the whole capitalist world—they been trying to smash the Soviet Union for twenty years. They let Hitler take Spain and Austria and Czechoslovakia to build him up for the job."

"Then why do you bastards just start squawking now for?"

"I been squawking since I was old enough to open my mouth. What do you think we were doing in Spain?"

Red opened his newspaper to the comic section as if he were not listening; then he folded the paper and got up from the table. "I want to catch some sleep," he said. "I still work for a living even if you don't." They tossed the money for the beer on the table and walked outside. Dave, feeling part of the other's question still unanswered, groped for the place to begin again. "You want to know why I got confidence in the Soviet Union? Because it's a socialist state—because it was set up by a workers' revolution—"

Red cut him off. "I'm all for you, boy, but I think you commies got caught with your pants down."

Dave spun around and they faced each other, scowling and blocking the sidewalk. "You ask me a lot of questions and then won't listen to the answers I give you," Dave shouted. His anger flashed up suddenly out of his control. "You knew how things were going to work out a year ago, did you?"

"Go on," Red said. "I won't argue with you. You bastards always got your own answers."

They turned, walking along without looking at each other; but Dave saw that Red was satisfied now he had finally provoked him. As they reached the corner, Red lurched sideways, bumping Dave against a woman who was passing; then giggled like a kid when the woman stopped and Dave had to apologize.

"Here's where I take off," Red said. "I don't want to be seen on the street with you, you drunken bum."

"So long."

But Red stopped and tugged at his arm. "Listen, Dave—"

"What's the matter?"

"I'm not kidding, boy. You ain't going to enlist for a hitch, or go to sea, or some damn thing? The guys are ready to walk out for you. By Christ, we'll make 'em put you back."

Dave shook his head. "It's not worth it for one man's job. You got the Lodge in good shape, Red. The wage movement's coming into line. You don't need me around here."

"The hell we don't." Red pressed Dave's arm hard for a moment. Then, shaking his head, walked off down the side street.

■ ■

It was late evening when Dave returned to the Koviaks' house. A light was burning in the kitchen, but he did not want to talk to Mrs. Koviak or Rosa. He went up the stairs to the room in the attic. On the bed were Stephanie's hat and brief case; she must have come home without going to her class, he thought. Stepping to the window, he looked out over the tracks behind the house.

Stephanie was standing there. He whistled and she turned around, then waved to him to come out.

The sky hung smoky and lavender with a faint glow of twilight fading over the rooftops. As he reached the crest of the cinder slope, she said, "Now ask me about my class. Go ahead. I know that'll be the first thing."

"All right, I will. What about it?"

"I didn't go, that's all. I didn't feel like going and I didn't go."

He tried to hold his voice level. "I wasn't worrying whether you went or not. What's the matter, Stephanie?"

"Nothing's the matter. Why should anything be the matter?" He put his arm around her, but she pulled away from him. "Don't lean on me. I'm tired enough as it is."

Laughing, Dave asked, "Why did you want me up here anyway?" He turned and started down the slope; she stood watching him, but before he reached the bottom, she called to him and he came back.

"I'm sorry, Davey. I didn't mean to get angry again."

"I can sure get a day's exercise running up and down here, can't I?"

She slipped her hand under his arm. "Come, take me for a walk on our promenade." Her voice had a tense, uneasy sound; but her eyes and her teeth flashed as if she were laughing. "Isn't it a nice evening? See, the stars are out and the moon's rising. Doesn't it make you feel romantic? We could lie down here in the cinders and make love. Would you like to?"

He shook his head.

"Did you ever read *Hamlet,* Davey? I feel like Ophelia—giddy and lightheaded. If we walked all night down the tracks, do you suppose we could be out in the country by morning?"

Along the embankment, the red and green signal lamps stepped away one after another into the southwest. "Almost," Dave said. The evening had darkened into night and they stumbled sometimes as they walked.

"I used to read a poem, Davey, about two people who went to live in the country and they lived beside a little stream and all day and all night the stream rippled under their window. After a while they didn't hear it any more, because to them the sound of the stream became silence. Isn't that a nice way to put it? *The sound of the stream was silence.*" He nodded without answering and she said, "You and me, we live beside the railroad tracks, and I guess the noise of the trains almost is silence for us."

"Would you like to live in the country?" he asked.

"Not for always. But I sure would like to go for a while. Do you remember a long time ago, you took me to the country and we sat beside a brook under some trees? It was before you went to Spain. Do you remember that?"

"Yes, I remember it."

"Do you really?"

"Why not?"

"I didn't know you remembered things like that. I thought you remembered only facts and quotations you could use in speeches."

"Cut it out, Stephanie. Let's go back and get some sleep."

"What do you want sleep for?"

"Come on. Let's go back."

"What do you want sleep for? You don't need to get up in the morning. We live on love. No job, no money, and we have a nice home with my mother and my sister-in-law." Dave caught her by the shoulders. She threw herself back against his hands. In the darkness, he could scarcely see her face, but she whispered, "Go ahead, shake me. See if you can shake some of that fine resolution of yours into me."

His anger flared up and faded.

It's as if there were a million miles between us, he thought. If I was to get down and put my arms around her knees, she'd laugh at me; and if I beat her until she couldn't stand, she'd stare back and never make a sound. He knew she acted the way she did because she was miserable, and he kept saying over to himself, I made her come with me when I could have let her go. He pulled her around and they returned along the embankment. Far in the distance were the lighted towers of the Loop, but directly beneath them lay the black gulf of the coal yard. The streetlamp on the corner struck a blue gleam here and there from the heaps of coal, and Stephanie, as they passed the yard, stared down into the darkness.

"You never told me anything about Spain," she said suddenly. "Why is it you never talk about that?"

"I never felt much like talking about it."

"Did you sleep with all the Spanish girls?"

"Only a few."

"And how many fascists did you kill?"

"I don't know."

"Didn't you count them? Didn't you carve notches in your gun?"

He shook his head. On the opposite side of the tracks, an engine puffed past, and they watched the boxcars rumble by one after another.

"I think that's the secret of your success," Stephanie said. "Anything that bothers you, you put it out of your mind. Forget it; better luck next time!"

Dave stood silent, watching the red taillights of the caboose as they crept around the curve of the embankment.

"What are you doing now?" she asked. "Putting *me* out of your mind?"

"I wish I could."

"Well, who's stopping you?" After a moment, she said in a petulant, childish voice, "What are you thinking?"

"Nothing." He peered down at her face, lifted his hands to pull her towards him, but let them drop again.

"What are you thinking? You're angry at what I said about Spain?"

"What you said was all right: better luck next time."

"You're angry at what I said."

"No."

"Of course you are. That's why I said it."

"Then you'd better try again."

"Oh, Dave, I don't know why I say things like that to you. But sometimes it seems all so useless. You fight in Spain—and for what? The fascists win out. And here—night after night—meetings, organizations, speeches. And each night I wonder, will they bring you home to me with your legs sliced off by the trains, or with your head split open by a club in some dark alley? And what's the use? My God, what's the use? The company throws you out like a dog and no one lifts a hand to help you."

"The Lodge is fighting for me."

"The Lodge. And when you're gone, the stupid old men will come back to the Lodge, just like the weeds over the vacant lots."

He shook his head. "Maybe we feel that way sometimes; but it's not true. When we're gone there'll be plenty more to take our place." They had come back now to the brink of the slope that dropped down into the back yard. Across from them on the level of the tracks, was the window of the attic bedroom. Dave had left the light burning; they saw the bulb hanging from the ceiling by its black wire, and they could see the patchwork quilt on the bed.

Stephanie took him by the wrist and swung out her other hand, pointing to the houses with their lighted windows, the whole jumble of roofs and chimneys and towers under the night sky. "God, Dave, how can you go on day after day so stolid and unbending?" Then, letting her head drop forward, she began to kick at the wet and muddy cinders beneath her feet. He guessed what she was thinking, and whispered, "Don't do that."

But she said, "All winter there was the black ice over the streets, and I watched it melt, and I watched it freeze again. Twenty-seven years beside the embankment, Dave; I guess the sound of the trains really is silence for us. But it doesn't come easy; it breaks something inside you. It grinds your guts under the wheels and then you don't hear them any more." Her voice had grown low and quiet. Bending his head, he listened now without trying to stop her. "You never saw it, but I'm going to tell you. Maybe I never said anything about it either, but I didn't forget it. It was snowing, and there was snow all across the tracks under the bridge. At first I thought he was all right. His face looked red and as if he'd been drinking, and you could smell the whiskey they'd given him. He was worried about the brakemen for fear they'd think it was their fault. 'Take care of yourself, Stevie,' he said, and 'You and Dave come to see me.' " She stopped and he felt her shoulders shaking under his hands. Turning suddenly, she dropped her head against his chest. "I'm no good to you, am I? I've gone to pieces like a bundle of weeds."

Rocking her in his arms, he whispered, "You're all right, Stephanie."

"Help me, Dave. For the love of God, take me away from here, now, tonight—"

They slid down the embankment and walked through the passage between Mrs. Koviak's house and the house next door. Stephanie's legs gave way under her. She clung to him, and with his arm around her waist, he half carried her along the blocks towards Halsted Street. While they waited for the streetcar, Stephanie hovered in the lighted doorway of the jeweler's store as if she were warming herself before a fire.

"How much money have you got?" Dave asked.

She gave him a couple of dollars and he put them in his wallet alongside his five-dollar bill.

They rode south and east to the little hotel on Stony Island Avenue. The same old man behind the desk stared at them from under his green eyeshade just as he had stared after them when they had gone out twelve months before. He took them up in the elevator and they walked through the dark corridor, peering at the numbers on the doors.

Inside their room, Stephanie sat down at the mirror, smoothed her hair, put on powder and lipstick. Then she turned to face him, smiling slightly, her mouth looking very red against her white face. "See, now I feel safe again," she said. "I guess I have the soul of a traveling salesman's girl. With a lobby full of mangy palms and overstuffed chairs between me and the outside, I feel safe again. Tell me, how did you know I wanted to come here?"

"I didn't; but we had to stay somewhere."

She shook her head. "I've thought you stupid sometimes, Dave. I guess I called you that a little while ago. And sometimes I think you know me better than I know myself." Standing up, she brushed the dandruff from the collar of his jacket. "I don't know what to make of you. You scare me sometimes. Come now, play the traveling salesman for one night. Take me to the bar and buy me some whiskey."

In the tavern next the hotel lobby, they sat in one of the chromium and imitation leather booths. Dave ordered whiskey and, emptying his glass at a gulp, gave it back to the bartender for a refill.

"I guess we need it tonight, Stephanie."

"I think so. Can we afford it?"

"We've four dollars left. I'll save fifty cents for breakfast."

"Then I'm going to get a jag on tonight." As she held her glass up between her fingers, her hand shook slightly, but the whiskey did not spill. Dave saw the color slipping back over her cheekbones and the high bridge of her nose. He wanted to reach out to her across the table.

"I never knew I could get the way I've been," she said. "I do things, I know I'm doing them, I don't want to do them, and I keep right on doing them anyway. Does that seem impossible to you?"

"No, I know what you mean."

"I don't think you really do. I think you're the only person I've ever known who seemed to have no divisions within his soul. But

311

with me, everything inside me moves in different directions. I'm like the woman who wanted to stay thin, but she loved her cake so well . . . Why? Why is it that way with me, Dave?"

"You must want one thing most of all, Stephanie."

"And I should know what that is and subordinate everything else to it? That's discipline, isn't it? I used to be disciplined like that. I worked my way ever since high school, and now I've almost got a Ph.D. But it's all gone, Dave, all gone. I sit in the library and stare out the window; I haven't cut a lecture on purpose in five years, but I did it today, and not for any reason at all. And my class downtown, I suppose that's gone to hell too, hasn't it?"

He nodded.

"Then Rita Hanson was right, wasn't she? She said I was unreliable and I was. She was right."

"They don't expect you to come when you're sick."

"Yes, of course, I was sick."

She stared past him, biting at her lips. "Now I'm going to tell you what you probably know already, Dave. I really was sick. But I wanted to be sick, the first time in my life I ever wanted to be sick and I used it as a club against Rosa and my mother—and—"

"Against me," Dave said.

"Yes. You knew it, didn't you? Against you most of all. When you got fired and we had to stay at my mother's house, I didn't want to stay." Her voice had turned dry and toneless, like a schoolgirl, he thought, reciting some lesson by heart. "My mother doesn't like you, nor like me either very well. But as soon as we came inside the house, I began to act like a little girl. I let my mother wait on me and take care of me—I let her see me pestering you so she thought it was all right for her to pester you too. We nagged you with questions—where are you going? How long will you be away? Why couldn't you ever stay home evenings? That's true, isn't it, Dave?"

"Yes, it's true."

"And I stopped everything because I was sick, and my mother and Rosa took care of me. And I went to the Art Institute again, and brooded all through the galleries. I knew what I was doing, but I did it anyway. Do you understand why?"

"I think so."

"Why?"

"Because you were unhappy."

"Because I was unhappy." She laughed, shaking her head. "That's a good reason, isn't it? And maybe I wanted to be unhappy. I don't know. Oh Jesus, I don't know." He watched her sitting across from him with her elbows on the table, her forehead pressed against the palms of her hands. Wondering what it would be like living without her, he remembered the long months in Spain: when she was gone, he would be on foreign soil once more.

"Inside me," she said, "I've been making believe I was a little girl again. I've been acting the part. I feel as if hands came up out of the darkness pulling strings to make me jump and whistle and hop like a little monkey on strings." She rubbed her fingers across her eyes. "I thought the whiskey would clear my head. I wanted to talk to you, but now I'm drunk as an owl already. Say something to me, Dave."

He did not know what to say to her; the silence grew heavy between them.

She leaned forward across the table at last. "I'm getting like my crazy friend Marguerite; I keep thinking about things. I told you how I watched the black ice melting and freezing on the ground. You knew what I meant right away, didn't you? There must have been something. I feel as if we were walking along the brink of a great dark gulf. Why should I think about that? We're young yet. Maybe we've half our lives still to go. But that's not much, is it? Then what we are evaporates into nothing, even the lights and the mangy palms in the lobby won't fence us in."

"Don't do that, Stephanie."

"You don't see it. You're like a machine that goes on running until it breaks apart from old age. Don't you ever wonder how there can be anything against that nothing? The things we see and touch and taste might as well never have happened. Everything that ever happened dissolves as if there had not been anything. . . ." Her voice was rising; people at the other tables began glancing towards them.

She stopped abruptly, stared into his face, and Dave put his hand on hers. "I'm frightened," she told him. "I feel myself breaking up like a piece of clay between my own fingers."

They got up, and Dave took her back to the hotel. In their room, she dropped down on the bed and he sat beside her. "Tell me," he asked. "Why did you come back to me?"

"Why did I come back to you? Because I love you, I guess. Because I wanted to get in bed with you and make love to you with everything in the world. Those rotten little North Shore bitches couldn't love that much in a million years."

Dave took off his jacket; but a moment later when he turned back to the bed, she was fast asleep. He slipped off her shoes and tucked the blankets around her. Then he lay down by her side, kissing her throat and the soft hair over her ears. "Stephanie," he whispered. "Oh, Stevie, Stevie, how can I let you go?"

1941

WHEN Billy came home on his first furlough from Camp Grant, Ruby threw a party for him. He was a husky, barrel-chested kid who looked good in his khaki uniform. And he looked good to Pledger, who felt a warm surge of pride as he shook hands with the boy. Then he cuffed him around; and they wrestled and laughed and shouted together all over the Chile Parlor. After the Sunday service, Andrew Masters came over from the chapel along with a lot of the congregation and Billy's friends from high school and the members of Pledger's railroad Lodge. They pushed all the tables together and Ruby dished up the food—fried chicken and baked ham, greens and corn bread, coffee and wine and apple pie and chocolate cake. The Lodge members all brought bottles of whiskey for the celebration. Andrew Masters got drunk and made a speech, while everybody laughed and slapped their legs because no one had seen old Andrew take a drink in fifteen years. Word went around the neighborhood that Billy McAdams was home on furlough, and the young people swarmed into the Chile Parlor. Ruby gave away free slugs for the juke box, they moved the tables against the wall to make room so the young people could dance. Then Ruby got up by herself in her black silk dress, pink beads, and green earrings. All the couples cleared out of her way, and Ruby whirled around the floor, swinging her arms and slapping her great square buttocks.

Pledger noticed that Billy was drinking a lot of whiskey, but the boy remained shy and quiet. However, the party got louder all the time until one of the neighbors fell through the plate glass of the front door. He cut a gash in his forehead and they had to call an ambulance to keep him from bleeding to death. One of the girls keeled over, and somebody yelled, "You seen your first blood, Billy. Can you stand it?"

But Billy had disappeared. Everybody began looking for him, and Pledger finally located him in the back yard, vomiting the evening's food and liquor against the trunk of the cottonwood tree. He seemed sober enough. Pledger waited till he had got rid of his load and then helped him to bed.

"Guess I can't hold it very good," the boy said.

"You did all right," Pledger told him. "But a man's bound to hit the jackpot if he keeps at it long enough." They both laughed, which started the boy off again, and he barely made the window in time to let the second batch go. He was shaking all over when he finished. "Didn't know I had any more in me," he whispered; and Pledger helped the boy off with his jacket, pulled his boots off, and stretched him on the bed. Then he went down to the Chile Parlor again; the party broke up about three in the morning, and Pledger helped Ruby clean up the wreckage.

Most of the next day the boy spent sleeping it off. He had to catch an evening train back to camp, but before leaving, he stopped at the railroad yard to say good bye to Pledger. He still felt kind of shaky, he admitted, and hadn't been able to hold any food down. Pledger's partner offered him a pork sandwich and rocked with laughter at the look of the boy's face as he shook his head.

"No man in his right mind would lay a finger on one of your sandwiches," Pledger said. "Let alone eat it." During the eight o'clock supper period, he took the boy all over the yard, introduced him to his friends, telling everybody they met, "This is my boy Billy, just back from the army." And Billy grinned and nodded, shifting his feet in the cinders. When the eight-thirty whistle blew, Pledger said,

"Well, good luck to you, boy."

They shook hands, and from the doorway of the wheel-pit house, Pledger watched the figure in khaki uniform crossing the yard through the bright cones of light of the overhead flood lamps, disappearing at last into the shadows beyond the roundhouse. The boy didn't look like a soldier, Pledger thought; he still ambled along like a high-school boy. They'd break him of that soon enough; marching was the easiest thing to learn about soldiering.

Maybe the country would never get into the war, Pledger thought; maybe the boy would stay in camp without ever hearing a shot. Or maybe he would go to war and come back; or maybe he would go and wouldn't come back. There were all those chances and nothing to do but wait and see. Just so he fights on the right side, Pledger said to himself. There would be plenty of fighting for the boy to take on yet, just so the fighting was on the right side.

And as he stood in the doorway, he remembered when he had worn a soldier's uniform himself and he thought again of the men he had marched with—how many million times they had picked up their tired feet and set them down again to the stamp and swing of the song:

"He is trampling out the vintage where the grapes of wrath
    are stored—"

Coming over the crest of a hill, he had seen the column stretching out ahead of him, between the double line of poplar trees, through the town of stone houses and slate roofs, across the railroad track, across the plowed fields and into the hills beyond. He saw the endless column of the black soldiers from America, the black men who had been denied by their own country and who asked each other what they were fighting for. American soldiers with French rifles over their shoulders, stamping their boots on the cobblestones and dusty roads of a foreign country. But he had known in his heart that these were the fighters and diers for a world that would not be lost. The soldiers of freedom, and he was one of them. He had watched the line of men crossing the valley, winding up into the hills that lay towards the Rhine. He had heard their voices pour back down the column like the great rushing of waves:

"He has loosed the fateful lightning of his terrible swift sword,
    And his truth goes marching on."

Now his own boy who had never worried about anything much except playing baseball in the yard behind the school building— now his own boy was going off to war; and Pledger wished that for him the battles might be easier to understand and the end more clear to see.

Pledger and his partner finished their work a few minutes before midnight. The little switch engine chugged down the hill, tied on to the cars they had repaired, and dragged them off to the ready track to go down to the depot. Pledger put away the tools in the wheel-pit house, then went to change his clothes in the locker room, where Andrew Masters was waiting for him.

"That's a fine boy you got," Andrew told him.

He and Andrew headed home together across the embankment. The moon was up, round and yellow in the center of the sky, casting their shadows over the cinders in front of them. Along the crest of the embankment, a line of red boxcars stood up in the moonlight. The boxcars were parked on a siding, and Pledger looked in each direction to make sure no engine was hitched to them. They found an empty car with both its sliding doors open, and climbed in. On the floor beneath their feet was sawdust which appeared yellow as gold in the square of moonlight falling through the doorway. The car smelled of newly cut pine boards. Pledger jumped down from the opposite doorway and helped Andrew down after him. On this side ran the two tracks of the main line, and beyond the curve of the embankment, the can factory thrust up its twin smokestacks. Andrew Masters steadied himself on Pledger's arm as they stepped over the rails.

A voice behind them said, "What you looking for in those boxcars?"

Pledger swung around. They were standing now in the bright moonlight between the two tracks. For a moment he could see no one. Then he heard the sound of a foot on the cinders. A thin figure stepped out of the shadow under the line of boxcars. Pledger remained motionless, only opening and closing his hands at his sides. The figure moved towards him and he saw that it was the railroad detective, Morgan.

24

DAVE and Stephanie came down from the hotel and walked along Stony Island Avenue looking for a place to eat breakfast. The morning was windy and sharp. Over the fronts of the buildings, the flood of sunlight brightened and darkened from one moment to the next as the spring wind drove clouds across the sky. They stopped in a drugstore on Sixty-Third Street and sat down at the counter.

"Well," Stephanie asked. "What are we going to do now?"

"I don't know. We better decide soon."

"Yes, we had."

"If you'll come," Dave said, "I'm going to take you to the dunes for a few days. Maybe it will help us think things out."

"Are you sure you can spare the time from your work?" He noticed the dry and hostile undertone of her voice; we've sobered up since last night, he thought.

That morning he drew out the rest of the cash they had in the bank and they took the electric train around the bottom of Lake Michigan. The stacks of the steel mills thrust up against the blue June sky. Beyond South Chicago the market garden fields stretched out, a mist of young green shoots spreading over the plowed earth. Then the first dunes rippled up from the prairie, climbing higher until they marched along opposite the railroad like a range of hills. At their whistle stop, Dave and Stephanie dropped down stiff-legged, and watched the little train of orange-colored cars hoot off through a cut in the sand dunes. The wind was chilly in the open country; but as they followed the road to the farmhouse, they saw the grass springing up thick and green through the dead leaves in the ditches. "I wasn't expecting anybody today, it's been so cold for the end of June," the landlady told them, and she gave them a room over the kitchen, warmed by the stovepipe from the kitchen range.

That afternoon, Stephanie and Dave took cigarettes and a couple of chocolate bars from their grip, and walked up into the dunes. Where the road dwindled out, they chose one of the many paths through the underbrush. The flanks of the sand hills, the thick growth of poplars and oak trees, broke the wind. Between the hills, they found deep clefts of black earth, where iris and violets unfolded like plants in a hotbed. Stephanie knelt beside them and brushed her finger tips against the blossoms. Then, with their feet sinking and sliding, they climbed a wall of sand to come out on the backbone of the whole range. Ahead of them, beyond the tumbled yellow-green slopes, the lake sparkled, flecked with whitecaps.

They scrambled down the outer slope into a cup-shaped hollow which sheltered them from the wind. The hollow was hot with sunlight, and on Stephanie's face, Dave noticed the forming beads of sweat. He took one of the chocolate bars from his pocket, broke it in half, and they sat down lighting cigarettes. Over their heads, the wind rose and fell in the branches of the trees. Neither of them spoke. But glancing up suddenly, he found her eyes fixed on him, suspicious and hostile; in silence they stared at each other. His throat turned dry and his tongue glued itself to the roof of his mouth. Then he broke his eyes away from hers, bent down, smoothed the sand in the bottom of the hollow, and spread his sweater over it.

"What's that for?" Stephanie asked.

"So you won't get sand in your hair."

She put out her cigarette and carefully buried it. When she looked up, the anger was still in her face, but her eyes were wide and her lips parted over her teeth. Reaching out to him, she pulled him down on top of her. The hunger that had come over them never left them even when they were exhausted, and as he looked into her eyes close under his, he did not know whether it had been the hunger to make love to her or the hunger to kill her.

"And were the Spanish girls better than that?" she asked.

"None that I met."

"I'm honored," she said.

They rolled apart at last and lay soaking up the spring sunshine. At the end of the afternoon, they returned across the ridge. The shadows lengthened over the sand dunes; the sun dropped down into the haze that lay in the direction of Gary and South Chicago. Dave felt tired and hungry. In the farmhouse, the landlady was setting dinner on the kitchen table and they sat down with her in front of the coal range, listening while she told them about the crops in her two fields, and how fine the tourist trade would be come the Fourth of July.

Afterwards, Dave and Stephanie walked outside again, towards the highway this time. All day he had wanted to talk to her, to break through the barrier of tension and hostility that separated them. Somehow during these few days away from the city, they would have to cut through, to settle this thing one way or another. But in his mind nothing was settled; everything turned over and over again.

"Stephanie." He stopped her and they stood facing each other. "What are we going to do?"

"I thought you were busy figuring that out."

"I was trying to figure it out, but I haven't got anywhere. That friend of yours, he asked you to go East with him—"

"I'm still here, aren't I?"

"You're still here, but you don't act as if you want to be."

"I don't. I don't."

"Then why didn't you go?" he demanded angrily.

"Oh, Dave, for God's sake let me alone."

"We've got to come out of this somewhere."

"All right, but not tonight. I can't talk to you tonight. Tomorrow we'll talk—"

As she turned back toward the farmhouse, he remained where he was for a moment, staring at the ground. Then he followed quickly, and when he caught up with her, said, "They're trying to buy you off the same way they bought off Jennison with a union job and a little money. They want to make you think you're better than other people because you can sit in your pigeonhole and pour one test tube into another. That's what they've always done to scientists and teachers. Just don't teach anybody to think anything out of line. But science doesn't belong to them. Don't you believe what you teach, yourself?" He stopped for a moment, picking his words carefully. "You're making a smoke screen inside your own head, that's all. That's what they try to dope you with so you won't know what you're doing."

"Stop it, Dave! Stop it!"

"Maybe it *is* my fault," he said. "Maybe we can't get along together. But you busted up your class at the People's School. That wasn't my fault."

They had reached the front steps of the farmhouse. She took his hand now and asked, "Please, Dave, let's talk tomorrow."

He felt surprised, himself, at what he had told her. When he had started, he had not known where he would finish; but he had finished by saying something which had been gnawing in his mind for many weeks—the answer he should have made to her friend Martin the night when they had walked between the snowdrifts. If what he said had not reached her, he thought, there probably was no way he ever could reach her. And he felt now that it had *not* reached her—as if she had been too far away to hear.

"All right," he said. "We'll talk tomorrow."

They went up to their room, and as they lay in bed after they had turned out the light, she seemed to fall asleep at once; but Dave remained awake for a long time. Down below them he heard coals dropping in the kitchen stove. A train wailed in the distance; a cat padded across the porch roof outside the window.

At the sound of knocking on their door, Dave woke. He saw that it was daylight.

"Telegram for you," the landlady called.

He got out of bed, took the envelope through the crack under the door, and Stephanie, sitting up, watched him while he opened it. "What is it?" she asked.

He stared at the message in silence.

"What is it? Can't you answer me?"

"It's from Ruby," Dave said. "Pledger McAdams was shot."

"Oh, Jesus."

Dave started putting on his clothes.

"Is he alive?" Stephanie asked.

"He's in the hospital. Ruby didn't say how bad."

"And are you going?"

"Of course." He saw the look of bitterness come over her face.

"You don't think I might need you, do you? Are you going to leave me here?"

"Unless you want to come with me, Stephanie. But I'll come back as soon as I can."

Getting out of bed, she put on her dress and walked to the window. "This has always happened," she cried. "Always, always. And it always will as long as we live unless we put an end to it."

Dave did not answer; he was lacing his shoes.

"Go ahead," Stephanie said. "But I'm not kidding this time. If you leave me here, you don't need to come back."

"Then you'd better come to the city with me."

When he straightened up, she was sitting in the chair by the window. He stood above her for a moment, looking at her black hair and her head turned away from him. She did not move. He crumpled the telegram, threw it on the floor, and left the room. Downstairs he told the landlady he had to go back to the city, but his wife might stay a few days longer. She gave him a cup of coffee, and he hurried up the road to the whistle stop to catch the next train.

25

RUBY had just come back to the Chile Parlor. She told Dave how they had called her at midnight and she had rushed to the hospital and remained there almost steadily ever since. She had not slept in thirty hours, so she stumbled off to bed while Dave went to wait at the hospital. But the doctors would not allow any visitors to see Pledger except for his wife. The next day, the doctors reported Pledger "improving," and Dave decided it was useless for him to spend his time in the hospital waiting room. Already meetings were being held all over the city to protest the shooting; he threw himself into the job of helping to organize them.

He and old Andrew Masters set up a sort of campaign headquarters in the Chile Parlor. All day the phone was ringing, the typewriter clattered on the corner table, people were coming in from unions, councils, churches. Dave borrowed Hanson's car so he could move around more easily. After the first few days he had faced so many meetings and committees and men across office desks that he hardly noticed whom he was speaking to or what he said. His voice almost spoke by itself. He would catch himself up, peer into the faces of his audience, trying to guess if they knew what he was talking about. Feathered and beady-eyed, the ladies of some local civic organization stared back at him. Then the chairwoman of the ladies would be shaking his hand: "Thank you, Mr. Spaas, you've given us something to think about. One of the terrible problems of our community—"

Finally, at the end of each day, he drove Hanson's car across the city through the dark blocks and bright intersections. The opposing line of traffic glared past. A streetcar blocked the road, then clattered away and the bunched traffic streamed out beyond, the red taillights weaving a crooked pattern before him. He parked the car in front of the Chile Parlor, and Ruby brought him a cup of coffee and some food.

Every night he asked the same question: "How's Pledger?"

And Ruby told him, "He seemed pretty good today. He's coming along all right."

But it was the end of the week before the doctor let Dave visit Pledger. He found him lying flat in bed, his chest wrapped in bandages. Pledger stretched out his hand, his grip answering Dave's strongly, and his eyes and teeth flashed in the old smile. One of the doctors waited beside the bed.

"I kept asking for you, Dave, but these damn doctors wouldn't let you in."

"How do you feel?"

"Like a mule had kicked me. I guess this is old stuff to you. You ask this doctor when he aims to let me out. I got no business in here."

The doctor smiled and shook his head. "We'll let you out as soon as we get you put together again."

"That's all the answer I can get from these fellows. What are you doing, Dave? Tell me what you're doing out there?"

"We're doing all right," Dave said. "Don't worry about that. They give you enough to eat in here?"

But Pledger insisted on his question. "I want to know what you're doing out there. Don't you try to put me off."

Dave glanced at the doctor, who nodded assent. From his pocket, Dave took the clippings and handbills he had brought. He showed Pledger first the stories from the city dailies, a few lines each headed, BOXCAR VANDAL SHOT or, WATCHMAN WOUNDS NEGRO PROWLER. Then he gave him the full-page headlines from the Negro papers of the South Side: RACE SHOOTING BY GREAT MIDLAND KILLER—DEMAND INDICTMENT OF RAILROAD GUNMAN. After that, Dave spread out on the bed the batch of handbills. Some were printed and some mimeographed. They carried the names of most of the Negro churches of the city; the Negro organizations, unions, and the Chicago CIO Council; there were some from the Wage Movement Committee; some from the South Side Section of the Communist Party. All were calls for meetings to fight discrimination on the railroads, to demand the firing of the detective Morgan, and his trial for attempted murder.

"I been to a dozen different meetings in the last day and a half," Dave said. "And that's only a few of them. Tomorrow Red and some of the officials from the white lodges are going to see the superintendent downtown."

"Regan? He won't do anything."

"Maybe not."

"Of course he won't. And what you aim to do after that?"

"Then we'll try something else," Dave said.

"See, doctor, you got to let me out, that's all."

The doctor patted Pledger on the knee. "You take it easy, my friend. Why, if you were out, they'd have to call off all these meetings."

Pledger did not smile at the doctor's joke. He watched Dave anxiously, twisted as if he were trying to come up to a sitting position, then dropped back on the pillow. "All that ain't for me. That's not the thing—"

"Of course it isn't. We're fighting an issue. Everybody knows that."

For several moments Pledger did not speak. The expression of his face changed, and the doctor moved quickly to the head of the bed. At last Pledger asked in a low voice, "The Russians, Dave? They won't let me have no newspapers in here." Dave told him the Russians were retreating, the Nazis had crossed the Soviet frontier from Poland. "They'll hold them," Pledger said. "They'll drop back and then they'll hold 'em."

Dave nodded. He understood what was in Pledger's mind. It wasn't that anyone knew for sure they could; but now it was useless thinking any different. Once a fight began there was no use to calculate the chance of losing. Pledger had rocked forward now, straining against the bandages. He brushed the pile of leaflets to one side of the bed, and Dave saw how the sweat gleamed on the knotted muscles on his neck.

The doctor was motioning him to leave. He gathered up the leaflets, pressed Pledger's hand, and turned away. But as he walked down the long aisle of the ward, he could hear Pledger's voice calling, "I got no business in here. You got to let me out!" Dave turned back for a moment and saw the doctor and a nurse bending over the bed.

All that week no word reached him from Stephanie. He wrote her at the farmhouse in the dunes, but the letter came back marked, *no forwarding address.*

When he went to Mrs. Koviak's house to find if there were any message for him, Mrs. Koviak shut herself in her bedroom and refused even to speak to him through the door. Dave laughed angrily. "Just like her daughter," he told Rosa. Rosa had two letters for him, but neither from Stephanie. One was the formal notice of his suspension from the union, telling him a trial board would meet the second week of September, to which, if he chose, he could appeal his case. The other was from New York, in a handwriting he did not recognize. He sat down at the kitchen table to read it, while Rosa moved about the room picking things up and putting them down. In the corner of the kitchen, her new baby rocked back and forth, butting his head against the bars of his pen; and through the open window, Dave could see the other one, the little boy, sunburned and sooty, scrambling along the slope of the embankment.

He ripped open the letter. It was from the little Englishman Ardwick, who had returned with him from Spain, in answer to the letter Dave had written several weeks before. ". . . if you may soon be shipping again with things like they are," Ardwick wrote. "I'll be in New York another fortnight, and I've no objection to shipping with you, if you've no objection yourself."

Rosa watched him uneasily. "Is it bad news?" she asked.

Dave shook his head. "Somebody I used to sail with." Then he pointed towards the room above where Mrs. Koviak had shut herself in. "Is she hiding any letters from me?"

"I don't think so," Rosa said. "I look every morning."

He wrote down the phone number of the Chile Parlor on a slip of paper and gave it her. "Will you do something for me, Rosa? If a letter comes from Stephanie, try to get hold of it first and call me?" Rosa nodded. He stood up, took her hand for a moment, then went out through the kitchen door into the back yard. The little boy was waiting for him, and Dave swung him first by the heels and then by the wrists and left him spinning about dizzily, shrieking with laughter and calling for more.

"Tomorrow," Dave told him. "More tomorrow."

He climbed the slope to the crest of the embankment, from which he could see the city stretching out on each side, a plain of roofs and chimneys with here and there a tree or water tank thrusting above the level. Overhead hung a gray lattice of smoke, and shafts of morning sunlight filtered through gaps in the lattice. Puffs of dust drifted up from the cinders. Dave was sweating already after the short climb. A windless heat, smelling of coal smoke, dust, and the stockyards, lay over the city. Stopping, he looked back at a line of trackworkers far down the embankment.

They were spiking down rails, and the clang of their hammers reached him faintly.

He remembered it was less than two weeks, less than ten days ago, he had found her here. What was she doing now? he wondered. Had she stayed in some boardinghouse, or come back to Chicago without telling him? Now it was up to him to say what came next; and there was not much left to say. He had waited, always hoping something might happen to set things different. It seemed strange to him now how casually the decision shaped itself. Almost as a matter of course he was agreeing to an action he had struggled for more than a year to avoid. More than a year? This had been hanging in front of him for almost ten years, he thought, ever since he had known her. A spasm of regret shook him. He stood biting the skin of his lips, thinking how often she had waited by herself while he went to the meetings and committee sessions; and when she said, Please, Dave, stay home tonight, he told her he could not stay. It had been tough for her, he had no doubt of that; he had asked too much. Maybe a long time ago, he thought, they could have worked things out differently, but it was too late now. He remembered that summer when he had studied engineering in the night school—if he had gone on with that, if he had become an engineer instead of a hobo, railroad worker, professional fighter, then things might have been different; but not since then.

Turning abruptly, Dave slid down through the cinders to the street on the far side of the embankment. Yes, the son of a bitch had been right. Neither one could change to suit the other. And if she had been made to be a professor and professor's wife, a learned liberal, a tennis player on the courts of universities, he could not ask her to go with him.

That evening, Dave waited for Red at the lunch counter of the Great Midland depot. While he waited, he took out a piece of paper and pencil.

"Dear Stephanie," he wrote,

> Pledger seems to be coming through all right. I have one more thing here to take care of. Then I am going to New York and will go to sea again. With the war the way it is, I could not stay much longer anyhow. This was not right for you, but something else will be. We tried, but it did not work.

I hope your mother will send you this letter wherever you are. Good luck to you.

Dave sealed the letter and slipped it in his pocket. A few minutes before eleven, Red sat down at the counter beside him.

"What happened?" Dave asked. "Will they fire him?"

"No, they won't fire him. Did you think they would?"

"They might."

"They might, but they ain't going to. We had a real nice time with the superintendent." Red chewed at the stub of his cigar a moment before he went on. "Secretary finally lets us in, we'all march into the office, and Regan, real democratic bastard he is, gets up and shakes hands with us over the desk. 'We appreciate the interest you men take.' He tells us that, see, after he's kept us waiting fifty minutes while every son of a bitch from the office boy to the milkman comes in ahead of us. What are you grinning about?"

"Regan's a busy man."

"Busy, my eye! Listen, you ever hear of an instruction sheet from the company telling employees not to go on parts of the property where they got no business?"

Dave nodded.

"That's Regan's angle. They should have hiked two blocks down to the underpass and two blocks back the other side instead of walking across the tracks. So it was an accident, and Regan's sorry it happened. But of course it was all McAdams' fault."

"Guys have been walking to work across that embankment since I was a kid," Dave said.

"Maybe Regan wasn't around that long. Says he doesn't see how the company could fire a faithful employee that was only trying to do his duty like he seen it. Particularly since there weren't any criminal charges against Morgan."

"Sure, I guess he was doing his duty." Dave sat silent for a time, looking up at the neon sign over the gateway to the train shed which blinked on and off: CHICAGO GREAT MIDLAND RAILROAD— SOUTH SOUTHWEST— Finally he said, "That takes care of that, Red. How about the rest of it?"

"It's all fixed. You be there Monday."

They got up from the counter. Red went off to work through the gate under the blinking sign, and Dave walked out to the street.

327

On the corner, he stopped in front of a mailbox and took the letter from his pocket. He thrust the letter halfway into the slot, then drew back his hand, studied the address, made certain the stamp was glued firmly. At last he dropped the letter into the box, the lid clanged shut after it.

He remained leaning with one hand against the mailbox, feeling too tired to move. Then he walked away, down the dark and empty street under the elevated tracks.

THE SECOND WAR

26

AFTER Dave had left the room, Stephanie remained in the chair by the window looking out at the sand hills in the morning sunlight. At last she got up, picked up the telegram which Dave had thrown on the floor, opened and read it. Slowly the understanding of what it said penetrated. She thought of Pledger Mc-Adams as she had seen him so often, waiting for her at one of the tables of their cafeteria near Randolph Street. And she thought of Ruby. Walking to the mirror, she stared at herself in the glass. Now she felt a rising fear at what the next few hours and days held for her. It was as if she had met herself face to face in a dream, with that glaring comprehension which dreams can bring. The things she had described two nights ago to Dave wove themselves into a pattern before her eyes—the drying-up of ambition and discipline, the effort to act the little girl again, to turn back the pages to another time. *And she had sat still in her chair, while Dave had gone.*

Stephanie packed her grip and went downstairs. In the kitchen the landlady was waiting for her with breakfast ready, but Stephanie said she was not hungry, and walked off along the dirt road to the railway crossing. She felt bitterly ashamed. Yet she could give herself no answer to the question of what to do next. To face Chicago on this day seemed to her more than she could endure. Tired and afraid, she wanted to be alone, and at the same time was afraid to be alone. She kept wishing for some person who would stay with her, but ask no questions and ask nothing of her. She remembered Ann Spaas.

The trains to Chicago ran every hour, but beyond the tracks, the highway led in one direction to the city—but in the other, north towards Michigan. Crossing over to the café and gas station, Stephanie asked for the next bus to Ludington. In a couple of hours, the man told her, and she sat down at the counter to wait.

Now she thought of sending word to Dave, but again the doubt checked her. What could she say to him? Had she meant what she told him when he had thrown down the telegram and left her in the room? She did not know. So she comforted herself with the thought: I'll let it rest for today and decide tomorrow.

Cars pulled up from time to time at the gas pump outside. A few truck drivers stopped for coffee and apple pie. At last the gas-pump man called her outside, a big gray bus rumbled up the highway, he flagged it to a halt, and she climbed in. The hours, the little towns, the stretches of rolling country slipped past. She tried to think about herself, but her mind had turned numb. No starting point she could select led her further than some meaningless repetition of phrases. Words in her mind meshed themselves into the hum of the motor and thrummed endlessly in her ears. She tried to break through into some reasonable chain of thought, but the effort wore her out at last and she sat staring out the window at the telephone poles reeling in their wires.

Ludington, which she reached in the late afternoon, was a town of quiet streets lined with trees like pictures of New England. She hunted up the address Ann Spaas had given her—clear across town and into the country beyond. In front of the last house, where the road dwindled off between the fruit orchards, she recognized Ann Spaas' little girl Sally, playing with half a dozen black-haired kids. As she passed, the kids fell solemnly into step behind and followed her towards the house, while Sally raced ahead shrieking, "Mummy, Stephanie's come to see us." Ann Spaas appeared in the doorway, shooed the kids back to the road again, and took Stephanie into the kitchen.

"Those kids all yours?" Stephanie asked.

Ann smiled and shook her head and Stephanie asked whether she could stay a few days in the house. She saw the other watch her closely, although she asked no questions. "Sure you can, if you don't mind sleeping on the couch; it's not much of a bed." Ann showed her around the few rooms and out to the back yard which opened into a fruit orchard. The long rows of trees stretched away farther than Stephanie could see. Late afternoon sunlight streamed down across the treetops; the air was fragrant with the smell of blossoms.

"You're not sorry you left Chicago, then?" Stephanie asked.

"No, I like it better here," Ann told her. "Don't you?"

A few chickens scratched around their feet, and from beyond

the house, the sound of children playing reached them. Stephanie nodded her head. "I like it very well—for a while."

"I'm thinking of getting married again," Ann said.

"You're thinking of what?"

"Getting married again."

Stephanie stared at her. "I thought you'd had enough the first time?"

Ann Spaas shrugged her shoulders. "There's lots of different kinds of people. I guess it won't hurt to try again."

"Who's the guy?" Stephanie asked.

"You'll see him. He comes for supper every night." And she added. "You can tell me what you think."

When they went back into the house, Ann Spaas set ten places around the kitchen table. Towards five o'clock, Stephanie heard a truck stop outside, then a deep voice bellowing in what sounded to her like Italian, and a chorus of shrieks and cackles from the kids. A moment later the door banged open, a man appeared, so short and broad he filled the door halfway up and all the way across. At the sight of Stephanie, he stopped, whipped off his hat and made her a bow, while the kids squirmed in past his knees.

"This is Mr. Salvivi," Ann said.

Mr. Salvivi entered, kissed Ann Spaas gallantly on the cheek, put one arm around Stephanie while he pumped her hand with the other. Then he took his place at the table, the kids scrambled into theirs, and Ann and Stephanie dished up the food. Stephanie saw that Mr. Salvivi was a man of unquenchable good spirits. He named a hundred or so of his relatives in Chicago; but she knew none of them. Then he asked her about the weather in Indiana, the traffic on the highway, the prices of fruit and vegetables in the city. When the kids hollered so loud no one else could make themselves heard, Mr. Salvivi simply raised his voice a notch and drowned them out. But Ann Spaas waved her hands angrily at the noise; Mr. Salvivi smashed his fist down on the table.

"Be silence!" he roared.

In the sudden stillness, his youngest child let out a frightened wail. "I scare him," Mr. Salvivi said humbly, and planted the little boy on his knee, soothed him with his gigantic black-bristled hands, feeding him soup out of his own dish.

After supper, Mr. Salvivi roped the seven kids into the back of his truck. He put Ann Spaas and Stephanie into the front seat and they boomed off to see the sights of Ludington. The truck rattled through the streets, the kids whistling and shrieking behind and Mr. Salvivi nudging Stephanie with his elbow to point out the stores and houses, the trucks of his competitors, the roads leading down to the Lake Michigan car ferry. When it grew too dark to see, he drove them home and they sat in front of his house which was next to Ann's, drinking a glass of wine from Mr. Salvivi's cellar. He began explaining his assets and prospects to Stephanie as if she were Ann Spaas' elder sister.

"She couldn't do any better than me, eh, could she? All over this state, she couldn't find six fine kids like mine, I bet? And a man with his own house and a truck almost new and ten acres of orchard? But that's nothing!" He dismissed all that he had said with a clap of his hands. "She don't get married to a house, eh? Or she don't get married to my kids either. A woman gets married, she wants to get married to a *man*. So I say to her, look me over, make sure what kind of a man you're looking at. A real husband, I say to her, a man with big muscle, a tiger for work—" He jumped up, pounding his barrel chest and shouting with laughter. "What you think, eh?"

"You better ask her," Stephanie said. "I've got no vote."

"Ah well, you put in a little good word for me, please."

Stephanie understood that Mr. Salvivi set much pride in having ladies beside him in the cab of his truck. In the mornings after the kids went to school, he took her and Ann Spaas along with him on his route; they drove out into the country, stopping at farms along the way to pick up batches of fruit and vegetables. The truck wheezed and popped over the country roads while Mr. Salvivi's inexhaustible voice boomed along telling stories about himself, his customers, neighbors, brothers and sisters.

". . . . My brother that owned this truck," he explained to them, "he don't understand nothing about motor vehicles, that's how come I got it from him. My brother say she burns too much oil, he tears her apart, and when he puts her back, he's got all the gears mixed up and nobody knows whether she's going to start forward or backward until you try her out. That makes it very hard. One day he takes his girl friend to a dance . . ." Mr. Salvivi leaned suddenly across Ann and roared in Stephanie's ear, "But myself, I fix her up like new, I used to work in Detroit. . . . Like I'm telling you my brother is taking his girl to a dance, they stop at a traffic light in the middle of town. Traffic light turns green, my brother puts her in first speed forward like you always got to start, but this time she goes backward instead. He grabs the brake, only it's not the brake he gets ahold of, it's this girl's leg. Now if she knows him real good, maybe she don't mind like women don't sometimes. But she's only known him a couple of days; she thinks, this monkey don't even know my first name yet, he's got his hand up my leg already. So she let's him have one in his eye, and my brother has his foot on the gas but he don't know it. Then crash!" Mr. Salvivi lifted his hands from the wheel, an expression of amazement lighting his face. "Mother of Jesus, what a crash! And it's the traffic cop right behind them driving his own vehicle to the dance. My brother shoves him backwards all the way up Main Street before he can get this truck stopped." Mr. Salvivi swung the truck into another farmyard, and when he brought it to a stop beside the barn, he explained, "That's how come I take her over, my brother don't want her any more after that. . . . Good morning, Mr. Galucca. What you got for me today? . . ."

Stephanie did not try much to think. The days drifted past; she soaked up the sunlight and the wind and watched with delight the clouds floating across the summer sky. In the afternoons, Mr. Salvivi returned them to the house before he delivered his cargo to the markets or the freight shed. Sometimes she helped Ann with the housework; sometimes she walked out into the orchard, lay down and slept under the blossoming fruit trees. Sometimes she sat on the front doorstep watching Ann's little girl Sally playing with the six black-haired children of Mr. Salvivi.

But she knew she could not stay forever. The thoughts stirred uneasily beneath the surface. At the end of the week, Mr. Salvivi announced he had a consignment of greens and onions for some Italian markets on Halsted Street, and Stephanie said she would ride back to the city with him. He parked his loaded truck in front of the house late in the afternoon of the day they were to leave, and he and the kids came in for supper. As a going-away present he brought Stephanie a jug of wine, which they polished off among the three of them. The wine set them dancing and shouting about the kitchen. Mr. Salvivi caught Ann Spaas like a twig between his hands, lifted her up, bumping her head against the ceiling. The kids all shrieked with laughter and he had to bump each of their seven heads against the ceiling, also. Then he made Stephanie promise she would come to the wedding when they got married;

he kissed his bride-to-be, kissed Stephanie, and kissed all the children in rotation. After that, they ate supper and went to the movies. Entering the movie theater, Stephanie felt as if she were part of a small parade. But the kids broke ranks immediately and scampered past the knees of the ticket chopper, while Mr. Salvivi, with a magnificent gesture, extended a yard-long ribbon of tickets. Inside the theater, the ten of them occupied an entire row. Mr. Salvivi put his arm around Ann, the kids nudged and cuffed each other in the darkness.

The theater smelled of chocolate and perfume and popcorn. Stephanie sat twisting her hands on her lap. She stared above her at the shafts of light which slanted down through clouds of tobacco smoke. Her giddiness from the wine faded quickly. For tomorrow she would be in Chicago again. The vacation was over, she thought, the interim ended. What she had tried to leave behind only awaited her return. Abruptly the fear and tension resumed possession of her mind. When she got down from the truck in Chicago, she wondered, where would she go then? To Richmond Court? To her mother's? To the University? She felt as if she were racing time, struggling to reach some point of clarity before the hours ran out against her.

Martin had left Chicago; certainly she could follow him. But she had never considered Martin's offer seriously, and even now did not consider it so. She knew that she had not loved Martin, nor regretted leaving him. But what did it mean, loving? Was it some random and accidental affect? By such an accident, might she as easily have tied herself to a bond salesman or a professional follower of race tracks? Had she then fallen in love with Dave by accident—in contradiction to the sense of her own personality? That was what Martin had told her; and that, she knew, was what Dave himself was coming to believe. Perhaps Martin had told him also. Perhaps Martin was right. And if so, then it would be better for them both that she should leave him.

She closed her eyes. The newsreel had shown the pictures of war, the marching men, the skyline of London against a mass of flames. It could not be long now, she thought; Dave would go, one way or another he would go. All around her the theater buzzed with laughter, the kids giggled and hooted at each other. There came into her mind the recollection of the evening when she had walked with Dave to the railroad depot and they had talked about death. She remembered being startled by that conversation; she had set it aside to think about later—and then forgotten it. But now the words came back to her. Partly in joke, she had said, "Isn't death a stage in the dialectical process? Why should we struggle against it?"

He had taken her seriously. "It isn't part of any dialectics to go in peace. People fight to stay alive."

"To cram into themselves enough living to last for eternity, you mean?"

But that had angered him. "No, that's not what I mean at all. People fight to stay alive." (He had repeated it stubbornly as if saying it over several times would convey the meaning the words did not fully express.) "To live better and longer. I guess that's what people have always fought for."

How precisely their words had described their opposite states of mind! She realized now why she had been impressed by the conversation at the time—and why she had been careful to forget about it. On one hand was the despairing mood, self-consciousness, deliberately conscious of nothing but itself, gripped in the sudden terror of realizing the true dimensions of self-consciousness, how tiny and how brief these were. So she had defined life as the struggle to cram into each individual enough living to last for eternity. She had intended that to be humorous and cynical. It was as if she had asked: "What can you offer for an antidote to death?"

And Dave, who was no theoretician, had not grasped the meaning of her question, any more than she herself had grasped it at the time. Yet his answer suited him perfectly. Who needed any antidote to death? Life elbowed and slugged its way forward, rejoiced at being alive. He had not even understood what she was worrying about. He could not conceive an individual pondering this matter of death. He saw a whole march of people from the beginning of history—noisy, impatient, alive. He saw them fighting cold and hunger, fighting to wipe out the few who exploited the many, fighting disease and suffering, fighting to learn the nature of the universe they lived in. He figured himself as one of them, and why shouldn't he? He saw the wonders they had already achieved —and he looked forward to more. It was very simple, and indeed she had often accused him of being simple.

From the beginning of her relationship with Dave, she had struggled against him. Part of herself had said of Dave, that's for me, and part of herself had said, stay clear of him. When she was with him, she had tried to break away; when she was away, she

337

had dragged herself back. Against their will or with their will, they had been closely bound together. She had known from the beginning that somehow he was of the same blood as herself, carrying the same love and hope, the same hatred and determination that she carried—or would wish to carry. The conflict then was not between herself and Dave, as Martin had described it to her. It was inside herself. Her relation to Dave had mirrored the conflict. If she had never known Dave, or Martin either, the conflict could not have been very different. Coldly and precisely now, she saw that division stretching back to the first days she could remember, assuming a hundred different forms, but always the same. It had pushed her to accomplishment past every obstacle. It had driven her into devious passages of escape. And now as she reached the blank end of these passages, it drove her to the brink of destroying everything she had accomplished.

Stephanie sat for a long while with her eyes closed. When she opened them, the second feature was beginning. Beside her Mr. Salvivi's kids chewed on their caramel corn, chumping like a row of small horses eating oats. Stephanie reached out for a handful of popcorn from the kids and crunched it while she watched the picture.

They returned to the house after the movie. Ann brewed them a pot of coffee against the night ride; and when Mr. Salvivi had kissed Ann and all the kids good bye, he and Stephanie climbed into the truck. The lights of the town faded quickly behind them; the highway came pouring out of the darkness into the bright beam of headlamps. Mr. Salvivi lit a cigar, and over the crashing motor, he talked to Stephanie about the virtues of his bride-to-be, with which, she gathered, he had already made fairly complete acquaintance. She listened for a time, then rolled a blanket behind her head and settled into the corner of the cab. As she drifted towards sleep, she realized that with all her thinking she had reached no conclusion, and decided nothing. For there was nothing to decide. She had invoked magic, not fact; she had been hoping for some magic amulet to ease the hostile factions without effort on her own part. But naturally the amulets of St. Christopher refused their services to one who did not believe in the saint himself. She had heard no angels singing in the trees of Ludington, and so returned as she had come. For she had known the decision from the beginning; she found it rooted inside her as irrevocably as the conflict itself. One with a crippled foot did not appeal to angels; but learned to walk in the one way possible: by walking—

When she woke, Mr. Salvivi had lighted a new cigar. The night was dissolving into the liquid gray of daybreak, and a single greenish star burned over the horizon. Stephanie sat up, wide-awake at once, rolled down the window of the cab, and thrust her head out. Fresh and sweet, the wind streamed across her face, rippled her hair back from her ears. The fields lay misty gray, houses and trees floated half formed against the pale wash of dawn. She thought how beautiful the morning was, breathed deep to drink it in. The truck ran past a cluster of buildings at a crossroad; there were a few lighted windows; she saw a woman at a kitchen door, and smelled the odor of coffee and wood smoke. Then, stretching and laughing, she dropped back into her seat.

"Good morning, Mr. Salvivi."

He jerked his head and beamed at her.

"Where are we?" she asked.

"Just pass Gary."

The magic of sunrise turned quickly into the familiar clatter of Chicago Monday morning. Mr. Salvivi's truck growled along in low gear, bucking the lines of traffic. A feeling of urgency took hold of Stephanie; she found herself counting the stoplights, and straining in her seat as if to push the truck more rapidly forward. When at last they reached Halsted and Thirty-Sixth Street, she waved good bye and jumped down to the sidewalk almost before the truck had stopped. Mr. Salvivi, however, did not accept such informal leave-taking. He climbed down after her.

"Now listen, Salvivi," she said; "don't you be fooling around with Ann Spaas. You get married to her."

He thumped his fist against his breast. "That's what I say to her myself. I say, why we don't get married right now?"

Stephanie held out her hand; but the other threw his arms around her, and when she finally broke loose, a circle of grinning spectators surrounded them. Mr. Salvivi whipped off his hat, made her a formal bow, and heaved himself back into his truck. As it sputtered and backfired into the stream of traffic, she watched it out of sight, then turned down Thirty-Sixth Street towards her mother's house.

To her relief, she found her mother not at home; but Rosa gave her the letter from Dave. Stephanie ripped open the envelope, and as she read his note, the feeling of urgency turned to panic. That he was going away did not surprise her. She had known he would go. With the war as it was, he could do nothing else. But it had not occurred to her that he might leave Chicago before she returned. After the agony of the last few days, the thought of missing him seemed suddenly more terrible to her than anything else that could happen. Even for an hour, she thought, for five minutes, she had to find him. She stared down suddenly at the paper in her hands. And when she found him, what would she say? She did not know.

"Rosa, when did this letter come?"

"Yesterday."

"And has he been here?"

"About a week ago. He left a telephone number."

Rosa showed her the number, which Stephanie recognized as the number of the Chile Parlor. She went there immediately. A girl working behind the counter told her that Ruby was at the hospital and usually came back about noontime. The girl did not know anything about Dave. It was only eleven o'clock and Stephanie, as she waited, tried to drink a cup of coffee, but she could not sit still. The panic of uncertainty gnawed into her mind. She whispered over and over to herself: He can't have gone. In another hour, I'll know where he is. Or the door will open and he'll walk in while I'm sitting here. He'll walk in and I'll wait here till he sees me. . . . Each time she heard the door open, she hunched down in her seat, trying to recognize the sound of his step, afraid to lift her eyes. And at the same time, she was certain he had already gone; he had boarded a ship and it would be months, miserable and endless months before he would return. But this was more than she could endure and she came back again to the starting point: He can't have gone; it could not happen that way. If only she had not stayed so long in Ludington, she thought—

She rose from the counter and walked outside with the idea of following Ruby to the hospital, but changed her mind for fear she might miss her on the way. Through the hot and crowded blocks along State Street, she wandered back and forth waiting till noon. When at last the factory sirens blew for midday, she forced herself to wait an extra half hour to make certain Ruby would have returned. Then the notion struck her that Ruby might come and go out again. She hurried back to the Chile Parlor almost at a run.

Now the girl behind the counter looked at her strangely and nodded her head towards the door at the rear. Stephanie went through into the back yard, where she saw Ruby sitting by herself on the bench under the cottonwood tree.

"Ruby," she cried. "Ruby!"

Ruby raised her square black face from her hands.

"Ruby, where's Dave? Have you seen him?"

"He was with me this morning, Stephanie. I don't know where he is now."

"But he hasn't gone away? He hasn't left for New York?"

"No, he told me he'd come here this evening."

"Oh, thank God, Ruby! I was afraid I'd missed him."

Stephanie's knees turned weak and she began to laugh and shake at the same time. Then she stared into Ruby's face and dropped down on the bench beside her.

"What happened?"

"Pledger died this morning," Ruby said.

27

THE moon hung round and yellow in the center of the sky. It rode up over the rooftops big as a dinner plate, so bright the whole sky glowed and the stars disappeared. Dave parked the car under the embankment where the shadow swallowed up the sidewalk and half the street. But opposite them, moonlight spread a network of angles and shadows across the faces of the buildings. The street was empty. A streetlamp burned dully at the far corner. Dave glanced at his watch, then looked up again at the place in the darkness where the stairway led down the side of the embankment. Directly across from the stairway was the red neon sign of Walter's Tavern.

". . . now this guy has a tic in his eye," Red Brogan told them. "You've seen people like that, they're always winking without they intend to. He gets into St. Louis and wants a hotel, so he says to the taxi driver, Take me to a good hotel, Mac. He says it like this, see—"

"Don't bother acting it out. We can't see you in the dark."

"Well anyhow, this fellow goes into the hotel, see, and he says to the room clerk, gimme a nice room; and he winks his eye again on account of this tic. But the room clerk winks right back, and he says, You want it with or without, mister? And the guy says, With or without what? The room clerk thinks that's a howl. He says, With or without running water." Red clapped his hand on his knee. "With or without running water! Haw, haw haw—"

"For Christ's sake," Dave said, "pipe down. You want 'em to hear you all the way up to the yard office?"

"Aw, go fly a kite. Anyhow, the bellboy shows this guy up to his room and the guy tells the bellboy, I hope this is a quiet room, I'm very tired. But he winks again, see, on account of this tic he's got."

One of the men asked: "What time is it, Dave?"

Dave looked at his watch again. "Ten minutes to one."

"He's just about going to sleep when there's a knock on the door—"

Across the street, the neon light above Walter's Tavern went out.

"Is he closing up?"

"Naw, he stays open all night," Red said. "So pretty soon, like I was saying, there's a knock on the door and in pops a skirt—"

"How the hell do we know he's coming down here?" one of the men demanded. "Maybe he went home some other way."

Dave pointed in front of them. "That's his car parked right ahead of us."

"He's as regular as a dose of salts," Red said. "Don't worry, he'll be along. Anyhow, where was I? A blonde. Yeah, it's a blonde this time and she's got on one of these kimonos that opens down the front. Anything I can do for you, mister? she wants to know—"

"Look!"

They could hear someone moving on the stairway down the side of the embankment. Then they heard voices, and a moment later two men came out into the moonlit half of the street, stood arguing for a moment, and walked off towards the corner.

Red propped his feet on the back of the front seat. "Couple of goddamn brakemen, that's all."

"Well, what happened to this guy, Red? Didn't he wink that time?"

"Oh, sure. I forgot to tell you he winked on account of his tic. And this girl goes out and he's just getting to sleep again when there's a knock on the door and in comes another skirt. But he really sits up this time because she's in the nude, see—a redhead and she ain't got a stitch on—"

"Here he is," Dave said.

Dave unlatched his door and held it open a crack. The five men peered forward through the windows of the car. For a moment they saw a man's head and shoulders silhouetted in the moonlight at the top of the embankment. Then they heard steps coming slowly down the stairway. They waited, listening. At last the thin figure for which Dave had been watching stepped from the shadow of the embankment into the moonlight, crossed the street, opened the door of Walter's Tavern, and went inside.

"Stopping for a drink."

"He generally does that," Red said. Unfolding his arms and legs, Red climbed out of the car, but stuck his head back through the open window. "Tavern's as good a place as any for a quiet chat, unless there's a lot of people around. I'll stop in for a beer. If there's too many people, I'll come right out again. Okay, Dave?"

"We'll wait five minutes, Red. If you're not out, we'll come in."

Red winked and grinned.

"But what happened to this guy with the tic?" one of the men asked.

"Aw, Christ, I don't know. He caught a dose for himself, I guess."

Red giggled, crossed the street, and disappeared into the tavern. Dave held his watch in his hand. At the end of five minutes, Red had not come out. They left the car and followed him across the street.

Dave pushed open the door of the tavern. He glanced quickly around him, noticing that the tables and booths were empty. Red and the detective Morgan were standing at the bar, close together as if they had been talking. Walter was on the other side of the bar.

"Why it's Davey Spaas," Walter cried. "How you doing, old man . . . ?"

Dave saw Morgan's face contort suddenly in fear. Morgan jumped away from the bar, reaching for the pocket of his black suit coat. At the same instant, Red pinned his arm from behind, Dave jumped and struck. His fist, landing high on the cheek, knocked Morgan sideways into Red, who clamped his arms up behind his back and held them. One of the other men slipped the gun from Morgan's pocket and threw it on the floor.

"Let him go," Dave said.

343

Red released his grip and Morgan, crouching slightly, glared into Dave's face.

"Pick your gun up," Dave told him. "I'd make a good mark if I had my back turned." Morgan broke his eyes away from Dave's and turned back to the bar as if to finish his drink; but in the same movement, he ducked and lunged for the gun. Dave hit him, knocked him the full length of the bar. He jumped after him, pulled him to his feet, and shoved him against the rear wall.

Dave stood in front of him waiting. But now Morgan only stooped down, covering his face with his hands. Dave punched his stomach, and when the hands dropped down, smashed him in the face. Then he moved in, rocking on the balls of his feet, swinging with both fists. When the others at last pulled him away, Morgan fell forward on his hands and knees. A spasm of retching shook him and he spat out a few black gobs of blood.

Dave was breathing hard. For a moment, as he rubbed the cut knuckles of his hands, he stared down at Morgan; then he turned suddenly on Walter who had not stirred from his position behind the bar. "You saw him try to pull a gun on me, didn't you?"

Walter's round, pink-rimmed eyes wavered sideways for a moment and snapped back. "Sure I did," Walter told him. "Sure I seen it, Dave."

"Make sure you remember it."

The clock over the bar said quarter after one. Red prodded Morgan with his foot. "Get up, we want to talk to you." They pulled Morgan to his feet and propped him on one of the stools, where he sat sprawled backwards against the bar. From his smashed lips and nose, blood oozed down the lines of his jaw.

"We ought to work him over a little better," one of the men said.

Red thrust his face close to Morgan's. "You want any more of this treatment?"

The other made no sound.

"Answer me!" Red shouted. "You want some more?"

Morgan shook his head.

"There's only five of us here tonight," Red said. "But I know fifty men would have been glad to do this job. See, your gun ain't any use to you any more, is it?"

Red stopped; then yelled into Morgan's face, "You know what you're going to do tomorrow? You're going to cash in your chips and get off this railroad. Understand me? If anybody sees you around this yard after tomorrow, Morgan, it's going to be tough.

We don't want you around here, and one way or another—*one way or another*—you ain't going to be around."

Catching him by the collar of his coat, Red yanked him from the bar stool and threw him down on the floor. Morgan lay still where he had fallen. Then Red picked up the pistol and the five of them went back to the car.

As Dave drove south along Halsted Street, one of the men asked, "You think he'll try to pin anything on us, Dave?"

"No, I don't think so."

"Why not?"

"Well, let him try," Dave said. "That tavern's not on company property. I got as good a right to go in there as anybody else. He tried to pull a gun on me and I knocked his goddamn teeth in for it. We got six people to swear to that."

On the bridge over the Chicago River, Dave stopped the car for a moment and Red sent the pistol spinning through the window, high over the railing of the bridge. They saw it wink in the moonlight and heard it splash into the water below.

Dave returned Red and each of the other three to their homes, then drove himself back to the Chile Parlor. His hands throbbed sharply from the cuts in his knuckles. Now that the appointment with Morgan was over, there remained a sickish taste in his throat and he kept hearing again the crunch of Morgan's bony mouth when he had struck it. He had planned beforehand to do exactly what he did and he was not sorry for it. But he felt slightly sick at his stomach, as if he had crushed a frog with his bare foot. It would have been better to have taken the gun and shot Morgan, except they would have gone to jail for it instead of getting the citation they deserved. And he said to himself, We waited too long. When you get soft and slow, somebody pays for it. Pledger would be alive today if we had taken care of Morgan a long time ago.

He parked the car in front of the Chile Parlor. The door was closed and the lights were out. Ruby must have gone to bed, he thought; she would be up in her room, sitting by herself, her head in her hands as he had seen her sitting in the hospital, sweating her way through. He unlocked the door and stepped inside.

"Dave."

Someone rose from the counter and moved towards him in the darkness. "Dave," the voice said again. For a moment he did not know who it was. Then he asked,

"It's you, Stephanie? What are you doing here?"

"Waiting for you."

"Is Ruby asleep?"

"Not likely."

He closed the door behind him and snapped the lock. "That letter," he said. "Didn't you get it?"

"Yes, I got it."

"I'm going to New York in a few days."

"I know."

"Did you read the letter?" he asked angrily. "I told you I was leaving you."

"No, Dave. No, you're not leaving me." They faced each other in silence in the dark room. She took his hand, drew him through the back door of the Chile Parlor into the yard, where they sat on the bench under the moon-speckled leaves of the cottonwood.

"I left you once and I came back," she told him. "Now you feel you'll do me a good turn by making a clean decision of your own and slicing through all our problems. But that's not the right way, Dave. I've thought it all over. You couldn't do us a worse turn than that. You'll go to sea if you must because of the war, but not to leave me, oh no, not to leave me—"

He sat silent, listening to the flood of her words. Then he leaned towards her, pressed his face into the hollow of her shoulder and throat. The terrible strain of the last few days left him shaking uncontrollably; slowly he began to understand what she had suffered during these months.

"I'm glad you came," he said, and tightened his arms around her, until, half laughing, she gasped into his ear,

"Easy, Dave, I can't breathe—"

1942

B Y the end of the year, Eddie decided he couldn't stand the Great Midland any longer.

He tried to persuade Paddy Gallagher to go west with him, but Paddy said he was due for his pension in another eight months and he wasn't going anywhere. Uncle Jennison told him it was a crack-brained idea to give up all his years of seniority for some job he wouldn't be able to hold except while the war lasted.

So Eddie went down all by himself to the SP office and signed up for a job as switchtender in a little town he'd never heard of down in the Arizona desert. They gave him a ticket to wherever it was he was going, and Eddie turned in his keys on the Great Midland and said good bye to everybody he knew around the yard. He took off a few days after New Year's. Uncle Jennison and his Norwegian wife came down to the station to see him off. Eddie waved to them a couple of times, then boarded the train with his suitcase in his hand and his guitar clamped under his arm.

The coaches were all crowded with young soldiers heading for the Pacific, but Eddie finally found a seat and rubbed himself a peephole on the frosted pane so he could see the last of Chicago. As the train pulled out of the yard, Eddie made out a few familiar buildings through the clouds of smoke and steam. But these faded quickly from sight and there was only the clatter of wheels and the blur of lights in the winter twilight.

The young soldiers began joking about how quick they aimed to square things up for Pearl Harbor. They were handing liquor bottles back and forth and throwing a party. One of the soldiers had a harmonica. Eddie unlimbered his guitar and he and the harmonica player cranked out all the songs they could think of and drank any liquor that came their way. The soldiers sang the same songs over and over again and shouted and raised hell to pass the long hours of the night.

■ ▨

Dave Spaas came off watch at four o'clock in the morning. As he climbed the ladder from the engine room, he met the little Englishman Ardwick on his way down, looking sleepy-eyed and with his few wisps of hair standing on end.

"Good night, Ardwick," Dave said.

"What do you mean, good night? Wake up, matey. It's the marning already." And Ardwick called after him, "You know where we'll be in the marning?"

"Sure I know."

Dave went to the mess hall for a cup of coffee before he turned in. A couple of sailors at the sideboard were making themselves peanut-butter sandwiches, while the bos'un and one of the Navy gunners still worked over the same game of chess they had been playing four hours before when Dave went on watch. The mess hall was thick with tobacco smoke. Two fans at opposite ends of the room barely rippled the hot air which baked up from the galley and the engine room; the portholes were dogged down tight for the blackout.

Dave stepped out on deck with his cup of coffee. At first, as he ducked under the blackout curtains which shielded the end of the passageway, he could see nothing at all. The darkness pressed heavily against his eyes; the wind, which he heard humming in the rigging above him, drove splatters of rain and salt spray into his face. Then gradually he made out the shapes of the deck cargo; and over his head, saw the crosstrees of the mast swinging like a pendulum across the low-hanging clouds. As always, when he stood for a few moments alone, he thought of Stephanie, imagined how it would feel to reach out and touch her in the darkness; and then the anticipation of returning to her moved in a warm flood from his finger tips through the rest of his body. He leaned against the bulwark, sipping his coffee. As the ship rolled, the sea boiled up close beside him along the outer face of the bulwark, then sank from sight in the darkness. After a time, the wind chilled him and he went inside and to bed. He slept with his shoes and clothes on, dozing and waking.

When the depth charges began to thump again in the distance, Dave rolled out of the bunk, grabbed his coat and lifejacket, and was on deck before the ship's alarm sounded. There was a faint wash of dawn over the sea now. The ships in the next line of the convoy hovered like shadows. The Navy boys and the merchant crewmen ran for their gun stations. They unlimbered the guns and stood waiting, straining their eyes against the small circle of rolling ocean beyond which they could see nothing. Dave clapped his hands and stamped his feet in the cold.

Suddenly through the gray darkness ahead sparkled a flare of light. A needle of red flame blazed up and died down. A moment later came the noise of the distant explosion—a small, sharp sound like the cracking of a dry stick. The men beside Dave strained and shifted their feet. Depth charges rumbled in all directions, then dwindled away, leaving only the wind and the thrum of the engines.

At eight o'clock Ardwick came up from watch to join Dave and the others in the after gun tub. "It's a bloody pain in the head, below," he told them. "Like somebody whacking the hull plates with a sledgehammer when those depth bombs start popping." The men laughed. It was full daylight now. The ocean heaved out under the lead-colored sky, slashed gray and white by the wind. Ahead and behind, the rusty-flanked ships butted into the seas. Along the eastern horizon, stretched a bank of cloud; and beyond these clouds, Dave knew, lay the coast of Spain where it sloped in towards the Strait of Gibraltar. He thought of the people in the hills who would watch this convoy of ships roll through the straits: some watching with fear, and many with a stir of hope.

Already the convoy was forming double column for the entrance of the straits; and as Dave looked back, he saw the masts and funnels of these ships stretching away as far as he could see. Off to one side, left behind by the convoy, the single ship which had been torpedoed at dawn wallowed into the seas. She was burning sullenly, and the smoke from her cast a black smear across the sky.

28

THE snow came again over Chicago. The days glowed briefly through the curtains of vapor and smoke. At the winter convocation, Stephanie took her doctor's degree, marched up through the chapel with the group of gold-tasseled doctorate candidates who led the procession. Afterwards, she returned her gown to the rental office, ate lunch, and went back to her job in the laboratory. She remembered how she had looked forward to this day on which she would receive her doctorate; but it came and went like many others.

Evenings with the stream of people from the laboratories, laughing and talking, pulling on their gloves and turning up their coat collars, she came down the stairs and out through the archway to Fifty-Seventh Street. Sometimes snow blurred across the streetlamps; and sometimes the sky glowed clear and green behind the grandstands of Stagg Field. The bells rang out from the chapel tower. People moved past her in the direction of Hutchinson Commons dining room. Crossing the street, she hurried along, her heels crunching in the packed snow; the boom of the chapel bells following her all the way to the car stop. She counted the days at first, but gave that up because she did not know what day to count them towards. Letters reached her without date or postmark, and she and Ruby tried to guess from what port they might have come.

Sometimes, as she closed her eyes, she saw before her the picture of a ship rolling across a gray sea. All the colors of the world seemed to have faded to that one color. Around her the vast city of Chicago lay wrapped in the blanket of winter. And she understood the other cities she had never seen, the roofless buildings, the people in dark doorways who waited for the coming of something. Gray was the color of watching and waiting; a world stripped of the bright sunlight she once had longed for.

Day by day increased the urgency of the waiting. The few days they had spent together before he left, she felt had brought them closer together than all the previous years. She knew that he had felt this, but not fully understood; nor had she, either, fully understood. A few crowded words before departure gave but a fragmentary communication; while inside her the store of things to say and look and understand accumulated, and she could only press them back and wait.

On the surface of moment to moment, she felt herself not unhappy. She tried to tread lightly on that surface to avoid breaking through. For often some familiar object, or the touch of her own hand against her skin, or the coldness of the sheets at night as she crawled into bed, would shatter the surface beneath her. Then the bitter hunger for him poured up through, and in the agony of loneliness, she buried her face in the pillow, biting the knuckles of her hands. The picture of the gray ocean rose again before her eyes; the fear that was never more than half suppressed set her repeating his name, fevered and shaking, wrapping her arms around the pillow. Sometimes Ruby heard her and came in, and then Stephanie wept like a child, although she knew Ruby had more to weep about than she.

For hard though it was to wait, she knew it would be better than, like Ruby, having nothing to wait for. But Ruby's laughter boomed as loud as ever through the Chile Parlor. She talked often of Pledger, and Stephanie noticed that she never reserved him any special or tragic tone of voice. In her flowered dress and gigantic pink beads, she switched up and down between the tables, taking care of her customers. The juke box blared out music, the stove glowed red hot, the place was thick with tobacco smoke and the steamy smells of food. Every evening when Stephanie came at suppertime, Ruby met her and clamped an arm around her, the black face beamed into hers, the beads flashed on the square bosom. At the table in the corner, a place was waiting and Ruby brought over what she thought was most suitable on the menu. She sat down for a few moments, but then was up again, stamping and shouting around the Chile Parlor, stopping at one table and another, helping out the waitresses if they needed help. Stephanie, when she finished eating, went up to her room in Ruby's apartment. There she stretched out on the bed long enough to smoke a cigarette; then collected her papers for the evening class and went downtown to the new Labor School.

She found herself working steadily and well, and the days passed quickly. The crisis of the summer, she knew, had not changed her much; there remained within her the same divisions, fears, conflicting desires, which she had come to recognize as repercussions in her own mind of the gigantic conflict outside. But that she had weathered summer and fall and winter, taught her something she had not known before; she too could be tough and resilient; she also could meet worse than she had yet come through. Slowly her confidence in herself returned. Her life became more closely knit than it had ever been before. Although she felt no great excitement at receiving her doctor's degree, she knew the years of work it cost had not been wasted. A dozen different jobs opened up in the war research projects in the University laboratories, and she could choose the one she wanted. Her two classes at the new Labor School, in evolution and race relations, went well and she was proud of them.

Sometimes even, she felt moments of elation when the fire blazed up through the gray surface. Then in the flickering light the faces of the crowd around her seemed to reach out forever across the world; she felt herself one with the vast throngs who waited in the darkness in all the dark cities around the globe, and on the ships, and in the lines of marching men, feeding their hope with hatred. For love and fear, hatred and hope, twined together like the stems of a vine. Her eyes lifted to the vision of what the world might be—the city they had once planned with wide streets and houses for people to live in, the sunlight in the windows of the houses, the trees along the river; a world where people could live and work and learn; where science and understanding would be to

351

some other purpose than to destroy themselves. She had wondered in certain gloomy moments if all this were not simply a dream, the solace of an empty mind which heard no angels singing in the treetops and so came seeking some other revelation, some new millennium. She laughed and shook her head. If Ulysses Grant drank that whiskey, then send a barrel to all my generals. For any dream that gave the strength to fight to men like Pledger and her own husband Dave was a dream to hold on to.

But as she climbed the steps to the elevated station and from the platform looked out over the rooftops and the blurred lights in the falling snow, she knew these were no dreams; the reality was sharp and precise as the winter wind. Life had been fighting to stay alive these many years, she thought, elbowing and slugging its way forward; and surely it would go on doing so. One day, one day, out of the gray snow, out of the yards and alleys and the little houses whose roofs stretched endlessly beyond the embankment, the fire would crackle up. Waste and failure and misery and death demanded a bitter harvest. That was no dream. And no dream either was the compound she found inside herself, the mixture of hatred and hope, love and fear; these were her dowry and her inheritance, the first things she remembered, and the last she would remember.

Shivering, she heard the engines in the distance stumping along the embankments; she glanced at her watch and paced up and down the platform, waiting for the elevated train.

(1)

ALEXANDER SAXTON, professor emeritus of history at UCLA, is the author of *The Indispensable Enemy: Labor and the Anti-Chinese Movement in California* (1971, 1995) and *The Rise and Fall of the White Republic: Class Politics and Mass Culture in Nineteenth Century America* (1990).

CONSTANCE COINER (1948–96) was associate professor of English at SUNY-Binghampton and the author of *Better Red: The Writing and Resistance of Tillie Olsen and Meridel Le Sueur* (1995).

ALAN WALD, professor of English literature and American culture at the University of Michigan, is the author of *James T. Farrell* (1978), *The Revolutionary Imagination* (1983), *The New York Intellectuals* (1987), *The Responsibility of Intellectuals* (1992), and *Writing from the Left* (1994).